Admission to Higher Education: Issues and Practice

ADMISSION TO HIGHER EDUCATION:

Issues and Practice

THOMAS KELLAGHAN
EDITOR

EDUCATIONAL RESEARCH CENTRE, DUBLIN

INTERNATIONAL ASSOCIATION FOR EDUCATIONAL ASSESSMENT, PRINCETON, NJ

Copyright © 1995, International Association for Educational Assessment

Cataloguing-in-Publication Data

International Association for Educational Assessment. Annual Conference (18th : 1992 : Dublin, Ireland)
Admission to higher education: issues and practice / Thomas Kellaghan, editor
Dublin: Educational Research Centre ; Princeton, NJ: International Association for Educational Assessment

x, 323p ; 23 cm
Includes bibliographical references and index
1. Universities and colleges - Admission - Congresses
I. Title II. Kellaghan, Thomas
378.1056 - dc20 1995
ISBN 0 900440 05 8

Cover Design
Identikit design consultants

Printing
Leinster Leader

CONTENTS

ISSUES

PRACTICE

AFRICA

THE AMERICAS

ASIA

AUSTRALIA

EUROPE

CONCLUSION

PREFACE

In the 17 Annual Conferences which the International Association for Educational Assessment (IAEA) sponsored between 1976 and 1992, only one topic appears more than once. That topic is admission to higher education which was the subject of a Conference in 1976, 1989, and 1992.

This attention to issues relating to admission to higher education is testimony of the importance to the assessment community of the topic. Indeed, not only is it of interest to those involved in assessment, it is also of very considerable interest to the general public, many of whom, directly or indirectly, would have had experience of procedures used for selection to higher education. Since important decisions relating to the life chances of so many people can rest on a selection procedure, it behoves those responsible to do all they can to ensure that the procedures do what they are designed to do, accurately and fairly.

The fact that admission to higher education has been the topic of an IAEA Annual Conference on three occasions can also be taken as an indication of the fact that, in many countries, admission procedures are under review. Substantial increases in the numbers of students applying for admission to third-level institutions, together with changing curricula in second- and third-level institutions, raise questions about the appropriateness of traditional procedures for contemporary circumstances. Many countries have revised their systems of selection or experimented with alternative procedures since the publication of the proceedings of the 1976 Conference[1]. Conferences, such as those organised by the IAEA, and ensuing publications provide important opportunities for those engaged in these exercises to learn about what is happening in other countries and to reflect on their own practice.

The present volume contains a selection of the papers presented at the 18th Annual Conference which was held in Dublin in 1992. It was possible to include only about half of the papers presented. Many presenters did not submit their papers for publication and restrictions on space did not permit the inclusion of all that were

1 Ottobre, F. (1976). *Admission to higher education in sixteen countries and some international developments.* Princeton NJ: International Association for Educational Assessment.

submitted. Because of space restrictions, it was also necessary in editing to shorten many of the papers.

The book is divided into two parts. In the first, issues relating to admission are discussed: criteria used for selection; the relative weights given to school-leaving examination results and to teachers' judgments; the role of scholastic aptitude and achievement tests; the comparability of students' achievements when these are measured in different ways; the validity and reliability of assessments; equity in selection; and the effects of selection procedures on curricula in second-level schools. In the second part of the book, admission procedures in a variety of countries are described. Seven papers describe procedures in African countries; three papers are from Asia; three are from the Americas; two deal with the Australian situation; and five deal with European countries (including countries in Eastern Europe).

The editor wishes to express his appreciation to all who submitted papers for this volume, and who returned edited manuscripts promptly. The assistance of Séamus Ó hUallacháin and Muireann Joy in editing is also gratefully acknowledged. So also is the assistance of Teresa Bell, Hilary Walshe, and Mary Rohan who prepared the manuscript for publication.

1. INTRODUCTION

Thomas Kellaghan
Educational Research Centre
St Patrick's College, Dublin

Throughout the world today, social demand for education is high. At no stage in the educational process is that demand more obvious than in the scramble for places in higher education. Individuals realise, what research confirms, that one's personal development, life chances, earnings, status, and life style are likely to be considerably enhanced by having a higher education qualification. Governments too are concerned from a national perspective to ensure that their work forces are sufficiently educated to compete in the international market place. In a world in which economic hegemony depends less and less on natural resources, military power, or strategic geographical location and more and more on the 'educated intelligence' of workers, educational provision is being assigned a key role in developing that intelligence.

As a consequence, one finds throughout the world great commitment, often under difficult financial circumstances, to the expansion and improvement of educational opportunities for young people. Some countries are still struggling to improve provision at secondary, and even at primary level. Others are more fortunate and can provide primary and secondary education for most of their young people. All, however, realise that it is necessary to provide third-level education for some students, even before education at lower levels is universally available. Difficult decisions have to be made in these circumstances about the proportion of students that are to be admitted to third-level education and the kinds of courses that are to be offered.

Because of the perceived role of higher education in economic and social development, many countries have accorded a high priority to its provision, and numbers of students have been increasing in recent years. This kind of expansion requires very considerable financial investment, both by the state and by individuals. Hence, it is important not only to get the balance right between higher education and other sectors of the educational system, but to do all that can be done to ensure that a high level of quality is achieved and maintained in the education that is provided in third-level institutions.

In this context, the theme of the papers in the present volume assumes a particular significance. The quality of education that an institution can provide is to some extent a function of the quality of the students it recruits. In some respects, third-level institutions can be regarded as fortunate insofar as they can choose their students since the number of applicants is usually considerably in excess of the number of available places. This tends to be particularly true of some courses. In these situations, one would expect the level of student quality to be high.

The extent to which an institution succeeds in recruiting students of high quality must be, at least in part, a function of the quality of its admission procedures. A variety of strategies is available for this purpose but not all would have the same effect on student quality. Besides, student quality, however one might define that term, may not be the only consideration for an institution in selecting students. It may also be necessary, given the amount of public investment in higher education and the value to individuals of its benefits, to consider the implications of selection procedures for fairness.

The papers in this volume address these and other issues relating to admission to higher education. The first part of the volume contains papers which deal with general issues. These include the kind of criteria that are used for selection; the relative weights given to school leaving examination results and to teachers' judgments in making admission decisions; the role of scholastic aptitude and achievement tests in deciding who will be selected and who will not; the comparability of students' achievements when these are measured in different ways; the validity and reliability of assessments; and the possibility that selection procedures may discriminate against students on the basis of their gender, ethnic background, or educational background.

Since higher education is not an oasis, isolated from other sectors of the educational system, it is important to consider how it interacts with and affects other sectors. Of particular interest in this context, especially at a time when participation in secondary education is increasing and not all participants are destined for higher education, is the theme of papers that deal with the relationship between selection procedures and curricula in second-level schools.

One of the unusual features of the papers in this volume is the range of countries that is represented. This would lead us to expect that wide-ranging and diverse perspectives would be brought to bear on the issues that are discussed. It also provides the opportunity of describing admission procedures in a variety of countries and such descriptions comprise the second part of the volume. Seven papers describe procedures in African countries; three papers are from Asia (relating to China and Hong Kong); three are from the Americas (two deal with the United States, one with three countries in Latin America); two papers deal with the Australian situation; and five deal with Europe (including one which focuses on three Eastern European countries).

It is clear that all countries do not go about the process of selection to third-level education in the same way. Most, however, are based on the concept of merit, though they may differ in how merit is assessed. Further, most use school-related criteria to determine who will be admitted and who will not. All strive in their own way to deal with problems of cost, time constraints, validity, and fairness. Attention to the approaches of the countries represented in this volume to dealing with these problems should serve to remind us that we have much to learn from each other. No country has a perfect system, and in most there is a consciousness of the need to refine existing procedures or find better ways.

ISSUES

2. PRINCIPLES AND PRACTICE IN SELECTION FOR ADMISSION TO HIGHER EDUCATION

Günter Trost
Institute for Test Development and Talent Research, Bonn, Federal Republic of Germany

THE PROBLEM

There is hardly any country in the world where the number of applicants for admission to higher education, at least for certain courses, does not exceed the number of available places. No society, not even the wealthiest, can afford to offer places in higher education in unlimited numbers to meet the demands of academically oriented young people. This statement holds true particularly for medical and natural science courses which require expensive laboratory equipment, but it is also true for the non-experimental, non-technical courses where lecture-halls and libraries and a reasonable number of faculty staff have to be provided. Therefore, selection of some kind has to take place.

The sheer economic impossibility of accepting each and every candidate is, in principle, incompatible with the fundamental right of free choice of profession. In the former Federal Republic of Germany, for example, Article 12 of the constitution which proclaimed this right is unanimously interpreted as including the right of free choice of courses at all stages of the educational system, provided that the formal requirements are fulfilled (for university entrance, this means holding the *Abitur* certificate or an equivalent). Attempts by the German legislature and educational administration to escape the consequences of this constitutional provision will be described later.

I will begin by describing some principles underlying the various attempts that different countries have made to solve the problem of selection for admission to higher education. Then I will examine the different procedures from psychometric as well as from economic and acceptability perspectives. Finally, I will describe the German practice of admission to higher education as an example of a complex system applying a diversity of criteria.

SOLUTIONS: THE PRINCIPLES

Selection During the Early Years of Higher Education

First I will look at a special, i.e. rather untypical, way of solving the selection problem which is being practised in a few European countries such as Belgium and, to a certain extent, France. In this approach, no selection at all takes place at the entrance to higher education: all applicants who have completed secondary education or comprehensive school are admitted. However, during the first two years of higher education the majority of students are rejected because of unsatisfactory performance in the college or university courses they have taken.

At first glance, the advantage of this strategy is that the decision to retain or not retain students is based on actual performance in their courses of study. However, after an inspection of the curricula in these courses, one may question the underlying assumption that the requirements in the first or second year are representative of those of the following years. The main disadvantage of this solution is, without doubt, that the majority of students leave without a qualification, having already devoted time and effort to their studies, and have to start anew in another course or turn to vocational training.

Selection at the Entry to Higher Education

In most countries, selection takes place at entry to higher education. A wide variety of criteria is used for selection decisions. The criteria can be classified according to the following categories: school-related achievement, scholastic aptitude, personality factors, formal criteria such as waiting-time, and chance. I shall look briefly at each of these categories.

School-related achievement is by far the most common criterion for selection at the threshold to higher education. For example, in most developing countries, it is the only one. But even in systems where other criteria, such as scholastic aptitude, are used, school-related achievement is always taken into account also. It is mainly assessed in one of three ways: average marks or grade point averages in upper secondary school; rank in class in the final school year; and subject-based achievement tests.

Among the nations in which achievement tests are used are Brazil, the People's Republic of China, Greece, Japan, South Korea, Turkey, and the United States. The selection procedure for admission to the French *grandes écoles* includes the assessment of achievement in non-standardised written and oral examinations *(concours d'entrée)*.

In some countries (e.g., the United Kingdom), minimum marks in particular school subjects or weighted combinations of single marks are used for the decision regarding admission to certain college or university courses. However, research has shown that the use of single marks or of weighted combinations of selected marks does not improve the prediction of academic success when compared with the use of the unweighted total average mark or grade-point average (Lissmann, 1977).

Tests of general knowledge are sometimes used (e.g., in some Italian universities). However, in Israel, a subtest of general knowledge has recently been removed from the Psychometric Entrance Test due to its low validity coefficients.

Achievement tests are based on courses of education which have been completed. Aptitude tests, on the other hand, are oriented towards the requirements of courses about to be undertaken. Scholastic aptitudes are usually measured by means of multiple-choice tests, but occasionally also through essay-type examinations. Interviews are also used to estimate scholastic aptitude.

Scholastic aptitude tests are of two main kinds: general scholastic aptitude tests and specific scholastic aptitude tests. The general type, aimed at central cognitive functions that are considered relevant for most courses in higher education, is used in Australia, Israel, Turkey, the Philippines, Sweden, and the United States of America. Specific scholastic aptitude tests are used in a smaller number of countries. In the United States and Canada, tests such as the Graduate Management Admission Test, the Medical College Admission Test, and the Law School Admission Test, are elements in the selection procedure for admission to graduate school. In Germany, all who wish to apply for admission to university courses in medicine, dentistry, or veterinary science must take the Test for Medical Studies.

In a completely different approach, an attempt is made to assess desired personality characteristics such as motives, attitudes, and values. The approach is used in addition to, but hardly ever instead of, achievement or aptitude measures. Most frequently, personality variables are assessed in interview. Also used are testimonials or letters of recommendation written by teachers or other persons who know the candidates well, application essays, biographical questionnaires and, very rarely, personality questionnaires. Interviews are used for certain courses or universities in France (*grandes écoles*), Germany (medical studies), Japan, South Korea, Spain, and in Anglo-Saxon countries.

While the criteria just described are educational and psychological in nature, the criterion waiting-time is a purely formal one. The length of time that has elapsed — 'queueing time' — since a candidate first applied for admission is taken into account for selection for higher education in Germany. The use of this criterion enables public institutions of higher education that have more applicants than available places to solve the dilemma arising from the fundamental right of free choice in education and the lack of places. Applicants, who are not immediately admitted by virtue of high achievement or aptitude, are guaranteed admission provided they are prepared to wait for a number of years. In the long run, however, the procedure ensures the admission of a reduced number of applicants for the simple reason that a considerable portion of those in the queue change their minds and turn to another career.

Yet another non-educational criterion for selection which is used in the Netherlands is chance. In courses that are restricted by *numerus fixus*, a lottery determines which applicants will be admitted from among those who do not meet a certain minimum requirement of average marks in the secondary school leaving certificate. During the first half of the 1980s it also played a part in the German system of admission to medical studies, but an individual's chances of being selected also depended upon the average mark in the school leaving certificate because candidates with better marks could draw more lottery tickets.

In most countries combinations of more than one criterion are used for selection decisions. Procedures may consist of a single stage. This may take several forms. In one, all applicants are placed in rank order according to a (weighted) linear combination of different scores and those with the highest combined scores are admitted. Or all applicants that meet certain minimum standards in each of several criteria are admitted. Single stage systems may also involve a quota system, in which certain proportions of the available places are awarded, each according to a different criterion. Procedures may also be multi-stage. This occurs when different criteria are applied in several steps of the selection process. For example, initial selection may depend on high school rank or total score on a scholastic aptitude test. Further and final selection may be based on the results of an interview.

A BRIEF EVALUATION OF PRACTICE

I will now try to evaluate briefly the selection practices based on the criteria described above in terms of reliability, objectivity, validity, cost, and acceptability. The reliability and objectivity of external tests, both of achievement and aptitude, for selection are generally high. The reliability coefficients of total tests or test sections are mostly greater than .90. By virtue of clearly defined scoring criteria, precise scoring instructions, and highly sophisticated scoring and monitoring techniques, even essay tests for the assessment of aptitudes or achievement can attain satisfactory levels of objectivity and reliability. Marks obtained from school-based assessment are notoriously less objective and less reliable than external tests (Ingenkamp, 1989). The average mark in the school leaving certificate or rank in class seems to be somewhat more reliable than single marks in individual subjects.

The objectivity and reliability of most of the procedures that attempt to assess motives, attitudes, and values are rather low. This is true for the interview as well as for essays, when their avowed purpose is the assessment of attitudes and motives, for testimonials, and for letters of recommendation. The reliability of questionnaires, which can be quite high when used in other contexts, is seriously impaired in selection situations because applicants will provide the responses that they think will further their chances of selection. It goes without saying that waiting-time is a reliable criterion for selection while the lottery is characterized by perfect unreliability.

Predictive validity is the most important feature of selection procedures. If not all applicants can be admitted, it makes sense to accept those who are most likely to succeed in the courses for which they are applying. Instruments with good predictive validity are needed for such selection. The results of the vast majority of longitudinal studies indicate that overall performance in secondary school is the best single predictor of success in higher education. This is usually operationalised as grade-point average or examination marks (Baron-Boldt, 1989; Trost, 1975; Whitney, 1989). The coefficients of correlation vary around and above .50 for short-term prediction and around .45 for longer-term prediction. After performance in secondary school, performance on a scholastic aptitude test best predicts success in higher education. Correlations between the two variables range between .40 and .50 (Donlon, 1984; Willingham, 1985). In a number of studies they are as strong or even stronger than the relationship between performance in secondary school and success in higher education. General and specific scholastic aptitude tests do not appear to differ markedly in their predictive power. The predictive validity coefficients for achievement tests have been found to be as high and even higher than those for scholastic aptitude tests. However, when indicators of performance in secondary school were combined with the results of a scholastic aptitude test, the overall predictive validity was higher than when they were combined with the results of achievement tests.

The predictive validity of decisions about selection based on interviews is low. Most coefficients that have been obtained in a number of countries are lower than .20 (Trost, 1986, 1994). The validity of testimonials and letters of recommendation seems similar to the validity of interviews; again coefficients of the order of .20 have been reported (Breland, 1981). For personality questionnaires, somewhat higher coefficients were found (Breland, 1981), but the faking and ethical problems remain unresolved. Lottery, by definition, has no predictive validity, nor has the length of time an applicant has spent queueing for admission, as this is determined by the number of candidates ahead of him or her in the queue.

Besides the criteria of objectivity, reliability and validity, other features, including relative cost and acceptability, are relevant in judging the usefulness of a given selection procedure. The most economical selection procedure is one which uses information that is already available, for example, marks in secondary school or rank in class. A lottery is also inexpensive, as it is easily carried out on a computer. Waiting-time does not cost institutions of higher education anything, but is very costly for candidates. The development, pre-testing, and administration of standardised tests are all very expensive. In many countries, candidates pay to take the test and thus bear part of the cost; in others (e.g., Germany), there is no charge for taking an admission test. The interview is one of the most expensive assessment procedures. Because of this, it is usually reserved for a small number of applicants who have been preselected on the basis of other criteria.

Considerations of economy must always be balanced against the effects of the selection procedures. Use of an expensive, but valid, aptitude test may be very economical if it results in low rates of failure and dropout among those admitted, while the use of an inexpensive procedure, such as a lottery, can result in high costs to both the institution and the individual if a large proportion of admitted candidates are poorly qualified.

Even the most reliable, most valid, and most economical selection procedure has little chance of being implemented or continued if it is not acceptable to students, staff, and the public. Acceptability has much to do with the face validity of the assessment instruments as well as with the transparency and fairness of the decision process. I cannot go into details on this multi-faceted issue, but will report some general findings on the acceptability of some selection practices.

All available evidence suggests that the interview is highly acceptable world-wide, in spite of its limited reliability and validity (Trost, 1986, 1994), perhaps because it allows for presentation of the 'full person' in face-to-face communication. The acceptability of scholastic aptitude tests and achievement tests appears to be moderate (Trost, 1992).

I could not find international data on the acceptability of the average mark in school or rank in class as selection criteria. German studies in the early 1980s indicate approval by half of the applicant population. However, objections against the use of the average mark as the only criterion were strong. About the same proportion favoured waiting-time, but only one-fifth were in favour of the lottery as a selection device (Fay, 1984).

AN EXAMPLE: ADMISSION TO HIGHER EDUCATION IN GERMANY

I will now describe very briefly the present German system of admission to higher education, which contains many of the elements I have already discussed, though the combination of these elements is rather unique.

The normal route leading to university involves 13 years of school (four years of primary, six years of lower secondary and three years of upper secondary school). The main entrance qualification is the school leaving certificate which is awarded after the final examination (*Abitur*), and may be taken in two modes. The general mode entitles the holder to apply to all institutions of higher education without restriction with regard to subjects, while the subject-restricted mode grants the holder the right to apply for enrolment in specific programmes of study. The entrance qualification for a second type of institution offering more practically oriented courses (*Fachhochschule*) can be acquired after 12 years of school.

Almost all institutions of higher education in Germany are state institutions; admission procedures are therefore uniform and regulated by law. Only a few private institutions are free to determine their own admission procedures. Seventy percent of all courses or subjects at state universities and 15% of courses at state *Fachhochschulen* offer open admission to anyone holding the appropriate school leaving certificate. Candidates apply directly to the institution of their choice for enrolment.

For the remaining courses or subjects, three different kinds of procedure, known as *distribution, general selection*, and *special selection*, are used. For these courses, admission decisions are not, as a rule, made by the respective faculties but by a central agency for the distribution of study places, an administrative interstate institution of the states (*Länder*).

The procedures operate as follows. The distribution procedure is used when there are more applicants than places in some universities or *Fachhochschulen* while there are vacancies at others. A number of applicants are referred to universities or *Fachhochschulen* other than those of their first choice. The only criterion used in this procedure, and this is at present used only for computer science, is the proximity of the respective university to the student's home.

The general selection procedure is used for a considerable number of courses, excluding medical courses, when there are more applicants than places nationwide. Selection is made in a quota system on the basis of two criteria: the average mark in the school leaving certificate, which places all candidates in rank order according to their average mark, is used until 60% of the places in a given university are filled; and waiting time under which remaining applicants are put on a waiting list and admitted according to the length of their waiting time until the remaining 40% of places are filled.

This procedure is in operation for the following courses at universities: architecture, biology, business/management studies, economics, pharmacy, psychology, and for some further subject areas with small numbers of places as well as for 85% of all *Fachhochschule* courses. At present, the cut-off points for the average marks (on a scale from 1.0, best, to 4.3, poorest) fluctuate mostly between 1.5 and 2.5. The minimum waiting-time needed for admission is two to six semesters (one to three years) depending on the course.

The special selection procedure was introduced in 1986 for three courses: medicine, dentistry, and veterinary science, where for a long time competition was stiffest (Trost, 1989). At each university, the available places are awarded within five quotas according to five criteria: weighted combination of average marks in the school leaving certificate (55% of weight) and total score in a specific scholastic aptitude test (Test for Medical Studies) (45% of weight) (45% of the places are reserved to this quota); total score in the Test for Medical Studies alone (10% of places); waiting-time (20% of places); result of an interview conducted by two members of the faculty staff (15% of places); and special cases (e.g., foreigners, hardship cases) (10% of places). The overall selection ratio in the three courses is

1:2·3. Complicated and expensive as this special selection procedure may appear, it at least ensures that candidates with very different types of aptitude, achievement, and motivation have a chance of admission, and thus prevents the student body from being uniform.

REFERENCES

Baron-Boldt, J. (1989). *Die Validität von Schulabschlußnoten für die Prognose von Ausbildungs- und Studienerfolg* [Validity of marks in school leaving certificates for the prediction of success in vocational training and higher education]. Frankfurt: Lang.

Breland, H. M. (1981). *Assessing student characteristics in admission to higher education: A review of procedures* (Research Monograph No. 9). New York: College Entrance Examination Board.

Donlon, F.T. (Ed.). (1984). *The College Board technical handbook for the Scholastic Aptitude and Achievement Tests.* New York: College Entrance Examination Board.

Fay, E. (1984). Einstellungen zum Vergabeverfahren [Attitudes towards admission procedures]. In G. Trost (Ed.), *Test für Medizinische Studiengänge. Studien zur Evaluation* [Test for Medical Studies: Evaluation Studies] (pp. 157-161). Bonn: Institut für Test- und Begabungsforschung.

Ingenkamp, K. (Ed.). (1989). *Die Fragwürdigkeit der Zensurengebung* [The questionableness of marking in school] (8th ed.). Weinheim: Beltz.

Lissmann, U. (1977). *Gewichtung von Abiturnoten und Studienerfolg* [Weighting of marks in the secondary school leaving certificate and success in higher education]. Weinheim: Beltz.

Trost, G. (1975). *Vorhersage des Studienerfolgs* [Prediction of academic success]. Braunschweig: Westermann.

Trost, G. (1986). Die Bedeutung des Interviews für die Diagnose der Studieneignung. Darstellung der internationalen Forschungsergebnisse [The relevance of interviews for the assessment of academic aptitudes. Review of international findings]. In R. Lohölter (Ed.), *Das Interview im Zulassungsverfahren zum Medizinstudium* [The interview for admission to medical schools] (pp. 49-80). Stuttgart: Schattauer.

Trost, G. (1989). A nationwide testing program for admission to medical schools in West Germany. In R. C. King & J. K. Collins (Eds.), *Social applications and issues in psychology* (pp. 131-137). Amsterdam: Elsevier Science Publishers.

Trost, G. (1992). Attitudes and reactions of West German students with respect to scholastic aptitude tests in selection and counseling programs. In B. Nevo & R. S. Jäger (Eds.), *Psychological testing: The examinee perspective* (pp. 148-169). Frankfurt: Deutsches Institut für Internationale Pädagogische Forschung.

Trost, G. (1994). Interview. In K. Pawlik (Ed.), *Differentielle Psychologie, Bd. 1: Grundlagan und Methoden. Enzyklopädie der Psychologie.* [Differential psychology, vol. 1: Foundations and methods. Encyclopedia of Psychology] (pp. 381-421). Göttingen: Hogrefe.

Whitney, D. R. (1989). Educational admissions and placement. In R. Linn (Ed.), *Educational measurement*. (pp. 527-543). New York: Macmillan.

Willingham, W.W. (1985). *Success in college. The role of personal qualities and academic ability.* New York: College Entrance Examination Board.

3. COMBINING DISPARATE INFORMATION FOR SELECTION PURPOSES: CHALLENGES TO VALIDITY

John Izard
Australian Council for Educational Research,
Camberwell, Victoria

The educational practices of schools are coming under increasing scrutiny by administrators, governments, and taxpayers. Concern with evaluating what schools do has resulted in national and international focuses on assessment that is seen to provide a measure of what students (and therefore schools) do. Assessment is considered to provide valid evidence of learning achievement to inform students, to facilitate provision of further learning, or to certify that a required level has been reached (Izard, 1992). However, the procedures used to obtain the final assessments may not justify the faith we have in the assessments. This paper examines some of the implications of particular approaches to obtaining final assessments and suggests ways in which the combination of information for assessment purposes might be monitored.

EXTENDING THE RANGE OF ASSESSMENT INFORMATION

In efforts to provide a more comprehensive picture of a student's learning achievements, assessment strategies are being extended to cover knowledge, understandings, skills, and personal qualities not usually assessed by traditional tests. This extension to include tasks to assess the development of initiative, taking responsibility for learning, and applying problem-solving strategies relies on the reasonable presumption that assessment tasks should be representative of tasks implied in curriculum intentions. Use of more realistic tasks in assessment has the potential for ensuring that the tasks mirror the desired skills, hence contributing to valid assessment. However, variety in the range of possible responses makes the use of such assessment strategies problematic. Academic audits (both external and internal) at British universities and polytechnics have provided comments such as: 'It is extremely difficult to compare projects on widely differing topics' (external examiner, 1990); 'It is difficult to compare different projects and hence mark them fairly. I would like to see a much more detailed report from the ... examiners justifying the marks awarded ... ensuring disciplined marking' (external examiner, 1991), and 'The committee considered that the absence of a numerical mark, and of feedback, provided no guidance ... [to students]' (internal review, 1991).

The media play an important part in influencing public views of the assessment process, raising concerns about the acceptability of particular examinations. Their role has already been in evidence in Australia, Canada, Great Britain, and the United States. Often, however, it is difficult to distinguish between facts, media hype, and politicians (from all sides) scoring points against each other. It should be remembered that good results are rarely considered newsworthy. Australian newspapers, which reported declining standards from the evidence collected in the first Australian study of literacy and numeracy in 1975, ignored the second study in 1980 which provided the first real evidence that there had been no decline (and that in some cases there had been an improvement).

Assessment procedures need to deal with complexity, encourage better communication between examinee and examiner, and lead to more consistent and relevant assessment. Such procedures have to be representative so that reasonable inferences about learning achievements that are not assessed can be made from the component of achievements that have been assessed. The procedures should be feasible and should provide information about the examiner's confidence in the precision of the assessments. Assessment strategies should be fair to each student so that students are rewarded in accordance with their genuine knowledge and skill. They should provide students with information to support their own learning as well as trustworthy certification that will inform those who will use the assessments as part of the selection process for entry to later stages of education. 'The information provided by assessment should do more than portray a learner's level of performance. It should inform the actions of all participants in the learning situation. ... Links must be forged between the assessment, the instruction it reviews, and the instruction it anticipates' (Clarke, 1989, p.4).

WHO IS TO USE RESULTS?

Examination boards often have no say in who is to use the information they provide and very little control of the way in which information is used. A number of questions arise. Are some results the private property of the candidate? Are some results the private property of the school? Should results derived during the learning process have as much currency as the results at the end of a stage of learning? Is it reasonable to compare students on an (unstated) assumed equivalence of subjects (if the examinations are subject based)? Other questions relating to the qualifications of those who would use the information include: How should those wishing to use test results be prepared before being allowed to make their decisions? Does one rank order suit all vocations as well as further education and community service? Can place in class be interpreted in a meaningful way? Do employers have a responsibility to make their selection criteria explicit? Is wastage of trainees a function of inappropriate selection criteria? Should employers and further education authorities have to demonstrate that their judgments are reliable? I cannot offer any easy solutions, but draw attention to the fact that these issues impinge on validity.

THE IMPORTANCE OF ASSESSMENT PRACTICES

Gasking (1948) has argued that examinations exert considerable pressure on the subjects and the topics within those subjects that are taught, and on the teaching strategies which are used. He draws two conclusions. 'First, a reformer, a teacher or an administrator, who wishes to introduce certain changes into school education, will, if the examinations remain the same, find his efforts defeated in the long run, unless the changes he introduces increase the chance of examination success' (p.10). 'But conversely, if a reformer succeeds in introducing changes in the type of examination, he will automatically tend to bring about such changes in the content and method of education as are likely to make for success in the changed type of examination' (p.10). Gasking also discussed the effects of indirect measurement as compared with the direct measurement of relevant skills and knowledge. 'The easiest way ... for teachers to get good results is to concentrate on imparting those capacities which are directly measured in the examination, even if these are not the real objectives of the course, but are merely capacities which the examiners are trying to use as indirect measures. Thus education is perverted away from its real objectives, on to those which the examiners use as indirect measures' (p.14).

Since the easiest things to measure relatively objectively are knowledge of facts (particularly isolated facts rather than interrelationships) and knowledge of the verbal expression of theories, generalisations and definitions, examinations tend to have high proportions of such questions, rather than questions which test understanding or applications in novel circumstances. Initially, using factual recall provides an indirect measure of the higher order skills based on the assumption of a reasonably high correlation between the intended skills and those actually measured. However, intensive coaching in the indirect criterion tends to reduce this correlation, and the indirect measure ceases to be a valid indicator of the true objectives (Gasking, 1948, p.15). Gasking pointed out that when examiners perceive that students without the intended skills are passing, they may raise the standard required in the indirect criterion. This diverts schools even more from the intended skills and makes the examination an even less valid measure of those skills. His advice is to have direct measures wherever possible.

Madaus (1988) reaches similar conclusions when considering the literature on the power of testing practices to influence curriculum, teaching, and learning. Where students, teachers, and administrators believe that the results of an examination are important, their actions are guided by this perceived importance. Where measurement of learning achievement is used for important decisions, teachers are likely to teach to the test, developing test-taking skills rather than improving the educational process, and treating the test results themselves as the major goal rather than the achievement itself.

THE VALIDITY OF EXAMINATION MARKS

Examination boards tend not to pay explicit attention to the topic of the validity of examination marks. Strategies for assessing the validity of examination marks, underlying assumptions, the effects of aggregation of examination marks, and the scaling of marks for selection, whether outside the control of the examinee's examination authority or not, do not appear to be issues of immediate concern. Boards tend to provide reports of marks (whether standardised, re-scaled, or not) and a variety of descriptive statistics about individual subjects or courses, and about the marks obtained by anonymous groups of students. However, the approaches used in the scoring of papers, in the aggregation of marks, and in the scaling of results can have profound effects on particular individuals.

What is meant by validity in this context? The basic question must be: Is this student's result a true indication of the student's skill or knowledge at the time the examination was administered? From the student's perspective, the extent to which responses are typical of the student is probably of most interest to the student (and parents and teachers). From the examination board perspective, the extent to which the sample of skills and knowledge is representative of the curriculum intention is the major concern. The examination board probably has to assume that it is the candidate's responsibility to respond in an appropriate way, but obtaining a representative result at the time of testing depends upon both sources of variation. Clearly there are hosts of related questions, for example: Is the result an indication that the candidate will retain the skill or knowledge for a specified period of time? Is the result an indication that the candidate has a high probability of being able to use that skill or knowledge in a new context at a future point in time? How long will these results remain current?

Many published validity studies are concerned with either results on a single assessment instrument (perhaps by comparison with accepted instruments) or results from sets of instruments in conjunction with other performance data. The analyses from a study of a single instrument may be concerned with internal consistency — the extent to which the items which make up the instrument have similar properties. Such analyses might use computer packages such as Bigsteps (Wright & Linacre, 1991) or QUEST (Adams & Khoo, 1991, 1993). Analyses of sets of instruments may concentrate on variance shared in common or on unique variance. Analyses might involve such techniques as regression (Darlington, 1968) or factor analysis. There may be limited opportunities for examination boards to undertake such analyses of sets of instruments because the analyses require large numbers of candidates to attempt a common battery of tests; examination boards may not be in a position to ask candidates to attempt tasks not directly related to that year's assessments.

Examination boards are likely to use item analysis to examine the characteristics of items before use, particularly if the proposed examination papers are of the multiple-choice type. However, appropriate procedures are less likely to be used if questions are open-ended, although our knowledge of assessment practice suggests greater problems when the complexity of examiner variation is introduced. Examination boards may have an opportunity to provide specialised training for those hired to mark papers, but procedures also need to be in place to monitor the performance of examiners (just as flight crew employed by airlines have to be checked to ensure that they are continuing to operate in an appropriate way).

The use of school-based assessments is intended to access a wider range of information than that measured by a traditional examination and to allow such information to be collected over a period of time. Such assessments are presumed to be more accurate descriptions of a person's achievements because they invole more diverse and multiple sampling of assessment tasks. As with other forms of assessment there are critical issues to be addressed. How can we ensure that the evidence collected in schools is relevant and valid? Does similar performance on similar tasks result in similar assessments? How do we take account of a wider diversity of tasks and still ensure comparability? Is superior performance recognised (regardless of school) in a fair way? Internal consistency research is less likely to be carried out by examination boards for coursework options, implying that coursework is not considered important in the eyes of the examination authorities. Yet examination boards often make use of information provided by others who may not have had training for the task. Note that reducing the proportion of marks assigned to coursework options does not solve the problem; it merely tends to distort the curriculum intentions in subtle ways.

Where information from multiple-choice examinations and/or open-ended examinations is aggregated to provide a subject result, it is important to investigate the contribution of each part to the total result. Aggregation of subjects to give an overall score for selection purposes (or for deciding whether a certificate is to be issued) needs scrutiny too. The nominal weightings given to the candidates may not be reflected in the marks actually awarded and the aggregation effect can distort the assessment from the intended balance (see Izard, 1991). If appropriate monitoring is not carried out, examination boards may well be conveying misleading advice to candidates, employers, and further education authorities.

For example, advocates of the teaching of mathematics through modelling activities in the classroom consider that these activities are more authentic, and address situations where there are multiple (correct) solutions, where there is a diversity of problem-solving approaches, or where skills cannot be demonstrated easily in pencil-and-paper format. Those who judge the projects should also share the same meanings for all or most of the descriptors. As projects differ in the demands they make on candidates, choosing a project which makes less demand may give a student an advantage by allowing mastery of a topic to be demonstrated more easily. If each person does a different project, and no person does more than one project, there is no way in which the influence of the project can be separated from the achievement of the candidate. The assessment process adds its own problems. Examiners look for different features, give those features differing emphasis, have different views of complexity, and therefore assign differing values to the work and vary in their assigned marks. It is common practice for examiners to partition the marks to different sections of the work or categories of tasks (see Haines, 1992).

EFFECTS OF PARTICULAR PRACTICES

There are a number of practices which occur frequently in examination procedures that require careful monitoring.

Restricting the range of tasks being assessed. Tasks that are assessed are explicit indications of the topics and issues that an examining authority considers to be of major importance. Curriculum intentions may be ignored in order to meet the requirements of the examination. If the examination assesses only a part of the curriculum, that part becomes the *de facto* entire curriculum. Accordingly, valid assessment requires that all aspects of the curriculum be assessed (or at least a representative sample).

Assuming intended weights are actual weights. Procedures are needed for combining and aggregating scores so that one component does not exert undue influence (Izard, 1991). When examination boards place statements on examination papers to indicate the number of marks allocated to individual questions, or parts of questions, there is an assumption that the full range of these marks will be used when examiners are assigning scores. In other words, a 1-mark question is to be worth one-fifth of a 5-mark question. This assumption is reasonable when there are large candidatures (unless the information required is trivial). However, if examiners do not use the full range of scores in this way (for example, when every candidate obtains full marks on this question, regardless of their level of skill on all other questions), the information provided to the candidates is misleading. In fact, in such a case the weights presented on the examination paper do not appear to be followed. Litigation might follow if a statistically sophisticated candidate considers that due credit was not awarded for getting that question correct. Izard & Griffin (1989) have shown that sub-tests with low between-subtest correlations can be interpreted in a reasonable way provided that the scaling process used to combine the scores does, in fact, ensure that the intended weights are the actual weights.

Combining different components to obtain a subject score. How should results on disparate subjects be combined? To extend an analogy with money presented by Viviani (1990), a score of three obtained by combining one US dollar with two sterling pounds will have a different value to a score of three obtained by combining two US dollars with one sterling pound. The relationship between the two currencies (at a particular time) must be known so that the combined value can be expressed in a comparable way. As McGaw, Eyers, Montgomery, Nicholls, and Poole (1990, p.30) have observed, 'The aggregation of unscaled marks is inappropriate and unjustifiable. If individual subjects are too different for scaling of their results on a common scale to make sense, then it makes no sense to add the results. Another way to make this point is to say that whenever it is believed appropriate to add results then it is appropriate to express them on a common scale before doing so'.

Monitoring scoring. Examination boards generally accept scores based on objective tests and are happy to allocate high proportions of the marks to such test results. In such cases it might be said that the board 'trusts' the questions, and since the answers appear to be tamper-proof, the results obtained can be trusted too. In the case of open-ended questions, many boards check the capabilities of their examiner panels before the task commences. This is admirable as it attempts to ensure that incompetent examiners will be detected before they tackle 'real' examination scripts. However, quality control is also necessary during the process of the marking to ensure that problems that arise at this stage are detected as they occur. For example, while one examiner may be consistent with others in the sense that there is general agreement about which responses are best and which are not, he/she could still vary considerably in stringency or leniency. Candidates examined by this examiner will be less likely to receive the credit awarded by other examiners for the same knowledge and skill. If such an examiner is found in a checking procedure, there is an obligation to rectify the problem in the interest of fairness to candidates.

DESIRABLE PRACTICE

One essential element in achieving valid examination results is to ensure use of procedures which lead to comparable standards. Candidates expect that the task of reaching a particular standard will not become more difficult in the year that they sit for their examination. Some examination boards seek to achieve this by using group consensus at meetings of examiners. At such meetings, sample examination scripts are assessed by all, and the examination board's staff check to see whether there is general agreement on standards. Simple measures of location and spread are not sufficient in this context, because they cannot distinguish between erratic marking and consistent but stringent (or lenient) marking. One needs an analytic technique which considers all of the sample passages together, all of the assessors together, and identifies erratic assessors together with the type of examination script with which they have difficulty. This is one way of testing the assumption that the marks awarded correlate with the quality of the examinee responses.

Some educational programmes seek to encourage students to take more responsibility for their own learning. Falchikov and Boud (1989) observe that 'Life-long learning requires that individuals be able not only to work independently, but also to assess their own performance and progress' (p. 395). Although they identified both substantive and methodological problems in the self-assessment literature (relating to higher education), they considered that 'self-assessment may be regarded as a skill and, as such, needs to be developed' (p. 425). They recommend that good assessment practice should include training of assessors whether ratings are made by students or teachers. They conclude that experienced teachers are not reliable markers in all situations and, therefore, it might be reasonable to expect inexperienced students to lack such skills.

There are other sound educational reasons why more emphasis should be placed on self-assessment skills. Withers and McCurry (1990) argue that student participation in determining the broad structure of a course and the details of its progress (such as content, assessment, and reporting procedures) is superior to present approaches where syllabuses and assessment are imposed from above. They assert that such participation enhances the quality of a student's life (real and perceived), makes positive changes in what is learned in school, increases the validity and utility of a course, and helps students, parents, and teachers develop a common understanding of how assessments were obtained and what the reports mean. Research by Batten (1989) has demonstrated that, relative to their peers in traditional secondary school classes, students participating in this way value the improvement in quality of their school life, take greater control over their learning, have a better self-image, and are better judges of their knowledge, skills, and achievements.

Incorporating self-assessment may well be one of the most difficult tasks facing examination boards but the problem is well worth investigation. It could go a considerable way towards changing the face of examination boards from measures of how full the 'bucket' is to measures of the skills and powers of individuals to participate fully in the community.

REFERENCES

Adams, R. J., & Khoo, S. T. (1991, 1993). *QUEST: The interactive test analysis system.* Melbourne: Australian Council for Educational Research.

Batten, M. (1989). *Year 12: Student expectations and experiences.* (ACER Research Monograph No. 33). Hawthorn: Australian Council for Educational Research.

Clarke, D. J. (1989). *Mathematics curriculum and teaching program (MCTP): Alternatives in mathematics.* Canberra: Curriculum Development Centre.

Darlington, R. B. (1968). Multiple regression in psychological research and practice. *Psychological Bulletin, 69,* 161-182.

Falchikov, N., & Boud, D. (1989). Student self-assessment in higher education: A meta-analysis. *Review of Educational Research, 59,* 395-430.

Gasking, D. A. T. (1948). *Examinations and the aims of education.* Carlton: Melbourne University Press.

Haines, C. R. (1992). Developing assessment strategies for mathematics projects. In M. Stephens & J. Izard (Eds.), *Reshaping assessment practices: Assessment in the mathematical sciences under challenge.* (pp. 127-141). Hawthorn: Australian Council for Educational Research.

Izard, J. (1991). Issues in the assessment of non-objective and objective examination tasks. In A. J. M. Luitjen (Ed.), *Issues in public examinations. Proceedings of the Sixteenth IAEA Conference.* (pp. 73-83). Utrecht: Lemma, B.V.

Izard, J. (1992). *Assessing learning achievement.* Paris: United Nations Educational, Scientific and Cultural Organization.

Izard, J., & Griffin, P. E. (1989, November). *Spatial tests for tertiary selection: A pilot study.* Paper presented at the Fifteenth International Conference of the International Association for Educational Assessment, Sydney.

Madaus, G. F. (1988). The influence of testing on the curriculum. In L. N. Tanner (Ed.), *Critical issues in curriculum. Eighty-seventh Yearbook of the National Society for the Study of Education, Part 1.* (pp. 83-121). Chicago, Il.: National Society for the Study of Education.

McGaw, B., Eyers, V., Montgomery, J., Nicholls, B., & Poole, M. (1990). *Assessment in the Victorian Certificate of Education: Report of a review commissioned by the Victorian Minister for Education and the Victorian Curriculum and Assessment Board.* Melbourne: Victorian Curriculum and Assessment Board.

Viviani, N. (1990). *The review of tertiary entrance in Queensland.* Report submitted to the Minister of Education. Brisbane: Queensland Department of Education.

Withers, G., & McCurry, D. (1990). Student participation in assessment in a co-operative climate. In B. Low & G. Withers (Eds.), *Developments in school and public assessment. Australian Education Review, 31,* 77-101. Hawthorn: Australian Council for Educational Research.

Wright, B. D., & Linacre, J. M. (1991). *A user's guide to BIGSTEPS: Rasch-model computer program.* Chicago, Il.: MESA Press.

4. ADMISSION TO HIGHER EDUCATION: CURRENT DILEMMAS AND PROPOSED SOLUTIONS

Michal Beller
National Institute for Testing and Evaluation, Jerusalem

University admission is only one of the areas that raise issues involving the fair distribution of rare and highly-valued resources that preoccupy society (Klitgraad, 1986). Several approaches to solving such problems have been adopted.

One invokes the free market. In this the solution is based on the principle that the payer of the highest price wins. This is the situation, for example, in all auctions. A second approach is based on the concept of equal probability. This is used when it seems that a lottery may be the proper solution; for instance, a lottery for tickets to a particularly popular concert, or to decide who will serve in the army (as in the U.S. during the Vietnam War). A third approach is based on seniority-based rating. In this situation, the 'first-come, first-served' principle or seniority is the basis for distributing benefits. It is used when promotions are based on seniority or when the most recently employed lose their jobs in cutbacks. A fourth approach, based on meritocracy, is very popular and is used by most of the world's universities in making admissions decisions. 'Merit' is what matters — quality of performance or excellence.

There is almost no country in the world in which the number of candidates for higher education does not exceed the number of available places (at least in some areas of study). No society (no matter how affluent) can afford to offer unlimited opportunity for higher education to all. This is particularly true in the case of medicine and the natural sciences, for which laboratories and expensive technological equipment are required. Thus, reality necessitates some sort of selection and sifting process.

THE SITUATION IN ISRAEL

In public discussions regarding the admissions policies of Israeli universities, statements such as the following have frequently been made: 'The government should ensure that all Israelis with matriculation certificates have the opportunity to test their abilities in higher education in universities or colleges,' and 'Psychometric tests may erect a barrier in the paths of young people who deserve to enter higher education.' However, it must be noted that needs are almost entirely met at present. Over 80% of Israelis with matriculation certificates receive higher education, most of them at university and a minority at other academic institutions. The real barrier standing between young people and higher education is the matriculation certificate, which is a *sine qua non* for entrance to academic institutions (except the open university), and is earned by only one third of all 18-year-olds today. Removal of this barrier is not an issue of current debate, although consideration is being given to ways of making the certificate more attainable.

Although anyone with a matriculation certificate can acquire a higher education, not everyone can study in the field or institution of one's choice. The existence of selective fields (i.e., fields which do not accept all candidates) is mainly because of quotas or limits on the number of students that a department can absorb and teach. Such limits may result from restrictions within the department (such as a shortage of teachers or laboratories) or from external circumstances (such as a shortage of places available for professional training or counselling). In any case, popular departments must use some method to choose their students from the population of applicants. It is appropriate to consider the nature of this method, but one must not confuse the question of whether or not, or to what extent, there is a need for selection of candidates, with the issue of which instruments will provide the basis upon which the selection is being made. The obstacle hindering some young people from realising their ambitions in the area of higher education is the existence of an admissions quota (and the fact that the number of applicants exceeds it) and not the selection instrument.

One radical suggestion for solving this problem is to adopt a model of completely 'open admission.' Following such a model, all applicants would be accepted to their departments of choice and would be able to continue in them as long as they achieved 'passing' grades in their studies. Adoption of this method would mean, in the short run, that classes would be large and crowded, that the average achievement level of students would be lower, and, therefore, that the level of teaching would probably suffer. Moreover, the number of people signing up for popular departments might even exceed what it is today, since the sign-up process currently involves 'natural selection.' Many students decide in advance not to apply for a course if they believe their chances of being admitted are small. It may seem that some of the problems of open admission might be solved in the long term if greater resources were invested in higher education. But the budgets that would be required to realize this dream are not available, and such a proposal is not being seriously considered today. In addition, it is worth mentioning that even allowing everyone to study in his or her field of choice would still not remove all barriers to self-realization since the capacity of the Israeli job market to absorb psychologists, doctors, lawyers, film directors, and so on, is very limited and thus not all graduates would be able to find work in their field.

A more practical and frequently made proposal suggests that open admission should be allowed for the first year of study only, selection being used for entry to the second year based on students' first year achievements. The opening of all departments in this way, even for one year, would involve great costs, but this approach, like the former, recognises the real need for quotas in various departments. However, although it seems to many that selection based on academic achievement is more just and more appropriate than selection which precedes admission to university studies, this method exacts a heavy price from the students who are accepted. This is because, as long as such quotas exist, continuity of studies cannot be ensured for every student, but only for the very best. Imagine, for instance, that a certain department accepts 500 students to first year studies and that, among those, 300 successfully pass their courses, but that only 100 can be accepted for continuing studies. In this situation, two-thirds of the 'passing' students are rejected.

A selection process based on first year achievement has already been tried in several places in Israel. For example, one university ran a pre-law programme for several years. The number of students accepted to the preliminary course far exceeded the quota allotted for its graduates by the law school. The students in the programme found out that it was not sufficient to be 'good', but that it was necessary to be 'better' than other students in the programme, since only the best would be accepted for law school. This competition fostered a harsh, unpleasant atmosphere among the students and between students and teachers (an atmosphere of 'every student for him/herself'), and the programme was cancelled after several trial years. Another example of the disadvantages of this method is provided by the Psychology departments in Israeli universities. Because of certain objective restrictions, only one half of the graduates of these departments are accepted for the masters programme, but a masters degree is necessary for membership of the Psychological Association and for receiving a work licence as a psychologist. Since the admissions cut-off for bachelors programmes in the Psychology departments is very high (due to factors of supply and demand), students are usually of very high calibre, and, therefore, in the transition from bachelors to masters programmes, candidates with final grades averaging above 90 are sometimes rejected, a fact which is discouraging and to many seems unfair. Those who are not accepted to the masters programme cannot continue work in their chosen field even though they have already invested in three years of study.

Given such considerations, and assuming that the desire is to select candidates before they invest time and money in studies the future of which is uncertain, the question arises of how, and based on what criteria, students should be selected. The issue has both social and professional aspects. The question of who deserves a place in a selective department is a social question, which depends on the selection approach adopted by society. It may be decided, for example, that every candidate who wants to, has an equal right to study a certain subject. In that case, if in a certain department 400 candidates are competing for 100 places (a realistic supposition in certain departments), and each candidate is to be given an equal chance of being accepted, then candidates must be selected by lottery. This method, like open admission, would lower the academic level of the admitted class since selection is not based on quality. And so, even though it is 'fair' on a certain level, it is not practical in a society which strives for quality. And, indeed, there are no (serious) proposals today for university admissions that exclude quality considerations.

Universities have adopted the meritocratic approach to accepting students and have decided to give precedence in admissions to the 'best' students. Ideally, this means the acceptance by each department of those who will be the 'best' students in that department. Since universities lack prior knowledge about each candidate's likely future success, however, a means has to be found of predicting candidates' achievements and of choosing those whose chances of success are high. In this case, there is general agreement that candidates should be rated using the most objective and valid rating methods, i.e., using the best available predictive tools for success in academic studies.

A DESCRIPTION OF THE UNIVERSITY ADMISSIONS PROCESS IN ISRAEL

Each university in Israel independently determines its own admissions policies and quotas for each area of study. It may be stated, generally, that in most fields of study admissions decisions involve a ranking of candidates from 'best' to 'weakest' based on composite scores comprised of two components (usually given equal weight): the high school matriculation certificate and the Psychometric Entrance Test (designed by the National Institute for Testing and Evaluation, founded by the universities in 1981). Based on the ranked list of candidates, a minimum admissions point is determined by the number of students that each department has decided to accept. When necessary, other means of selection may be used, such as tests of knowledge or of specific abilities (in Music, Mathematics, or languages), interviews, and personality assessments (in Medicine). In certain fields of study, a minimum cut-off point for admissions is determined irrespective of quotas, to ensure that students are able to meet certain basic requirements (Mathematics, English, Hebrew, or matriculation grades). The cut-off points for admissions may vary from year to year, as a function of the selection ratio (the ratio of the number of candidates to the number of available places). In other words, the cut-off points for admission are a function of supply and demand: the larger the number of applicants and the smaller the number of available places, the higher the admissions cut-off points.

In recent years, the cut-off points for admission to Law and Medical schools, Engineering, Computer Studies, Business Management, Accounting, and Psychology have been relatively high (1.5-2.0 standard deviations above the mean), whereas in other fields of study, the admissions cut-off points have been in the range close to one standard deviation above or below the mean.

The Psychometric Entrance Test (PET)

The Psychometric Entrance Test (PET) measures various cognitive and scholastic abilities, in order to estimate future success in academic studies. As of October 1990, the test battery comprises three subtests:

(i) Verbal Reasoning (V). This subtest is comprised of 60 items which focus on verbal skills and abilities needed for academic studies: the ability to analyze and understand complex written material, the ability to think systematically and logically, and the ability to perceive fine distinctions in meaning among words and concepts. The verbal sections generally contain a number of different types of questions, such as antonyms, analogies, sentence completion, logic, and reading comprehension.

(ii) Quantitative Reasoning (Q). This subtest is comprised of 50 items. It focuses on the ability to use numbers and mathematical concepts — algebraic problems and equations as well as geometrical ones — to solve quantitative problems, and the ability to analyze information presented in the form of graphs, tables, and charts. Solving problems in this area requires only basic knowledge of mathematics — the mathematical level acquired in the 9th or 10th grades in most high schools in Israel. Formulas and explanations of mathematical terms which may be needed in the course of the examination appear in the test booklet.

(iii) English (E). The English (as a foreign language) subtest serves a dual purpose: it is a component of the PET total score and is also used for placement of students in remedial English classes. The test is comprised of 54 items that are designed to test command of the English language, to the extent that this is required for reading and understanding texts at an academic level. The English subtest contains three types of questions: sentence completion, restatements, and reading comprehension.

All PET items are multiple-choice. Each subtest is separately scored, using number-right formulas, and standardized on a scale which had a mean of 100 and a standard deviation of 20 for the original norming group in 1984. The total PET score is a weighted average of the scores on the three subtests (40%V, 40%Q, 20%E), transformed on to a scale ranging from 200 to 800, which originally had a mean of 500 and a standard deviation of 100.

In establishing admissions policy for universities in Israel, policy-makers and psychometricians have been faced with the question of finding the best method for predicting the academic success of non-Hebrew-speaking applicants in institutions of higher education, where the language of instruction is Hebrew. It was decided to translate PET into the languages spoken by large numbers of non-Hebrew-speaking applicants. Currently, the test is translated into Arabic, Russian, English, French, and Spanish. A combined Hebrew and English (H & E) version is offered to applicants who are not proficient in any of the aforementioned languages. Around 20% (of 56,883 examinees in 1991/92) chose to take PET in a foreign language (10% in Arabic, 7.5% in Russian, and 2.5% in other foreign languages). The non-Hebrew versions of PET are essentially translations of the Hebrew form, and thus have a similar structure. The accuracy of the translation is checked by translating the non-Hebrew version back into Hebrew and comparing it with the original. In addition, items that do not meet specified psychometric standards are removed, *post hoc*, from the test. Scores on the different language versions are equated to those of the Hebrew version. The examinees who choose to take PET in a foreign language are required to take an additional Hebrew proficiency test which is scored separately.

EVALUATION OF THE ADMISSIONS PROCESS

Klitgraad's (1986) approach may be adopted in order to evaluate the selection method used in Israel in relation to three aspects: efficiency, bias, and indirect effects (personal, social, educational) (see Beller, 1994).

Efficiency

A broad perspective on the efficiency of a selection method may be obtained by examining the expected general utility of one selection process as compared to that of other processes. Predictive validity is an important factor in such a perspective, but not the only one. Other factors also taken into consideration are the cost of the system, the selection ratio, and the basic success rate in studies, all of which contribute to the utility of the selection procedure.

Predictive Validity. The most important consideration in the examination of the efficiency of a selection system is its predictive validity. Predictive validity is an expression of the test's success rate in predicting that which it is supposed to predict. In university admissions, it is appropriate to predict final grade point averages (at the end of the first year or at the end of the degree) as the best measure of success in studies. Given a group of candidates and a fixed number of acceptances, the higher the predictive validity of the applied selection method, the higher the average final grades of those who were chosen according to it.

Broad reviews of research based on an analysis of the academic achievement of all students (82,389 students in 1,031 units of study) who began their studies at

Israeli universities in the eight years between 1985 and 1992, show that the correlation between average matriculation grade and the criterion (average grade at the end of the first year of university studies) ranges across different faculties on average between 0.21 and 0.37 (Oren, 1992a; Oren, Bronner, & Kennet-Cohen, 1993). The correlation between the PET score and the criterion ranges between 0.22 and 0.40. The correlation between the composite score (in which equal weight is given to the components) and the criterion ranges between 0.32 and 0.46.

For obvious reasons, the students included in the validity studies were only those whose acceptance to university was based on the tests and who completed at least their first year of study. Hence, the correlations cited will underestimate the true validity coefficients because of the restriction of range determined by the selection ratio. After statistical correction for restriction of range, the following meta-analytical results emerge. The predictive validity of the matriculation certificate ranges on average between 0.35 and 0.51; the predictive validity of PET ranges on average between 0.40 and 0.54; and the predictive validity of the composite score ranges on average between 0.51 and 0.62. These data indicate that excluding one of the components would necessarily decrease predictive validity and the ability to make precise predictions about academic achievement in all areas of study.

Higher validity coefficients were found in other studies which included not only those accepted to universities but also representative groups found beneath the admissions cut-off points. These studies clearly indicate that the chances for academic success decrease as the acceptance score (based on a combination of the psychometric test and the matriculation certificate) decreases. This is expressed in a decrease in average academic achievements and in an increase in drop-out rates for academic reasons (Ben-Shakhar & Beller, 1983).

It is important to emphasise that the validity coefficients reported by the selection system used in Israel today meet international standards, and are similar to those reported by the most sophisticated selection systems available today, such as the Scholastic Aptitude Test system used in the U.S. for selection of candidates to the top universities (Donlon, 1984; Linn, 1990).

A criticism often levelled at psychometric tests and at the entire admissions process is based on examples of mistakes in prediction. Critics are correct in claiming that, under the present system, some students who could have succeeded are rejected. But every selection process with imperfect validity involves such eventualities. The difference between selection based exclusively on matriculation grades and selection based on a weighted score or on first year grades, lies only in the relative number of such errors in prediction: the higher the validity, the lower the chances of such errors. As of now, there is no known method for exposing prediction errors ahead of time. If there were, it would immediately be adopted. Moreover, even if we had a system of perfect predictive validity, the existence of quotas would necessitate the rejection of some who could succeed in their studies, but who would be less successful, on average, than those who were accepted.

It is important to emphasise that, apart from other effects of leaving the selection of students to the end of the first year of study, it is doubtful if the adoption of such a system would improve predictive validity. It is known that the correlation between first and second year grades within a department is not perfect (0.6-0.7), and that the correlation between first year grades in a general studies programme (such as a programme involving all departments in a given faculty) and the continuation of studies in a given department is even lower (due among other reasons, to a lack of uniformity in the standards for grades given in the first year of a general programme). Thus, first year grades are nothing more than predictions of a student's ultimate success, and their imagined advantage over prior selection is nullified

Utility. A broad examination of the efficiency of the admissions system includes not only a discussion of the system's predictive validity, but also of its utility. Ben-Shakhar and Beller (1983) conducted a study in which they applied a threshold utility model to assess the student selection procedure in the Faculty of Humanities at the Hebrew University, assuming that no quota restrictions existed. The approach adopted avoided exact estimation of the utility function, estimating instead the range of utility ratios (i.e., the ratio between the utilities of false-positive and false-negative errors) for which the predictor is useful. A usefulness index was defined for the predictor in terms of its contribution to the expected utility of the possible outcomes of the decision problem. The ranges of utility ratios for which the predictor is useful were computed for several values of operating costs and for three dichotomous definitions of student success. The results demonstrated fairly large ranges of usefulness, meaning that under a moderate estimate of its costs, expected utility is larger when selection is based on the predictor as compared with an *a priori* strategy to either accept or reject all applicants. The results also demonstrate that because of the negative relationship that exists between the probability of achieving a certain academic criterion and the utility of that criterion, utility ratios and prior probabilities of success tend to neutralise one another. For this reason, even moderate gains in validity are often sufficient for justifying additional selection tools.

It should be noted that conclusions from this study are limited since they compared a selection procedure that was based on a certain predictor with an *a priori* strategy of either accepting or rejecting all applicants, a strategy that is rarely adopted in university admissions. An alternative selection procedure that is less valid but less costly typically exists. Therefore, an additional study was carried out by Ben-Shakhar, Kiderman, and Beller (1983), which deals with a more realistic situation where the utility of a more valid, but more expensive, selection procedure is compared with that of a less valid and less costly one. The main question raised in this study was whether adding the PET to matriculation grades is beneficial. PET, which is specifically administered for student admission, is costly, and the real question faced by the university authorities is whether the increase in validity (or decrease in decision errors) justifies the additional costs. The threshold utility model was applied to determine the conditions under which the use of the additional test (PET) was justified (under a quota-free situation).

The results revealed that despite only moderate gains in validity which resulted from the additional test, the test is clearly justified, from an expected utility perspective, if the primary goal of higher education is seen as that of producing excellent graduates. If the goal is to provide basic post high-school education to masses of students (and hence 'success' involves graduating with minimal passing marks), then it is quite clear that admissions can be based exclusively on high school achievements.

Bias

The first question one can raise in the social context is whether a university selection system is biased against any particular group. Claims about the existence of bias are based largely on the feeling or the observation that there are noticeable differences between the success rates of different groups on the tests. The tendency to criticise selection tests increases when the groups whose success rates are relatively low are also the groups which are socially disadvantaged and the focus of public attention.

Unfortunately, much of the public discussion about the problem of test bias tends to confuse several issues. Differences in success rates on tests between different groups are often regarded by the groups themselves as evidence of bias in the test, totally disregarding the success of these groups on the external criterion which the test is supposed to predict. It is often the case that groups, whose success rate on the tests is relatively low, tend to exhibit equally low (or even lower) success in measures of the relevant criterion (such as academic achievement). There is also a tendency to confuse the issue of test bias with the possibility of bias in the content of certain items included in the test. When differences in success rates on tests between groups are related to specific content, what often happens is that, instead of systematically eliminating problematic items (i.e., checking all items to expose those which are associated with differential performance), a proposal is made to reject entire batteries of tests which are reliable and valid.

Empirical evidence, gathered in studies conducted by Israeli universities and by the National Institute for Testing and Evaluation, indicates that, from a psychometric point of view, there is no problem of test bias in the selection process used by the universities (Beller & Ben-Shakhar, 1983; Gafni & Beller, 1989; Kennet, Oren, & Pavlov, 1988; Kennet-Cohen, 1993; Zeidner, 1986, 1987). According to accepted definitions of test bias (Cleary, 1968), it has been found that the Psychometric Entrance Test in particular, and the admissions process in general, are equally valid for and fair to the different groups of examinees (characterised by differences in sex, language, and country of origin). In most situations in which there were differences between groups they were not accompanied by significant 'overestimation' or 'underestimation' of the relevant criterion scores (success in academic studies). In other words, candidates of different ethnic backgrounds (or of different gender, or speakers of different languages) whose entrance examination scores were identical, had a similar average rate of success in their university studies.

These results are complex and not always easy to present and explain to the public. It is important to clarify that the choice of a certain selection method should be made on the basis of its validity and the degree to which it is appropriate in terms of predicting the criterion (for example, level of academic success). Social and political considerations may also be included in the selection process, but these considerations must be explicitly and quantitatively defined in conjunction with a determination of the general admissions policy (a task which may be difficult). It is legitimate that policy-makers should favour different approaches to different social groups, but the determination of the way in which the scores of candidates from different groups are used (for example, determining different cut-off points for different groups) must be independent of the determination of which tests are to be used. The tests must be chosen exclusively according to psychometric criteria, whereas the policy dictating the process and manner in which decisions are made must reflect the values of society and should be determined by decision-makers at the social policy level (Petersen & Novick, 1976).

Indirect Effects

Each model for the allocation of precious resources, particularly educational resources, has an effect on the entire system. A merit-based admissions method, for example, creates competition among candidates. Questions may also be raised about the effect of rejection on those who are not accepted. Another important issue relates to the effect of university admissions requirements on programmes of study in high schools. Finally, if the number of prestigious and sought-after places is limited, and the competition is intense, some will strive to attain them at any cost, raising concerns about possible corruption.

These and other questions naturally arise regarding the selection system used in Israel. In particular, questions arise regarding matriculation examinations and the educational impact (positive and negative) of their use in selecting students. Additional questions arise regarding the use of psychometric tests as a tool for giving students a second chance (beyond high school achievements) and regarding preparation for the tests and their effects (Bond, 1989; Oren, 1992b; Powers, 1985, 1993).

CONCLUSION

University admissions policies are often the subject of public discussion in Israel. On the one hand, there are those who argue that it would be preferable to adopt a policy of admitting all candidates to most departments, thus giving everyone the opportunity to compete. On the other hand, there are those who argue that the cost of failure, both to the university and to the student, is too high, and that the university must therefore try to limit in advance the number of students who are likely to fail in their academic studies.

Universities have decided that once a set quota for admissions has been established and the number of applicants exceeds it, preference will be given to high calibre students who are most likely to achieve excellence. In such a situation, it is agreed that the candidates must be evaluated using the most objective and valid evaluation methods available for predicting success in academic studies. Currently, the score (usually a combination of equally-weighted matriculation grades and the psychometric test score used for admission to Israeli universities) predicts success in academic studies better than any other predictive method which has been investigated (and notably better than matriculation grades alone).

There are those who believe that interviews are a good method of candidate assessment and suggest incorporating them into the selection process. No doubt, an interview may reveal things that are not apparent in the matriculation certificate or in the psychometric test scores. But, however surprising it may seem, the validity of interviews in predicting academic success is in many cases close to zero and, under optimal conditions (for example, when all candidates are interviewed by the same interviewers, an implausible condition when there are tens of thousands of candidates), is at best 0.2. Moreover, the interview procedure, because of its inherently subjective nature, may cause bias in selection, depending on the specific make-up of admissions committees and the values and positions of their members. Another factor meriting consideration is the interviewer's vulnerability to personal pressures and favouritism (Ben-Shakhar & Beller, 1993). The selection of candidates on the basis of various personality tests or graphological analysis is advocated by some but the available evidence suggests that the validity of these in predicting academic success is negligible.

The solution for alleviating the distress of the many students who cannot study in their fields of choice can only come through an increase in the places available in those fields. This is a question of policy to be determined by the higher education system, policy which depends, among other things, on the allocation of resources to the universities, and is independent of the choice of selection instruments (including the psychometric tests). However, as long as the shortage of places necessitates selection, that selection should be carried out in an optimal way. Those who believe that the quality of candidates is the correct basis for their selection recognise the advantages of the present system of candidate selection. At the same time, the search for alternative selection methods with high validity and attempts to improve the system are carried on unceasingly by psychometric experts at the National Institute for Testing and Evaluation and by those responsible for the selection and admissions processes at the universities.

REFERENCES

Beller, M. (1994). Psychometric and social issues in admissions to Israeli universities. *Educational Measurement: Issues and Practice, 13*(2), 12-20.

Beller, M., & Ben-Shakhar, G. (1983). On the fair use of psychological tests. *Megamot, 28*, 42-56. (In Hebrew).

Ben-Shakhar, G., & Beller, M. (1983). An application of a decision-theoretic model to a quota-free selection problem. *Journal of Applied Psychology, 68*, 137-146.

Ben-Shakhar, G., & Beller, M. (1993). On the personal interview as means for selection and classification. *Megamot, 35*, 246-259. (In Hebrew).

Ben-Shakhar, G., Kiderman, I., & Beller, M. (1993, April). *Comparing the utility of two selection procedures in a quota-free situation: An application of decision-theoretic models*. Paper presented at the annual meeting of the American Educational Research Association, Atlanta, GA.

Bond, L. (1989). The effects of special preparation on measures of scholastic ability. In R. L. Linn (Ed.), *Educational measurement*. (3rd ed.) (pp. 429-444). New York: Macmillan.

Cleary, T. A. (1968). Test bias: Prediction of grades of negro and white students in integrated colleges. *Journal of Educational Measurement, 5*, 115-124.

Donlon, F. T. (Ed.). (1984). *The College Board technical handbook for the Scholastic Aptitude Test and Achievement Tests*. New York: College Entrance Examinations Board.

Gafni, N., & Beller, M. (1989). *Investigating the fairness of the Psychometric Entrance Test with respect to males and females.* (Report No. 95). Jerusalem: National Institute for Testing and Evaluation. (In Hebrew).

Kennet, T., Oren, C., & Pavlov, Y. (1988). *Analysis of the culture fairness of the selection procedure in two Israeli universities* (Report No. 78). Jerusalem: National Institute for Testing and Evaluation. (In Hebrew).

Kennet-Cohen, T. (1993, June). *An examination of predictive bias: The Russian version of the Psychometric Entrance Test for Israeli universities*. Paper presented at a conference of the International Test Commission, Oxford.

Klitgraad, R. (1986). *Elitism and meritocracy in developing countries: Selection policies for higher education*. Baltimore, MD: Johns Hopkins University Press.

Linn, R. L. (1990). Admissions testing: Recommended uses, validity, differential prediction, and coaching. *Applied Measurement in Education, 3*, 297-318.

Oren, C. (1992a). *On the validity of PET: A meta analysis (1984-1989).* (Report No. 160). Jerusalem: National Institute for Testing and Evaluation. (In Hebrew).

Oren, C. (1992b). *On the effect of various preparation modes on PET scores*. (Report No.170). Jerusalem: National Institute for Testing and Evaluation. (In Hebrew).

Oren, C., Bronner, S., & Kennet-Cohen, T. (1993, October). *On the reliability and validity of new PET*. Paper presented at the annual meeting of the Israeli Psychological Association, Ramat-Gan, Israel.

Petersen, N. S., & Novick, M. R. (1976). An evaluation of some models for culture-fair selection. *Journal of Educational Measurement*, *13*, 3-29.

Powers, D. E. (1985). Effects of test preparation on the validity of a graduate admissions test. *Applied Psychological Measurement*, *9*, 179-190.

Powers, D. E. (1993). Coaching for the SAT: A summary of the summaries and an update. *Educational Measurement: Issues and Practice*, *12*(2), 24-30.

Zeidner, M. (1986). Sex differences in scholastic ability in Jewish and Arab college students in Israel. *Journal of Social Psychology*, *7*, 847-852.

Zeidner, M. (1987). A test of the cultural bias hypothesis: Some Israeli findings. *Journal of Applied Psychology*, *72*, 38-48.

5. TECHNICAL AND EDUCATIONAL IMPLICATIONS OF USING PUBLIC EXAMINATIONS FOR SELECTION TO HIGHER EDUCATION

M.J. Cresswell
Associated Examining Board,
Guildford, Surrey

General Certificate of Education (GCE) A-Level examinations are the principal selection devices for higher education in England and Wales. This paper discusses some of the requirements which this use of the examinations places upon them, such as the apparent need for predictive validity, high perceived reliability, and close comparability of standards between different A-Level examinations. It is argued that these requirements have a considerable influence on the assessment techniques that are used and that recent developments in England and Wales can be understood more easily if the role of public examinations in selection is taken into account.

THE SELECTIVE FUNCTION OF PUBLIC EXAMINATIONS AND FAIRNESS

Public examinations, like most educational assessments, have a number of purposes and functions (e.g., Ingenkamp, 1977). They are said (a) to provide formative information for students concerning their progress, to enable them to improve their learning; (b) to motivate students; (c) to provide information for selection, in order to distinguish between students with differing abilities so as to provide appropriate further education, training, or specific employment; (d) to provide information for assessing the effectiveness of teaching methods, curricula, forms of organisation of schools; (e) to provide information about the performance of the education system as a whole; and (f) to provide curriculum control.

For British A-Level examinations, there is little doubt that the selective function is the predominant one. It is identified as the 'principal historical function of school examinations' by Orr and Nuttall (1983); as the 'historical function of the GCE examination system' by Christie and Forrest (1981); as the function which 'outweighs all others' by Ingenkamp (1977); and as 'most important' by Broadfoot (1986).

Ever since Edgeworth's (1890) pioneering study there has been a considerable amount of research into the technical quality of public examinations. Their role in providing information for selection has motivated much of this concern because of the need for the examinations, and consequential selection decisions, to be 'fair.' It is therefore important to consider, albeit briefly, how 'fairness' is conceived in the public examination context so that the consequences of this for the technical demands which are made upon the examinations can be better understood. Broadfoot (1986) argued that the development of public examinations in the late nineteenth and early twentieth centuries reflected a growing belief in meritocracy as a social organising principle, coupled with the notion that it was appropriate for schools to provide for the selection which such an ideology implies. Both of these beliefs are still evidently widespread in the late twentieth century. For example, random lotteries, although accepted as 'fair' for some purposes, are not generally considered appropriate for allocating places in higher education. In this paper, it is taken as axiomatic that a meritocratic philosophy underpins the use of examination results for selection purposes and that the fairness of examinations must be judged in this light.

BIAS

From a meritocratic point of view, it is clearly undesirable that examination grades should be biased in such a way that they do not correctly report the achievements of members of a particular social group. However, the problems of bias extend beyond the examinations themselves. It is well established that social variables (e.g., social class, race, and gender) are related to school achievement and, given the social nature of schooling, members of different social groups have different educational experiences which are likely to produce different measured achievements in examinations (Mathews, 1985).

To take a concrete example, schooling does not completely ameliorate the effects of social disadvantage; indeed, it may even widen the gap between some social groups. Disadvantaged pupils, as a group, are proportionally under-represented among those with good public examination grades (see, for example, Blackstone & Mortimore, 1982). The question is: should they be under-represented in this way? Mathews (1985) argues strongly that they should because examination grades should reflect current achievement and socially disadvantaged pupils have, as a group, relatively low achievement. However, this argument begs the question of what achievements examinations should report. It is clear, for example, that changes in the extent to which coursework contributes to an examination will change the measured difference between boys' and girls' achievements (Cresswell, 1990; Stobart, Elwood, & Quinlan, 1992). Thus, it would be quite possible to design examinations that would eliminate average differences between boys' and girls' measured achievements. However, the British legal system would appear to prohibit this approach, at least for gender. The old practice of using separate standardisation tables for boys and girls in selection tests is now illegal. As Goldstein (1986a) pointed out, to use particular assessment techniques or to assess particular achievements in order to engineer equal outcomes for boys and girls would be no different, in effect or spirit, from using different standardisation tables for boys and girls.

The position which has traditionally been taken by public examining boards is that the achievements measured by public examinations, and the assessment techniques used, should be determined without explicit reference to their effect in terms of the performance of different social groups. Rather, what is being assessed should be determined on pedagogical grounds and how it is assessed is a technical question which involves finding the best techniques for the purpose. Examining board procedures then involve simply making every effort to remove overt signs of bias such as any preponderance of, say, masculine contexts for problems. Once this has been done, any remaining differences in the outcomes for different sub-groups of candidates for public examinations are seen as a reflection of the way in which subjects are defined. Clearly, this position ignores many historical questions concerning why the subjects are defined as they are. Moreover, the philosophical difficulties surrounding the notions of equality of opportunity and equality of outcome still bedevil attempts to measure any residual bias due to assessment techniques when the subject definition is given.

From the point of view of purely meritocratic selection, of course, acknowledgement that social biases may exist in examination results is theoretically disastrous since it is precisely the social biases evident in other selection procedures that examinations are intended to eliminate. In terms of policy-making, however, the practical question is whether social selections are more or less biased when public examination results contribute to them. The technical and procedural consequences of concern about overt bias tend to support the use of standardised procedures involving examiners who are not involved in teaching the candidates.

RELIABILITY

A necessary feature of fair meritocratic selection systems is that the selections should be replicable. If the same individuals are considered on a different occasion, the same subset of them should be selected. It follows that the same individuals examined on different occasions must receive the same results if subsequent selections are to be seen to be fair.

The reliability of marking has been extensively studied. Wilmut (1986) compiled an extensive bibliography of over 240 studies or reviews relating to it.

The requirement of high reliability has, of course, profound effects upon the examinations. It is commonly observed that highly replicable assessments tend to be associated with standardized conditions of administration. In general, the need for standardized administration predisposes the examination towards the use of written examination papers with fixed time limits. Of course, the use of timed written papers imposes its own restrictions upon the sort of knowledge, skills, and understanding that can be assessed.

One of the more profound effects of the need for public examinations results to be replicable concerns the number of grades (categories) used to report candidates' achievements. Cresswell (1986) showed that the use of a relatively small number of grades decreases the reliability and validity of examination results when these are measured in conventional correlational terms. However, using a few, relatively coarse, grades to describe candidates' results means that a greater proportion of the candidates receive the identical grade upon retesting. The social need for the public examination system to be perceived by the users as meritocratically fair, therefore, tends to lead to the use of a small number of grades despite the adverse effects that this has upon the technical quality of the results.

COMPARABILITY

Mention of the use of grades to report results leads naturally to the question of grade comparability. Selectors frequently use a system of points that treats grades from different A-Level examinations as interchangeable but this is fair from a meritocratic point of view only if the examinations concerned are comparable in the sense that the same grade represents equal merit regardless of the examination from which it comes.

Several ways of defining equal merit have been implicitly used by those studying examination comparability. For example, comparability can be defined as having been achieved if students who followed Course A and took associated Examination A obtained the same average grade as students with the same achievement at the beginning of their courses who took Course B and the associated Examination B. However, from the point of view of meritocratic selection, this definition is problematic because, in the limit, it defines those who have followed an irrelevant or trivial course as equal in merit to those who have followed a demanding course relevant to that for which they are being selected.

An alternative is to define comparability as having been achieved if students with the same achievement at the end of their courses receive the same grade from either examination. This second definition is probably the sense in which the term is usually used. Unfortunately, as Goldstein (1986a) has pointed out, it is theoretically impossible to test for comparability defined in this way. The reason is that since the two examinations do not assess identical objectives, it is impossible ever to establish in an objective, empirical manner the extent to which candidates who enter for one examination have similar achievements to those entered for the other. In any attempt to do so, like is not being compared with like.

Given their selective purpose, examination grades can be likened to a currency with which candidates buy entry into higher education or employment. Developing this analogy a little further, the intrinsic value of banknotes does not match their face value but commerce functions because it is commonly agreed to accept them at face value. (This agreement is greatly strengthened, but not guaranteed, by the underwriting of a national bank.) Similarly, educational and vocational selection processes can proceed provided that there is common consent that comparability exists between different examinations. That is to say, it must be accepted that a given grade from one examination represents achievement which is equal in merit to the achievement which earns the same grade in other examinations. From this starting point, it is possible to define comparability in purely social terms as follows: comparability between two examinations has been achieved if candidates for one of them receive the same grades as candidates for the other whose assessed achievements are accorded the same value by all interested certificate users.

From the point of view of this paper, the important point to note about this definition of comparability is that, in philosophical terms, it is relativistic. This means that comparability is defined only for a particular group of certificate users in a particular time and place. There is no reason why others who do not value achievements similarly should accept that comparability has been established. Clearly, however, the wider the group that shares the consensus, the more useful are the examination certificates. The certificate users referred to in the definition must include candidates, parents, teachers, and selectors, if the examination system is to function optimally.

Those setting grade standards must therefore either faithfully represent the views of most users or persuade the users that the standards which they set are comparable. The importance which examining boards have always attached to studying and reporting upon comparability can be seen as an implicit recognition of these requirements. In the case of British A-Levels, most certificate users accept the judgments of public examining board grade awarders for most examinations. (Note that this is not to say that every individual user would necessarily express preferences about the candidates' achievements which were identical to the awarders' preferences; they each merely agree to abide by the examining board view for as long as it differs only to some small extent from their own.)

The maintenance of public confidence is thus critical to the operation of a public examination system for selection purposes. The result is that procedures must be relatively simple, straightforward and open to scrutiny by non-experts in measurement. They might not, therefore, be technically optimal but must appear fair. The need for comparability also adds to the pressure for external involvement in the assessment process and the use of standardised conditions of administration.

Moreover, the need to make comparability manifest leads to a desire for standardisation of administration conditions across different examinations.

NORM AND CRITERION REFERENCING

One of the most profound effects of the use of public examinations for selection purposes lies in the area of the referencing system that is used. It is necessary in this connection to be clear what is meant by criterion referencing. The term has, at least in the UK, two distinct meanings. The meanings flow from two different meanings of the word criterion itself. Criterion can mean the variable being measured (the criterion variable of psychometrics) or it can mean a standard (the criterion to be met for acceptability).

The possibility that public examinations for selection could be criterion-referenced in the second of these senses seems, at first sight, to be high. It was argued earlier that public examination grades are awarded for work which meets particular standards of merit. However, the definition of these standards is mysterious. In particular, because the variable being assessed is very broad, it is not possible to articulate grading standards (in this sense of the word, the criteria which candidates must meet) with any precision. Rather, they represent a general consensus of what are reasonable standards to expect from candidates taking the examinations. Inevitably, therefore, the standards applied shift over time in a way that reflects changing expectations that are, themselves, based upon the changing experience of the grade awarders of pupils' achievements. As a result, the proportion of candidates in each grade tends to remain much the same over a very long period of time. This effect can be seen in the results from British A-Levels over the past 40 years.

Viewed historically, therefore, A-Level examinations appear to be more norm- than criterion-referenced. Moreover, from the point of view of selectors this is a desirable property. It means that when they set similar entrance requirements in terms of examination grades, they get similar proportions of successful applicants from one year to the next. If more absolute grading criteria were to be used, then changes in educational standards over time would require constant adjustment of entry requirements by selectors. At the extreme, after a long period of improving educational provision, so many candidates might begin to pass absolute grade boundaries that the examinations would become useless as a basis for selecting amongst them.

When criterion referencing refers to the first of the two meanings set out earlier, the selective role of public examinations is relevant because of the need for criterion variables to be well (and hence, narrowly) defined. It is clear from Goacher's (1984) study, and from other evidence (for example, Harrison, 1983) that selectors do not wish to make complex selection decisions involving simultaneous consideration of many different well-defined aspects of achievement within a subject. Rather, they require a single summarising measure — a subject grade. As a result, public examinations used for selection purposes cannot be criterion-referenced in this sense.

Further implications of this for the examining process relate to methods of aggregation. Most public examinations cover a variety of topics in a number of components such as written papers, coursework, and multiple-choice tests. Performance on the components must be aggregated to produce the overall subject grade. Methods of aggregation can be grouped into two classes: those that permit compensation to operate freely between components (so that candidates can compensate for weakness in one area by strength in another) and methods that limit the operation of such compensation (by making the award of a particular grade dependent upon achieving some specified level in one individual component or more). Cresswell (1988), who analysed these two classes and the reliability of the overall grades which they produce, showed that systems which limit the operation of compensation carry with them a substantially increased likelihood that some candidates will receive an incorrect overall grade. He observed that limiting compensation might be desirable in some contexts.

> If an overall pass qualifies candidates to practice surgery for example, it may be thought desirable [by inhibiting compensation] to stack the odds against awarding incorrect passes even at the expense of increasing the likelihood of incorrect failures.

However,

> in a general educational context the unreliability of the resulting overall grades for certain types of candidate makes preferable methods which permit good performances in some components to compensate for poor ones in others and *inter alia* permit positive errors of measurement to compensate for negative ones.

In an earlier study, Cresswell (1987) had already demonstrated that the usual motive for using aggregation methods which inhibit compensation was naive. This motive is the desire to make the overall grades carry specific information about the relative strengths and weaknesses of the candidates. Cresswell showed that when achievement is reported in terms of a multi-grade scale (as it is for public examinations) some grades can be made to carry specific interpretations of this type only at the expense of increased ambiguity for other grades in the scale. On this basis, it can be concluded that the only way effectively to report specific information about candidates' strengths and weaknesses within a subject is to do so directly in the form of a profile and that the overall grade is most useful to selectors if it records each candidate's mean achievement. For selection purposes, an aggregation method which permits compensation to operate freely between the various examination components is to be preferred. A similar conclusion was reached by Thyne (1974) using different, but related, arguments.

VALIDITY

The use of A-Level grades for selection purposes appears to presuppose that they are positively related to success in the university course concerned. Houston (1987) reviewed the large amount of work which has been done on the relationship between GCE A-Level grades and performance in higher education. In particular, he cited a major study by Choppin and Orr (1976) as demonstrating that, of the available measures that might be used for this selection purpose, GCE A-Level grades were the best single predictor of future success. No better single predictor had been identified in any of the studies which Houston reviewed. Similar results were also found by Miles (1979) in a study of the ability of GCE O-Level grades to predict later results at A-Level. It is difficult to avoid the unsurprising conclusion from the various studies in this area that only weak predictions of future performance are possible. This should not be forgotten. The validity of public examination results for selection purposes may be relatively high but in absolute terms examination results do not give rise to highly accurate predictions of future performance.

However, there is a sense in which this is to miss at least part of the point. The meritocratic philosophy which underpins the use of examination results for selection purposes contains a strand which holds that future rewards for an individual should, for moral reasons, reflect that individual's current achievements — that success must be earned (Young, 1961). In response to this, it might be argued that examinations fail to take into account students' investment of great effort, which should be rewarded in some way. However, the meritocratic view is that those with the highest marks are more deserving of selection than others. For example, Young (1961), in his original satire, wrote:

> ... the eminent know that success is *just reward* for their own capacity, for their own efforts, and for their own undeniable achievement. They *deserve* to belong to a superior class. (p. 106, emphases added)

From the meritocratic perspective, therefore, the validity of public examination grades as measures of current achievement is as important to their role in social selection as their predictive power. There is, however, scant empirical evidence of the validity of public examinations in this sense. Because public examination candidates rarely take more than one examination in a given subject on one examining occasion, there are no data sets of any size that might provide correlational measures of concurrent validity. The strong claim to validity made by public examinations rests principally on their content. It is for this reason that examining boards place great procedural emphasis on establishing relevance and representativeness in this sense and have, as a result, increasingly come to specify in detail the content and objectives of their syllabuses. This practice also has the social advantage that the basis upon which candidates are to be assessed, and by implication selected, is both public and standardised.

CONCLUSION

In the light of the preceding discussion, it is, perhaps, easy to see why British public examinations in general, and A-Levels in particular: (a) emphasise assessment by examiners unknown to the candidates; (b) use tasks common to all candidates; (c) use standardised administration conditions; (d) report results in terms of a coarse scale of grades; (e) are not criterion-referenced; (f) use compensatory aggregation methods; and (g) are based upon the detailed specification of syllabus content and objectives.

Essentially, examinations that are used for selection purposes are likely to exhibit these features because they have to be seen to be fair in meritocratic terms. The selection process must command consent in society at large and the techniques used in public examinations are a legitimate matter for public discussion. Perhaps regrettably, it is therefore unrealistic to expect that the procedures used will necessarily be the best on technical or general educational grounds. The merits of particular assessment techniques must be argued at a level suitable for a non-specialist audience and from the meritocratic perspective, if the techniques are to gain widespread acceptance.

This case is well illustrated by the fate of teacher-assessment coursework in public examinations in England and Wales. From the point of view of the selective function of examinations, the use of non-standard assessment tasks taken under non-standard conditions and assessed by a teacher who knows the candidate raises questions concerning bias, reliability, and comparability. The British government has recently announced a restriction upon the amount of each A-Level examination which can take the form of teacher-assessed coursework, at least partly as a result of concerns about these matters; the standard limitation is to be 20 percent.

The proponents of teacher-assessed coursework argue that because it is embedded in normal learning processes it can cover a much wider range of work in a much wider context and, as a result, has higher validity than more controlled approaches to assessment. They also argue that there are many educational benefits in using teacher assessment which flow from the greater control which it gives to teachers over the curriculum which they deliver and from the enhancement of their professional role. Unfortunately, the second of these arguments is irrelevant, except in a most indirect sense, from the perspective of the selective function. The argument about validity is relevant in terms of the moral aspect of meritocracy which was discussed above and is generally accepted. In terms of the predictive aspects of the validity argument, however, the case is much harder to make simply because of the inevitable limitations on any attempt to predict the future. Moreover, the proponents of teacher-assessed coursework have signally failed to produce empirical evidence of the reliability of their preferred technique. Indeed, the naturalistic nature of teacher-assessed coursework assessments (which is their strength) makes such data extremely difficult to collect.

As a result, policy makers have been in the position of trading off relatively sophisticated arguments about improving one aspect of validity against easily visible potential problems of bias, reliability, and comparability without, in any of these cases, any knowledge of the size of the effects concerned. Given the key need for the selection system as a whole to command public consent, retrenchment towards less naturalistic assessment techniques is not surprising once policy makers focus upon the selective function of public examinations.

REFERENCES

Blackstone, T., & Mortimore, J. (1982). *Disadvantage and education.* London: Heinemann.

Broadfoot, P. M. (1986). Alternatives to public examinations. In D. L. Nuttall (Ed.), *Assessing educational achievement.* London: Falmer.

Choppin, B., & Orr, L. (1976). *Aptitude testing at eighteen plus.* Windsor, Berks: National Foundation for Educational Research.

Christie, T., & Forrest, G. M. (1981). *Defining public examination standards.* London: Macmillan.

Cresswell, M. J. (1986). Examination grades: How many should there be? *British Educational Research Journal, 12,* 37-54.

Cresswell, M. J. (1987). Describing examination performance: Grade criteria in public examinations. *Educational Studies, 13,* 247-265.

Cresswell, M. J. (1988). Combining grades from different assessments - how reliable is the result? *Educational Review, 40,* 361-383.

Cresswell, M. J. (1990). *Gender effects in GCSE - Some initial analyses.* (Research Report RAC/517). Guildford, Surrey: Associated Examining Board.

Edgeworth, F. Y. (1890). The elements of chance in competitive examinations: Parts I and II. *Journal of the Royal Statistical Society, 53,* 460-475 and 644-663.

Goacher, B. (1984). Selection post-16: The role of examination results. In *Schools Council Examinations Bulletin 45.* London: Methuen.

Goldstein, H. (1986a). Gender bias and test norms in educational selection. *Research Intelligence. BERA Newsletter,* pp 2-4.

Goldstein, H. (1986b). Models for equating test scores and for studying the comparability of public examinations. In D. L. Nuttall (Ed.), *Assessing educational achievement.* London: Falmer.

Harrison, A. (1983). *Profile reporting of examination results.* London: Methuen.

Houston, J. G. (1987). *Advanced level grades as predictors of degree performance.* Paper prepared as part of the GCE Examining Boards evidence to a Government Committee of Inquiry into A-level examinations chaired by Professor G. Higginson during 1987-88.

Ingenkamp, K. (1977). *Educational assessment.* Windsor, Berks: National Foundation for Educational Research.

Mathews, J. C. (1985). *Examinations. A commentary.* London: George Allen & Unwin.

Miles, H. B. (1979). *Some factors affecting attainment at 18+*. Oxford: Pergamon.

Orr, L., & Nuttall, D. L. (1983). *Determining standards in the proposed single system of examining at 16+*. London: Schools Council.

Stobart, G., Elwood, J., & Quinlan, M. (1992). Gender bias in examinations: How equal are the opportunities? *British Educational Research Journal, 18,* 261-276.

Thyne, J. M. (1974). *Principles of examining*. London: University of London Press.

Wilmut, J. (1986). *Marking reliability: A bibliography.* (Research Report RAC/403). Guildford, Surrey: Associated Examining Board.

Young, M. (1961). *The rise of the meritocracy 1870-2033.* London: Pelican.

6. ACHIEVING COMPARABILITY OF SCHOOL-BASED ASSESSMENTS IN ADMISSIONS PROCEDURES TO HIGHER EDUCATION

Graeme Withers
Australian Council for Educational Research,
Camberwell, Victoria

Why do assessment, certification, and admissions systems go to sometimes extraordinary lengths to ensure the comparability of the various individual results which pour in from candidates within the system? At root, this is an ethical question. Sheer justice demands that certificates or lists of successful applicants for tertiary places should be comparable. We sometimes forget this in the stress engendered in designing and mounting the complex systems and annual programmes which process these results.

It is the view of the author that the school-based nature of widely-used current systems of educational delivery does not need to be demeaned by the intrusion of external examinations or mass testing. Why force students, with different needs, aspirations, educational backgrounds and personalities into a single process whereby these differences are submerged, discounted, or even ignored? Examinations may seem to guarantee comparability between results, or at least they represent attempts to achieve a greater measure of it. Those who have worked with such examinations, however, know the truth of the matter, or could, if they mounted the research necessary to verify it. Often there are educational policy or direct political imperatives relating to assessment that cannot be ignored by those who design and operate an assessment system. However, where such imperatives are absent, school-based systems can and do operate well and are sympathetic to the needs of both students and other users of the credentials. There are more ways of solving the ethical problem than by administering a pencil-and-paper test, or even a battery of more sophisticated instruments. However, to take the view that key curriculum and assessment decisions may be largely left with schools does not mean leaving a school and its teachers quite alone. They do not deliver their own learning programmes in happy isolation from other institutions whose students will also appear on the candidate roll for a credential or a place. Moderation becomes an imperative, in some form or another, for acceptability of each school's contribution to the pool of data.

A look at a few first principles suggests that the person who knows most about the actual quality of the performances and achievements of a student is the student himself or herself. The student knows how much learning has been done, how much is yet to come, and in broad terms how it rates against the criteria which will be used to assess it. A potentially fuller and more powerful view of learning, however, can be achieved by the student by working in consort with teachers through the introduction of criteria for judgment about the quality of learning which teachers have developed as professional educators.

When a student shares a learning experience with teachers, judgments regarding the quality of achievement become unavoidably subject to the exercise of common criteria shared by the teachers. When the learning is limited to a single class with one teacher, this is not a huge problem. But when the learning is common to many students, in different classes and schools, with many different professional assessment inputs by different teachers, the problems of achieving comparability escalate in number and severity. This is not to say that they are insoluble, however. Various sorts and stages of moderation, together with monitoring and research, allow one to make public accountability statements regarding comparability between different students' results. However, we need, perhaps, to expand our views of what 'validity' means in this context (Withers, 1989). It should also be noted that the costs of a school-based system are less than those of an externally-examined system. There are hidden costs, of course, in the school-based system in terms of teacher time and effort paid for by schools. However, there are also pay-offs in terms of genuine teacher professional development.

STRUCTURE OF AUSTRALIAN EDUCATION

There are seven systems of curriculum, assessment, and certification leading to tertiary entrance for students in Australian schools. One system covers two state legislatures, and has even been transplanted to Malaysia. States' rights in education have been maintained with some vehemence since the country was federated in 1901, but appear to be rapidly losing out to the pressures of centralised tax gathering and distribution, and a new inclination to centralised decision-making about truly national initiatives.

How the specifically school-oriented systems differ in details of procedure between states is too big an issue to be gone into here. [For a current summary, see Australian Curriculum Assessment and Certification Authorities (ACACA), 1991]. Two systems are the focus of particular attention in this paper, and a third will be mentioned from time to time. The three states involved in these systems provide a cross-section of the major structures for provision in Years 11 and 12 which are to be found across the nation.

Queensland's structure for its 'mainstream' students allows individual schools freedom to design and deliver course offerings, or 'work programmes' as they are called. These are written by classroom teachers in response to template 'syllabuses' prepared and offered in 44 subjects (so-called 'Board Subjects', after the Board of Senior Secondary School Studies, which administers the system). The work programmes are then subject to peer accreditation. This effort, together with the learning and teaching which then ensue, is supported by school-designed and conducted assessments. Student work is collected in 'folios', and samples of these are peer-moderated at the district and state levels in two stages. The first occurs towards the end of a student's Year 11 (Monitoring) and the second a year later (Review or exit Moderation). This sequence of school-based processes is followed by a state-wide test for scaling the results of those students who wish to apply for tertiary entrance (see McCurry, 1992). A summary of the processes involving Board subjects is given in Figure 6.1 [Committee to Review Assessment and Moderation Processes (CRAMP), 1992]. Schools may also conduct other, alternative courses of their own devising and assess students' performance in these 'Board registered' or 'Recorded subjects.' However, such results - though recorded on certificates - do not have the same status as mainstream courses when it comes to processing for tertiary entrance. Students may do a mixture of both sorts of course.

FIGURE 6.1

SEQUENCE OF PROCESSES FOR BOARD SUBJECTS LEADING TO CERTIFICATION IN QUEENSLAND

1. Approval of syllabus
2. School writes work programme, including assessment plan
3. District accreditation of work programme by review panellists
4. State accreditation of work programmes
   (10% of work programmes sampled)
5. Conduct of learning and teaching, including formative assessment
6. Assessments of achievement leading to exit assessment
7. District monitoring of sample folios (5 student folios per school)
8. District review of sample exit folios (9 student folios per school)
9. State review of district sample folios (2 schools per district)
10. Confirmation of statewide standards by panels and the Board
11. Exit assessment of student achievement
12. Certification of individual students

All courses must involve assessments based on what the authority calls its 'criteria-and-standards model.' This term acknowledges and focuses attention on the duality within any assessment process: the establishment of clear criteria for judgment occurring before (not intermingled with) the application of a standards statement (mark, grade, verbal description) with reference to the criterion or criteria under review. Standards statements in Queensland are verbal, are called Levels of Achievement, and five are common to every Board subject.

Victoria offers its schools a rather more prescriptive set (also more restricted in subject range) of what are in effect syllabuses, although called 'Study Designs.' These are grouped into Fields of Study. Certification of achievement is somewhat detached from tertiary entrance, in that the former is based on completion of stipulated Work Requirements for each study, while the latter requires the further undertaking of specified Common Assessment Tasks in each study. (As in Queensland, a student can get a certificate without qualifying for tertiary entrance, but not the reverse). Some of these common tasks are school-assessed and moderated; some are externally set and assessed. In both cases, clear guidelines are in place regarding the criteria that should be used during assessment. Schools may no longer (since 1991) develop and assess their own courses alongside these arrangements. A separate standards-statement — in Victoria's case a grade in the range A to E — is reported for every common assessment task in every subject.

The provision in South Australia involves a two-tier arrangement, whereby some subjects on offer follow the school-assessed Queensland model and some the mixture of school-assessed and publicly-examined models of the Victorian system. Courses in both tiers may 'count' for tertiary entrance, and students may take a mixture of courses across the tiers, but scores obtained in school-assessed courses are subject to discount during the processing of results.

It will be seen that school-based assessment plays some part in each of these three systems. The proportion varies between systems, and between subjects within systems, but none disregards it entirely. Some distinction is made, as will be seen, between processes for those who desire tertiary admission and those who want merely certification, but the processes are essentially the same.

THE EXTENT TO WHICH PARALLEL EDUCATIONAL EXPERIENCES LEAD TO COMPARABLE ASSESSMENT OUTCOMES

Nine hypothetical cases are considered below in which students have been exposed to parallel courses, to different teachers or different assessment procedures or have been awarded the same assessment grade. The inherent assumption that parallel educational experiences or even the same assessment grade are really comparable is analysed. Suggestions are occasionally made as to how the existing situation might be improved.

1. *At the end of Year 10, one student chooses subject A for study in Years 11 and 12, while another student chooses subject B. Are the two courses, as described*

in their respective syllabuses, comparable in quality and appropriateness as vehicles for learning at senior secondary level?

The issue here is the relative academic value of diverse curriculum offerings. All subjects should provide an appropriate challenge, in terms of intellectual or academic content, for students in Years 11 and 12. Where a subject (or its syllabus) has been identified as so deficient as to make it unworthy of a place in the roster, it should be immediately redeveloped or removed.

In Queensland, there is little or no complaint about the overall, relative academic quality of the syllabus designs for Board subjects. There are sporadic criticisms of some specific subjects, based usually on imperfect and often elitist perceptions of their value to students, and occasionally of their delivery in particular schools. Doubts, however, have been expressed about the validity of some school-developed courses (so-called 'Board registered subjects'). To meet these reservations, a moderation process has been recently recommended for all such subjects to improve the validity of this segment of the overall provision.

In Victoria, the situation is somewhat different. The whole system is under continuous and strenuous attack from party-political sources, and from one institution within the tertiary sector, which attracts a high level of media coverage. This has led to an undermining of public confidence in the system, the Victorian Certificate of Education (VCE), and its constituent subjects which in this author's view is unwarranted. Aspects of the implementation procedures might deserve some criticism but not the quality of the course designs.

2. *In one school, two students who have elected to study the same subject are assigned to different classes taken by different teachers. Are the educational experiences on offer to the students likely to be comparable in content and in the calibre of the teaching?*

It will take more than just the efforts of a senior curriculum and assessment agency to solve the problems of comparability which arise here. Teacher education, registration, and evaluation processes need to be in place to ensure a positive answer to the question about calibre of teaching, to ensure a base level of expertise in teaching quality. Variations will inevitably exist between the competence of any two professionals (in education as in any other profession), and it is impossible to legislate to achieve absolute uniformity. The procedures defined by the various Boards of Teacher Registration in the states of Australia seem to guarantee the base levels, though there are various moves at the national level to define more rigorously, and perhaps erect a system of appraisal of, the expertise (or 'competencies', to use current jargon) required of professionals.

As far as the content of courses is concerned, it is not necessarily the case in Queensland that exactly the same learning experiences take place in the two classes. The same work programme will be applied but the two teachers would have some freedom to vary the learning experiences in minor ways (text-choice; sequence of learning stages; applications of learning styles) to suit the needs and aspirations of students. System-wide peer accreditation processes are in place to ensure the value of the content of all school work programmes in all subjects as prescriptions for learning.

In Victoria, the variations between classes would, overall, be fewer and have less impact on individual students. Course designs, their work requirements, the format and scope of assessment tasks, and the criteria for dealing with the products of learning are much more rigidly specified for all schools. This has led to a large problem within the system — authentication that the products of learning presented for assessment are indeed the student's own work, and not 'borrowed' from a student in another school doing the same course. Queensland schools do not have this problem, since the work is school-designed and continuously assessed, with less emphasis on large and important tasks.

3. *Two students in different schools are enrolled in the same subject. Are the school-based assessment programmes the schools deliver likely to be comparable in validity, overall appropriateness, and stringency?*

Regulations and guidelines for schools need to be in place to support local delivery and implementation of assessment procedures. Some of these will be aimed at ensuring the relevant authority's oversight of the actual delivery in schools; others will aim to validate the quality of the actual assessments performed by teachers, both at the planning stage and the enactment stage. This is particularly crucial where an authority devolves full responsibility for raw assessments to schools (as in Queensland), rather than prescribing or imposing common instruments or occasions (as in Victoria, and to some extent South Australia). What all systems also need to do is to collect research evidence that might eventually confirm (or refute) the comparability aimed at.

Several aspects of the current processes in Queensland are designed to ensure comparability (see Figure 6.1). At the syllabus level, guidelines for assessment are offered. Each work programme must both conform to these and offer precise details of the assessment procedures to be followed. Accreditation allows a view of the quality of the programmes, and at various other times (such as those entitled Monitoring and Review) the instruments themselves come under external scrutiny. Every occasion for assessment can then be verified as consistent with the school's prescriptions and as conforming in general terms to the system-wide 'criteria-and-standards' model applied within syllabuses for all Board subjects.

The Victorian procedures, in essence more prescriptive, do not need the checks and monitoring that are required in Queensland. They are school-based in conduct, rather than school-based in design. They do, however, require school principals to testify that the full programme was carried out in accordance with prescriptions.

4. *Two students in different schools are enrolled in the same subject. What comparability exists between the amounts of assessment each student will be required to undertake in the assessment programmes which the schools deliver?*

In Queensland, work programmes and their assessment plans are accredited to ensure that minimum amounts of assessment take place in schools. Where the evidence presented at the monitoring stage suggests that this minimum has not or might not be met, a school's plan will be subject to special consultation between the monitoring panel and the school. In the same state, the situation regarding over-assessment is much less clear, both as to why it occurs and how serious it might be. There is research under way to determine the amount of assessment within certain subjects, based on the evidence of the contents of students' folios of work submitted for final review moderation. Even that may not reveal the whole picture, given the nature of much learning, teaching, and formative assessment in Year 11.

Students and parents report two principal manifestations of 'over-assessment.' One is the practice in some schools of administering a series of assignments during a term or semester and following this up with a solid block of tests and mini-exams at the end of the period which covers essentially the same learning. The other is the practice of mounting a virtually continuous series of assessment occasions. Schools may well argue that such practices are 'built into the system' and that they are necessary to comply with the authority's requirements for selective updating of records of student achievement as well as to offer students opportunities for improving their record. Others will argue that their students' educational experience (in Year 12 particularly) is incomplete without formal examinations to prepare them for similar instruments at the tertiary level.

Two issues are crucial in any discussion of the matter of over-assessment. The first is to acknowledge the relative complexity and breadth of the process, content, and skill specifications within many syllabuses. There is, indeed, a lot to be assessed at senior secondary level. However, the intention of continuous assessment is not to enforce the continuous drudgery of one formal assessment following closely after another. The drudgery, where it occurs, is manifestly unfair in handicapping students who perform less well in formal situations than they might otherwise do. It also makes serious inroads into student free time and social life. Those teachers who would argue the necessity for prior experience of formal examinations for students would do well to investigate the range of other assessment practices used in contemporary tertiary institutions. They might ask themselves whether prior experience of all these types is required of schools as well. They might also ask themselves just how much practice is really necessary.

However, another issue with regard to over-assessment is the absolute requirement, in a fully school-based system, to allow schools to design their own assessment programmes to suit, clearly and appropriately, the syllabus-related courses they have designed. In Queensland, schools are left free, and the fact that some are over-zealous in assessing their students has to be faced. In Victoria, where the freedom of schools to design their own instruments is much more circumscribed, the issue is less sharply felt by teachers.

The problem at present is to find some way of controlling or directing the vast amounts of work which some individual students are prepared to do for the common assessment tasks in some subjects, to the detriment of their other learning and assessments in other subjects. It is possible to legislate to limit the amount of summative assessment, but this needs to be accompanied by encouragement of a greater emphasis on formative styles of assessment in schools where this is not already a feature of their practice. Where there is too much assessment, the problem is often that it is too much of the wrong kind.

5. *A student is enrolled in two different subjects. Are the stipulations for assessment and moderation proposed in each syllabus comparable in the degree to which they cover all the required and appropriate learnings of that course?*

Insofar as school assessment in Queensland is concerned, the answer is yes. However, some products of learning and demonstrations of achievement cannot be put into a student's review folio for moderation, especially student work during practical activities. Thus, in many mainstream subjects which include such practical work, when it comes to moderation at the review stage the answer to the question must be no. Student work and teacher judgments that were made are reviewed on written evidence of the learning. However, the authority may move to implement a set of procedures whereby practical work (activities, performances of various kinds) will become the subject of special review. It remains to be seen how this will be done. Two main methods are proposed: moderation by visitation from an external expert (such as a teacher of the same subject in another school, or a community member with special expertise in the subject), or video/audio records of the particular performances assessed. It may be that samples of such work are all that are necessary to confirm that the assessing teacher is aware of appropriate standards and makes appropriate judgments.

In Victoria, the common assessment tasks are designed in such a way that they reflect major learnings within each course. What schools and teachers do by way of assessment to prepare students for the tasks and to support their learning generally is left up to them. The work resulting from tasks administered within schools is subject to two stages of moderation. The first is authentication by the teacher that it was indeed the student's own work, and the second is verification of the grades awarded by teachers. Until 1994 the latter was done during an inter-school process using peer panels similar in some respects to the Queensland one. It is now done by statistical moderation against a common cross-curricular test.

6. *Two folios of student work come forward to a district panel from two students in different schools who have been enrolled in the same subject. The students have been awarded the same grade or level of achievement by the schools concerned. Are the two results directly comparable with regard to the quality of the achievements?*

The question here focuses on the intrinsic quality of the results. If we lived in an ideal world, the answer to this question for every pair of students would be yes. For the vast majority of cases the existence of measures such as a common syllabus or work programme, accreditation procedures for any school-based work programmes where these occur (as in Queensland), common moderation or review processes, and a 5-point (rather than a larger) scale for reporting achievement implies such comparability to some degree.

Without research, however, we do not know the degree of consistency, and perhaps in a thoroughly school-based system we never can know (though we can estimate it). In the current circumstances in both Queensland and Victoria, there are no research data from the past against which we might compare the consistency of the present. Furthermore, even where the authorities do obtain some contemporary data, it will still be difficult to make comparisons with any future data.

Whatever the case, the degree of comparability can never be reduced to a single index, covering all subjects and all cases. In terms of validity, and indeed integrity and accountability, this leaves the authorities in a somewhat awkward position. They have to fall back on professional principle. Their duty is to assume that the current situation in regard to the comparability of teacher judgments is not as good as it could and therefore should be.

Queensland currently does this by providing some teacher development and informational activities and by conducting research into current practice. There are also moves in the state to erect stronger safeguards against poor practice, involving random sampling of review folios, the direct improvement of teacher assessment expertise, articulation of more precise statements of acceptable standards in syllabus statements, and direct sharing of understanding of those standards through the availability of exemplars of folios.

What happens in Victoria currently, or will happen, is not yet clear. There is perhaps little or no research or on-going monitoring given the trauma of implementing what are in essence 43 new syllabuses in a single year (1992).

Measures adopted so far might appear to be unduly suspicious or critical of school practice, and such suspicions and criticisms are sometimes voiced. Generally they come from the tertiary sector bewailing 'declining standards' or perceiving poor quality amongst successive intakes of undergraduates. The authorities themselves do not operate from motives of suspicion. The measures are undertaken because the authorities have the responsibility of accounting for standards at each stage of the system they administer.

7. *Two review folios come forward to a state-moderating panel from two students in different districts who have been enrolled in the same subject. The two schools have awarded the same grade or level of achievement to the students and this has been ratified by the district panels concerned. Are the two results directly comparable with regard to the quality of the processing each receives and the judgments made?*

The question here focuses on the quality of the operation of the moderation processes themselves. In Queensland, the authority is conducting research in a limited number of subjects into the comparability of review judgments between district panels. The results of this study are not yet to hand. Neither are there any data from the past to report, with which the new data could reasonably be compared. As in the previous section (and for the same reasons) the situation in Victoria is not yet clear, the system is too new.

Any authority operating a school-based system has to be able to verify that, at least, the degree of comparability is as high as it might be. Such a body need not do this in any punitive or negative sense. The basic premise is simply that current procedures should clearly be consistent in quality, and the criteria which underlie the judgments of standard should be commonly understood, shared, and used. Where the shared understandings of both criteria and standards across districts could clearly be improved, it is worth doing so in the interests both of individual students and of public accountability.

Authorities will certainly have to look at district and state panel training. They may have to consider the accreditation of individual teachers as panellists. A monitoring of students' performance based on random sampling will contribute some further evidence. There will be benefit, too, from provision of maximum opportunity for interaction between teachers, district and state panellists to clarify and increase understanding of the standards which are made manifest during assessment of actual student work. In dual tier systems, such as in Queensland and South Australia, the measures would be expensive and would have to apply within every school-assessed subject, but as noted, they should also have spin-off effects on teacher expertise.

8. *On the official certificate, a student is shown to have achieved the same grade or level of achievement in two different subjects. Are the two results directly comparable?*

In a broad common-sense sort of way, since a common descriptor has been used for the level achieved, one might presume that the results are comparable. However, they may not be, for two main reasons. One is that subjects are indeed very different in what they offer, and each is designed to be adapted to different sets of learning and teaching experiences in schools. Furthermore, they are designed to yield different sorts of performances, be assessed according to different criteria, and cater for a wide range of student abilities and interests. The other reason is that there will always be marked differences in ability between the student groups that enrol for different subjects. The comparability implied in the question cannot and should not be assumed.

Every Australian state in its recent educational history has made some provision for direct inter-subject scaling in an attempt to achieve comparability. Some still do. It is the view of the author that such attempts are vain, indeed doomed to failure, because of the untenable assumption of parity in assessment criteria, standards, and work values across subjects that underlies each attempt. What authorities can say (and should say more loudly, perhaps) is that, whatever the subject and whatever the grade or level awarded, the results have been subjected to the same basic set of assessment and moderation processes (such as those outlined for Queensland in Figure 6.1 above) to enable certification to proceed. The procedures, checks, and controls need to be publicized, with a commentary, and should be readily available to all users of the certificate.

Unfortunately, one of the plagues affecting Australian assessment and certification systems is the fervent desire of tertiary admissions officers to obtain a single-index indicator of student performance, not just for each individual subject but one which summarises performance in all subjects undertaken. This requires inter-subject scaling processes of enormous statistical and logistical complexity (even given the insertion of a common scaling test taken by all candidates), but defies the logic of what actually happens in schools. Most certifying authorities have not so far had the political clout to resist such processes, but at least Queensland has been able to break with the tradition. It seems possible that others will do likewise.

9. *On the student's certificate, the achievements in two subjects are shown to have been awarded the same grade or level of achievement, one being a school-assessed subject and one being a publicly-examined subject. Are the two results directly comparable?*

The two reasons advanced for answering no to the same question when posed in situation 8 also apply here. Any user of the certificate, such as an employer during an employment interview or a tertiary admissions officer, who makes the assumption that the two results in this situation are directly comparable or in some way 'equivalent' does so in error. Such an answer sits uncomfortably in the minds of teachers in South Australia, whose students face a direct discount on their efforts in school-assessed subjects when processing of results for tertiary entrance occurs.

Nevertheless it is a negative answer that has to be faced. Not that one necessarily agrees with the rough bench-mark basis of the discounting process. In its arbitrariness and its base on the false assumption about parity, it is about as silly (and unjust) as inter-subject scaling. (One would like to see the research evidence - if it exists - which the authority uses to justify the discount. Are such students really less able than their similar-scoring peers? In every subject? Do they perform worse in particular tertiary courses alongside those who were given the same grade in publicly-assessed courses during Year 12?) Only a massive change to the admissions procedures themselves, to include perhaps student interviews, probationary entry into tertiary courses and screening during such work, a sharper focus on school performance in particular pre-requisite subjects, or a dramatic lessening of the competition for scarce places would actually right matters. It simply will not do justice to students to hand such procedures over to computer operators and clerks.

COMPARABILITY: WHAT ACTUALLY IS IT?

As the foregoing discussion indicates, comparability is many things. At various times in a student's career, it may include: opportunity to study a course and/or its component subjects; treatment in school (the availability of courses; parity between schools in learning and teaching resources; teaching quality; common curriculum delivery procedures); comparable assessments in terms of quality, degree of task difficulty and the application of common procedural measures to verify and moderate their accuracy; outcomes during certification; long-term outcomes in terms of just and equitable access to tertiary courses and employment opportunities.

Thus it can be seen that 'comparability' is relevant to, or part of (or very easily confused with) concepts such as equality, equity and social justice, commonality, and equivalence, depending on whether one might be talking to a student, a parent, an employer, a teacher, a school administrator, a systemic administrator, or a tertiary admissions officer.

Parents and students want comparability. The desire is expressed often in the context of ensuring that other students in 'the school in the next town' are not receiving favours from the operation of the system. Since some will even go so far as to argue that external examinations are 'fairer,' authorities need to be able to demonstrate the thorough-going fairness of a school-based system.

With regard to comparability of opportunity, enrolment in educational institutions is widely and freely available, as it is in all developed countries. The inability of some students and their families to bear the costs involved is ameliorated by the provision of allowances. In terms of outcomes comparability, care is taken that assessments (and their moderation) within subjects within schools; within subjects across schools; between subjects, within schools; and between subjects, across schools receive attention from both the curricular and processing points of view.

MAXIMISING THE LIKELIHOOD OF VARIOUS KINDS OF COMPARABILITY

Any assessing and certifying authority, whether it uses a thorough-going system of school-based assessment or not, must try to ensure fairness within all the systemically-ordained aspects of a student's educational progress and the protection of his or her rights to fairness. Australian school-based systems have much to teach others when it comes to protecting the validity of the system and the reliability of assessments made within it, at the same time as protecting the rights of individuals.

What maximises the likelihood that due and appropriate comparabilities will ensue from school-based programmes? The Australian experience points to the following, in a properly sequenced programme:

(i) real, not token, devolution of responsibility for assessment design and conduct to the students' own teachers, respected throughout all subsequent stages of the system, and supported by appropriate teacher development programmes;

(ii)the provision of sensitive, thorough moderation opportunities: (a) enhanced by provision of common syllabuses and/or subject-specifications which nevertheless allow for some school curriculum development; (b)promoted (and supported) within schools, prior to public exposure of the assessments; (c) promoted within a district, in circumstances attached to opportunities for on-going development of teacher understandings about criteria, standards, and the system generally; (d) promoted on a system-wide basis, to ensure that common understandings are shared across as well as within districts.

The presence of external scaling instruments or devices is a red herring. It is seriously flawed in its operation and in its fundamental misconception about what other forms of moderation are intended to do — to keep the human scale at all times within the formulation and reporting of educational assessments.

At a conference in the United States recently, a presenter was heard to remark that various new overarching structures of programme development, including the possibility of a national curriculum in that country, were necessary to 'stop teachers wasting their time in curriculum development and its assessment.' However, far from being a waste of time, devolution of responsibility for curriculum development and assessment to teachers, given a reasonable and benign set of checks, may in fact enrich a school's curriculum — a truly worthy national aim. It will do this by facilitating the development of a curriculum and assessment programme that is truly responsive to the school's clientele, yet moderated and enhanced by contacts with other schools. At the same time, if appropriately conducted, with due respect for individual differences amongst both teachers and students, it will heighten the full development of each professional practitioner.

REFERENCES

ACACA. (Australasian Curriculum Assessment and Certification Authorities). (1991). *Leaving school 1991: A guide to Year 12 certificates and tertiary entrance statements in Australia.* North Sydney: Board of Studies.

CRAMP. (Committee to Review Assessment and Moderation Processes). (1992). *The review of assessment and moderation processes in Queensland senior secondary education, 1991-92.* Report to the Minister of Education, Queensland. Brisbane: Author.

McCurry, D. M. (1992, September). *Common curriculum elements within a scaling test for tertiary entrance: The Queensland Core Skills Test.* Paper presented at the 18th annual conference of the International Association for Educational Assessment, Dublin.

Withers, G. P. (1989). *''How happy would I be with either . . .'': The validity and reliability of new types of assessment procedure for use in selection.* Paper presented at the 15th annual conference of the International Association for Educational Assessment, Sydney.

7. MULTIPLE-ENTRY PATHWAYS TO HIGHER EDUCATION: IMPLICATIONS FOR THE DESIGN OF SENIOR SECONDARY CURRICULUM AND ASSESSMENT

R. John Halsey[1]
Senior Secondary Assessment Board of South Australia
Wayville, Southern Australia

One of the most significant advances in Australian education in recent years has been the development of multiple-entry pathways to higher education. I make this claim because this development has boldly demonstrated that entry to higher education can be achieved in a variety of ways.

The primary purpose of this paper is to consider the implications and potential for change flowing from the development of multiple-entry pathways to higher education particularly as it affects the way in which senior secondary education curriculum and assessment are designed and delivered. The significance of this development now needs to be fully grasped and utilised to further enhance educational opportunities for all aspiring Year 12 graduates.

To place this development in context, it is useful to present an overview of some critical aspects of Australian society, and to describe the essential structure of

1 I would like to thank my SSABSA colleagues who assisted with the preparation of this paper and acknowledge three in particular: Ms Judith Lydeamore, Co-ordinator of Assessment Services and the Equity in Senior Secondary School Assessment Project, for extensive advice on the overall structure and focus of the paper; Mr Antonio Mercurio, Co-ordinator of Curriculum Development, Accreditation and Publications; Dr Margaret Cominos, Research Officer, who provided valuable editorial advice and service. I would also like to acknowledge the work of Ms Kathryn Tolhurst-Thomas who entered, arranged, and produced the finished document. Finally, I would like to recognize the assistance given to me in preparing this paper by colleagues who work in the tertiary system and in other statutory assessment authorities.

education services in Australia at the secondary and tertiary levels. I have also included a brief 'position statement' in the paper in order to draw some inferences and conclusions about what I believe to be the ideals that Australia needs to work towards insofar as educational provision is concerned. Finally, while the paper necessarily draws upon my knowledge and experience of the Australian education scene (and particularly that of South Australia), the issues being raised by the changes we are currently experiencing and the solutions being proposed also, I believe, have relevance to other countries and other circumstances. Because I am conscious of the limitations of trying to address a very complex set of circumstances within a limited framework, I find it helpful to remember the words of Sir Karl Popper, who, when responding to a compendium of critiques of his extensive philosophical output replied, 'no one should be expected to say, all the time, at the same time, everything that is to be said!' (cited in Halpin, 1992).

AUSTRALIA IN BRIEF

Physically, Australia is a country of approximately 7.68 million square kilometres and 17.5 million people. Although the popular 'media' image of the country is rural and sunburnt, with a semi-frontier lifestyle, in reality, most Australians live near the seaboard in urban centres. With the steady influx of migrants, first from England and other parts of Europe, and latterly from Southeast Asia, Australian society has taken on a multicultural flavour, which has led to increasing diversity in lifestyle, the arts, and the general social fabric.

Australians' growing perception of themselves as part of Southeast Asia has led to a weakening of some of their ties with Europe and America. This has been reinforced by the attitude of Prime Minister Paul Keating who has expressed his determination to make Australia an internationally recognised nation, with a major role to play in Asia, and the Pacific area in particular, where Australia has established a position for itself as a country interested in the protection of the sovereignty of small nations, the exploitation of natural resources, and the advocacy of nuclear-free zones.

To place Australia in a competitive trade position internationally, the federal government has recognised the need to restructure both industry and education. Prior to the present Labour government's coming to power, Australia enjoyed high tariff protection and a fixed rate of exchange, which was closely controlled by the government through its monetary regulation agencies. To stimulate the economy and accelerate restructuring, the government has embraced a policy of greatly reduced tariffs and has deregulated the money market. The worldwide economic recession has taken its toll of jobs as in most other industrialised countries. This has affected Labour's image in the eyes of the Australian public, who have always viewed it as a people's party, representing the working classes and the trade unions. The general perception of many is that the party has sold out on the fundamental principles of job protection through tariffs and wage preservation. The basic defence of the government in relation to this claim is that these measures were necessary to restructure industry, increase productivity, and make Australia a more viable commercial competitor on the international scene.

With the expressed desire of making Australia a 'clever country' and of exploiting its intellectual capacity, there has been more focus by the federal government on education and vocational training schemes at the national level than probably at any other time in this century. To appreciate this development, it is important to have some understanding of the respective levels of government in Australia. There are three tiers of government - federal, state, and local. However, in terms of this paper, it is only necessary to focus on the federal and state levels, since these are the two key players in education and are responsible for the generation and allocation of resources for it.

Most of the taxing powers and procedures reside with the federal government which disburses revenue at two levels: nationally for policies and programmes that are its responsibility and via the individual states for state-based programmes. In this dual federal-state model, there is huge scope for negotiation, particularly when state governments can be of a different political persuasion to the national ruling party.

At the state level, education is the biggest expenditure line. It is also one of the human services that the federal constitution principally allocates to the states. This can make for very considerable tension as the federal government attempts to shape and implement national priorities which directly require the co-operation of state education and training systems, which, in turn, depend upon various levels of decentralised decision making. Notwithstanding this, in recent years there has been a significant trend towards greater co-operation in education and training between the federal and state governments which has created an environment that is now more conducive to establishing a further dimension of commonality of curriculum and assessment nationally, with significant implications for preparation for higher education.

HIGHER EDUCATION SYSTEM

Australia now has a unified system of universities developed from an amalgamation of existing universities with former colleges of advanced education (that is, institutions which predominantly ran diploma and first degree programs with a heavy applied emphasis). This federal government initiative was implemented at considerable political and financial expense, ultimately gaining the acceptance of the universities by manipulating their grants. However, universities, although heavily dependent on federal funding, generate a considerable amount of their revenue from both private and overseas students and enterprise programmes of various kinds, many of which are off-shore. They continue to exercise considerable autonomy within the educational community and are essentially self-accrediting and self-regulating.

In addition, at the tertiary level, there is a system of technical and further education which provides the majority of the nation's structured training programmes at skilled tradesperson and paraprofessional levels. The Department of Employment and Technical and Further Education works very closely with employers and industry and is at present being recast by the federal government to play a greater and more extensive role in the area of vocational preparation. In terms of the percentage of the population who access and receive a recognised vocational award, as distinct from a tertiary award, Australia is considerably below the OECD average. In recent years, there has been a growth in the nexus between senior secondary education and technical and further education, which has resulted in quite significant credit transfer into various awards from secondary courses. However, the relationship is nowhere near as strong or well-developed as that which has traditionally existed between senior secondary education and the universities.

RETENTION RATES

For a number of reasons, economic and otherwise, during the past decade in Australia, there has been a steady rise in student retention rates in the latter years of secondary education, particularly at Year 12. As this is the level of study immediately preceding university entrance, the increased retention rate has contributed towards the restructuring of senior secondary education and the development of multiple higher-education entry pathways. Table 7.1 presents the apparent growth in retention rates from 1980 to 1991.

TABLE 7.1

APPARENT RETENTION RATES TO YEAR 12 BY STATE (PERCENTAGES)

	1980	1985	1989	1990	1991
NSW	32.9	41.7	54.4	56.8	61.4
Victoria	32.5	45.4	60.5	65.4	75.7
Queensland	38.6	55.1	69.7	73.8	79.6
SA	38.3	51.2	66.7	72.1	83.5
WA	34.0	47.25	61.8	64.2	71.1
Tasmania	26.9	28.7	39.7	44.7	57.5
NT	20.1	30.1	42.7	47.7	57.5
ACT	66.6	77.1	85.6	86.9	95.6
Australia	**34.5**	**46.4**	**60.3**	**64.0**	**71.3**

The increased retention rates through to Year 12 have been somewhat parallelled by an increase in the overall number of students who have sought university entrance. For example, in 1980 in South Australia, 5,950 sought admission to university and 3,214 were eventually enrolled in undergraduate courses. For 1991, the figures were 11,219 admissions applications, resulting in a total of 4,981 offers of enrolment (Australian College of Education, 1992).

CHANGES IN EDUCATIONAL ASPIRATIONS

Changes in educational aspirations comprise one of the main reasons for the increase in the number of Year 12 students seeking and subsequently gaining entry to university. Among other incentives have been the overall increase in the number of university places funded by government and the general change in the nature of the labour market, which requires increasingly higher levels of education and training. As in most industrialised countries, the most sensitive political issue in Australia is unemployment which is around 10% nationally, varying from about 8% to 13% among the states.

Lack of employment opportunities and employer demands for higher levels of education and training have had the effect of increasing the number of school leavers seeking entry to university. The same economic conditions have resulted also in increased mature-age enrolments. However, the fact that school leavers comprise only 43% of these enrolments indicates clearly the trend towards university entrance via alternative pathways.

Statistical evidence covering the period from 1979 to the present indicates that this has been a relatively long-term trend (Australia. Department of Employment, Education and Training, 1992). That is, although the number of school leavers seeking university enrolment has been increasing steadily over this period, the proportion actually entering university has remained around the 43% mark.

South Australian figures reflect the overall national picture, which shows that, although there has been a substantial growth in Year 12 student numbers over recent years, the proportion of these moving directly into higher education grew by only 1%, compared with a growth of more than 8% for other undergraduates, presumably entering higher education from alternative pathways.

UNIVERSITY SELECTION/ADMISSION

Historically, universities in Australia have always reserved the right to determine entry requirements to undergraduate and graduate programmes. In most instances, for undergraduate programmes, this has meant that matriculation required completion of secondary education to Year 12 to the satisfaction of the university; while for graduate courses, the possession of relevant or related prior award(s) has been required. However, in relatively recent years there has been a significant growth in the extent to which universities are willing to grant entry to undergraduate and graduate programmes on the basis of a range of comparable but different criteria.

By way of illustration, the University of Adelaide now has two broad admission categories to undergraduate programmes. These are known as Standard and Special. Within the Standard category are located the pathways that require applicants to gain a competitive ranked score based on performance at Year 12, or its interstate equivalent. In summary, the Standard pathways include: successful completion of Year 12 Studies and the scaled subject achievement aggregate required for the particular programme; adult Year 12 Studies - in this pathway, adults are defined by age (21 years or over) and allowed to complete their entry requirements over a longer time period (at least three years as compared to two for non-adult students); interstate or overseas equivalents to successful completion of Year 12 studies; and status granted for previous study undertaken at another institution of higher education. Each of these pathways may, in addition, require students to have successfully completed some prerequisites, to undertake an audition (e.g., music or dance), or to satisfy specific work experience requirements (e.g., for programmes in farm management or labour studies).

In the Special admissions category the entry pathways include: the Aboriginal and Torres Strait Islander Scheme; the Fairway Scheme which encourages the participation in higher education of students from schools that have traditionally been under-represented in the university's student population; the special-entry scheme which is reserved for mature-age applicants (21 years and older) who have not satisfied the academic entry requirements and are therefore required to undertake all or some of the following: a Special Tertiary Admissions Test (STAT) and an essay test; an audition; and to present evidence of previous study or work or other experience and reasons for wishing to study the course(s) chosen.

Finally, spreading across both entry categories is the pathway for students whose pre-tertiary studies have been affected by a severe and continuing disability. Such applicants may be exempted from some of the entry requirements.

Both of the other universities in South Australia also have a range of entry pathways for undergraduate programmes, which are very similar to those of the University of Adelaide, and account for a similar percentage of students in the first year of undergraduate programmes. The same generally applies nationally.

SCHOOL SYSTEMS

There are three main school systems of education in Australia: government, catholic, and independent (usually based on a protestant religion, though this category includes others such as Waldorf and Montessori schools as well as various kinds of 'finishing' schools, e.g. dance, drama, business). Approximately 70% of all students attend government schools. The other two systems account for the rest, where fees for tuition are met by parents and government grants, which are allocated to schools on a sliding scale, based on the wealth of the supporting school community and the quality of the school's facilities. In terms of a national 'who's who', students from independent schools are still decidedly advantaged in private enterprise and public life in Australia. This is an important point to note because it emphasises the disproportionately high impact on the shaping of Australian society by the non-government sector.

Until relatively recently in South Australia (1984), and elsewhere in Australia, accredited courses at Year 12 level were partitioned into two very distinct groups and were often managed and assessed by two different bodies.

Non-university approved syllabuses and courses, culminating in a Senior Secondary Certificate or similar qualification, were developed, assessed, and reported on by the state-based Education Department for use in its schools. The certificate was designed generally for students who stayed on to Year 12, but who either did not aspire to higher education or were considered to be incapable of coping with preuniversity syllabuses.

For entry to a university, students were required to take a specified programme of studies endorsed by the universities (and, to a lesser extent, agreed to by the schools because they were essentially the junior partner in the arrangement) which were externally examined and reported upon by a body known as the Public Examinations Board or its equivalent. Students in all the school sectors were assessed by public examination. Results were (and still are in many ways) used as an important gauge of school-system performance, and hence public standing. They were scaled to form a single aggregate (and still are in most states) for ranking purposes in a competitive selection process.

SENIOR SECONDARY CURRICULUM ASSESSMENT AND CERTIFICATION AUTHORITIES

In addition to the school sectors, each State and Territory also has a statutory authority, which is responsible for developing curriculum appropriate for senior secondary students (usually considered to be Years 11 and 12, or 16- to 18-year olds) and for assessing and accrediting student performance. In some states, such as New South Wales and Western Australia, the mandate of the statutory authority extends into the compulsory years of schooling. However, for the purpose of this paper, it is sufficient to focus upon their responsibilities in the area of senior secondary schooling.

Each of the statutory authorities assesses and issues certificates to recognise student achievement from each of the school systems. Though different emphases exist within each system, for religious, philosophical, or pedagogical reasons, as well as socioeconomic factors, the overlay of statutory authority programmes and assessments provides a degree of commonality of educational experience in the final years of schooling. Each statutory authority has a Board, which comprises representatives from the school systems, higher education, practising teachers, parent groups, employers, trade unions, technical and further education and, in some instances, a representative of the state's Equal Opportunity Commission or the equivalent.

The functions of the Boards are quite similar and include approving all major policies of the authorities, and accrediting syllabuses with their respective assessment, reporting, and certification procedures. An amplification of these functions can be found in the initial charter of the Senior Secondary Assessment Board of South Australia (SSABSA) of 1984:

> the provision of a challenging high level of general senior secondary education for all students;
> the development and approval of high quality syllabuses in order to engender public and professional confidence in the subjects available;
> the facilitation of equal opportunity of access to education for all students regardless of sex, ethnic background, geographical location or physical impairment, age and aspiration;
> the provision of a variety of methods of assessment which meet the requirements of students, employers, post-secondary tertiary education institutions and the expectations of the community;
> the production of a clear statement of student achievement which is recognised statewide and is portable across the Commonwealth;
> the acceptance of leadership in the field of educational assessment by undertaking and commissioning research into assessment. (p. 2)

REDESIGNING SENIOR SECONDARY EDUCATION

In recent years, statutory authorities have played a very important role in the redesigning of secondary education, especially in Victoria, where, following the Blackburn Report, a dramatic and controversial overhaul of the structure of curriculum and assessment in Years 11 and 12 has taken place (Victoria. Ministerial Review of Post-Compulsory Schooling, 1985). In South Australia, the Gilding Enquiry into immediate post-compulsory education has led to very significant changes at the senior secondary level, consistent with the development of multiple pathways at the tertiary levels (South Australia. Committee of Enquiry into Immediate Post-Compulsory Education, 1988, 1989).

In 1989, the state government gave SSABSA the task of developing, in co-operation with all member groups of the educational and wider community, the curriculum, assessment, and reporting policies and procedures for the new South Australian Certificate of Education (SACE). The successful completion of this certificate by students signifies the end of secondary education. The SACE was required to be a certificate programme that would profitably engage all students in the senior secondary years of schooling (Years 11 and 12) and provide for a range of post-secondary options: tertiary entry, training, vocational, direct employment, as well as providing a sound general education appropriate to the needs of individuals and the nation as a whole. A very important function assigned to it was the provision of quality educational experiences for the vast majority of students (approximately 85%) who would not, for a wide range of reasons, enter university from Year 12. In these very important senses then, the design of the new certificate was required to reduce the demarcation and status differential between university and non-university programmes and students and move towards the provision of a more genuinely 'seamless' curriculum.

The development of the new certificate in South Australia (and its counterparts in other states such as Victoria and Western Australia) has produced a context for ongoing challenges to the single scaled aggregate score method of selection, which is used virtually accross the nation for university entrance from Year 12. Some changes made and issues to be resolved have been summarised by Elliot, Meade, Power, & Toomey (1987).

> The passage into higher education, or moving from school or work into tertiary education, is presently unnecessarily difficult and restrictive for the majority of Australians. The current monolithic, elitist and unjust procedures used to select people for higher education are presently under attack.
>
> .... the Davids have emerged in a number of forms: members of a number of visible new groups are now forcing their ways into tertiary education through a variety of alternative pathways, aided and abetted by widespread doubts and a measure of disgust about existing admission procedures. The previous Goliath of the 'selection process' - the rank-order aggregate score - is beginning to totter under the onslaught of the growing number of Davids.
>
> ... the difficulty is, (however) that these aggregate scores continue to have a powerful selection effect even though it is now generally regarded that they have relatively low predictive and content validity. [A study by Meade reported in 1971 found that correlation coefficients between terminal school results and tertiary success ranged between 0.3 and 0.4. In 1984, a study by Beswick in Victoria reported the correlation between success in Year 12 and subsequent tertiary success at 0.5]... Several unwanted curricular and social outcomes flow from the preoccupation of upper secondary school life with obtaining good scores for admission purposes. These include the way teacher, student and parent anxiety about the rating system for tertiary entrance artificially affects subject choice; divides pupils into the well regarded and the poorly regarded; separates teachers and students; separates students and students; and has a very negative impact upon sound evaluation, teaching methodologies and the quality of learning (pp. 85-6).

I now want to identify some of the possible implications for the design of senior secondary curriculum and assessment which flow from this change in the profile of entry pathways to university together with the other relevant contextual items. However, I would like to precede this with a brief 'position statement' of my personal view of

Australian society and how education might address the needs of individuals, as individuals and as participants in a democratic society.

POSITION STATEMENT

Raymond Williams (1966) states that 'an education curriculum .... expresses a compromise between an inherited selection of interests and the emphasis of new interests'(p. 150). Any move beyond what currently exists at the senior secondary level of education in Australia as a result of the development of alternative higher education entry pathways in particular must take this into account and have the potential to further enhance democratic values and a diversity of sustainable lifestyles.

In trying to outline what needs to happen to bring about this ideal, I feel somewhat aligned with the Byzantines who, when attempting to define God developed what became known as 'negative theology'; that is, rather than limit the concept of God by trying to describe what it is, they defined their idea of God by saying what the concept is not. In a similar way, I often find it easier to describe what I believe ought to be the case for the role of education and the role of society by dwelling on what they are not.

Although Australian society emphasises and values co-operation and team work, it is very competitive so that the needs and aspirations of individuals are favoured over those of the group or community. There is also a tendency to value instrumental and measurable outcomes above those of a more problematic, reflective, non-quantifiable, and creative nature. Resources tend to be directed to economic ends and justified in terms of either maintaining or improving the nation's general standard of living.

This relates especially to Australia's exploitation of its natural resources. In common with many developed countries, however, Australians are becoming more aware of the particular fragility of the Australian ecosystem and are balancing this against some of the more exploitative industrial, commercial, and social practices. And though cultural diversity exists and is encouraged, Australia is still, in the words of the eminent historian Manning Clark (1989), trying to find its own clock, its own sense of identity, that encompasses earlier epochs than European settlement.

Education in Australia is currently poised to move either in significantly new ways or regroup and retreat into the somewhat familiar, but I believe inappropriate, past where class structures and divisions of labour were fairly clearly defined and the formal education system functioned as a giant sorting and allocating machine. What needs to be understood is that, notwithstanding the economic and demographic pressures for change, I believe that the maintenance of, or a return to, the conservative models of educational provision is a possibility that cannot be excluded.

However, leaving aside this note of caution, I am somewhat optimistic about the future opportunities in Australian education while stressing that at the crucial senior secondary/higher education interface, the gains made to date through the

Blackburn and Gilding enquiries in Victoria and South Australia respectively, and related elements of change that have occurred in other states of Australia, need to be consolidated and further developed if they are not to be lost.

Cherry Collins places Australian states into one of three categories in relation to policy developments that are currently taking place: conservative, progressive, and 'common culture' states. Briefly, the conservative states have adopted a policy line of different solutions for different kinds of young people, with those bound for university being at the top of the hierarchy. The progressive states follow a minimal centralist intervention approach to policy and have attempted to deal with the linear and mechanistic relationship between senior secondary and university placement. The 'common culture' states have attempted to develop policy about the kind of Australia the upper secondary system might help to create and about how to reconcile national needs with a system which offers dignity and purposeful learning to all young people. The common culture model of education is intended 'to ensure for all young people, access to cultural understandings and intellectual tools necessary for their full and confident participation as adults in a democratic society' (Collins, 1992, p. 255).

I strongly believe that the ideal that needs to be vigorously pursued is the common culture model, because, at its best, it primarily serves the dual purposes of individualism and collectivism. The model comprises studies considered essential for all students as well as scope for specialisation, without resorting to very extreme forms of subject and course partitioning and their attendant hierarchy of knowledge and associated status differentials. Common culture education is designed to enhance access and value diversity, while stressing the national obligations of an adult population towards the new generations. It is highly vocational and pragmatic as well as academically rigorous. At best, it creates appropriate opportunities across all areas of the curriculum for all students to be successful in the key broad areas of learning considered to be essential for their full participation in society.

A COMMON CULTURE MODEL AND SENIOR SECONDARY EDUCATION

The new certificate in South Australia is compatible with a common culture model of education with its agreed pattern of studies for all students, and has the support of each of the main groups involved in the provision of secondary education. Irrespective of their intended post-school option(s), to gain a SACE all students must: at the first stage (Year 11) study English or English as a second language or Communication for the Hearing Impaired, Australian Studies, Mathematics, and two additional units from each of two groups - Arts/Humanities/Social and Cultural Studies and Mathematics/Science/Technology; at the second stage (Year 12) study at least two units of a 'language rich' subject and two units of a 'quantitative experimental' subject; study and record achievement in 22 semester units (each of 50-60 contact hours); gain successful achievement in at least 16 of these, 6 units or more at Stage 2 (Year 12) level; satisfactorily complete a writing-based literacy assessment which is determined by evaluating written work drawn from across the curriculum to match the pattern of the certificate which is marked at the school level against Board -approved exemplars; sample moderation is conducted to verify results.

The design of the new certificate and its inbuilt flexibility of interpretation is intended to serve various purposes including strengthening the nexus and inter-relationships between senior secondary programmes and technical and further education programmes, that is, between general education and vocational education/preparation. Consequently, high priority has been given to the development of vocationally-oriented pathways of study, using the range of studies available for SACE as well as developing new syllabuses such as Tourism, and enhancing credit transfer arrangements with technical and further education. These pathways have increased the options for students who take the SACE, by providing a set of quality alternatives to the traditional academic/tertiary pathways, by giving access to post-school awards at the sub-degree level, which, in turn, open up alternative entry pathways to university study that, in some instances, can be used to articulate into the second or third year of a degree.

Finally, perhaps the most important development associated with the new South Australian certificate, and its counterparts, has been some changes to the methods used for calculating the single scaled higher education entry aggregate, although it must be conceded that the use of a score for Year 12 entry into university remains firmly entrenched in spite of warnings referred to earlier. It should be noted that the gains that have been made have only come after considerable debate, discussion, and expenditure of resources. In South Australia, the following has been agreed to. Of the five Stage 2 (Year 12) subjects required to calculate an aggregate score, only four need be acceptable to the university to which entry is sought. An aggregate, however, is developed using all five subjects by scaling the best three of those acceptable to the university; allocating 'bonus' points on a sliding scale from 1 to 5 for the other two subjects based upon subject-achievement scores. The 'bonus' points begin to operate when a student reaches at least 10 on a 20-point achievement scale. Both categories of subjects (that is, publicly examined and school assessed) can be used in the score calculation process but, in many instances, the universities exclude the school-assessed subjects by classifying them as inappropriate for most of their programmes.

MULTIPLE-PATHWAYS GROWTH: SOME CONTEXTUAL FACTORS

The development of multiple higher-education entry pathways in Australia has been, in part, a recognition of the fact that appropriate preparation for study at university level occurs in a variety of ways and contexts. The development has also been a response to general pressure exerted by the community, and more especially by government and its policy advisers and managers, for universities to be active in the area of social justice by enhancing access for disadvantaged or marginalised individuals and groups. In short, the universities have been challenged to use their autonomy, together with some persuasion through various categories of funding entitlements, to become more flexible with their entry procedures.

The overall percentage decline in the number of students entering first year university programmes direct from Year 12 has, however, resulted in increasing competition for limited places because applications for admissions have basically outstripped the availability of places. Pure market force advocates would see this as a Darwinian situation, in which a kind of natural selection operates, enabling only the 'best' prepared students to gain access to a university education.

Australia does not yet have, at the post-secondary level, a technical and further education system that enjoys parity of esteem with universities. This situation is now, however, being redressed through the many changes currently taking place at the senior secondary/higher education and vocational training interface. These changes also reflect the government's willingness to provide the necessary resources (an example is the recent injection of funding for the upgrading of the national vocational training scheme), through restructuring of the technical and further education system. This reassessment of the value of vocational skills and training represents an important aspect of the government's commitment to making Australia a 'clever country.'

MULTIPLE-PATHWAYS GROWTH: SOME IMPLICATIONS

The implementation of multiple pathways to higher education has several very important interrelated implications for the future design and delivery of senior secondary level curriculum and assessment. First, the growth of alternative entry pathways can be used to reduce the overall pressure on Year 12 students, most of whom feel compelled to maximise their scores at the expense of all else. As well, the 'trickle down' model of curriculum where one elite purpose/design is used to serve multiple purposes is seriously challenged when other viable higher education entry options exist. The creation of alternative entry pathways to tertiary studies, other than through Year 12 (even though most of them do not begin to operate until a certain adult age threshold is reached, for example 18 or 21) provides a safety net for aspiring students, allowing them more time for critical decision making, and thereby keeping open life possibilities that can be revisited or renegotiated as their circumstances change, due to factors such as maturity, economic imperatives, and career aspiration.

Second, now that the practice of alternative entry pathways to higher education has been accepted, the way is open for the creative redesigning of Year 12 curriculum and assessment. The traditional continuum from senior secondary into undergraduate programmes is gradually being replaced by a set of intermediate options, not unlike those offered to travellers at a large airport that services passengers on continuing journeys as well as those who have to change or renegotiate flights and destinations. The existence of alternative pathways, I believe, needs to be exploited further as a key ingredient in the task of creating productive space for reconceptualising the nexus between senior education and the requirements of undergraduate study.

Third, the effect of this shift in emphasis means that preparation for study at university level is not now exclusively confined to a formal educational programme immediately preceding it at Year 12 level or equivalent, in which the curriculum has been framed to conform to university requirements. This allows more attention to be focused on the quality of the outcomes for students from an undergraduate programme, rather than expending disproportionate energy on getting the inputs 'right.' Though the input side of the equation has become quite differentiated, the output has remained quite specific, that is the attainment of a degree or a postgraduate diploma of a particular kind. Quality control procedures still remain with the university.

Fourth, the steady growth of multiple entry pathways to university-level study raises the issue of parity between the different sets of entry criteria and establishes an environment for a continuing evaluation of the single scaled aggregate score method for selection, particularly in terms of any comparative analysis of success rates from the various entry pathways. Questions about the appropriateness of the selection procedures as well as their fairness, in terms of social justice and equity, become increasingly pressing as well. So too do questions about the way in which major changes brought about by policy and procedural shifts of a fundamental kind ought to be managed, so that the further transition from the old and known to the new, unknown, and untried, does not produce dysfunctional unintended outcomes.

Finally, the growth of entry pathways to university level study has established a reservoir of precedents which can, in turn, provide the impetus for the exploration of other forms of entry pathways and preparation as well as providing an important source of stimulus for redesigning senior secondary education.

WHERE TO NEXT?

The changing nature of Australian society, recent developments in senior secondary education, changes to higher education and the development of multiple-entry pathways and national curriculum and delivery restructuring now mean that educators in Australia must grasp a very large nettle indeed and continue to build towards a common curriculum structure at the senior secondary level of education. Until quite recently, the prestige of the universities and the power they exercised over curriculum and delivery made this an unrealistic goal. Now, however, this goal is within reach. Further reinforcement has come from the industrial/commercial sector of the Australian community whose powerful nationally-based lobby groups have collectively articulated a very persuasive bottom line: 'our taxes pay for public education which includes grants to universities, and we want better and different services from them!'

Essentially, the proliferation of different entry pathways is, as I have already stated, an acknowledgement that preparation for study at university level can occur in many and varied settings and ways. While conceding the desirability of maintaining the traditional school-based Year 12 performance option, the hard-edged and sharply categorised university versus non-university subjects model must be significantly modified; in addition, the single aggregated scaled score for selection purposes must be replaced by a more appropriate indicator. The question becomes then: what action should take place to achieve this goal?

Though the answer cannot, I believe, be supplied in too much detail at present, it is possible to outline a number of the key components. Others, I believe, will emerge once the project has commenced. This, of course, does not absolve educators from the responsibility to be as clear as they can about what needs to be done to bring about the proposed changes.

From my perspective, there are at least three main tasks that need to be undertaken to capitalise on the growth of multiple-entry pathways to higher education, which have consequences for changing the design and delivery of senior secondary curriculum and assessment. The first is to continue to build upon current structures and processes that support a common-culture approach to senior secondary education. The common-culture advocates the need to work with the conservatives and the progressives to develop a coalition of support for a common model of education. However, we do not have to wait for further changes in attitudes and practices before continuing developments can take place in the preferred direction.

As a corollary, the second task is to design the senior secondary curriculum and assessment procedures in such a way that the hard-edged partitioning referred to earlier is further diminished and genuinely allows for alternative articulated pathways within the overall framework. Here, I believe, the study-design model rather than separate highly refined and prescribed subject syllabuses is what is required. Several states already use the study-design model for some of the major secondary curriculum areas but, especially in high status university areas such as mathematics and the physical sciences, it has generally met with limited enthusiasm and support.

Study designs define the parameters of an area of curriculum through key features such as aims, objectives, areas of study, work and assessment requirements, and reporting of performance. They have an internal set of procedures and structures that enable users (and clients) to tailor programmes to meet the needs and interests of students (both individually and in groups) and also to meet the requirements of external audiences (the wider public in terms of accountability and confidence about the outcomes) and end-on users, such as employers and universities. The SSABSA has developed a wide range of study designs for use at Stage 1 (Year 11) of the new certificate and has, for some years, also used the model in the non-publicly examined subjects. A major task now is to bridge the gap between the university/non-university categories of subjects using this approach.

The Victorian Curriculum and Assessment Board (VCAB) (1989) has described its version of a study design approach to curriculum as follows:

> The study structure [design] approach is an attempt to accommodate diversity without sacrificing commonality. The essential difference between this new approach and the arrangements it will replace is that the demands of diversity are accommodated within a single curriculum structure, rather than by the provision of choice among a range of structures. The key to the approach is to provide flexibility in the design of the curriculum so that it can be shaped at the local level to suit local circumstances. This has involved drawing a distinction between curriculum design and course development; distinguishing between those elements that are essential to a curriculum, and which can and should be prescribed centrally, and the elements which can be varied and are better left to schools and providers to determine. (p. 1)

Given the historical, and what will be the continuing importance, of support at the university level for any new further developments in senior secondary education, I believe that the VCAB statement needs to be strengthened to ensure that the legitimate performance entry requirements set by universities can be clearly ascertained. But, this must be done in ways that do not overpower and devalue so called non-university ways of knowing and doing, and the assessment thereof. Further, both the advantages and limitations of study designs have to be closely analysed and considered in the process of moving forward.

Some of the advantages of study designs include:

opportunities to consolidate areas of knowledge rather than have a proliferation of subjects as new needs emerge and pressures are brought to bear by lobby groups;

enhanced flexibility for short-term options (e.g., semester or 1/2 semester rather than full year-length courses). It needs to be clearly recognised, however, that flexibility can be used to exclude students as well as to include them in the mainstream;

the use of variants from a single coherently designed framework statement;

a reduction of duplication of content usually present in the partitioning approach to curriculum (e.g., mathematics for university versus mathematics for direct employment) can be more effectively dealt with;

a reduction of the status differential between university and non-university oriented programmes, if both of these broad post-school pathways are derived from the same study design;

an enhancement of articulation with other awards (e.g., those issued by the Department of Employment and Technical and Further Education as well as other providers) is facilitated because the scope of each study design is intended to capture relatively broad areas of knowledge and skill rather than those which are highly refined and specialised; and

the facilitation of future national developments, particularly if agreement is reached about the components of the study designs.

Some of the disadvantages of study designs could include:

the possible loss of public confidence particularly during the transition phase ('what is being packaged? what is inside the package? I can't recognise my subject/what I need to teach/ what I was taught!')

the need for a high level of teacher competence in transforming study designs to programmes of learning for students. There are major implications flowing from this for teacher preservice and continuing inservice training and development;

the potential need for more sophisticated (more complicated?) student enrolment, tracking, and reporting procedures, especially where a study design encourages highly individualistic responses; and

the forming of status judgments when essentially different forms of content and possibly different modes of assessment are derived from the same design.

The third main task in capitalising on the growth of multiple-entry pathways to higher education is that of replacing the single scaled Year 12 subject achievement score for competitive entry to university with a more sensitive and educationally defensible procedure. In making this stipulation, I am mindful of how relatively easy it would be in the Australian context to move outside the present system and replace it with one that is even more traumatic for students with further possibilities of inhibiting good teaching and learning at the senior secondary level. However, there are some developments occurring at present which need to be supported and others which need to be considered. One such development is based on the premise that students perform better in some areas of the curriculum than in others and that this differentiation should be preserved in some overall profiling of performance rather than collapsed into a single scaled score. The details of how this should be done have yet to be worked out. However, the work of Howard Gardner (1983) seems particularly relevant because it exposes the limitations of using a single measure for an 'intelligence test' and extrapolating from this into all areas of complex human performance. Essentially Gardner defines six broad categories of intelligence: linguistic, musical, logical-mathematical, spatial, bodily-kinesthetic, and personal intelligences. Although there are many and varied ways of measuring and reporting upon intelligence, it would seem that there are some connections between what Gardner argues and proposes and the directions that need to be taken in replacing the single scaled aggregate score for university selection.

CONCLUSION

The situation has now been reached in Australia where entry to higher education can be achieved in many different ways. However, until quite recently, the climate did not exist in which this could be capitalised upon in terms of redesigning curriculum and assessment procedures at the senior secondary level. Now that this is changing, it is critical that lively discussion and debate on policy and procedural proposals at the senior secondary/university interface occur.

The present state of developments in senior secondary education and the acceptance of alternative pathways for selection to higher education has demonstrated that there are acceptable ways of accessing a university education other than through the traditional Year 12/matriculation route. These alternative pathways have brought in their wake a potential for further rethinking and redesigning of curriculum and assessment procedures for senior secondary students which, in the long term, will take Australia further along the path of providing an equitable and appropriate education for all of its citizens. Study designs, I believe, offer very real opportunities for overcoming the hard-edged partitioning of knowledge into 'high status' and 'other and low status' which has bedevilled education in Australia at the senior secondary level and beyond. For my final statement, I want to return to the commentary of Raymond Williams (1966):

> Instead of the sorting and grading process ... we should regard human learning in a genuinely open way, as the most valuable real resource we have and therefore as something which we should have to provide a special argument to *limit* rather than a special argument to extend. (p. 147) (emphasis added)

REFERENCES

Australia. Department of Employment, Education and Training. (1992). *Higher education report, No 16.* Canberra: Author

Australian College of Education (1992). *ACE News*, *11*(2), p. 11. Australian College of Education, Curtin, ACT.

Clark, M. (1989). *The 1988 Boyer lectures postscripts.* Sydney: Australian Broadcasting Corporation.

Collins, C. (1992). Upper secondary education in Australia: Differing responses to a common challenge. *Journal of Curriculum Studies, 24*, 247-260.

Elliot, B., Meade, P., Power, C., & Toomey, R. (1987). Policy directions for the processes of selection for higher education in Australia. In R. Toomey (Ed.), *Passages from secondary school to higher education.* Hawthorn, Victoria: Australian Council for Educational Research.

Gardner, H. (1983). *Frames of mind: The theory of multiple intelligences.* London: Heinemann.

Halpin, D. (1992). The NUT's 'strategy for the curriculum': An appreciation. *Journal of Curriculum Studies, 24,* 457-61.

South Australia. Committee of Enquiry into Immediate Post-Compulsory Education (1988). *Report.* (Chair: Kevin R. Gilding). Adelaide: Education Department of South Australia.

South Australia. Committee of Enquiry into Immediate Post-Compulsory Education (1989) *Second Report.* (Chair: Kevin R. Gilding). Adelaide: Education Department of South Australia.

SSABSA. (Senior Secondary Assessment Board of South Australia) (1984). *Annual report.* Adelaide: Author.

VCAB. (Victorian Curriculum and Assessment Board) (1989). *The VCE planning guide.* Melbourne: Author.

Victoria. Ministerial Review of Postcompulsory Schooling (1985), *Report.* (Chair: Jean Blackburn). Melbourne: Author.

Williams, R. (1966). *The long revolution.* New York: Harper & Row.

8. TECHNICAL ISSUES IN CRITERION-REFERENCED ASSESSMENT: EVIDENTIAL AND CONSEQUENTIAL BASES

Dylan Wiliam
King's College,
London

The increasing use in many countries of criterion-referenced assessments in high stakes assessments, such as those used for entry into higher education, has, to a certain extent at least, proceeded in advance of the theoretical foundations that so firmly underpin the use of norm-referenced assessments. At the same time, the concept of validity has been subject to a sequence of extensions from a property of an assessment, to a property of the behaviours elicited by an assessment, to a property of the inferences made on the basis of the assessment. In the framework proposed by Messick (1980), validity is located within a framework that emphasises the social settings in which assessments are made. As well as the inferences attached to assessment outcomes, he argues that the process of validation must also consider the value implications of the interpretation of results, the evidence for the relevance of the construct, the utility of the particular applications, and the social consequences of the proposed and actual use of results.

He presents this view of validation as the result of a crossing of basis (i.e., evidential or consequential) with function (i.e., result interpretation and result use):

	result interpretation	result use
evidential basis	construct validity	construct validity relevance/utility
consequential basis	value implications	social consequences

Within this framework, it is possible to see that a consideration of the effects of the use of assessment outcomes on the subsequent behaviour of agents is also part of the validation process.

This paper presents some theoretical concepts that have been developed to inform the construction of assessments for the National Curriculum in England. The development of these high stakes assessments in criterion-referenced domains has necessitated paying particular attention to the consequential basis of the assessments, and it is the consequential basis of these concepts that is the particular focus of this paper. The paper deals with three major topics: the topology of criterion-referenced domains; combination, aggregation, and reconciliation of assessments; and the relationship between validity, reliability, and manageability.

THE TOPOLOGY OF CRITERION-REFERENCED DOMAINS

The term objective-referenced assessment is often used to describe assessments where the inferences made on the basis of results relate simply to the items assessed (Hambleton & Rogers, 1991). On the other hand, the results of criterion-referenced (also often called domain-referenced) assessments are intended to be generalisable beyond the immediate items assessed to some larger domain of interest. The use of generalisability theory in such contexts has often required the domains to be relatively homogenous in order to attain sufficiently high reliability in the assessments, although generalisability theory can, of course, be applied to non-homogeneous domains. The traditional approach to generalisability theory in non-homogeneous domains has been to increase the number of assessment items in order to achieve the required reliability. However, an alternative approach is to capitalise on the internal structure of the domain defined by the criterion.

For example, if we take as our criterion 'addition of two numbers under 100,' this gives rise to a domain *D* consisting of all possible additions of pairs of numbers under 100. However, some of these additions, such as 7+3 are clearly much easier than others, and indeed, are logical prerequisites for others such as 27+53. Since it is inconceivable that someone could be capable of adding 27 and 53, while being unable to add 7 and 3, we lose nothing by removing the 'easier' items from the assessment domain. We can therefore define a sub-domain *T* as the set of all possible two-digit additions which nevertheless preserves the 'essence' of the original domain. We can, in fact, go further, and define *C* as the set of all additions of pairs of two-digit numbers that require carrying, and *H* as the set of all additions of pairs of two-digit numbers that require carrying twice. These four sets are clearly nested within each other, and using the set-theoretic notation '$A \supset B$' to denote that set A contains set B, we can write $D \supset T \supset C \supset H$. Most importantly, the sub-domain H represents a kind of 'cover' for the whole domain, in the sense that if a student has 'covered' H by demonstrating mastery of this sub-domain, then that student has also demonstrated mastery of the whole domain *D*. If we are interested only in classifying students as masters or non-masters, then all our attention should focus on those items which require carrying twice.

More formally, any (proper) subset of an assessment domain which has the property that any individual achieving mastery of the subset would be regarded as having achieved mastery of the domain (however mastery is defined) is called a 'cover' for the domain. Any cover of a set that does not itself have a cover is a 'minimal cover.' Note that the minimality of a cover is a local property of the initial cover chosen. There is no guarantee that a minimal cover is a globally minimal cover (whatever that might mean). Furthermore, if we use the notation *A-B* to denote the set of all elements that are in *A* but not in *B* (Stoll, 1961), then the sequence of domains represented by *D-T, D-C, D-H,* and *D* represent a progressive hierarchy within the domain that can be used for sequencing teaching, or for defining levels of achievement within the domain, rather than simply classifying each student as master/non-master. In this definition it is intended that a cover is necessarily a logical, rather than an empirical construct. Empirical research might well disclose that a student who can successfully add all pairs of numbers between 90 and 100 can always add any pair of numbers under 100, but it would be wrong to use this smaller set as a proxy for the whole domain. The reason is clear when we consider the consequential basis of result use.

The result of any assessment is almost invariably used to make inferences beyond the immediate items assessed, in other words as an index of performance. If it is easier to increase a student's score on a test, without increasing the student's competence on the domain, and the results of the tests matter, then we should not be surprised that the teacher's efforts are directed towards the indicator rather than the indicated. Restricting the assessed items in a domain to a small set of especially difficult cases (critical indices) creates the possibility that teachers would change their teaching styles in order to concentrate on those cases. Indeed, the fact that certain items in a domain are (empirically) discovered to be easy and others hard may be a consequence of the teaching approaches used, and it is possible that a different teaching approach would lead to a different ranking of items (Booth, 1984; Hart, 1981).

A good example of this is the multiplication bond 9x7 which is used by many teachers as a critical index of whether students know all their multiplication bonds up to 10x10. This is, almost invariably, one of the last multiplication bonds acquired by children, but if it were used to select students for some important purpose, then we can be sure that it would become one of the first bonds to be taught. To distinguish them from 'covers', we can term these kinds of critical indices 'archetypes.' We would say that, currently, the bond 7x9 is an archetype for the domain of multiplication up to 10x10. The distinction between covers and archetypes centres around the strength of the relationship between indicator and what is indicated. If we accept that in high stakes criterion-referenced assessments, teachers will, for the best of motives, teach towards the test then we must attempt to assess the 'beneficence' of this course of action (L.R.B. Elton, personal communication, 1992). The important point about a cover is that one cannot increase the student's performance on the cover without a proportionate increase in performance across the whole domain. In contrast, if only archetypes are assessed then the transparent nature of criterion-referenced assessments renders the assessment predictable, and it is possible to increase a student's score on the indicator out of all proportion to the consequent increase in performance on the domain (Frederiksen & Collins, 1989). In this sense, performance on a cover is a robust performance indicator for the whole domain; performance on an archetype is not.

If these arguments are accepted, the optimal strategy for a criterion-referenced assessment is to divert a considerable time from item generation towards establishing a minimal cover for the domain, and then to sample randomly sufficient items from the minimal cover to achieve the reliability required.

COMBINATION, AGGREGATION, AND RECONCILIATION

The term domain is used here in its most general sense to describe any collection of learning objectives or outcomes; these need not be coherent in any sense or of a similar level of difficulty. A score is any assessment outcome that is reported on a measurement scale that is at least ordinal. The term aggregation is generally used to describe the process whereby scores on a variety of sub-domains are combined to give a single domain score. To preserve the continuity of the usage, we can use the term combination to describe the most general process whereby a number of assessment results on a set of sub-domains are collected together and used to provide a smaller number of results on the domain defined by the (set-theoretical) union of the sub-domains.

If we have k sub-domain scores (usually for an individual, but not necessarily so), then we can regard the process of combination as a procedure for representing these k pieces of data by some smaller number (k' pieces) of data. However, we can, without loss of generality, assume that each of the k' results arises from a separate combination procedure, so that we can define combination as a procedure for representing the performance on some (possibly trivial) subset of D by a single score. This score may, or may not, of course, be measured on the same measurement scale as used in the sub-domains.

Within this definition, it is useful to distinguish two different types of combination. The first, which we term 'reconciliation', is used when the sub-domain scores purport to be of the same sub-domain. The second, 'aggregation,' is used to describe the process of combination when the sub-domain scores purport to be of different (although not necessarily distinct) domains. Within this framework, reconciliation and aggregation can be seen to be the same process, applied to different situations, and most of the theoretical terms developed to discuss combination will be equally applicable to both. However, there is an asymmetry, in practice if not in theory, in that the examples of reconciliation procedures in which we will be interested will usually involve only two scores, whereas, typically, the aggregation processes will involve more than two scores.

Discretionary and Algorithmic Combinations

The first distinction that arises in considering combination schemes is whether the combination is algorithmic or discretionary. In most cases, the relationship between sub-domain and domain scores will be a direct relationship in the sense that defining the sub-domain scores uniquely defines the combined score. When this is the case, two individuals with the same sub-domain scores must be given the same combined score. However, there are also occasions when this is not an appropriate way to represent the combined score.

This apparent oxymoron arises when, in the partitioning of the domain into sub-domains, something has been lost. The 'glue' that binds the sub-domains together had not been taken into account, and we might therefore want two students with identical sub-domain scores to get different domain scores. No algorithm acting on the sub-domain scores can produce a domain score. At the very least, some discretion is required, and, in effect, a new assessment needs to be made. For this reason, we can term this process discretionary combination or combination by re-assessment. A discretionary combination scheme may be open or restricted. An open scheme allows the person exercising the discretion (the moderator) to award any score, while other schemes may restrict the choices that can be made.

The usefulness of imposing restrictions can be seen when we consider, for example, the use of discretionary schemes for reconciling scores derived from teachers' (possibly subjective) judgments with the results of externally set tests, as happens in the National Curriculum in England. With an open scheme for reconciling different assessments on the same domain, a moderator might be inclined to 'split the difference' between two assessments. This would create an incentive for teachers to inflate the scores awarded so as to 'drag' the mean upwards. A system that restricted the options open to the moderator might be better.

The term 'full-scale pendulum swing' was first applied in the United States to describe a system of arbitration used to settle pay disputes. The employers would make an offer and the employees would make a claim. The arbitrator would approve in full either the offer or the claim. The more extreme the offer or claim, the less chance it had of being chosen, and therefore provided a strong pressure towards moderation. In the context of assessment, full-scale pendulum swing reconciliation means accepting one or other of the sources as being 'correct.' The consequence of such a scheme is to exert a pressure towards moderation, since the more extreme an assessment, the less chance it has of being adopted. Arrangements for the reconciliation of teachers' judgments and externally set tests in the national assessment of 7-year-olds in England and Wales provides a good example of a full-scale pendulum swing discretionary reconciliation scheme (Great Britain. Department of Education and Science, 1991; Great Britain. Welsh Office, 1991).

In other cases, however, there will be a simple relationship between attainment in the sub-domains and the combined score and there may well be no reason why two students with the same sub-domain scores should not be regarded as equivalent. In this case, some direct procedure for deriving a combined domain score from the sub-domain scores will be entirely appropriate. The term algorithm is used in computer science to describe any process in which the action to be taken at any step is well defined by the existing state; in other words, one that could be implemented on a computer. For this reason, we can use the term combination by algorithm for any process in which the combined score is completely determined by sub-domain scores.

Enumerative and Arithmetic Combination. Algorithmic combination procedures can be further classified as either 'arithmetic' or 'enumerative.' Given a set of domain scores, enumerative methods are those that require that a certain number or proportion of the outcomes satisfy a given condition or set of conditions. These methods only require that the measurement scale is ordinal. For example, a 'trailing edge' model, also termed 'conjunctive' by Green and Wigdor (1988), requires that each of a series of logical conditions on the constituent sub-domains is satisfied. At the other extreme, a 'leading edge' or 'disjunctive' model would require that only *one* of the logical conditions on the constituent sub-domains is satisfied. In most educational applications, leading edge models are considered too lenient to be useful. On the other hand, trailing edge models, while preserving a high degree of criterion-referencing in the combined scores, are generally considered too harsh.

An interesting compromise between these two extremes (an example of what Green and Wigdor term a 'hybrid' model) was proposed by the National Curriculum Design and Technology Working Group (1988) in its interim report, which suggested that the overall domain level for technology should be the highest level achieved on all but one of the sub-domains, provided that the lowest sub-domain level was no more than one level below the overall domain level. This is likely to preserve a high degree of criterion-referencing, while at the same time allowing some compensation (see below). Enumerative models also include models that specify in advance all possible combinations (or permutations) of sub-domain scores such as the Open University's method of classifying its honours degrees (Open University, 1991), since any such system can be defined in terms of a (possibly lengthy) logical condition.

Arithmetic methods, on the other hand, produce a domain score by applying an arithmetical procedure or formula to the sub-domain scores. Because the procedures are arithmetical rather than logical, arithmetic procedures usually require the measurement scale to be at least linear (or at least, not to depart too much from linearity), and many of them require ratio scales. If we have a set of k sub-domains, on which we have sub-domain scores given by $x_1, x_2,..., x_k$, then any well-defined function $h(x_1, x_2,..., x_k)$ can serve as a combination rule, and since h must return an unambiguous domain score, we can use the term combination function to describe the most general possible such function. Such a combination function may have a number of additional properties, which are discussed below.

If there exists, for each individual's sub-domain scores, some value m such that:

$$h(x_1, x_2,..., x_k) = h(m,m,...,m) \qquad (1)$$

then it is clear that the value m is, in some way, representative of the set $(x_1, x_2,..., x_k)$, and may be called a mean. Examples are the arithmetic mean, the geometric mean, the harmonic mean, and the root mean square. In practice, almost all means, and in fact most combination functions, that are actually in use can be represented by a structure of the form:

$$h(x_1, x_2,..., x_k) = f^{-1}(g(f(x_1),f(x_2),...,f(x_k))) \qquad (2)$$

and we can term such a structure a norm.

When the reduction function g is symmetrical, all sub-domains are treated in the same way, i.e., all have the same normal weight, but different values of the sub-domain scores have differing effects on the domain score. For example, a root-mean-square combination function is obtained by setting $f(x) = x^2$ and $g(n_1, n_2,... n_n) = (x_1 + x_2 + ... x_n)/n$ [i.e., g is simply the arithmetic mean in equation (2)]. When applied to an examination with two components, this rule would aggregate a score of 50 on each component to an overall score of 50, but scores of 40 and 60 on the two components would yield an overall score of 51. A student who scored 90 and 10 on the two components would gain an overall score of 64, but one who gained 100 marks on one and nothing on the other would be given an overall score of 71.

The above illustrates the behaviour of concave functions when used as combination functions; inconsistent or erratic behaviour is rewarded (Plackett, 1976). In contrast, when used as combination functions, convex functions have the effect of rewarding consistency of performance. The arithmetic mean is neither concave nor convex: an extension of the optical metaphor might be to describe it as planar.

Aggregation models also vary in the degree of compensation which they allow. Green and Wigdor (1988) refer to compensatory scoring models in which strengths in one domain can offset weaknesses in another, described by Wood (1991) as a 'roundabouts-and-swings.' However, compensation is better represented as trichotomous rather than dichotomous. At one extreme, an aggregation scheme is completely compensatory if there are no absolute requirements so that any poor performance in one sub-domain, no matter how bad, can always be compensated for by performance in the other sub-domains. Aggregation models are partially compensatory if there are some absolute requirements, but good performance in some sub-domains can offset poor performance in others. At the other extreme, conjunctive models allow no compensation at all.

All the analysis so far has dealt with combination rules where the reduction function is symmetric on the sub-domain scores. As a result of this symmetry, all domains are treated the same, but particular values or patterns of values are more or less significant. There will, however, be occasions when we wish to give increased weight to particular sub-domains. Where these can be represented as norms, i.e., they have a structure of the form shown in equation (2), then they can be termed weighted norms, and by definition, the function g cannot be symmetric.

In summary, the arithmetic mean is both unweighted, and planar. Building in more sophistication (or complexity) can either place value on particular domains on the one hand, by using weights, or on particular values or patterns of values on the other, by using concave or convex combination functions. We could, of course, do both, but such methods are unusual.

The relationship between the terms defined above can be represented using a technique developed for the analysis of qualitative data (Bliss, Monk, & Ogborn, 1983). In this representation, a left square bracket ([) is used to denote a choice between mutually exclusive alternatives, and a left brace ({) is used to denote parallel or simultaneous aspects for classification, so that within the brace, several choices must be made. For example, a school can be classified as either primary or secondary or middle, but can also be simultaneously classified as either single-sex or coeducational and also as either state or private.

Using the conventions outlined above, the relationship between the various terms introduced so far in this chapter can be presented as shown in Figure 8.1.

The Manipulability of Combination Schemes

The effects of aggregation rules can be examined in terms of impact on domains, on individuals, and on the interaction between the two. Here are examples of each.

Impact on Domains In the British national curriculum, there are four domains in Design and Technology. It was originally proposed to weight all the domains equally, but it was decided that this placed insufficient weight on 'making.' Accordingly, for the first national assessment, the four sub-domains are weighted in the ratio 3:5:8:4. This is very close to 1:1:2:1. In fact, calculations on the final domain scores, with actual sub-domain scores from 6,000 students, show that only 3% get a different mark with weightings of 3:5:8:4 when compared with 1:1:2:1. Only 10% change levels when all the sub-domains are equally weighted.

The original proposals for English specified that the three sub-domains (speaking and listening; reading; and writing) should be equally weighted. However, this was unacceptable to government advisers who insisted that reading and writing are more important than speaking and listening. When weights were changed to 30:35:35, only two pupils out of a sample of 2,000 changed level. It is clear that the reason for changing the weights has little to do with the evidential basis of the result use and interpretation, and has everything to do with the consequential basis of result use, and is thus being used as an instrument of educational policy.

FIGURE 8.1

CLASSIFICATION OF COMBINATION SCHEMES

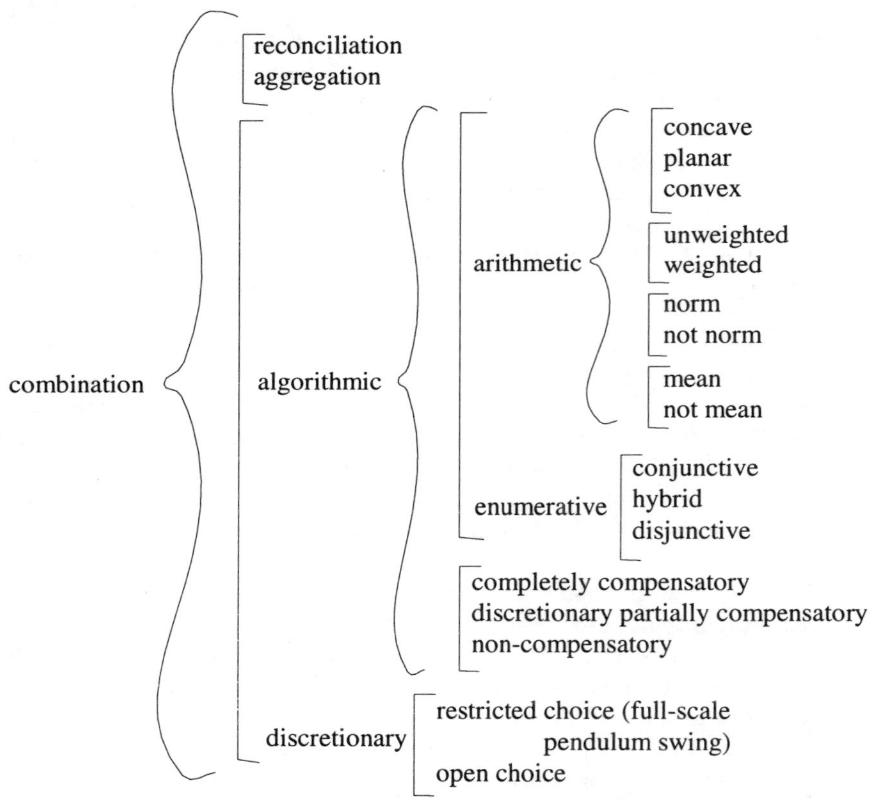

The most extreme example of the use of an aggregation rule as an instrument of educational policy is in the assessment of Welsh as a second language for 7-year olds in Wales. The subject has three sub-domains: speaking, listening, and viewing; reading; and writing and a score on a scale of 1 to 4 is recorded for each sub-domain. However, the government has determined that the overall score for the whole domain should be the score on the first sub-domain alone. Presumably, it believes that teachers are paying insufficient attention to speaking, listening, and viewing and that making it the only component that contributes to the overall score will persuade them to spend more time on these activities in future.

Impact on Individuals We have some limited, and at the moment only anecdotal, evidence that the effect of publishing the aggregated results of a school's assessment of pupils at age 7 on a scale of 1-4, with all numbers being rounded to the nearest whole number, is to pressure teachers into paying special attention to certain pupils. For example, a pupil whose attainment is around 2.4 just before the final assessment merits a great deal of attention because a small amount of extra attainment will lift the child's level to 2.5, which will be rounded up to 3 for reporting purposes.

Interactions Between Domains and Individuals For many combination schemes, there is no particular incentive for teachers to focus on particular pupils across all domains or to focus on particular domains for all pupils. For certain such schemes, however, there is an incentive to focus on particular domains for particular pupils. A good example of this is the aggregation rule originally proposed for the assessment of mathematics and science, which was to take as the domain score the highest level attained on at least half of the sub-domain scores. If a pupil has a profile of 233566, then a concentration on the fourth sub-domain is likely to lead to the most rapid progress from level 5 overall to level 6. Indeed, if a teacher wanted to maximise the student's score in future years, it is likely that no further attention would be given to the first three domains since improvements here are unlikely to improve the overall reported level.

A Tentative Definition of Manipulability

Consider an aggregation scheme with k component scores or grades to be aggregated to a single domain score. For each individual, choose one sub-domain at random, increment that sub-domain score by one unit, and find the expected value of the increase in domain scores over the population. Next, for each individual, the sub-domain score to be incremented is selected by an 'expert' (who knows both the sub-domain scores and the aggregation rule), with a view to maximising the domain score, and the expected value of the increment in domain score with expert selection of sub-domain is calculated. The manipulability index of an aggregation rule is the ratio of these two expected values:

$$\text{domain manipulability} = \frac{\begin{array}{c}\text{expected value of the increment in domain score}\\ \text{with expert selection of sub-domain}\end{array}}{\begin{array}{c}\text{expected value of the increment in domain score}\\ \text{with random selection of sub-domain}\end{array}}$$

Using assessment outcomes on 950 students in the four sub-domains for Design and Technology, the index of manipulability was calculated for four different aggregation schemes. The four schemes were the 'half or more rule', the rule recommended by the interim report of the National Curriculum Design and Technology Working Group (1988) (the 'one small slip' rule), a disjunctive or 'leading edge' rule, and a conjunctive or 'trailing edge' rule. The results are shown in Table 8.1.

TABLE 8.1

MANIPULABILITY VALUES OF SOME AGGREGATION RULES

Rule	Manipulability
half or more rule	1.64
one small slip rule	2.13
disjunctive or leading edge rule	1.74
conjunctive or trailing edge rule	4.00

A conjunctive scheme will always have an index of manipulability equal to k, the number of sub-domains, since the domain score can change only if the lowest sub-domain score is unique, in which case this sub-domain will always be chosen by 'expert' selection, and be chosen with probability $1/k$ for random selection.

Note that no attempt has been made to standardise the measurement of manipulability so that two aggregation rules using the same manipulability measure applied to different assessment systems are in some sense comparable. Furthermore, no allowance has been made for the weighting of domains. With weighted aggregation rules, the random sampling can be weighted according to the nominal weights, since the essence of the definition of manipulability is the extra information we get as to which domain to increment as a result of knowing both the aggregation rule and the individual's scores.

In this sense, the manipulability index does give an indication of the likely benefits to the student if the teacher were to direct teaching towards particular sub-domains. Thus, the measure of manipulability contributes to the process of consequential validation proposed by Messick (1980). The critical issue then becomes: if there is a pressure to manipulate the assessment, do teachers do so? This is clearly an issue which merits further research.

THE RELATIONSHIP BETWEEN VALIDITY, RELIABILITY, AND MANAGEABILITY

The relationship between reliability, validity, and manageability is subtle and complex. On the one hand, they are widely regarded as being in tension, with attempts to increase an assessment's reliability or manageability resulting in decreased validity. This can be illustrated using 'triangular co-ordinates' based on the idea that in any equilateral triangle, the sum of the length of the altitudes from any internal point is fixed. So, for example in Figure 8.2, assessment A is highly manageable, with moderate validity and low reliability, while assessment B is highly reliable and manageable, but not very valid.

FIGURE 8.2

THE RELATIONSHIP BETWEEN RELIABILITY, VALIDITY AND MANAGEABILITY

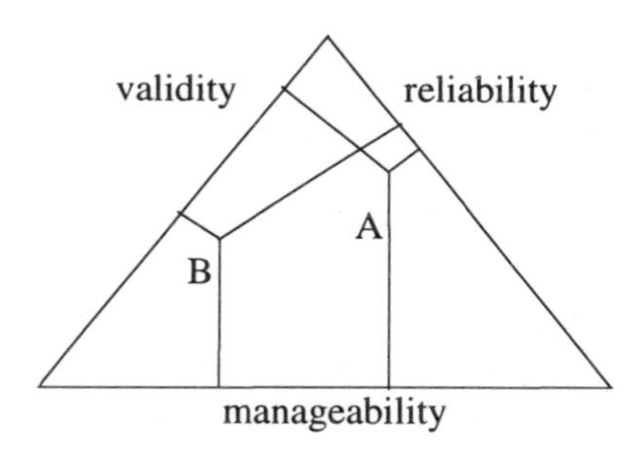

On the other hand, reliability is seen as a prerequisite for validity, since an unreliable assessment of an individual cannot be valid. Further, manageability is, itself, a prerequisite for reliability, since an assessment that is not easily manageable is unlikely to be implemented properly, leading to poor reliability. This apparent contradiction arises from a conflation of the evidential and consequential bases of validity. On an evidential basis, reliability is indeed a prerequisite for validity, and in turn, manageability is a prerequisite for reliability. However, when we come to examine the consequential basis for validity the situation is not so clear-cut. Consider the following example.

Let us assume for the moment that we have a paper-and-pencil test designed to assess performance in secondary school science. The possible marks on the test range from 0 to 100, with a mean of 55, and a standard deviation of 15. Let us also assume that we know the reliability of this test to be 0.9, so that the standard error of measurement is 4.74 (when $\sigma_E = \sigma\sqrt{1-r}$). We then modify the test and bring in the assessment of practical science skills such as observation, measurement, and implementing plans. A pilot study shows us that the reliability of the modified assessment is 0.75. The standard error of measurement of the modified assessment is therefore 7.5.

There is no doubt that the modified assessment is less reliable. The extent of construct validity is less clear. Inferences about performance related to material that was in the original test will be less warranted because the decreased reliability makes it more likely that we wrongly attribute a score to an individual. It is in this sense that the reliability is often said to provide an upper bound for validity. On the other hand, inferences about performance assessed only in the modified test will be more warranted.

However, the really important difference comes when we consider the consequential effects of the modified assessment on the actions of the teacher. The effectiveness of the teacher will be evaluated in terms of the classes that she or he teaches, i.e., in terms of the group means, which for a group of *n* individuals is related to the population standard deviation by the following formula:

$$\sigma_E = \frac{\sigma}{\sqrt{n}} \qquad (3)$$

So, if we have classes of 25 we have a standard error of 0.95 (=4.75÷5) for the original test and 1.5 for the modified test. We can therefore have much confidence in the group means as a reliable index of the group's performance, whether we use the original or modified test.

What about validity? Since the standard errors of measurement are so small, the inferences that we make are unlikely to be invalidated due to measurement error. Therefore, the modified test, with its greater coverage is likely to provide an increase in construct validity, without the usual trade-off in reliability. It is also likely to make teachers include more practical work in their teaching.

This brings in the idea of beneficence referred to earlier. Are the consequences of the use of the assessment beneficial? Are they ones we desire? If the modified assessment leads to more beneficial consequences, then the assessment procedure is validated. The difficulty here is who does the judging. Different actors will have different reactions; effects judged beneficial by some will be judged harmful by others. In the end, as Messick (1989) has pointed out, validity is not only multi-faceted; it is also inherently and intrinsically subjective. It is ultimately a question of the match of epistemologies. When the epistemology implicit in an assessment is consonant with that of the person performing the validation, validity is likely to be established. Where the epistemology implicit in the assessment is dissonant with that of the person performing the validation, validity is likely to be denied. We can therefore summarise all the aspects of validity in a single sentence: A test is valid if you are happy for teachers to teach towards the test.

REFERENCES

Bliss, J., Monk, M., & Ogborn, J. (1983). *Qualitative data analysis for educational research: A guide to the use of systemic networks.* London: Croom Helm.

Booth, L.R. (1984). *Algebra: Children's strategies and errors.* Windsor: NFER-Nelson.

Frederiksen, J.R., & Collins, A. (1989). A systems approach to educational testing. *Educational Researcher, 18*(9), 27-32.

Great Britain. Department of Education and Science (1991). *The education (national curriculum) (assessment arrangements for English, mathematics and science) (key stage 1) order 1991.* London: Her Majesty's Stationery Office.

Great Britain. Welsh Office (1991). *The education (national curriculum) (assessment arrangements for English, Welsh, mathematics and science) (key stage 1) order 1991.* London: Her Majesty's Stationery Office.

Green, B.F., & Wigdor, A.K. (1988). *Measuring job competency.* Washington, DC: National Academy Press.

Hambleton, R.K., & Rogers, H.J. (1991). Advances in criterion-referenced measurement. In R.K. Hambleton & J.N. Zaal (Eds.), *Advances in educational and psychological testing.* (pp. 3-43). Boston, MA: Kluwer Academic.

Hart, K.M. (Ed.). (1981). Children's understanding of mathematics: 11-16. London: John Murray.

Messick, S. (1980). Test validity and the ethics of assessment. *American Psychologist, 35,* 1012-1027.

Messick, S. (1989). Validity. In R.L. Linn (Ed.), *Educational measurement.* (pp. 13-103). Washington, DC: American Council on Education/Macmillan.

National Curriculum Design and Technology Working Group (1988). *Interim report.* London: Department of Education and Science.

Open University (1991). *Handbook for students on undergraduate and nine-month associate courses.* Milton Keynes: Author.

Plackett, R.L. (1976). Discussion of a paper by Barnett. *Journal of the Royal Statistical Society, Series A (Statistics in Society), 139,* 344-346.

Stoll, R.R. (1961). *Sets, logic and axiomatic theories.* San Francisco, CA: Freeman.

Wood, R. (1991). *Assessment and testing.* Cambridge: Cambridge University Press.

9. DIFFERENTIAL ITEM FUNCTIONING, GENDER, AND PROBLEM-SOLVING STRATEGIES

Anita Wester
Department of Education
University of Umeå, Sweden

There have always been gender differences in favour of males on performance on the Swedish Scholastic Aptitude Test (SweSAT) which has been in use since 1977. (For a description of the test, see Wedman, 1994.) In the 1980s the difference amounted to an average of approximately 5 to 7 points (out of a total of 144). Three of the six subtests on the SweSAT account for most of the difference. One of them (DTM) is intended to measure the ability to read (and interpret) diagrams, tables, and maps. The maximum score on this subtest is 20 points and the average gender difference is between 1.5 and 2 points.

Quite a lot of research has been carried out aimed at understanding, explaining, and thus reducing gender differences in test achievement. The study reported in this paper is one such study. Its purpose is to find out if there is any systematic relationship between gender-related differential item functioning and problem-solving strategy. The specific question was: Is it possible to identify items with a problem-solving strategy favouring one or other gender? The study consists of two analyses. The first is based on the score of a group which is unselected with respect to educational background. The second is based on the scores of two groups selected on the basis of their educational background in upper secondary school, one of which had studied natural sciences and the other social sciences.

For the first set of analyses, a random sample of 20% of all test takers in the first three tests (89B, 90A 90B) and one of 10% of all test takers in the last two tests (91A, 91B) were used for the study. For the second set of analyses, a selection was made of test takers who had received an education in natural sciences, aged 24 years or younger, and of test takers who had received an education in the social sciences, aged 24 years or younger. The material consists of the items from the four DTM subtests, administered between spring 1990 and autumn 1991, i.e., the same as for the unselected groups with the exception of the material used in autumn 1989.

This means that the analysis was based on 80 items. A random sample of 20% of the relevant population was drawn for the 1990 tests and of 10% for the 1991 tests (see Table 9.1).

TABLE 9.1

NUMBERS OF MALES AND FEMALES IN SAMPLES OF UNSELECTED, NATURAL SCIENCE, AND SOCIAL SCIENCE GROUPS

	89B		90A		90B		91A		91B	
	M	F	M	F	M	F	M	F	M	F
Unselected	952	1483	1554	1460	2711	2548	3448	3511	2675	2945
Natural Science			323	277	664	628	607	593	491	512
Social Science			74	187	206	495	318	807	257	707

THE UNSELECTED GROUP STUDY

The material consists of the 20 items in the DTM subtest of SweSAT administered between the autumn of 1989 and the autumn of 1991 (a total of 100 items). (The test is held twice a year in May and November. The May test is designated by the letter A and the November test by the letter B after the year.) The study was carried out in two stages, of which the first was an analysis of gender-related differential item functioning using the Mantel-Haenszel method (see e.g., Holland & Wainer, 1993). An item is identified as functioning differentially if it functions differently in different groups of test takers, e.g., men and women, so that the actual score of one group differs from the expected score on the basis of a given criterion.

Stage Two of the study was based on the items identified as functioning differentially with respect to gender. These items were classified on the basis of the seven problem-solving strategies in the DTM test: reading, ticking, simple calculation, complicated calculation, estimate, own production, and measurement. They are defined as follows. *Reading* implies that the item requires reading one or a couple of items of numerical data in a table, a figure, on an axis/curve, or finding a spot on a map. An item referred to the category *ticking* requires several readings that must be compared between themselves and with a number of specified numerical data. Items requiring addition or subtraction are referred to as *simple calculation*. Calculation of percentages and fractions, multiplication and division are referred to the category *complicated calculation*. An *estimate* requires judgment of different proportions in a figure or a rough estimate. *Own production* means that the data in the figure have to be revised and transformed by the test taker (e.g., verbalizing the content of a table). *Measurement* requires, in addition to reading, the measuring of one or several distances on a map or in a number of columns (Jonsson, 1990). The last three strategies are very rarely required in the test.

The classification of the items into different problem-solving strategies was made by four persons, two test developers and two junior researchers within a group concerned with educational measurement. Since the categories are not mutually exclusive, an item could be classified into more than one category, e.g., reading + complicated calculation.

The Mantel-Haenszel analysis showed that 33 items were identified as functioning differentially in favour of either men or women. Nineteen favoured men (6 at the .01 level and 13 at the .001 level of significance) and 14 favoured women (6 at the .01 level and 8 at the .001 level). Following the Mantel-Haenszel analysis, a classification was made of the 33 items. This was done individually by the four persons mentioned above, who did not know in which direction the items showed a difference (in favour of men or women).

Eleven of the 19 items that favoured men were considered to include *complicated calculation* (in most cases combined with *reading*), whereas only one of the 14 items that favoured women was referred to this category. Of the 11 items favouring men that require complicated calculation, five require a knowledge of percentages and two a knowledge of indices. No item favouring women requires any of these operations. The item which favoured women included an element of division (185/5). Thus, the results show quite clearly that items requiring complicated calculation and, especially, calculation of percentages and a knowledge of indices favour men.

Eight of the 14 items favouring women include *simple calculation*, in combination with *reading* (6) or *ticking* (2), whereas only three of the items favouring men require this operation. An examination of the items favouring women shows that they often require accuracy, concentration, and precision ('proof-reading ability'). Examples of such items are a table with several, numerically adjacent data and a diagram requiring careful reading.

The unselected sample did not enable potential gender differences in educational background and age to be controlled for. This means that it is possible that the results could be explained by differences in educational background, by the fact that men more often have an education in natural sciences and/or technology. (We already know that people with that background do better in the SweSAT.) To study the significance of educational background for gender-related differential item functioning, some Mantel-Haenszel analyses were performed on selected groups with a homogeneous education.

THE SELECTED GROUP STUDY

Since the Mantel-Haenszel method is sensitive to group size (based on the chi-square technique) fewer items can be expected to exhibit differential functioning in the groups with a similar educational background than in the unselected group.

Table 9.2 shows the number of items identified as functioning differentially for men and women.

TABLE 9.2

NUMBER OF ITEMS FUNCTIONING DIFFERENTIALLY FOR MEN AND WOMEN IN GROUPS WITH A SIMILAR EDUCATIONAL BACKGROUND

Background	90A		90B		91A		91B		Total	
	M	F	M	F	M	F	M	F	M	F
Natural Science	2	1[1]	1	-	2	3	1	1	6	5
Social Science	1	1[1]	-	-	1	-	2	-	4	1
N + S	3	1[1]	1	-	3	3	3	1	10	5

[1]This item is the only one identified as functioning differentially in both groups (N and S).

In the Natural Science (N) group, 11 items were identified as functioning differentially, six in favour of men and five in favour of women. In the Social Science (S) group, five items exhibited this characteristic, four in favour of men and one in favour of women. We can see that the number of such items is reduced with smaller group sizes. In the N and the S groups taken together, 10 items favour men but no item is common to both groups. Five items favour women, and one of them functions differentially in both groups.

Four of the six items favouring men in the N group require *complicated calculation*; the fifth item can perhaps also be referred to this category. The sixth item, requiring only *reading*, is special in so far as it has an extremely high score, .99 for men and .94 for women. Therefore, owing to a slight gender difference, expressed in *p*-values, this item is identified as functioning differentially, which can be explained by the fact that the Mantel-Haenszel method is sensitive to extreme values. Of the four items favouring men in the S group, which are not the same items as in the N group, two require calculation of percentages and the other two a knowledge of indices.

Four of the five items favouring women in the N group require *reading* or *ticking* either in isolation or in combination with measurement. The fifth item requires *complicated calculation* in the form of division (185/5). (The only item in the S group favouring women can also be found among the items favouring women in the N group.) It is not easy to discern any clear-cut pattern for the items favouring women. Some of them require accuracy, others repeated procedures.

The N and the S groups taken together show that seven of the ten items favouring men require calculation of percentages or knowledge of indices, whereas four of the five items favouring women require reading or ticking, sometimes in combination with measurement.

CONCLUSION

Analysis of the problem-solving strategies involved in items that exhibit gender-related differential item functioning reveals that items requiring complicated calculation favour men. Items favouring women often include elements of accuracy, concentration, and precision. These results are valid in the unselected group as well as in groups selected with respect to educational background and age, which means that neither age nor educational background can explain the differences.

The conclusion is that a reduction (or the elimination) of the number of items requiring complicated calculation (e.g., calculation of percentages or a knowledge of indices) together with an increase in the number of items requiring concentration and accuracy, would probably contribute to reducing gender differences in performance on the DTM subtest. However, such a procedure would change the character of the test and would have to be considered (and analysed) in terms of validity and in relation to the objective of using the whole test battery, which is to rank applicants to higher education.

REFERENCES

Holland, P.W., & Wainer, H. (Eds.). (1993). *Differential item functioning*. Hillsdale, NJ: Lawrence Erlbaum.

Jonsson, I. (1990). Högskoleprovet - Delprov 4: DTK. Beskrivning av provets sammansättning och utfall. *Provmemoria,* 1990, nr 26. Pedagogiska Institutionen Umeä Universitet.

Wedman, J. (1994). The Swedish Scholastic Aptitude Test: Development, use, and research. *Educational Measurement: Issues and Practice, 13*(2), 5-11.

10. DIFFERENTIAL ITEM FUNCTIONING IN A MATRICULATION TEST

Liu Qingsi
National Education Examinations Authority, Beijing

The Matriculation English Test (MET) is taken by senior middle-school graduates who wish to enter university or college in China. About 3 million candidates take the test each year.

The study reported in the present paper uses empirical data to address issues relating to validity and differential item functioning in the MET. Data were obtained from the 1990 administration of the test which used the version known as MET90.

MET90 is composed of five subtests. Subtest 1 measures candidates' phonetic knowledge. It has 10 items, including 6 on phonemes, 2 on stress, and 2 on intonation. Subtest 2 assesses grammatical knowledge (20 items). Subtest 3 (a multiple-choice cloze test consisting of 25 items) measures practical knowledge of the use of English; Subtest 4 comprising 20 multiple-choice items (spread over three or more reading passages) tests several aspects of reading ability; Subtest 5 requires candidates to write a short passage of about 100 words (guided writing).

THE STUDY

The objective of our study was to examine whether items in MET90 functioned differentially for candidates of each ability level from different provinces and, if so, to examine its extent.

Three groups of candidates were chosen from three provinces to represent the three different English language teaching levels in China. Zhejiang represented the provinces in which English language teaching (ELT) level is comparatively high; Sichuan represented the provinces where the ELT is at an intermediate level; and Gansu represented the provinces where the ELT level is comparatively low. This classification was based on candidates' mean MET90 scores in the three provinces which were Zhejiang : 66.02; Sichuan : 58.3; and Gansu : 51.32.

Only multiple-choice items were included in analyses. Thus Subtest 5 (guided writing) was excluded. As a result, the full mark on the test was 85 points.

2,556 candidates were selected from each province. These were then divided into five ability levels in terms of their scores in the test: Level A (56-85); Level B (48-55); Level C (40-47); Level D (32-39); Level E (0-31) (Table 10.1). Analyses were carried out for each item to determine if the distribution of candidates across ability levels differed by province. Since MET is mainly used to select the top 20% of students for higher education we shall be especially interested in Level A and B candidates in our analyses.

TABLE 10.1

NUMBERS AND PERCENTAGES OF CANDIDATES FROM EACH PROVINCE, BY ABILITY LEVEL

Province	Ability Level					
	A (56-85)	B (48-55)	C (40-47)	D (32-39)	E (0-31)	N
Zhejiang	1,095 43%	632 25%	400 16%	218 8%	211 8%	2,556 100%
Sichuan	497 19%	495 19%	533 21%	403 16%	628 25%	2,556 100%
Gansu	290 11%	346 14%	304 12%	640 25%	976 38%	2,556 100%
Total	1,882 25%	1,473 19%	1,237 16%	1,261 16%	1,815 24%	7,668 100%

RESULTS

Only five items in the test do not function differently for each ability level on the basis of χ^2 values (df = 2) at all ability levels.

There was considerable variation in the number of items for which there was evidence of differential functioning at different ability levels. The number is relatively high for Level D and E candidates but low for A, B, and C candidates (Table 10.2).

TABLE 10.2

NUMBERS AND PERCENTAGES OF ITEMS EXHIBITING DIFFERENTIAL FUNCTIONING, BY ABILITY LEVEL

Ability Level	Number of Candidates	%
A	26	31
B	29	34
C	17	20
D	73	86
E	68	80

Indications of the range of variation in differential functioning between subtests of the MET90 can be obtained by examining the percentage of items exhibiting such functioning in each subtest (Table 10.3) for candidates of different ability levels. It can be seen that for each subtest, percentages are relatively high for Subtest 1 and for Ability Levels D and E.

TABLE 10.3

PERCENTAGES OF ITEMS EXHIBITING DIFFERENTIAL FUNCTIONING IN EACH SUBTEST FOR CANDIDATES OF DIFFERING ABILITY LEVELS

	Subtest			
Ability Level	1	2	3	4
A	70%	27%	32%	15%
B	70%	17%	24%	40%
C	50%	17%	24%	5%
D	70%	90%	92%	80%
E	80%	97%	68%	70%

Subtest 4 (Reading Comprehension) consists of reading passages belonging to different fields: Story, Industry, Biography, and Geography. It was found that each of the passages with the exception of Biography at E level showed evidence of differential item functioning at levels D and E. For A and C level candidates,

however, there was little evidence of differential item functioning. Items designed to test the literal and underlying meaning of the passages shared the greatest amount of differential item functioning for candidates at levels D and E.

CONCLUSION

In this study, we found that differential item functioning on the MET90 varied by province for candidates of the same ability level. Students from different provinces also varied in their level of performance, though this was less true for candidates of higher ability levels (A, B, and C) than for candidates of lower ability levels (D and E). These differences, however, do not affect matriculation levels in the different provinces since matriculation cut-off scores are determined uniquely for each province.

For candidates of lower ability levels, almost all items functioned differently. For higher ability level candidates, however, the number of items that functioned differently was much less. These findings may be explained by the more heterogeneous nature of the population at lower ability levels. Candidates at Levels D and E are not homogeneous even though they are grouped at the same ability level. According to a report from the State Education Commission, there are many middle schools in West China where students are not given any English lessons because of the shortage of English language teachers. Such candidates usually get a quite low or even a zero score on MET90. In spite of this, they are grouped at Level E, together with candidates from East China, who get low scores for other reasons. Candidates of higher ability levels, on the other hand, especially of A level, are less heterogeneous than the candidates of D or E level in English language ability. As distinct from the candidates of D or E level, A level candidates have achieved a knowledge of the English language appropriate to high-school graduates. To a certain extent, they have achieved a level of comprehension of the language where they no longer need sentence-by-sentence explanations from their teachers. As a result, they are less dependent on the language teaching in their provinces than are candidates at the lower levels.

11. GENDER DIFFERENCES ON ADMISSION INSTRUMENTS FOR HIGHER EDUCATION

Christina Stage
University of Umeå

Since 1991 applicants for higher education in Sweden have been selected either on the basis of their average marks from completed upper secondary school or of their results on the Swedish Scholastic Aptitude Test (SweSAT). Approximately 60% of places are allocated on marks and 40% on test results. In theory, it is optional to take the test. In reality, test results are regarded as necessary since only applicants with top marks can afford to risk not taking the test.

Most applicants for higher education have a leaving certificate from one of the five courses in three- or four-year upper secondary school. The five different academic courses are: Humanities, Social Science, Economics, Natural Science, and Engineering. All the courses last for three years but there is an optional fourth year in Engineering. Marks from the courses are regarded as equivalent. When applying for higher education it is only the average mark of students that is taken into account, not which courses they have followed. The marking system for the courses is norm-referenced on a scale from 1 to 5, where 1 is the lowest and 5 is the highest mark.

The SweSAT has been in use since 1977 but until 1991 was used only for special groups of applicants. In 1991, the test consisted of 144 multiple-choice items distributed over six subtests. The results are transformed to a standard scale from 0 to 2.0 where 2.0 is the highest result. (More detailed information on the test is contained in Appendix 11.1.)

The aim of the study reported in this paper was to compare average marks and test results for men and women and for five different courses in upper secondary school.

SUBJECTS

The total number of students who completed three-year upper secondary school in April 1991 was 41,251 of whom 17,860 took the SweSAT either in Spring or

Autumn 1991. That means that for the latter number there are test results and average marks available from approximately the same time. These students are the subjects in this study.

In Table 11.1 mean marks are shown for these students as well as for all students, distributed by sex and course.

TABLE 11.1

MEAN LEAVING CERTIFICATE MARKS OF STUDENTS WHO TOOK THE SweSAT (TESTTAKERS) AND OF ALL STUDENTS, BY COURSE AND GENDER, 1991

	Testtakers			All Students			
Course	M	F	Total	M	F	Total	Testtakers as % of All Students
Humanities	3.52	3.59	3.58	3.28	3.40	3.39	
N	95	891	986	371	2,864	3,235	30
Social Science	3.45	3.60	3.56	3.24	3.48	3.41	
N	942	2,651	3,595	2,396	5,531	7,927	45
Economics	3.46	3.54	3.51	3.18	3.30	3.25	
N	1,496	2,263	3,759	5,047	7,503	12,550	30
Natural Science	3.78	3.82	3.80	3.70	3.80	3.75	
N	2,350	2,667	5,017	3,309	3,538	6,847	73
Engineering	3.54	3.52	3.53	3.29	3.40	3.31	
N	3,379	1,126	4,505	8,524	2,168	10,692	42
Total	3.58	3.64	3.61	3.32	3.45	3.39	
N	8,262	9,598	17,860	19,647	21,604	41,251	43

Source: Statistiska Meddelanden (1991)

Although there is no formal or organisational sex differentiation in Swedish schools, boys and girls make different and rather sex-stereotyped choices of academic courses (see Table 11.1). Women dominate in the Humanities and Social Science courses in particular, but also in Economics, while men dominate very much in Engineering. In Natural Science, there is a fairly even distribution of men and women.

Women have higher mean marks than men in all courses except Engineering (testtakers). These differences, however, are greater in the total group of students than in the group of testtakers. Students who took the SweSAT had, in general, higher marks than the total group of school leavers. For male testtakers the average mark is .26 higher than for the total group of men while the difference for women is only .19.

In Table 11.2, the SweSAT test results for the subjects in this study are compared with the results for all testtakers in 1991. Perhaps not surprisingly the subjects in this study score somewhat lower than the total group, which includes testtakers who may have had reasonably long work experience or some years of higher education after leaving upper secondary school.

TABLE 11.2

MEAN SweSAT SCORES OF TESTTAKERS IN STUDY AND ALL TESTTAKERS BY COURSE AND GENDER, 1991

	Testtakers in the Study			All Testtakers		
Course	M	F	Total	M	F	Total
Humanities	98.1	88.8	89.7	103.8	94.6	96.0
N	95	891	986	669	3,981	4,650
Social Science	97.6	89.1	91.3	102.5	93.9	97.0
N	942	2,651	3,593	4,121	7,155	11,276
Economics	94.5	86.0	89.4	97.6	89.5	93.5
N	1,496	2,263	3,759	7,021	7,605	14,626
Natural Science	109.8	101.4	105.3	110.3	103.0	107.1
N	2,350	2,667	5,017	8,065	6,038	14,103
Engineering	99.8	93.7	98.3	104.4	99.3	103.4
N	3,379	1,126	4,505	11,990	2,920	14,910
Total	101.4	92.3	96.5	104.1	95.3	100.1
N	8,262	9,598	17,860	31,866	27,699	59,565

More interesting is the comparison of results for students who followed different courses. The highest marks were obtained by students in both groups on the Natural Science course and the next highest by Engineering students. This was not the case in the school-leaving marks, where Engineering students came second last (Table 11.1). On average, men scored between 5 and 9 points higher than women in both groups on the SweSAT (Table 11.2). It should also be noted that among the subjects in this study women from the Natural Science course scored higher than men from any other course.

RESULTS

Figure 11.1 shows SweSAT test scores for the men and women who were the subjects in this study in different intervals of average marks on the school leaving certificate. It is evident that within the same average examination mark interval, men score significantly higher than women on the scholastic aptitude test, but the difference is larger at the lower levels. It is also evident that there is a clear relationship between test scores and average marks. The correlation is a bit higher for women (r = .57) than for men (r=.52).

FIGURE 11.1

SweSAT SCORES FOR STUDENTS IN DIFFERENT INTERVALS OF AVERAGE MARKS ON THE SCHOOL LEAVING CERTIFICATE, BY GENDER

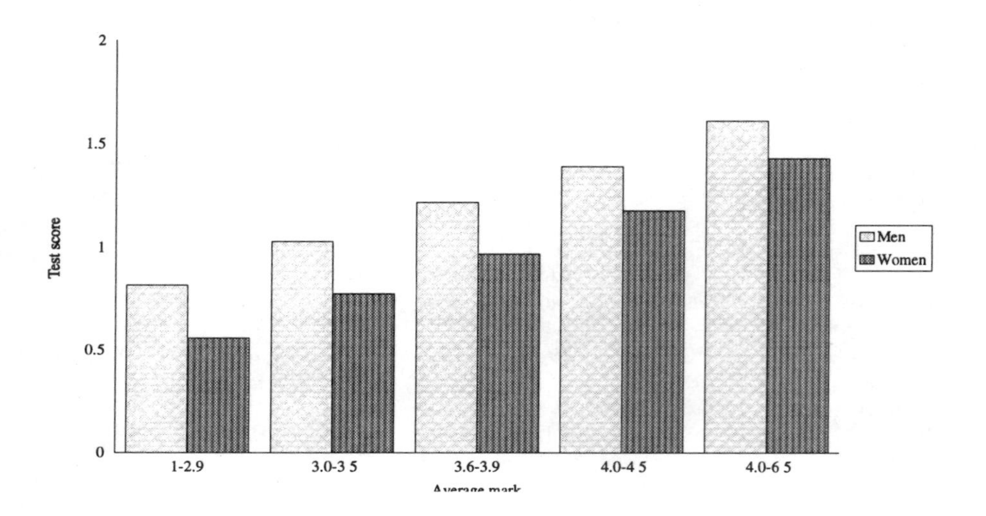

In Figure 11.2 the scholastic aptitude test scores for students who followed different courses are presented for different intervals of average marks on the school leaving certificate. Students from the Natural Science course had higher average marks on the leaving certificate than students from the other courses and they also achieve higher scholastic aptitude test scores within each average mark interval. It is evident that standardised test scores within each average mark interval are similar for students of Humanities, Social Science and Economics on the one hand and for students of Natural Science and Engineering on the other. Therefore, in Figure 11.3, data are collapsed for these two groups and results for men and women are compared. The difference between men and women is still notable, but the one between the two groups of academic courses is almost more striking.

The two most quantitative subtests on the SweSAT are DS and DTM and usually give rise to the largest differences in results between men and women. It might therefore be of interest to investigate the importance of knowledge of mathematics for students' performance on these subtests. The Natural Science and Engineering courses both have extensive mathematics courses while the Humanities, the Social Science and the Economics courses contain only limited courses in Mathematics. In

FIGURE 11.2

SweSAT SCORES FOR STUDENTS FROM DIFFERENT COURSES IN DIFFERENT INTERVALS OF AVERAGE MARKS ON THE SCHOOL LEAVING CERTIFICATE

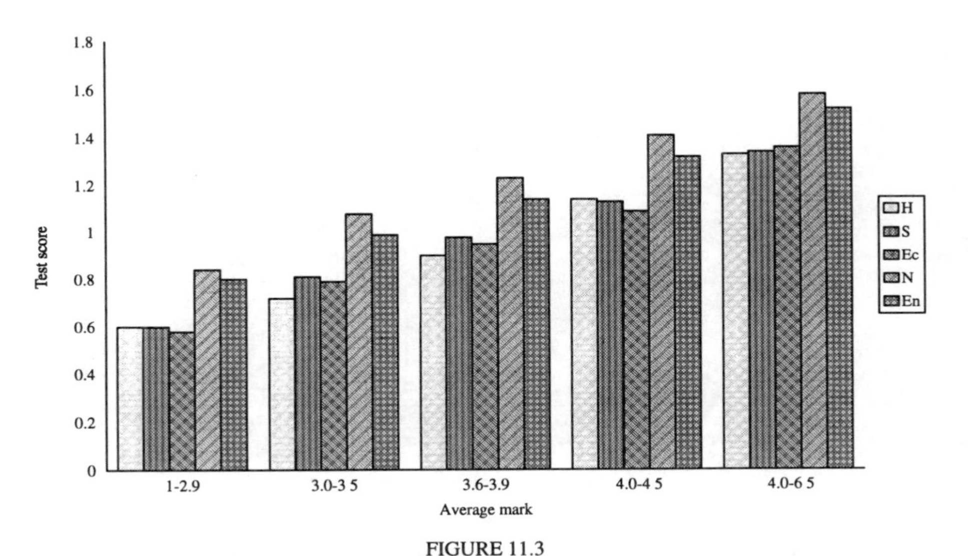

FIGURE 11.3

SweSAT SCORES OF STUDENTS IN DIFFERENT COMBINATIONS OF COURSES AND IN DIFFERENT INTERVALS OF AVERAGE MARKS, BY GENDER

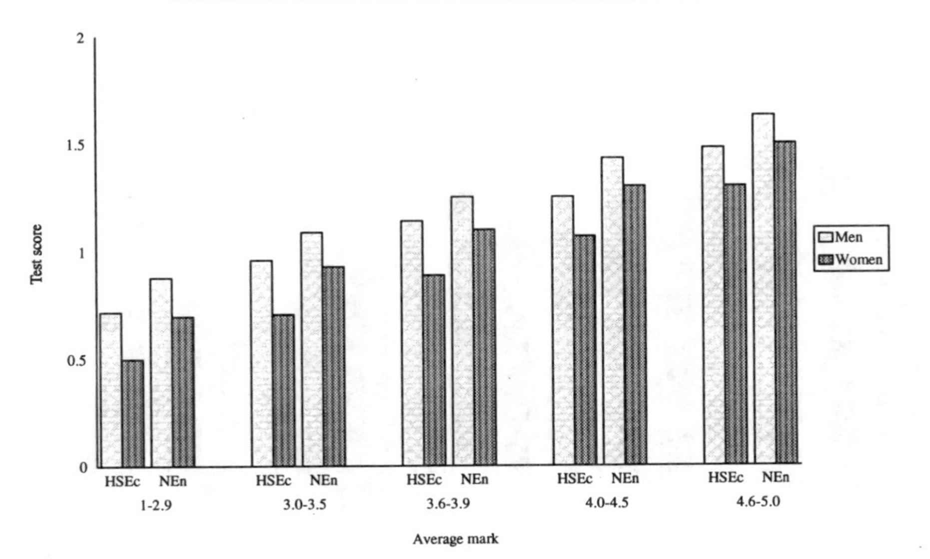

FIGURE 11.4

SCORES ON THE SweSAT SUBTEST DS OF STUDENTS IN DIFFERENT COMBINATIONS OF COURSES AND WITH DIFFERENT MARKS IN MATHEMATICS, BY GENDER

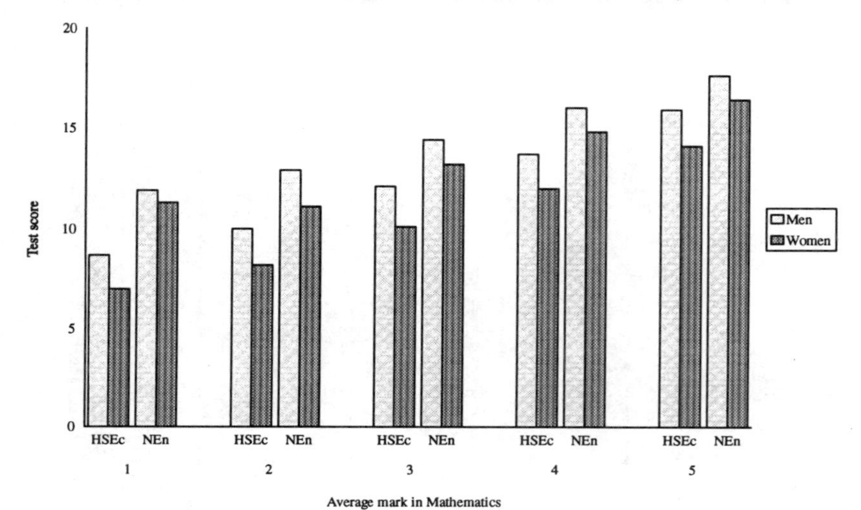

FIGURE 11.5

SCORES ON THE SweSAT SUBTEST DTM OF STUDENTS FROM DIFFERENT COMBINATIONS OF COURSES AND WITH DIFFERENT MARKS IN MATHEMATICS, BY GENDER

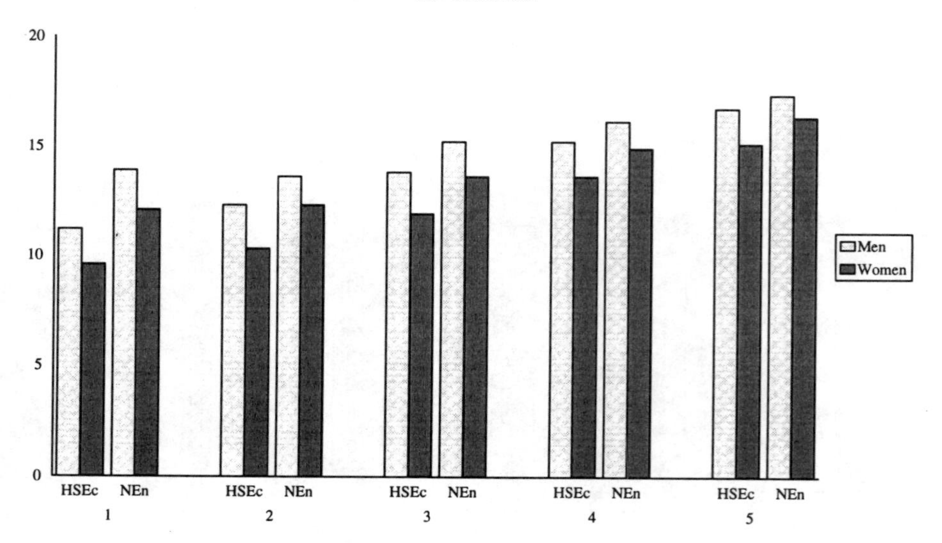

FIGURE 11.6

SCORES ON THE SweSAT SUBTEST WORD FOR MEN FROM DIFFERENT COURSES AND WITH DIFFERENT MARKS IN SCHOOL-BASED SWEDISH LANGUAGE ASSESSMENT

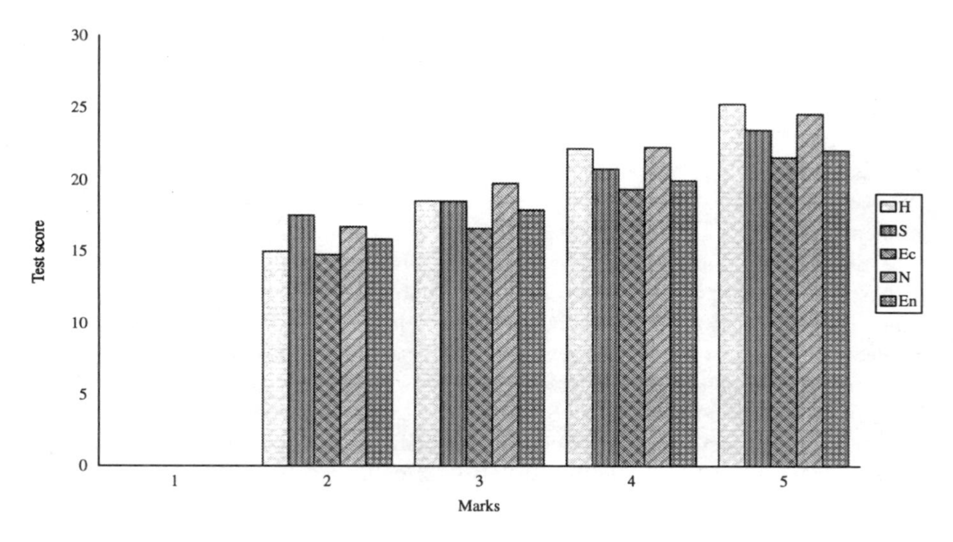

FIGURE 11.7

SCORES ON THE SweSAT SUBTEST WORD FOR WOMEN FROM DIFFERENT COURSES AND WITH DIFFERENT MARKS IN SCHOOL-BASED SWEDISH LANGUAGE ASSESSMENT

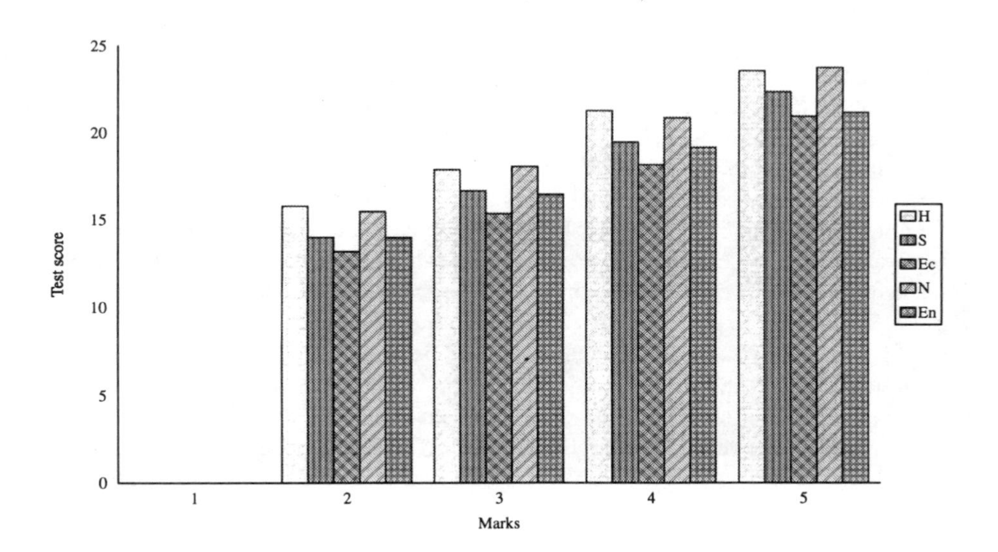

Figure 11.4 the results on the subtest DS are given for men and women in these two groups of courses at different intervals of average marks in mathematics.

It is evident that knowledge of mathematics is of great importance for performance on this subtest. The mark level is clearly related to the test score. Still women score lower than men with the same mark although women with higher marks in mathematics score significantly above men with low marks in mathematics on the same combination of courses.

In Figure 11.5 similar information is given for the subtest DTM. Here again there is a relationship between test results and mathematics but it is weaker than for DS. Results on this subtest do not seem to correlate as well with knowledge of mathematics.

Finally scores on the vocabulary subtest WORD of the SweSAT are compared with school leaving marks in the Swedish language for men (Figure 11.6) and women (Figure 11.7) distributed across different courses. There is a relationship between aptitude test scores and school marks in the Swedish language but it is not very strong. The pattern for different courses is also quite different from the one found for the quantitative subtests. Students on the Natural Science course still score high but on this test they are joined by Humanities students while Engineering students score much lower. On this test also, differences between men and women have almost disappeared.

CONCLUSION

A finding both in Sweden and in other countries, when measuring achievement with different instruments, is that males obtain higher scores on standardised multiple-choice tests, while females obtain higher marks on other forms of assessment, including ones based on essay-type examinations and teacher ratings (see Bolger & Kellaghan, 1990). This, in fact, is an adequate summary of the findings of this study as well.

Within each of the five courses in upper secondary school in Sweden, females obtain lower average standardised test scores than males who receive the same school leaving mark. However, it is important to note that women who have taken Natural Science and Engineering courses score as high or higher than men who have taken other courses. On the other hand, performance on the school leaving certificate gives a different picture. As a group, females obtain higher marks than males, and this is true for all subjects in upper secondary school except sports and physics; even in mathematics, females on average get higher marks than males.

A common but somewhat simplistic explanation of this phenomenon is that higher marks are a reward for the better classroom behaviour of girls. That is, the school marking system rewards well-adjusted and well-behaved students and punishes challenging and independent students.

A more obvious and perhaps more reasonable explanation is that the classroom achievement of girls is in fact superior to that of boys. But the important question still remains: why do girls achieve better in the classroom situation and why do boys achieve better in the test situation? In discussing this problem with regard to mathematics achievement, Kimball (1989) suggests three possible explanations. Here these explanations are applied to gender differences in marks and test results in general.

The first explanation relates to differences in experience. In the case of school leaving marks, it is mainly classroom learning that counts; experiences from outside the classroom are not likely to influence such marks to the same extent as they influence performance on an external standardised test. This hypothesis seems to explain at least part of the differences on standardised tests, but it does not explain why girls get higher marks when they are assessed in school. Do girls work harder in the classroom because they have less useful experiences from outside school and therefore less confidence? Do boys find classroom material boring compared to experiences outside class? And are they therefore less motivated to perform well in the classroom?

A second explanation relates to possible gender differences in learning style relating in particular to rote learning and autonomous learning. According to this hypothesis, boys' more autonomous ways of learning facilitate achievement on standardised tests which require the application and generalisation of old knowledge to new problems. Girls, on the other hand, make more use of the rote learning approach, which may be advantageous in classroom examinations which are often based on routine application of what has been taught in class. There is, however, no direct support for the hypothesis that there are gender-related differences in learning style, though there are some indications that girls' greater dependency and orientation towards the teacher may be related to a special learning style. Boys are often more antagonistic to teachers and this may be related to a more autonomous learning style.

A final possible explanation is that there are gender differences in dealing with unknown/novel and known/familiar material. According to this hypothesis, girls are more motivated and confident when working with known material but less confident and at times inhibited when working with new or unknown material. This could explain why girls achieve better on classroom tests and less well on external standardised multiple-choice tests. If, on the other hand, boys are more motivated and confident when working with new and challenging material they would perform better on standardised tests.

While test scores on the standardised SweSAT and school marks paint somewhat different pictures of the achievements of boys and girls, this does not necessarily mean that either instrument is faulty. It may be an indication that they measure different kinds of knowledge and abilities. The kinds of knowledge and abilities that are demanded in school and are reflected in school marks are on average mastered better by girls than by boys. In the SweSAT, the other kinds of knowledge and abilities that are included seem to be mastered better by boys.

REFERENCES

Bolger, N., & Kellaghan, T. (1990). Method of measurement and gender differences in scholastic achievement. *Journal of Educational Measurement, 27,* 165-174.

Kimball, M. (1989). A new perspective on women's math achievement. *Psychological Bulletin, 105,* 198-214.

Statistiska Meddelanden. (1991). Avgångna och avgångsbetyg från gymnasieskolans linjer läsåret 1990/91. *U 53 SM 9102.*

APPENDIX 11.1

The SweSAT 1991 consisted of 144 multiple-choice items distributed over six subtests:

Vocabulary (WORD) measures the understanding of words and concepts and consists of 30 items in which the task is to identify which of five presented words has the same meaning as a given word.

Data Sufficiency (DS) aims to measure numerical reasoning ability. In each of the 20 items a problem is presented, and the task is to decide whether the information given is sufficient for the solution of the problem.

Reading Comprehension (READ) measures comprehension of four texts elicited by six questions for each text.

Interpretations of Diagrams, Tables and Maps (DTM) consists of ten collections of tables, diagrams, and maps with two questions in relation to each collection.

General Information (GI) measures general knowledge and information. The test consists of 30 items.

Study Techniques (STECH) consists of a booklet (about 70 pages) which contains lists of figures and tables, different indices, etc. The test is made up of 20 questions, the answers to which are to be found in the booklet.

12. STAFF DEVELOPMENT AS A CATALYST FOR CHANGING ADMISSIONS PRACTICES

Henry G. Macintosh
West Sussex Institute of Higher Education,
Bognor Regis

The Enterprise in Higher Education (EHE) Programme was launched by the Education Division of the Department of Employment in late 1987 (see Great Britain. Department of Employment. Further and Higher Education Branch, 1992-93). It was supported from the outset by many organisations including the Committee of Vice-Chancellors and Principals of Universities (CVCP) and the Confederation of British Industry (CBI). The principal objectives of the programme are to give undergraduates a better understanding of industry and the world of work and to provide opportunities to improve personal skills in areas such as communication, numeracy, computer literacy, the ability to work in groups, and to take greater responsibility for their own learning, whilst still meeting the academic objectives of their chosen degree courses. These skills should in part be acquired through project-based work designed to be undertaken in a real economic setting and jointly assessed by employers and the students' own higher education institution.

'Enterprise' has been a word much in vogue in recent years and the overt development of an enterprise culture has been a major plank in the British government's plans to bring about radical change in the 1980s and 90s. Dictionary definitions of enterprise are varied but they always include: the wish, the power and the ability to begin and follow through a plan or task; an exciting often hazardous undertaking; and something undertaken that requires planning and work.

EHE offers financial support to higher education institutions within the United Kingdom up to a maximum of £1 million spread over five years. Eleven institutions were successful with bids which had to be made against stringent criteria, in the first year of the programme in 1988. A further 123 were successful in years two (26), three (41), and four (56). Ninety percent of eligible institutions applied but only some 50% have been successful to date. EHE is not intended as an addition to the academic curriculum, nor as a substitute for rigorous academic and vocational training. The initiative is a framework for change which each institution can develop in its own way in delivering the overall objectives. Building on existing ideas and good practice is every bit as important as devising new courses and programmes.

Delivery of EHE is based on a three-way partnership, involving the staff and students of the institution and employers. To obtain funding, institutions have to demonstrate strong commitment to their programme from institutional heads, departments, teaching staff, and employer partners. They have to devise plans for curriculum development, employer involvement, and staff development, which is a particular concern of this paper. They also have to carry out a thorough 'enterprise audit' of current courses and programmes.

THE GENERAL IMPACT OF THE EHE PROGRAMME ON STAFF DEVELOPMENT IN HIGHER EDUCATION

Any successful management of change within EHE is likely to depend upon the setting up initially of a core group within an institution which will need to address a number of major issues. Work to date has identified three in particular:

(i) a willingness to experiment with teaching and learning methods in co-operation with industry or other outside agencies;

(ii) the development of strategies for widening participation amongst staff; and

(iii) the development of staff training within the institution. Staff development provision will need to satisfy needs generated by the programme, including such things as projects, secondments, and exchanges with industry and outside agencies.

In broad terms, institutions have tackled staff development in two ways. One is product-oriented. The structure is formal with the emphasis on special events and activities. This parallels traditional methods of organising in-service training.

The second approach lays the stress on process. Development takes place through workshop sessions, meetings, networks, and informal contacts. The approach mirrors the changes in learning styles that students are experiencing. It is process driven and participants are involved in defining their own learning needs.

Evaluation has shown that some institutions which started by delivering event-driven staff training have shifted as the programme evolved to a more process-oriented view of staff development. In several institutions, staff development has pioneered new approaches. There has been a shift, for example, from individual tuition to the involvement of whole course teams. Staff development has also increasingly been seen as the acquisition by staff of the same range of personal enterprise qualities and skills as the programme sets out to facilitate for students.

For convenience, current provision for staff development can be considered under four broad headings: in-house provision; inter-institutional provision; regional provision; and national provision.

Three things are crucial to successful in-house provision: a commitment to the concept of staff development by the Vice-Chancellor and other senior officers; a policy of training and staff development which is communicated to all staff; and the appointment of a staff development co-ordinator with both time and seniority. The most common form of in-house provision are internal courses in which increasingly people from outside the institution itself are involved. Other areas of provision include external courses, job rotation and exchange schemes, on-the-job training, and trainee schemes.

A good example of inter-institutional provision is that provided by the M1/M69 corridor group which includes those universities and polytechnics linked by the two motorways. They currently run a joint staff development programme. Twelve universities in the North-east have also combined to run a four-module Management and Leadership Programme for senior academic and administrative staff.

Regional provision to date has concentrated on administrative staff training and five groups have been established which include most universities and polytechnics. There are signs that parallel developments will take place with respect to academic training.

As far as national provision is concerned the CVCP set up in January 1989 the University of Sheffield Development and Training Unit (USDTU) (see Guildford, 1990). Its main terms of reference include: the stimulation of training provision; the encouragement and publicising of existing initiatives; acting as a national resource centre for staff development; establishing networks; organising a restricted programme of national events; and the accreditation of courses run by other organisations. Whilst the EHE programme cannot claim to be responsible for all of these initiatives it has undoubtedly acted as a major catalyst for staff development. Successful enterprise programmes inevitably require reconsideration of the place and nature of staff development within higher education, as they also require a reconsideration of admissions policies, the introduction of more flexible course provision (probably modular in nature), a re-thinking of teaching methods, and the development of qualifications which allow for and encourage credit accumulation and transfer. This is no light agenda.

EHE AT LIVERPOOL UNIVERSITY

I now turn to a consideration of the impact of EHE upon a single institution. For this purpose the University of Liverpool has been chosen, not because it is typical or peculiar in any way – there is probably no such thing as a typical EHE programme – but because the writer of this paper has worked with another project at the university concerned with Curriculum Enrichment for students aged 16-19 and is in consequence more familiar with what is happening at Liverpool than elsewhere. The university has also always stressed the importance of formative evaluation in relation to what it does and seeks to do and this has formed a crucial part of EHE developments at Liverpool. It is in consequence beginning to provide important insights and markers for the future.

At Liverpool, the EHE Programme started in March 1990; it was in its second year when this paper was written. The paper relies in the main on the second Annual Report of the University's Steering Committee on Enterprise and Higher Education and covers the period 1 December 1990 to 30 December 1991 (*Annual report of the Steering Committee,* 1991). The picture it provides is thus dated as well as partial and can do no more than give an indication under the two interrelated headings of Staff Development and Curriculum Change of the kinds of activity that are going on in one institution of higher education as a result of the Enterprise Programme. Here it is important to stress that from the outset the university integrated the programme into its long-term development strategy and saw it as a vehicle through which to rethink a whole range of issues from curriculum structures (modular) through industrial links (wider and closer) to teaching and learning styles (more varied) at local, national, and European levels.

Staff Development

The most significant trends in the year under review have been the increased tailoring of staff development to meet individual departmental needs, the involvement of staff from other neighbouring higher education institutions and from local industry, an increase in the number of courses run by outside agencies in conjunction with the university, and the growing emphasis on the developmental needs of students. An example of this last has been the introduction of an induction programme for postgraduate students. This consisted of a suite of six half-day workshops which aimed to allow individuals to share/exchange ideas on a multi-disciplinary group basis; to involve postgraduates in more active styles of learning; and to provide the opportunity for individuals to improve personal skills such as teamwork, communication, and project management, and to initiate individual action planning with specific reference to business and enterprise skills.

Curriculum Change

In the year under review, initiatives and activities relating to curriculum change have involved some 3,000 students. The five departments involved in the first year (Geography, Psychology, Mathematics including Computing, Life Sciences, and Engineering Science) have built upon and extended their range of projects. A further two departments (Geography and Psychology) and two faculties (Engineering and Medicine) have joined the EHE Initiative. The projects being undertaken by all these departments are now appearing in the literature made available to prospective applicants to the university and there is a growing stress upon induction courses for first year students designed to emphasise the importance of personal and career development as an adjunct to an academic qualification. Feedback from students, both formal and informal, is being used to clarify needs and to plan future activities. Major emphasis has been laid upon the acquisition by students and staff of computer literacy and keyboard skills and this has resulted in the publication of a manual entitled *The Electronic Campus 1991* which has been issued to all first year, postgraduate, and overseas students. It is currently being evaluated. Parallel work is also being done in a number of departments (History has been particularly active) on developing personal study skills and in promoting economic and business-related skills. This last has involved co-operation with local and national firms. For example, accountants Coopers and Lybrand, Deloitte have devised and run a Management Training Module for Mathematics students in conjunction with the Mathematics Department.

The development of specific European links and the broadening of knowledge about Europe are both particularly strong themes in the Enterprise Programme at Liverpool. Opportunities are being provided for students in Engineering Science to gain work experience and training in continental Europe through project work at a university or in industry in collaboration with a local university. Students are also being offered language training courses which are provided by tutors from the Modern Languages Centre. The assessment of such courses is currently under discussion and it is hoped to develop a student Record of Achievement so that attendance at these courses, language training, work placement abroad, and other skills development can be credited to the student. This record will be adopted on a pilot basis by the Department of Engineering Science.

A branch of the *Association des États Generaux des Étudiants de l'Europe* (AEGEE) has been established with initial support from the EHE programme at the university. AEGEE is a multi-disciplinary European network established and run by students with 12,000 members. This initiative has already involved over 500 students from the university and neighbouring higher education institutions in a wide-ranging and extensive organisational exercise. It has stimulated interest in language training and will involve students in collaborative work with local, national, and international companies as they seek to establish sponsorship and run conferences on a variety of topics. All this has raised significant questions for language teaching at the university which are currently being addressed by senior management.

Possibly the most interesting and innovative initiative established at the university under the EHE programme is the Merseyside Community Research Exchange (MCRE). This was established in January 1991 and aims to link higher education with voluntary and community groups. Its purpose is to bring together students requiring access to organisations for projects as part of their assessed coursework and voluntary organisations requiring help or assistance with tasks which they would not be able to do with their own resources. The key element of MCRE is that of exchange. Students contribute to an objective agreed with an organisation and at the same time produce academic work which is submitted as part of their final assessment. The organisation receives a practical input and a definite outcome in the form of a report or piece of work undertaken while at the same time providing students with a learning environment. With initial funding, EHE has established a small office with administrative and secretarial support that will provide liaison between students and supervisors in higher education and in voluntary and community groups in Merseyside.

After preliminary work in the academic year 1990-1991, MCRE was launched with two half-day seminars held at the university in April 1991. The first of these looked at academic issues arising from assessment, particularly assessment of group project work of which the university had already considerable experience through its involvement in the 16-19 Curriculum Enrichment Programme. The second seminar was attended by representatives from 32 local voluntary and community groups and allowed those involved with MCRE at the university to establish links with possible users and to discuss with them the objects of the exchange. Close links have been developed with the Science Shop based at the Merseyside Innovation Centre and with the Action Resource Centre which seeks to place company executives with community groups on six-month to two-year secondments. All three organisations have complementary roles and work effectively together to provide a resource for Merseyside. Currently, projects are being carried out for Phoenix House, a drug rehabilitation centre, Rice Lane Community Centre, the One Parent Family Group, and the Healthy Cities Programme, to name but a few. Students are working both individually and in groups.

IMPLICATIONS FOR THE FUTURE

The kinds of initiatives briefly described above, which are of course replicated in other institutions, have inevitable consequences for the management both of institutions and of the learning environment. This in turn raises major questions about staff development, assessment methods, and course construction, to name but three significant areas. All of these in their turn have implications for admissions policies and practices.

Further stimulus to change in an admissions system, which is still largely dominated by use of single, terminal, external examinations, has been provided by work which has taken place in recent years in schools on Records of Achievement (increasingly linked with action, planning, and portfolios) and by government pressure backed by new funding arrangements to increase significantly the numbers in higher education. The first of these has made available a much wider range of descriptive evidence about potential applicants whilst at the same time providing the applicants with the skills needed to manage their own learning and assessment more effectively. The need to accommodate a much more diverse potential pool of applicants which is central to the second point will require *inter alia* a significant rethink of course design and the implementation of strategies for the accreditation of prior learning. This has already shown itself in the growing use of modular course provision and in the development of access courses, both increasingly described in terms of requirements and outcomes rather than content, with a consequential need to define success criteria.

This, in turn, can facilitate admissions policies couched in terms of meeting prerequisites, a trend that the growing localisation of higher education in Britain, stemming in part from the introduction of student loans, can accelerate through the use of 'compacts.' The growth of franchising courses between institutions is also likely to lead to increased use of student transcripts as a basis for transfer. In such circumstances, it would be both unreasonable and inadequate to retain university-dominated admissions procedures which tend to use sole selection instruments in the form more often than not of formal, graded, external examinations.

There are indeed clear signs that changes are on the way although there is much to be done, not least with respect to changing attitudes. The new centralised admissions system based on an amalgamation of the Polytechnics Central Admission System (PCAS) and the University Central Council for Admissions (UCCA) has drawn the attention of both applicants and institutions to the significance of Records of Achievement in its application arrangements. The admissions process within institutions is at this stage becoming increasingly professional through growing stress upon staff development and on the appointment of individuals with specific institution-wide responsibilities for areas such as Records of Achievement. The recent introduction of the National Record of Achievement (NRA) as a life-long record has meant that it will increasingly be used by teachers both in school and higher education as part of their own appraisal process and this in turn can only increase understanding and support. In this work, a number of projects funded by the Employment Department are playing an important part, notably the Recording Achievement and Higher Education Project (1993) based at Wigan and the Admissions to Higher Education Project (1992) based at the University of Sussex.

Further change will however take time, and it will be interesting to see over the next few years the extent to which over-reliance upon single instruments for selection will diminish; the degree to which the supremacy of the General Certificate of Education A-level Examination as a selection instrument will wither away; the extent to which interviews will be used to take advantage of the growing capacity of young people to sell themselves as a result of their experience with the NRA; and the speed or slowness with which British higher education institutions will move towards whole institution admissions policies.

Further moves will be as much a matter of changes in attitude as of changes in policy, although the practical pressures for change in response to government policies will if anything accelerate over the next few years. In changing attitudes, the EHE programme can play a crucial part and there are already clear signs in institutions such as Liverpool that these changes are starting to take place. As we move into the 21st century, the EHE Programme will, I believe, be seen to have constituted a major catalyst for change in the nature and operation of higher education, including its selection procedures, in Britain.

REFERENCES

Admissions to Higher Education Project. (1992). *Report.* Brighton: University of Sussex.

Annual report of the Steering Committee of the University of Liverpool Enterprise in Higher Education Programme: 1st December 1990 to 30th November 1991. (1991). University of Liverpool.

Great Britain. Department of Employment. Further and Higher Education Branch. (1992-93). *Key features.* Moorfoot, Sheffield: Author.

Guildford, P. (1990). *Staff development provision in universities of the United Kingdom.* Sheffield: University of Sheffield Development Training Unit.

Recording Achievement and Higher Education Project. (1993). *A report of the project and its evaluation 1 September 1991 to 31 August 1993.* (Project address: 39 Bridgeman Terrace, Wigan WN1 1TT).

13. GATEWAY OF OPPORTUNITY: THE ADMISSIONS PROFESSION IN THE 21ST CENTURY

Donald M. Stewart
The College Board
New York

I would like to begin with a quotation from John Millington Synge's introduction to his play *Playboy of the Western World,* 'When I was writing ... some years ago, I got more aid than any learning could have given me from a chink in the floor ... that let me hear what was being said by the servant girls in the kitchen.' What intrigues me about this quotation is that it identifies two worlds, the world of learning and the world of those without privilege, which too often have been held apart, as have been the people in them. And yet, as Synge recognised, they have so much to offer each other. Perhaps it is because of what is now happening in America that this quotation strikes me as apt. We are, at last, seeing the benefits of the arrival of poor and minority students — the metaphorical servant girls in the kitchen — in the halls of formal learning, and we have watched with pleasure as they have used the experience to transform their lives. Many more still need to be brought there.

As the world changes and becomes smaller, more complex, and more technological, and as, therefore, the value of education increases, our job in admissions is also changing. There are many technical issues we face with regard to the testing and selection of candidates. However, important as they are, we must allow our sights to encompass not only technical issues but also a larger horizon. Not only are there broader issues that we need to consider, but even the technical aspects of admissions have implications that take us beyond the day to day. The ways in which we solicit applications and admit candidates have implications that affect people's lives and happiness that go far beyond technical questions.

One of the glories of higher education in the United States is its independence. This is true even of so-called 'public institutions.' We enjoy remarkable, if endangered, freedoms of programmes and processes. It should be noted that recently a federal court handed down a ruling that makes it clear, with regard to awarding financial aid, that the U.S. government views higher education not as a public good or a public investment, but as a private business sector, subject to the laws and constraints of business. What effect this may have on admissions remains to be seen. Nevertheless, currently, an admissions officer, and an admissions strategy, can still make an enormous difference in the overall quality, character, and direction of a college or university.

I should further like to point out that the world of admissions in America consists of a great sorting process whereby more than a million and a half high-school graduates each year find their way to more than 3,000 colleges and universities nationwide. Between 1955 and 1990, enrolment in U.S. colleges and universities increased by 400% (Synder, 1993).

Three basic assumptions may be made in approaching the complex profession of admission. The first is that there is no longer a single norm in American society, whether a typical family, a common religious heritage, or even a common continent of origin. Rather, today, the only norm in American society is diversity. The college-going cohort is composed not just of the sons of society's elite, as was largely the case before World War II, but the daughters and sons of a mass — and increasingly diverse — society. Second, the transition to higher education is not strictly limited in time, starting in the junior year of high school and ending with acceptance to a college. It begins as early as the middle school, and, we now understand that successful admission must also mean success in college. Finally, as with everything else in our lives, new technologies are pointing the way to a future that will be different from the present. Whether in testing, transmission of data, transcripts, or the application form itself, new technologies have already begun to transform our professional lives.

I now believe that the primary goal of the profession of admission is finally to bring those without privilege — the servants in the kitchen — into full and equitable contact with the world of higher learning. I recognise that this is not an easy task, nor is it a 'greatness' that we necessarily chose when we entered this field. Rather, it is a case of greatness being thrust upon us. Choose it or not, it is our destiny to be the generation that made higher education the educational goal and experience of the many, not the few. In this way, we must also be statesmanlike believers in the cause of humanity, as well as being deliverers of next year's entering class of qualified students.

I make this assertion in ways that I hope will be useful in explaining what I have in mind. First, I want to speak briefly about how the history of our profession in the United States has brought us to this point, and why a statesmanlike approach is essential for the world of the 21st century. Then I would like to share some observations from an admissions colloquium which was recently hosted by the College Board.

THE DEVELOPMENT OF THE ADMISSIONS PROFESSION IN THE UNITED STATES

The organisation of which I am president, the College Board, was founded in the year 1900, a time of chaos in the admissions area in the U.S., a time in which there were no common standards, and when well-qualified candidates from less known schools or those distant from the great universities on our East Coast, had great difficulty in presenting themselves.

Originally composed of a handful of schools and colleges, our association was named the College Entrance Examination Board, and was brought into being to resolve this chaos. As the name itself suggests, the mechanism chosen was a common admissions examination, what today would be called an achievement test. Almost a century later, we number almost 3000 schools, colleges, universities, and educational associations, and part of the unique role we play in American education derives from the ongoing creative collaboration between secondary and post-secondary education that our structure makes possible. There has been a tremendous increase in the activities encompassed under the rubric of admissions in the U.S., such as the creation of the Scholastic Aptitude Test (SAT), the financial aid system, advanced placement, a growing complement of guidance tools including an increasing number on computer, and a series of products and services aimed at bringing the adult student to campus.

However, if my international studies in Switzerland and subsequently my years as a programme officer with the Ford Foundation in the Middle East and Africa taught me anything, it is the danger of viewing the world just through the perspective of one's own country's experience. Higher education in the United States, I fully recognise, has its own particular character. What sets it apart from some other systems in the world is that it is never too late to go to college or to get a graduate degree. Some institutions are highly selective, admitting less than 20% of those who apply, while many are essentially open to anyone with a high-school diploma or its equivalent. Who goes to college, and when, has changed radically in the past 20 years. In 1992, less than one-quarter of American college students were 18- to 24-year olds enrolled full-time in a four-year programme. Less than a quarter of today's cohort corresponds to what, until recently, had been the basic profile of the American college-going population.

A second major change has to do with public policy. Education, even higher education, is locally controlled in the United States, notwithstanding the growing involvement — some would say encroachments — of the federal government. Last year, however, a major national polling group threw a spanner in the works by reporting that the overwhelming majority of Americans now favour some national standards in education. Public sentiment being what it is, this could obviously swing back. But there is no longer a sense of business as usual.

Thirdly, Americans now understand that, pre-eminent as they may have been in the 20th century, they will not keep up with a United Europe or the Pacific Rim nations in the 21st century unless their educational system changes as well. The 20% of Americans who previously have been well educated, thanks to their preparation for and experience in higher education, simply will not be adequate in the future. In fact, experts now say that we must have at least 80% of our population skilled and educated, prepared to go to college and succeed.

Cumulatively, these changes and factors add up to a new world, coinciding with the end of the Cold War. Replacing the Cold War are economic battles and the search for markets. Making markets is not a simple matter. It requires all kinds of abilities and technologies, which require formal education and training.

Quality education for the majority of its citizens will be characteristic of societies that will be most successful in the marketplace in the 21st century. Increasingly, at least in the U.S., what defines quality education is adequate preparation for, and success in, college. Hence, admissions become an essential function, especially in a time of social and economic change. Because of this, the College Board in 1988 set about constructing a comprehensive review of what the now deceased pre-eminent theorist of admissions, Alden Thresher, called 'the great sorting.' In the past four years, with the advice of professions in counselling, admissions, financial aid, curriculum articulation, public policy, and professional associations, the College Board Study of Admission to American College and Universities in the 1990s — the formal name of the study — has produced two sets of monographs. The first set, the Selective Admissions Series, pertains to the practices at those institutions that select a class, and the second set, the Admissions Practice Series, addresses additional issues of importance to the educational community as a whole and the public at large.

As distinct from the comments in this paper, these monographs are quite specific, covering topics such as high ability students and college choice, academic standards, the college application and admissions process, and enrolment and recruitment patterns. In neither the series nor the subsequent meetings that we have had, however, can we really point to substantial unanimity within the American admissions or educational community on many basic issues.

In part, this is due to the wide diversity of American institutions, some of which must select a class from a large group of very talented candidates, and others that have to work to find a sufficient number of adequately prepared students to fill the classrooms. Our profession, and there is much debate on the extent to which it is in fact a profession, has entered a time of external challenge and internal soul searching which is appropriate to an era of enormous change.

THE OAK BROOK COLLOQUIUM

In response to this situation, the College Board hosted in June 1992 a colloquium in Oak Brook, Illinois, of 100 of the leading high-school counsellors and admissions officers from the full range of American institutions of higher learning (*The great sorting,* 1992). There were ideas aplenty, and issues percolating through the meeting included: the need to promote access and still maintain high standards; financial aid in the face of rising prices; the dissemination of accurate information in the face of over-simplified rankings that nevertheless influence student and parent choice; and finally, the role of the admissions officer as teacher/counsellor whose job is to support and nurture, to grow the crop, not just harvest it. Underlying much of the discussion was another question: what is the role of the admissions officer in the greater scheme of things? Is he or she a middle manager or a strategic policy officer? While the conference, not surprisingly, raised more questions than it answered, it may be useful to look in slightly more detail at some of the issues discussed. If any issue represents the delicate balancing act performed by admissions professionals, it is dealing with access versus standards. On the one hand, there is a concern that was strongly expressed at the colloquium by Carolyn Reid-Wallace, Assistant Secretary for Postsecondary Education, U.S. Department of Education, over what is perceived as an overall decline in academic standards in America — a decline that has had an effect on admissions policies. On the other hand, there is a genuine desire to guarantee access to all students and to ensure that the underrepresentation of certain groups is addressed.

As higher education grapples with the issues of standards, it must also recognise that it is not merely the passive recipient of what elementary and secondary schools have wrought. Colleges are also in a position to shape education, particularly through teacher training. Moreover, admission requirements, especially at state institutions, determine what courses students take in high school. Raising admission standards, and the clear communication of those standards, also have the effect of raising expectations at elementary and secondary levels.

A second major theme of the colloquium was sounded by James Ash, Jr., president of Whittier College. President Ash proposed that runaway costs are at the root of the loss of public confidence in higher education, and are seen as a manifestation of greed on the part of postsecondary institutions. Lying at the heart of this issue are reasons why students choose to attend college. Is higher education simply a means to the good life, or to the life of the mind? Are colleges in the business of maximising human capital or intellectual achievement? Certainly, students' enrolment patterns in the U.S. reflect a utilitarian attitude towards college. For a number of years, there has been a definite shift away from the liberal arts and sciences and towards majors that offer the possibility of a lucrative job at graduation.

A fact of life in late 20th century admissions offices nationwide is that, as James Scannell, vice-president for enrolment, placement, and alumni affairs at the University of Rochester, put it, 'the vast majority of colleges do not select a class so much as recruit one.' The emphasis on marketing postsecondary education institutions has raised ethical concerns within the admissions community and engendered criticism of it from without. Yet the change in the admissions function at many institutions — from selection to enrolment/management/recruitment — often works at cross-purposes with student needs. As one participant described it, 'Admission has become a vague process involving numbers. We aren't matching students' needs with programmes.'

In terms of public perceptions, the admissions process itself is surrounded by what has been described as a 'gaseous cloud,' leaving students and their parents uncertain about how to assess chances for admission or financial aid. Perceptions are further clouded by the fact that although selective institutions (defined here as those that admit fewer than 50% of applicants annually) comprise only 20% of U.S. postsecondary institutions, their admissions practices are seen as the paradigm by the public.

At the colloquium, technology, often viewed as a depersonalising force in contemporary society, was proposed as a potential contributor to revitalising the admissions profession. It was suggested that automating many of the mundane tasks that college admission entails could free personnel to deal with more students as individuals — 'high tech/high touch,' as one participant described it.

FACING THE FUTURE

I would sum all this up by saying that we are attempting to define the admissions profession for the next century. But we are doing it in a context in America, in which it is being suggested we are not educating our children very well, in which we are part of the problem. There is a school of economists, starting with Adam Smith, that would say that the public good is best defined in terms of the outcomes between and among competing interests in the marketplace. That sums up our situation quite well — institutions and systems seeking to maximise whatever benefits there are through competition for the best students possible.

A basic challenge facing American higher education is the following: will we, as self-regulating, autonomous institutions, be able to continue to function in an unfettered way even as our nation addresses the problem of how to educate its students? There is real concern that if we do not resolve some of these basic problems, government will step in and resolve them for us.

As we move to deal with these broader issues, we should also remember that admissions personnel are in a unique position to serve as catalysts for change. Our roles as gatekeeper, as advocate of the consumer, and as intermediary between students, faculty, and administration, make us uniquely aware of what needs to be done. With co-operation from our peers and recognition of their potential, we can accomplish much. In addition, the degree of uncertainty and fluidity that characterises our current situation provides opportunity for leadership, and the chance to shape our profession as it evolves in an international context.

As to the direction in which we should move, I believe that the admissions function should be viewed as high-level and strategic. Part of the difficulty we had at the session in Oak Brook was lack of clarity about what the public interest is. That is, indeed, a difficult question. We all want to progress, and yet, as the philosopher George Santayana commented: 'Progress, far from consisting in change, depends on retentiveness ... Those who cannot remember the past are condemned to repeat it'(cited in *The Oxford Dictionary of Quotations,* 1979, p.414). Therefore, let me suggest that we remember the past by reflecting on the ideas of that great admissions practitioner, Alden Thresher, former director of admissions at the Massachusetts Institute of Technology.

Thresher believed that education must serve the student first, and the institution, its faculty, or society second. He believed that it was the mission of counsellors and admissions officers to understand the whole system of education and to use that understanding to assist the students who use those services. Anything less, he argued, betrayed the public interest. Twenty-five years ago, at a time when he had retired from active duty, he gave a paper at an earlier College Board admissions colloquium held in Interlochen, Michigan. That paper may serve to guide us into the future.

Thresher (1968) noted: 'What college admissions people are currently doing [may] look extremely silly in the light of later and fuller knowledge' (p.16). He was also concerned that admissions policies tend to reinforce educational systems and faculty biases; and he hoped that in the future 'we may see less stress on the closed circle of prediction, selection, and validation that tends to confirm and intensify whatever scheme of education has taken hold' (p.20). He was very concerned that we rely too heavily on 'the assumption that the student who shines most brightly in high school or on tests, or on some combination of the two, is the one to go far' (p. 17). Pointing to academic ne'er-do-wells such as Darwin, Churchill, and Emily Dickinson, he cautioned that no system is foolproof, that some of the best fall between the cracks, and that we are fooling ourselves if we think otherwise.

But I think the part of his paper to which I respond most strongly is his comment about human ability: 'Talent to a much greater degree than anyone realized is not something stumbled upon and found here and there; it ... can be produced' (p.11). In other words, with the right educational and personal support, we can create a significantly broader pool of ability than has been the case to date. Needless to say, this has radical implications in the field of admissions. Should we be prospecting for a few, rare jewels to find and collect behind the strong walls of our universities, or should our goal be to plough all the fields, and sow the seeds widely, so that vast new crops come up strong enough to make the grade? To put this idea in Thresher's elegant and precise language: 'We need a more sociological view of the admissions process. As we come into an era in which the majority of high-school graduates will be continuing in some kind of further education ... we need to see admissions, not as a series of administrative devices, but as a social process by which the society moves a large segment of its youth into a wide range of educational experience'(p. 20).

I find that a tremendously important challenge. Obviously, it will have different ramifications in different nations. But given what is happening in the world, I believe, it is our common future. And that thought, to paraphrase the beginning of James Joyce's *Finnegan's Wake*, brings us, by a commodius vicus of recirculation, back to my opening quotation about the servants in the kitchen, the world of learning, and the need to unite them.

In the 20th century, we began our professional lives as gatekeepers, a variety of experts searching for the most reasonable ways to filter the finest of our students into the appropriate institutions of higher learning. For the 21st century, we will have to change from being guards before closed gates to being guardians of an open gateway to individual and societal well-being. We must think of our profession in broad sociological terms, a profession which we can lead and shape, the goals of which are to create the largest possible pool of ability and to promote educational achievement at the highest level for everyone.

REFERENCES

Synder, T. D. (Ed.). (1993). *120 years of American education: A statistical portrait.* Washington DC: National Center for Education Statistics.

Thresher, A. (1968). Frozen assumptions in admissions. In C. Vroman et al (Eds.), *College admission policies for the 1970s.* Papers delivered at the colloquium on college admissions policies, Interlochen MI. New York: College Entrance Examination Board.

The great sorting. (1992). A report on the College Board's admission study colloquium, Oak Brook, IL. New York: College Entrance Examination Board.

The Oxford Dictionary of Quotations. (1979). (3rd ed.). Oxford: Oxford University Press.

14. VALIDITY AND RELIABILITY ISSUES IN INTERNATIONAL BACCALAUREATE EXAMINATIONS

M. C. Hayden, P. N. Richards and J. J. Thompson
School of Education,
University of Bath

THE INTERNATIONAL BACCALAUREATE

The International Baccalaureate (IB) was developed in the early 1960s to meet the needs of the children of an increasingly internationally mobile workforce, who often found themselves in the situation of having studied and obtained qualifications in one country, and wishing to proceed to higher education in another. Staff in international schools and colleges in Switzerland, the USA, and UK, with support from Oxford University, devised the two-year IB programme to cater for the needs of such students in the 16-19-year old age range, with a view to providing a qualification that would have international recognition rather than being affiliated to one particular national education system. In 1992, the IB Diploma was offered by over 400 schools and colleges in more than 50 countries, and was recognised by more than 700 higher education institutions around the world.

While primarily designed to provide an internationally acceptable programme, the IB was devised as a deliberate compromise between the narrow over-specialisation of some systems and the broad over-generalisation of others. The resulting structure requires students embarking on the IB Diploma programme to follow one course from five different subject groups, including their best language (Language A) and a foreign language (Language B). A sixth subject must be chosen as shown in Figure 14.1 (Thompson, 1988).

Subjects are offered at two levels, Higher Level (HL) and Subsidiary Level (SL). In addition to the study of six subjects, students are required to write an Extended Essay of some 4,000 words on a subject of the IB programme, to engage in the compulsory study of a course in the Theory of Knowledge (ToK), and to engage in Creativity, Action, Service (CAS) activities that involve regular participation in non-academic pursuits.

FIGURE 14.1

STRUCTURE OF THE INTERNATIONAL BACCALAUREATE

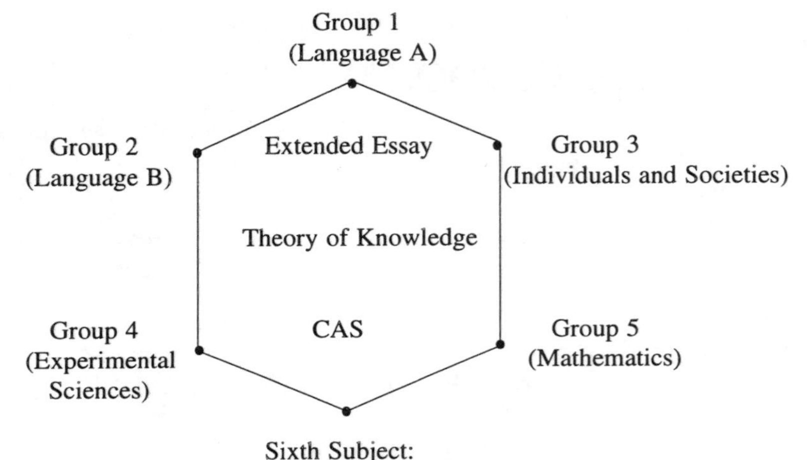

ASSESSMENT IN THE INTERNATIONAL BACCALAUREATE

Achievement in the six subjects taken by a student is reported on a scale of 1 point (minimum) to 7 points (maximum). Theory of Knowledge and the Extended Essay are both assessed on the basis that satisfactory performance results in a score of zero, while unsatisfactory performance attracts one penalty point. For Theory of Knowledge, good and excellent performance is rewarded with a bonus point, while for the Extended Essay good performance is rewarded with one bonus point and excellent performance with two bonus points. CAS is not assessed.

Each student's points from six subjects are added to form a total, to which bonus/penalty points from Theory of Knowledge and the Extended Essay are added or subtracted. The Diploma is awarded to students who have aggregated a minimum total of 24 points, and satisfied certain conditions. When the Diploma is not awarded, Certificates are issued which detail individual achievements. Modes of assessment used in IB subjects include, *inter alia,* multiple-choice, data analysis, structured and essay questions, as well as teacher assessment which contributes to most subjects.

The credibility of any form of assessment system relies on the confidence of its users (including students, teachers, and higher education institutions) in the integrity of the system. Unless the assessment system is believed to be reliable and valid, it will soon lose currency within the higher education sector and candidates holding its awards will find them worth little as evidence of their achievements. The routine procedures adopted by the International Baccalaureate Organisation (1985) in safeguarding the reliability of its assessment structures will be familiar to those involved in other external examination systems. Each subject is the primary responsibility of a Chief Examiner who, with the aid of assistant examiners, sets and marks written papers and awards overall grades. The marking of assistant examiners may be adjusted by the Chief Examiner to take into account variations of standard, as may the marking of teachers in internally assessed components.

The validity of the assessment process requires detailed consideration and to this end a study was completed in 1991 which focused on the validity of a total subject mark arrived at by aggregating results from a number of components.

ISSUES OF WEIGHTING

To arrive at the overall percentage figures on which grade boundaries for IB subjects are drawn, results from the various components are added together according to the prespecified 'weighting' of each component, i.e., the percentage of marks allocated to it as an indication of its relative importance in the overall framework of the knowledge and skills being assessed. The study reported in this paper investigated whether these prespecified weightings were actually realised in terms of the influence each component had on the overall result.

Work carried out in different contexts has highlighted the fact that the extent of the influence of one component on an aggregated total is determined not by the total number of marks attributed to it, but by the spread of marks of that component with respect to others contributing to the same total, as well as the intercorrelation between the various component distributions. Weightings assigned to a component can be described as 'intended', 'planned', or 'nominal' and the extent to which the component actually influences the final result as the 'achieved' or 'effective' weighting (Adams & Murphy, 1982; Adams & Wilmut, 1981; Cresswell, 1982; Fowles, 1974; Wilmott & Hall, 1975). Examination boards in England and Wales, as well as elsewhere, calculate the effective weightings of all subjects as part of their routine post-examination analysis of results data.

In our study, we investigated the effect of taking into account such considerations in the IB context, using the 'part with whole covariance' method advocated by, amongst others, Adams and Murphy (1982) where, for a given component:

$$\text{Effective weight} = \frac{\text{standard deviation x correlation with total mark}}{\text{sum of (standard deviation x correlation) for all components}} \times 100$$

Data for all candidates from the May 1988 and May 1989 examination sessions were analysed for a range of subjects. Table 14.1 lists the subjects and their respective candidate entries, by level.

TABLE 14.1

NUMBER OF CANDIDATES TAKING IB EXAMINATIONS IN MAY 1988 AND MAY 1989, BY SUBJECT AND LEVEL

Subject	Year and Level			
	1988		1989	
	HL	SL	HL	SL
English A	2,473	1,267	2,805	1,256
French B	384	1,489	400	1,637
Biology	1,169	1,538	1,178	1,556

For each subject and level the effective weightings of all components were calculated and compared with their intended weightings. Results are considered below, by grouping similar components together as a means of establishing the extent to which any trends emerged across subjects. It should be borne in mind in considering these results that, since effective weights for any examination must total 100%, the effective weight of any one component must be affected by, and affect, that of every other component of the same examination.

ANALYSIS OF INTENDED AND EFFECTIVE WEIGHTS ON IB EXAMINATIONS

Internal Assessment

All three subjects considered in this study include an internal assessment component. Analysis of each case showed that, while the extent of the discrepancy between intended and effective weights clearly varied from subject to subject, in every case the effective weight was lower than intended (Table 14.2). This pattern can probably be explained by the fact that marks awarded by teachers, often on a scale of 1-20, tend to be more bunched towards the top end of the scale than may be the case with a distribution of marks in the written examination paper component. This 'bunching' feature tends to be evident even after external moderation and is likely to be the cause, through the resulting relatively low standard deviations, of this component having a reduced influence on overall distributions with respect to that intended.

TABLE 14.2

INTENDED AND EFFECTIVE PERCENTAGE WEIGHTS ON THE IB EXAMINATIONS FOR INTERNAL ASSESSMENT, BY SUBJECT, LEVEL AND YEAR

Subject	Year	Intended Weight %	Effective Weight %	Diff %
Biology SL	1988	20	18.3	-1.7
Biology SL	1989	20	14.4	-5.6
Biology HL	1988	20	14.0	-6.0
Biology HL	1989	20	12.0	-8.0
French B SL	1988	15	11.4	-3.6
French B SL	1989	15	10.8	-4.2
French B HL	1988	15	11.5	-3.5
French B HL	1989	15	9.2	-5.8
English A SL	1988	20	13.3	-6.7
English A SL	1989	20	15.2	-4.8
English A HL	1988	20	14.9	-5.1
English A HL	1989	20	14.3	-5.7

Multiple-Choice Papers

In each of French B SL and HL and Biology SL and HL, one component is made up entirely of multiple-choice items. Analysis of these data show that in each case the effective weight of the multiple-choice component was, as in the case of internal assessment, lower than that intended (see Table 14.3). The explanation for the consistently lower effective than intended weights in this case could well be linked to the fact that, in IB multiple-choice papers, all items have four possible responses and since guessing is not penalised, all students have a theoretical chance of achieving a minimum of 25% of the total available score by guesswork alone. This factor tends to lead to the marks for these papers being less well-spread than they might otherwise be with the result that their influence on the total mark for the subject in question is reduced.

TABLE 14.3

INTENDED AND EFFECTIVE PERCENTAGE WEIGHTS ON IB EXAMINATIONS FOR MULTIPLE-CHOICE TESTS, BY SUBJECT, LEVEL, AND YEAR

Subject	Year	Intended Weight %	Effective Weight %	Diff %
Biology SL	1988	20	16.6	-3.4
Biology SL	1989	20	15.5	-4.5
Biology HL	1988	20	16.0	-4.0
Biology HL	1989	20	15.4	-4.6
French B SL	1988	20	15.8	-4.2
French B SL	1989	20	19.8	-0.2
French B HL	1988	20	19.4	-0.6
French B HL	1989	20	18.6	-1.4

Discrepancies were, overall, higher for Biology than for French. Moreover, at both levels of both subjects, as multiple-choice and internal assessment account for two of the four examination components, the reduced effective weight of both in each case must mean that at least one of the other two components has a higher effective than intended weight. For French B SL at both sessions the increased effective weight is shared by both the other components, Paper 2 and the external oral examination (see Appendix 14.1). The same effect is observed in Biology at both levels and for both sessions, where Paper 2 (data-based questions) and Paper 3 (essay-type questions) each have higher effective than intended weights (substantially so in the case of HL Paper 3, 1988 and 1989). The pattern in these three examinations at both sessions suggests that the components other than multiple-choice and internal assessment picked up the excess weight created by the reduced influence of multiple-choice and internal assessment. French B HL, however, the fourth of the subjects containing both multiple-choice and internal assessment, does not fit this pattern: here the weights 'lost' by Paper 1 (multiple-choice) and the internal assessment have been joined by a considerable weighting 'loss' by the oral component, all losses being absorbed by Paper 2. The suggestion that there is perhaps something about the oral component which causes it to have a reduced influence in this case was investigated further.

The Oral Component

The patterns so far observed in multiple-choice and internal assessment might suggest that a pattern would emerge with respect to the oral examination of English A and French B which, in 1988 and 1989 sessions, was conducted in most cases by a visiting external examiner. The figures, however, do not show the degree of similarity encountered elsewhere (Table 14.4).

TABLE 14.4

INTENDED AND EFFECTIVE PERCENTAGE WEIGHTS ON IB EXAMINATIONS FOR THE ORAL COMPONENT, BY SUBJECT, LEVEL, AND YEAR

Subject	Year	Intended Weight %	Effective Weight %	Diff %
French B SL	1988	35	38.7	3.7
French B SL	1989	35	37.2	2.2
French B HL	1988	25	18.6	-6.4
French B HL	1989	25	21.1	-3.9
English A SL	1988	30	28.9	-1.1
English A SL	1989	30	28.3	-1.7
English A HL	1988	30	27.4	-2.6
English A HL	1989	30	30.1	0.1

The discrepancies between intended and effective weights for English A, HL and SL, are not particularly marked and although for 1989 at HL effective weight is higher than intended, rather than *vice versa* as in 1988 HL and 1988/1989 SL, the difference is very small (0.1%). French B HL for both sessions shows a rather more marked effect, with effective weights lower than intended in both 1988 and 1989. French B SL results, however, follow a different pattern from French B HL or English A and the greater effective weight than intended weight for SL in both 1988 and 1989 bears closer consideration.

English A, at both SL and HL, is composed of a written paper, oral examination, and internally assessed components. Where the effect of the oral component is reduced, it could perhaps be attributed to the fact that there is a tendency for oral examiners to use the higher end of the scale to a greater extent than the lower end, causing a certain amount of 'bunching' and consequently a reduced effect on the total mark. At both levels and in both sessions, the written paper has 'absorbed' the weight by which both the orals and internally assessed components were reduced (Appendix 14.4). A similar, if more marked, effect could be attributed to the same factor for French B HL, where the written paper (Paper 2) 'absorbed' the weight 'lost' by each of the multiple-choice, oral and internally assessed components. For French B SL results in both 1988 and 1989, however, the weights 'lost' by the multiple-choice and internally assessed components have been absorbed by the written paper and the oral, suggesting that the French B oral marks are more widely spread at SL than they are at HL.

This discrepancy in the apparent spread of marks for the oral components at HL and SL may well be attributable to the populations of students entered for the respective examinations. HL, chosen by far fewer students than SL (e.g., 400 at HL in 1989 compared with 1,637 at SL) would tend to be selected by those intending to specialise in this area, while SL would tend to be selected by those who wish to study French B simply as one of their supporting subjects. When considered alongside the fact that the study of Language B is compulsory for all Diploma candidates, and that French B is the most widely-offered Language B in IB schools, it seems likely that a substantial number of students offering French B SL will be doing so, not because they are necessarily gifted or well motivated in the subject, but rather because its study is required as a means of conforming to the regulations governing the award of the IB Diploma. HL students, meanwhile, who have chosen to specialise, will be likely to be better motivated and possibly more gifted in the subject area. It would therefore seem reasonable to conclude that a wider range of ability might be evident in the distribution of marks for French B at SL than in those for HL, resulting in the marks for the oral component at SL not being reduced in influence on the total mark to the extent observed at HL.

CONCLUSION

The evidence gathered in this study suggests that the calculation of effective weights of examination components, as a routine part of post-examination analysis of results in every subject and at every examination session, would be a valuable contribution to the investigation of the validity of IB examinations. Such routine analysis for all future examination sessions is therefore recommended. Having established that discrepancies exist between intended and effective weightings, consideration needs to be given to what action should subsequently be taken. Possible strategies include adjusting candidates' marks for the component in question using scaling factors (referred to, albeit with reservations, by Adams and Wilmut, 1981) and the application of an interative process (Fowles, 1974). In a personal communication, M.J. Cresswell (1992) however confirmed that the policy of Examination Boards in England and Wales continues to be that referred to in his paper (Cresswell, 1982), of calculating routinely the effective weights of all examination components after each examination session, but of not subsequently making any adjustments to marks to bring intended and effective weights into line during the processing of examination data leading to the award of grades. Rather, information regarding discrepancies between intended and effective weights is communicated, after the award of grades, to those involved in the setting of future examinations as a form of feedback with respect to the validity of the previous examination.

Consistent with the policy adopted by Examination Boards in England and Wales, it can be further recommended in the IB context that the results of such analysis should be similarly fed back routinely, after grade awarding, to Chief Examiners and others responsible for the setting and marking of written examinations. Such feedback would serve to keep examiners and permanent staff better informed of the extent to which examinations are meeting their published aims (and thus of the extent of their validity). Where large discrepancies exist on a regular basis, such feedback could encourage, for example, the setting of papers with questions which better discriminate between candidates of different abilities. Again, consistent with the policy of Examination Boards in England and Wales, it is recommended that no action should be taken to adjust marks in the IB examination during the grade awarding process on the basis of this feedback. The question of what, if any, adjustment should be made to rectify discrepancies between intended and effective weights is clearly, however, the subject of on-going debate and one which should be kept under review.

REFERENCES

Adams, R. M., & Murphy, R. J. L. (1982). The achieved weights of examination components. *Educational Studies*, *8*, 15-22.

Adams, R. M., & Wilmut J. (1981). A measure of the weights of examination components and scaling to adjust them. *Statistician*, *30*, 263-269.

Cresswell, M. J. (1982). *Achieved and intended weights*. Paper based on an Associated Examining Board Research Unit Seminar, Guildford, Surrey.

Fowles, D. (1974). *The CSE: Two research studies*. London: Evans/Methuen.

International Baccalaureate Organisation. (1985). *General guide to the International Baccalaureate*. (5th edition). Geneva: Author.

Thompson, J. J. (1988). Presentation at International Baccalaureate Seminar, University of London.

Wilmott, A. S., & Hall, G. W. (1975). *O Level examined: The effect of question choice*. London: Schools Council Publications Macmillan Education.

APPENDIX 14.1

EFFECTIVE WEIGHTS OF SUBJECTS EXAMINED IN MAY 1988 AND MAY 1989, USING THE 'PART WITH WHOLE COVARIANCE' METHOD

BIOLOGY SL

	Paper 1 (mcq)	Paper 2 (data-based)	Paper 3 (essay)	I.A.	Year
Intended Weight (%)	20	20	40	20	1988/89
Effective Weight (%)	16.6	23.6	41.5	18.3	1988
	15.5	24.9	45.2	14.4	1989

BIOLOGY HL

	Paper 1 (mcq)	Paper 2 (data-based)	Paper 3 (essay)	I.A.	Year
Intended Weight (%)	20	20	40	20	1988/89
Effective Weight (%)	16.0	20.3	49.7	14.0	1988
	15.4	22.3	50.3	12.0	1989

FRENCH B SL

	Paper 1 (mcq)	Paper 2 (essay)	Oral	I.A.	Year
Intended Weight (%)	20	30	35	15	1988/89
Effective Weight (%)	15.8	34.1	38.7	11.4	1988
	19.8	32.2	37.2	10.8	1989

FRENCH B HL

	Paper 1 (mcq)	Paper 2 (essay)	Oral	I.A.	Year
Intended Weight (%)	20	40	25	15	1988/89
Effective Weight (%)	19.4	50.5	18.6	11.5	1988
	18.6	51.1	21.1	9.2	1989

ENGLISH A SL

	Paper 1 (essay)	Oral	I.A.	Year
Intended Weight (%)	50	30	20	1988/89
Effective Weight (%)	57.8	28.9	13.3	1988
	56.5	28.3	15.2	1989

ENGLISH A HL

	Paper 1 (essay)	Oral	I.A.	Year
Intended Weight (%)	50	30	20	1988/89
Effective Weight (%)	57.7	27.4	14.9	1988
	55.6	30.1	14.3	1989

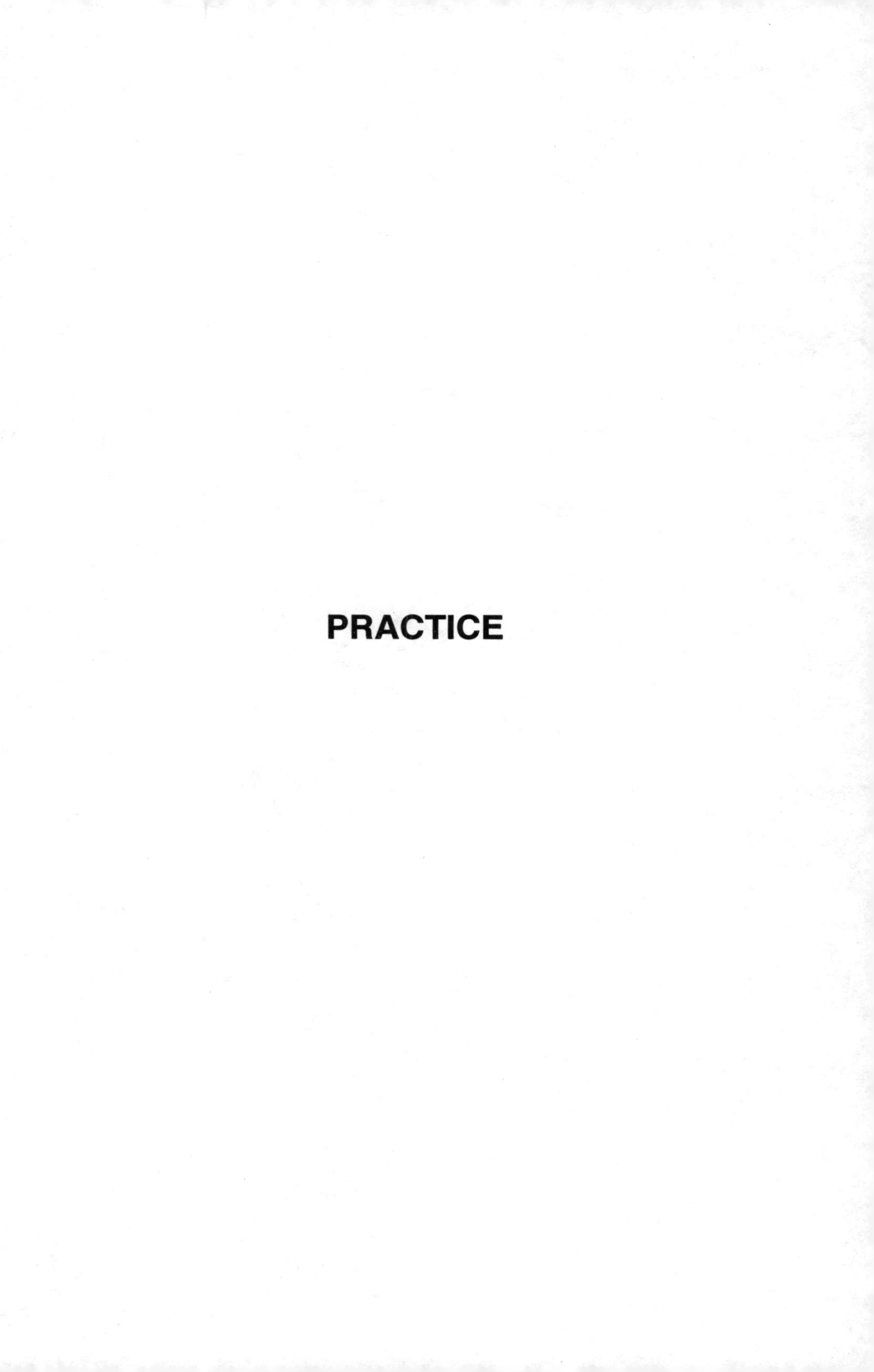

PRACTICE

AFRICA

15. SYSTEMS OF ADMISSION TO HIGHER EDUCATION IN ANGLOPHONE WEST AFRICAN COUNTRIES

S. A. Esezobor
West African Examinations Council,
Accra

Admission to higher education in Anglophone West African countries in the 1940s and 1950s (just before independence) was geared mainly towards the production of administrators, teachers, and even clergy. The universities were few in number—Fourah Bay College in Sierrra Leone, Legon in Ghana, Ibadan in Nigeria, and the University of Liberia. The first three were established in the tradition of British universities. Entry requirements were similar to those in British universities except that a concessionary entrance examination was offered to enable high achieving School Certificate (SC) or General Certificate of Education (GCE) O-level certificate holders to be admitted for a two-year inter-B.A. or inter-B.Sc. programme. Among the basic requirements for entry into Fourah Bay, Legon, and Ibadan in the early days were credits in the English language, Mathematics, and Latin.

In the late 1950s and in the 1960s, sixth forms blossomed to supply candidates for direct entry to West African universities. While Ghana adopted the system of admission through the possession of A-level qualifications, admissions in Nigeria and Sierra Leone were largely dominated by SC/GCE O-level qualifications. In Nigeria, the groundwork could be said to have been prepared by the University of Nigeria, Nsukka, which was established in 1960. It admitted students with SC/GCE O-level and similar qualifications, had no tutelage affiliations to U.K. universities and, therefore, awarded its own degrees from its inception.

ADMISSION CRITERIA

In general, admission criteria to West African universities are similar. A minimum of five passes in SC/GCE O-level subjects including English language and Mathematics is required for concessionary entry and a minimum of two good

GCE A-level passes for direct entry. In Ghana, three good GCE A-level passes and a pass in the General Paper are required. In Liberia, passes in four subject areas (Mathematics, Science, Language Arts, and Social Science) are the basic requirements. Departmental and faculty requirements have to be fulfilled by applicants in all cases. Mature students, usually 30 years old and over, are given special consideration. Entrance requirements for non-degree courses (diplomas and certificates) are usually lower than those for degree courses.

CONTROL OF ADMISSIONS

Each institution in Ghana, Nigeria, Sierra Leone, and Liberia has its own guidelines for admission and tends to control its admission processes using the results of O-level, A-level, Senior School Certificate, and Senior High School Certificate examinations conducted by the West African Examinations Council (WAEC). Under this system a candidate could apply to two or more institutions in the country during one academic year in the hope that, if not offered admission into one, there was the possibility of gaining admission into another. There have been many instances of candidates being offered admission to two or three universities in the country at the same time for the same or for different courses. In most cases, universities kept offers open till it was too late to get other qualified candidates to fill the resultant vacancies. This created loss of admission opportunities for many qualified candidates. However, the problem has now been resolved through the process of late admissions where the institution re-offers the vacancies to other candidates on the waiting list after a period of time.

To deal with the problem of multiple offers in Nigeria, the Joint Admissions and Matriculation Board (JAMB) was set up in 1977. It conducts matriculation examinations for all candidates seeking admission into universities in Nigeria. In practice, therefore, an applicant not only has to pass at credit level in the relevant subjects at the SC/GCE in Nigeria, but also has to reach certain minimum standards in the University Matriculation Examination (UME) conducted by the Board (see Joint Admissions and Matriculation Board, 1991). It is not uncommon to find a candidate attaining the minimum requirements in the University Matriculation Examination without obtaining the required credit passes in the SSC examination or the SC/GCE O-level examination.

It may be noted that the O-level, A-level, Senior High School, and Senior School Certificate examinations on which minimum entry requirements and the departmental/faculty requirements are based are terminal external examinations conducted by the West African Examinations Council. The Nigeria Senior School Certificate and the Liberia Senior High School Certificate examinations, however, have continuous assessment components which are school-based and are conducted by teachers in their individual schools.

The University Matriculation Examination in Nigeria, as the name implies, is an entrance examination which is also conducted by an external agency, the Joint Admissions and Matriculation Board (JAMB) referred to above. Other entrance examinations, including aptitude and placement tests, may be conducted individually by higher institutions. Personal interviews are similarly conducted individually by institutions, while age, post-school experience, and school recommendations are further considerations in the selection processes.

PROBLEMS OF ACCESS

A steady increase in the population of Ghana and difficult economic conditions are now affecting the system of admission to higher institutions. More and more students now possess the basic qualifications for university admission but the number of places available for any course of study remains limited. Less than 50% of qualified applicants gain admission. With continuous increase in the number of secondary school candidates this percentage will no doubt decrease and demand can be expected to outpace the number of places available in institutions for a long time.

Because of inadequate resources leading to inadequate facilities such as lecture rooms, library space, laboratory space, and equipment and because of unfavourable teacher-student ratios in the institutions of higher education, admission is very competitive and access is becoming more difficult. Possession of the minimum entry qualifications does not therefore necessarily guarantee admission to a chosen course and many qualified students are denied access. The recent opening of a university in Tamale in northern Ghana will go some way toward relieving the pressure on university space.

Policies relating to access must, however, always take account of employment opportunities. The call on the West African Examinations Council to conduct competitive examinations for appointment to certain positions in the civil service is an indication that there is an over-production of graduates with some qualifications.

TECHNICAL CONSIDERATIONS

The separate external examinations conducted by the West African Examinations Council (WAEC) and the Joint Admissions and Matriculation Board (JAMB) in Nigeria are of uniform standards and are on the whole the stepping stones for admission to higher education. The greatest concern seems to have been with the reliability and validity of these examinations. WAEC carried out some research studies, prominent among which was *The Reliability of O-level Examinations* (Soriyan, 1972). The results of this study showed that the reliability coefficients of O-level examinations for 1970-1972 were satisfactory in Mathematics, the Sciences, Art, English language, and Geography (mostly over 0.86).

A predictive validity study which related performance at the First University Examinations (FUE) at the University of Ghana to performance in O-level Mathematics and English language, which are additional requirements for admission, has also been carried out (Wuddah et al., 1991). The results of this study indicated that performance in O-level Mathematics predicts with reasonable accuracy performance at FUE in all faculties while performance in O-level English language predicts FUE performance in the Faculty of Arts only.

Comparability studies have also been carried out. Awomolo et al. (1987) reported that there were differences in standards between WAEC A-level subjects. More recent studies on comparability of standards confirm this finding and indicate further that grades awarded in A-level Science subjects are out of line with general standards (Wuddah et al., 1989). The findings suggest that a grade C in one subject may not be taken as equivalent to a Grade C in other subjects, a condition which is vital to the fairness of university admission procedures.

OTHER CONSIDERATIONS

Admission to higher education institutions is open to all without regard to sex, ethnicity, language, or socioeconomic background. In Nigeria, the federal government has directed that in federal universities, a percentage of candidates should be selected on merit and a further percentage on the basis of place of residence which in most cases is the geographical or socio-cultural area contiguous to the university. A proportion of places is also reserved for candidates from the educationally less developed states and for foreign applicants. There are nine state universities whose first obligation is to applicants indigenous to the states funding them.

An examination of applicants to the University of Ghana from 1989 to 1991 indicates that the number has increased over that time from 4,124 to 5,900. While the position of females improved over the period, the ratio of male to female applicants in 1991 was still 3 to 1. About three times more students apply each year to pursue courses in the Humanities than in the Sciences despite the government's avowed intention to shift emphasis from the Humanities to the Pure and Applied Sciences. (In Nigeria, government policy is to aim at 60% intake in the Sciences and 40% in the Humanities.)

In 1989, 44.23% of applicants were admitted to the University of Ghana. That figure had decreased slightly (to 42.15%) in 1990 and had further decreased (to 41.86%) in 1991. The percentages of females that were admitted were 44.89, 40.49, and 46.69 for 1989, 1990, and 1991 respectively (University of Ghana, 1989-1991).

A similar pattern is to be found in Fourah Bay College, Sierra Leone, where the numbers are much smaller than at the University of Ghana. The total numbers admitted were 561, 544, and 623 for the years 1989, 1990, and 1991 respectively.

In Sierra Leone, the disproportion between males and females is similar to that in Ghana. In 1991, it was 3.7 to 1.

More students are admitted to courses in the non-science subjects than in the science subjects (about 5 to 1 in 1991) because of lack of laboratory places and other facilities for science. The small proportion of females compared to males in science courses might also be due to the fact that some females are of the erroneous view that science-based subjects are difficult and that only males can study them. Efforts were, however, made in 1991 to increase the intake for the sciences so as to encourage and promote scientific and technological education for the development of the nation.

FOREIGN STUDENTS

Some provision is made each year to admit foreign students to universities in Ghana and Sierra Leone, though the numbers are small. Numbers admitted to the University of Ghana were 56, 94, and 78 in 1989, 1990, and 1991 respectively. Foreign student enrolment for the same years at Fourah Bay College in Sierra Leone were 51, 78, and 48.

SYSTEMS OF ADMISSION IN THE FUTURE

Under the national policy on education which became effective in 1987, the educational system in Ghana is being restructured to make it more relevant to the needs and aspirations of individuals and society. Under the new structure, at the conclusion of primary education, which has changed only a little, students enter a new three-year Junior Secondary programme which is replacing the first three years of lower secondary. The Basic Education Certificate examination is taken by students at the completion of Junior Secondary school. Students then transfer to a Senior Secondary programme at the end of which they sit for the Senior Secondary School Certificate Examination (SSSCE) for admission to four-year degree programmes in the universities.

The first Senior Secondary School Certificate Examination in Ghana was held in 1993. The first implication of this educational reform is that during a transition period, admission officers in higher institutions are faced with evaluating credentials from two somewhat different educational structures, one going back to 1966, the other introduced in 1993. Secondly, universities will be required to restructure their programmes in terms of content and duration to accommodate the change of programme in Senior Secondary schools.

Thirdly, the system of admission will change from reliance on O-level and A-level examination results to Senior Secondary School Certificate examinations. There are indications that universities will organise special courses to prepare applicants for the major study they will undertake. The situation will be similar to that in Nigeria on the commencement of the SSC examination in that country in 1988.

CONCLUSION

The first institutions of higher education in Anglophone West African countries served by the West African Examinations Council were few in number and had only a handful of students. Today, the number of higher institutions in some member countries has increased considerably as well as the number of applicants seeking admission to them.

The first university in Nigeria was established in 1948 with just a few hundred students. By 1962, the number of universities had increased to four. Now, 30 years later, there are 36 universities, six degree-awarding colleges (affiliated to a university), 26 polytechnics, and 19 colleges of education. The Joint Admissions and Matriculation Board handles applications to these institutions and the task of selection and placement is by no means easy. While more students now possess the basic qualifications for university admission, this does not necessarily guarantee admission to a chosen course because of the limited places.

The increase in the number of students completing secondary education each year is not matched by a corresponding increase in the number of higher education places, either through the expansion of existing institutions or the establishment of new ones. Accordingly, demand will for a long time to come outstrip the number of places available in higher education institutions.

REFERENCES

Awomolo, A. A. et al. (1987). *A report of the evaluation of the standards of WAEC GCE Advanced Level Examination*. Tedro:West African Examinations Council.

Joint Admissions and Matriculation Board. (1991). *Guidelines for admission to first degree courses in Nigerian universities.* Lagos: Author.

Soriyan, M. A. (1972). T*he reliability of Ordinary Level Examinations*. WAEC RR 107. Lagos: West African Examinations Council.

University of Ghana. (1989-1991). *Statistics of admission into the University of Ghana, Lagos.* Accra: Author.

Wuddah, A. A. et al. (1989). *Between-subject comparability of standards at the June GCE Advanced-Level Examinations*. WAEC RR 4. Accra: West African Examinations Council.

Wuddah, A. A. et al. (1991). *Performance at the First University Examination (FUE) relative to that at Ordinary Level English Language and Mathematics Examinations.* WAEC RR 9. Accra: West African Examinations Council.

16. ADMISSION TO HIGHER EDUCATION IN KENYA

Musau Kithuka[1]
Kenya National Examinations Council, Nairobi

The term 'higher education' is used within the Kenyan context to mean university education. In the African continent, and indeed in the world in general, higher education is seen as the source of highly qualified technical manpower and the pinnacle of human resource development in any economy. It may be argued that a highly developed human resource is of paramount importance since, unlike material resources, it cannot easily be provided at short notice (see Kamunge, 1988).

Higher education and training are associated in Kenya, as elsewhere, with higher economic returns to individuals. As a result, university education is the priority aspiration among Kenyans, followed by the aspiration to a post-schools' training which will impart marketable skills. These aspirations have led to a rapid expansion of education at all levels. Since about 60% of Kenya's population is below the age of 24 years, the demand for education at all levels far outstrips the available resources. Between 1965 and 1985, the percentage of an age cohort attending primary school increased from 54 to 94, the percentage attending secondary school from 4 to 20, and the percentage attending university from almost 0 to 1 (World Bank, 1988). Female enrolment trailed behind that of male enrolment in all cases. *Per capita* expenditure on higher education during the same period was much higher

1 I wish to acknowledge the support and assistance given to me by the British Council and the Association of Indian Universities through the Indian High Commission in Kenya in establishing contact with universities in the U.K. and India, Professor J.N.K Mugambi, the Academic Registrar, University of Nairobi, for providing data on admission in the local public universities and Professor M. Maleche, Deputy Vice-Chancellor, Moi University, for facilitating data collection.
Present address: Department of Educational Psychology, Laikipia College Campus, Egerton University, Nyahururu, Kenya.

than for the lower levels of education. Thus, the very small percentage of the population that was able to gain access to higher education received a larger share of the education budget.

Until recently, admission to higher education followed completion of a school career which consisted of seven years in primary school, four years in secondary school, and two years in high school working for A-level examinations. A minimum of three years was required in the university to qualify for a first degree. The system was commonly known as the 7:4:2:3 structure of education. It was often argued that the structure needed to be reformed on the grounds that it was too academic and irrelevant to the socioeconomic needs of the nation. A reform, launched in 1985, called for eight years primary education, four years secondary, and a minimum of four years university education. The reform placed greater emphasis on practical subjects at both primary and secondary levels with a view to promoting self-reliance, and as a prerequisite for further training.

The new structure, commonly known as the 8:4:4, makes provision for an achievement-based examination, the Kenya Certificate of Secondary Education (KCSE) examination at the end of the four-year secondary cycle.

In the old structure, the Kenya Advanced Certificate of Education (KACE) examination, also known as the A-level, was used for selection to university (Kenya. National Examinations Council, 1985-1986b). Candidates were required to sit at one and the same examination, the General Paper and either four principal subjects or three principal subjects and one subsidiary subject or two principal subjects and two subsidiary subjects (Kenya. National Examinations Council, 1985-1986a). No strict control was exercised on the combination of subjects a candidate was required to take. The minimum requirement for university entrance was two principal passes, which were graded at A, B, C, D, and E levels.

Because of the rapid expansion of secondary education in the 1970s and 1980s more candidates qualified for university education than could be admitted. The percentage of candidates who qualified for university entrance on the basis of their Advanced Certificate examination performance ranged between 39% and 49% in the years 1985 to 1988. At the same time, the number of undergraduates attending university in the country more than doubled (from 7,608 in 1985-86 to 18,883 in 1987-88) (Kenya. Central Bureau of Statistics, 1987). While one may assume that the candidates with the highest qualifications were selected, it may also be assumed that many of the other qualified but unsuccessful candidates sought admission to training institutions in Kenya or to foreign universities.

The Kenya Certificate of Secondary Education (KCSE) examination, like the KACE examination which it replaced in 1989, is also an achievement examination used as an instrument of selection for higher education (see Kenya. National Examinations Council, 1991-1992). Candidates are graded on a 12-point scale. Each interval on the point scale has a corresponding letter from A (12 points), A- (11 points), B+ (10 points) .... to E (1 point). By 1989, when the first KCSE examination was held, Kenya had four public universities. All candidates were required to sit 10 subjects which included practical and vocational subjects. To be considered for admission to a degree programme in the public universities, a candidate was required to achieve, at one sitting, a minimum average grade of C+ in the best 10 subjects which should include the five compulsory ones (English, Kiswahili, History and Government, Geography, and Mathematics). Between 1989 and 1991, approximately 10% of candidates have been able to meet this criterion. This criterion changed upwards to B- in 1993.

Candidates who satisfy the basic entry requirement enter a competition for a place on the course for which they have applied. The competition is based on a cluster of five specified subjects and the available places are allocated to candidates with the best results in those subjects. For example, for candidates for the Bachelor of Architecture degree programme, the relevant subjects are English, Geography, Physics or Physical Science, History and Government, and Mathematics.

The percentage of 'qualified' candidates who achieve university entrance has decreased dramatically since the changeover from A-level examinations to the KCSE—from between 40 and 50% to 10 percent. It would seem that if more university places were available, a considerably larger number of students could meet the demands of university education.

Since the introduction of the 8:4:4 reform in 1986, the public has argued that the curricula at the primary and secondary levels are too broad and demanding and are overloaded to the point that a lot of the content cannot be covered within the specified period. Many schools have had to hold classes in the evenings and over weekends. The secondary curriculum was evaluated in 1989 by the Kenya Institute of Education (KIE) which is the body charged with the development of national curricula. The findings showed that the curricula needed to be reviewed in terms of content and examination subjects. Following this evaluation, the government has reduced the number of examination subjects required from ten to eight and the compulsory subjects from five to three. This change affected candidates who sat the KCSE examination in 1993.

ADMISSION PROCEDURES AND CRITERIA

Due to the limited number of university vacancies, admissions are controlled centrally through the University Joint Admissions Board which consists of a rotational chair who is a vice-chancellor of one of the universities, principals of colleges and institutes, and deans of faculties. It is serviced by a secretariat. After the release of KCSE results, the board prepares an admissions list of all candidates who have satisfied the criterion of a mean grade of C+ and above for each degree programme. This list is in order of merit based on the cluster of five subjects appropriate to candidates' programme choices. For example, candidates whose first choice is Bachelor of Science in Agriculture are listed under this degree programme in order of their performance in the appropriate cluster of five subjects. The board decides on the cut-off point for admission to a programme. In the 1991/92 academic year, the cluster mean grade for this programme in the University of Nairobi was 30 points (an average of grade C in five subjects). There were 150 vacancies in the programme. The 93 candidates who met the criterion of C+ and who had applied for this degree programme as first choice were admitted. Those who had made this programme their second choice and met the cluster criteria were considered. If vacancies were still unfilled, applicants who gave the programme as their third choice were considered.

On the other hand, the number of applicants satisfying the C+ criterion may exceed the number of places on a course, as happened, for example, in the Bachelor of Science (Agricultural Engineering) degree (95 applicants for 34 vacancies). In this case the best 34 candidates were offered places and the other applicants were transferred to other degree programmes, specified as their second, third, or fourth choice, if vacancies existed.

Indices showing the comparative level of competition for degree programmes in the University of Nairobi in the 1991/92 academic year have been computed. The index (positive sign) is simply the percentage of applicants who are not offered a place and (negative sign) the percentage of non-applicants who were transferred into programmes against their first choice. Very high indices were recorded for B.P.H. (94%) and B.D.S. (92%) while very low indices were recorded for B.A. (-1432) and B.Sc. (-1127). Programmes such as B.P.H. and B.D.S. require very high grades for admission because of the disproportion between 'qualified' applicants and available places. B.A. and B.Sc. programmes, on the other hand, were unpopular and had to be filled with second, third, and possibly fourth choices.

Students who do not gain access to a public university are advised to seek admission to foreign universities. Applications to universities in India are co-ordinated by the Ministry of Education. Colleges and universities in India prefer to admit students holding KACE certificates into the three-year degree programme and those with KCSE qualifications into four-year programmes. The highest proportion of Kenyan students who attend a foreign university go to India. In 1991, the figure was 2,205. The next most popular countries are the United States of America (584 in 1991) and the United Kingdom (342 in 1991). Because of the large number of Kenyan applications to the Indian Universities, the Association of Indian Universities sent an evaluation team to Kenya in 1991 to evaluate KCSE standards for purposes of admission to universities in India. The team looked at curriculum development at the curriculum centre, the implementation of the curriculum in a sample of schools, and the curriculum evaluation procedures and awards of the Kenya National Examinations Council. Among the findings of the team was that an achievement of 5 C grades at KCSE level was equivalent to 2 A-level principal passes. A candidate with this level of achievement qualifies for admission into any Indian university degree programme provided the grades are attained in subjects which form the necessary combination for the programme.

For some years after 1989, Kenyan universities operated two degree programmes concurrently: a three-year programme for the 1989 A-level class and a four-year programme for holders of the KCSE. A recent survey carried out in some local and foreign universities in the UK and India has shown that most university lecturers (60%) feel that KCSE holders are capable of undertaking the degree programmes successfully, while 40% feel that they need a pre-university course. These findings should be regarded as preliminary given the comparatively short period of time that KCSE students have been at university and given that the four-year university cycle was introduced as recently as 1989.

REFERENCES

Kamunge, J. M. (1988). *Report of the presidential working party on education and manpower training for the next decade and beyond*. Nairobi: Government Printer.

Kenya. Central Bureau of Statistics. (1987). *Public universities*. Nairobi: Author.

Kenya. National Examinations Council. (1985-1986a). *Kenya Advanced Certificate of Education: Regulations and syllabuses*. Nairobi: Business Forms & Systems.

Kenya. National Examinations Council. (1985-1986b). *Kenya Certificate of Education: Regulations and syllabuses*. Nairobi: Business Forms & Systems.

Kenya. National Examinations Council. (1991-1992). *Kenya Certificate of Secondary Education: Regulations and syllabuses*. Nairobi: Business Forms & Systems.

World Bank. (1988). *World development report*. New York: Oxford University Press.

17. THE CHANGING NATURE OF SECOND LEVEL AND HIGHER EDUCATION IN KENYA

Jeckonia Opinya
Commission for Higher Education, Nairobi

Kenya's educational system has undergone major structural changes over the last decade which have had a significant effect on admission to higher education and, also, on the practical orientation of education and training in the country. The 7-4-2-3 system of education was replaced by an 8-4-4 system (Kenya. Ministry of Education, 1984). In essence, a year was added to the primary cycle which culminates in the Kenya Certificate of Primary Education (KCPE) after eight years. The former four-year O-level and two year A-level secondary programmes were merged into a four-year secondary cycle leading to the Kenya Certificate of Secondary Education (KCSE). A year was added to the undergraduate degree programme so that a bachelor's degree now takes a minimum of four years of study.

Change is also in evidence in the new curricula which were introduced for upper primary and secondary education and which were broad-based and included practical subjects. For example, the secondary education curriculum has the following subjects grouped under five main headings: (i) Communication: English, Kiswahili, foreign languages (e.g., French, German, Arabic); (ii) Mathematics; (iii) Sciences: Physical Sciences, Biological Sciences, Biology, Chemistry, Physics; (iv) Humanities: History and Government, Geography, Religious Education, Social Education and Ethics; (v) Applied Subjects: Accounting, Commerce, Economics, Typewriting and Office Practice, Home Science, Art and Design, Agriculture, Woodwork, Metalwork, Power Mechanics, Electricity, Drawing and Design, Music, Physical Education. The new curricula were introduced in 1986. Graduates of the second cycle were admitted to higher education (universities and training institutions) in 1990.

INSTITUTIONAL STRUCTURE OF POST-SECONDARY EDUCATION

There are about 629 post-secondary institutions in Kenya. These include 17 which use the term university in their title. There are four public universities and two university colleges (with about 41,000 students: 39,000 undergraduates and 2,000 post-graduates) and eleven private universities. There are three more under construction with a student population of 2,000.

The other institutions include 18 public teacher training colleges (15 primary with seven more under construction, and three secondary, with about 19,000 students); three private primary teacher training colleges (with 3,000 students); three public national polytechnics (with about 5,000 students); 126 public training institutions, run by various government ministries and state corporations (with about 15,000 students); and 462 private training institutions (with about 22,000 students). About 10,000 Kenyan students pursue higher education abroad, mainly in India, Britain, Canada, and the United States of America.

ISSUES ARISING FROM THE CHANGING NATURE OF SECOND-LEVEL AND HIGHER EDUCATION

There are five issues that have arisen as a result of the changing nature of second-level and higher education in Kenya. These relate to growth in enrolment and institutions; co-ordination of post-secondary institutions; cost-sharing in public institutions; admission requirements; and course duration.

Growth in Enrolment and Institutions.

The implementation of the reformed second cycle of the 8-4-4 system of education witnessed growth in the number of both public and private institutions and an increase in student population. This is consonant with the government's policy of expanding enrolment at the tertiary level. In 1989 for instance, there were five university level public institutions with a total enrolment of 27,294 students. However, in the following year, the number of institutions at this level had increased by three and the total number of students had risen to 41,000. Similar growth was experienced in other post-secondary institutions. The number of certificate and diploma-granting institutions rose from about 450 in 1989 to 600 in 1990. Most of the new institutions were established by entrepreneurs. The increase in the number of institutions has been accompanied by a rise in the student population. There were about 56,000 students in these institutions in 1989. A year later, the numbers had increased to 77,000.

Co-ordination of Post-Secondary Institutions

Expansion of post-secondary institutions ushered in great diversity in facilities, equipment, courses, and standards of training offered in these institutions. In 1985 the government, aware of the need for co-ordination of education in the institutions, established the Commission for Higher Education under the Universities Act, 1985 (Kenya, 1985). Its functions include the planning of higher education, the funding of public universities and accreditation of private universities.

Cost-sharing in Public Institutions

Until 1990, training in public post-secondary training institutions was free. In some institutions, trainees were given a stipend for their out-of-pocket expenses. At the university level, all students were eligible for loans which incorporated personal allowances. With increased enrolment at second level, the government introduced cost-sharing in its post-secondary training institutions, including the universities. Students admitted to these institutions are now expected to pay fees. In the case of university students, the government established a bursary scheme at each university to cater for financially needy students who cannot pay the fees.

Admission Requirements

Admission to higher education in Kenya depends, to a large extent, on results obtained in the Kenya Certificate of Secondary Education (KCSE) Examination. In this examination, candidates' performance in individual subjects is graded on the basis of a 12-point scale, with 12 points being the highest and 1 point the lowest score. Points are converted to grades represented by a letter in the following way: 12 (A), 11 (A-), 10 (B+), 9 (B), 8 (B-), 7(C+), 6 (C), 5 (C-), 4 (D+), 3 (D), 2 (D-), 1 (E). In addition students are awarded a single point score, which is the average of the total number of points scored on any ten subjects. This average score is also converted to a grade.

Universities. For a candidate to be eligible for admission to a university, public or private, he or she must have obtained at one sitting, a minimum average grade of C+ in the ten subjects in KCSE. In addition, the applicants must meet the entry requirements of individual programmes which are based on a cluster of five specified subjects. For example, in 1992 candidates wishing to be considered for the Bachelor of Commerce programme were expected to have a minimum of 45 points from the following cluster: English; History and Government; Geography; Mathematics; and another subject from a specified group.

Diploma Awarding Institutions. Candidates wishing to be considered for admission to diploma-awarding institutions are required to hold KCSE with an average grade of C taken at one sitting. Applicants also have to meet course requirements. These vary from programme to programme but a combination of at least three subjects in which an applicant must obtain at least a grade C is needed.

Other Acceptable Qualifications. Some post-secondary institutions admit students on the basis of a student's previous training qualifications or as mature students. Admission to higher education as mature students is mainly a feature of universities and theological colleges.

For instance, one of the minimum entry requirements for Diploma Courses at Egerton University, Njoro in Western Kenya, is a certificate from a recognised agricultural training institute or animal health training institution or equivalent, with distinction (Egerton University, 1989). The same university provides as one of the minimum entry requirements for degree programmes a diploma of Egerton University or equivalent with distinction or credit in a relevant field of specialisation.

Course Duration

The implementation of the 8-4-4 system of education affected the duration of programmes at tertiary level. The minimum duration of degree programmes at the universities is now four years. However, the adoption of the new system did not have an effect on the length of courses for other training institutions. The duration of diploma programmes is still generally three years and that of certificate programmes two years.

CONCLUSION

Kenya's experience resulting from changes to the structure of its education system is an inevitable corollary of broadening access to education and is not unique to the country. Increase in enrolments and in the number of secondary education institutions had a direct effect on admissions to higher education. Undergraduate admissions to public universities rose from 7,382 in 1989 to 21,450 in 1990 while those for other public training institutions increased from 37,000 in 1989 to 56,953 in 1990. This expansion called for co-ordination, which was entrusted to the Commission on Higher Education, to help ward off unplanned development in the country's higher education sector.

Expansion of the higher education sector also saw an increase in government expenditure on education. Indeed, the government spends 37% of the country's total voted recurrent budget on this sector. If no ceiling is imposed, the government may soon have no money to meet other commitments and a decision has been made to reduce the budget allocation for tertiary education to 20 percent. To implement this decision, the government has introduced fees in public post-secondary institutions.

The restructured curricula at second level ensure a broadly based education. The curricula are designed to meet the needs of students who wish to end their formal education at the end of secondary education as well as of those who wish to proceed to further and higher education and training. As has been pointed out it was decided to adopt a two-tier admission procedure. In order to be admitted into a post-secondary programme a person would have to fulfil both the average and cluster grade requirements. The average grade requirement establishes a minimum level of general education while the cluster grade requirements establish a candidate's suitability for a particular course of studies. It is hoped that the new arrangements will facilitate access for Kenyan students to post-secondary education.

REFERENCES

Egerton University. (1989). *Egerton University Catalogue, 1989/90.* Njoro: Author.
Kenya. (1985). *The Universities Act, 1985.* Nairobi: Government of Kenya.
Kenya. (1984). *Careers information booklet. Nairobi:* Ministry of Education.

18. ADMINISTRATION AND UPDATING OF ADMISSION TESTS FOR HIGHER EDUCATION IN LESOTHO

E. M. Sebatane
Institute of Education,
National University of Lesotho

A predominant mode of selecting and admitting students into higher education in Africa has been final high school examinations. These examinations are also used for certification purposes. Before and immediately after the colonial period, the examinations were conducted by Examinations Boards based in Europe. A well known examination body, the Cambridge Examinations Syndicate, conducted the Cambridge Overseas School Certificate (COSC) examinations for a number of English-speaking African countries for a long time. COSC, therefore, was the main selection mechanism. The majority of African countries now administer their own examinations, either at national or regional level. A good example of a regional examination body is the West African Examinations Council (WAEC).

By 1960, African governments had shown interest in tests as selection devices for training and employment (Irvine, 1966). However, until relatively recently, emphasis has always been on achievement tests rather than aptitude tests. An aptitude test is a test designed to assess an individual's ability to succeed in, or profit from, a given training programme or occupation. On the other hand, an achievement test is intended to measure the extent to which a student has attained a body of knowledge provided through systematic instruction.

In this paper, the experience of the National University of Lesotho (NUL) in using a battery of aptitude tests for selection and admission of a special group of potential students (mature age students) is outlined. Lesotho is a small country with a total population of 1.6 million. NUL, which is the only university, has faculties of Agriculture, Education, Humanities, Law, Social Sciences, and Science. There is also a School of Postgraduate Studies which co-ordinates graduate programmes offered by the various faculties. The enrolment is 1,500, of whom 1,000 constitute full-time and 500 part-time students.

The selection procedures adopted for the admission of applicants to the National University of Lesotho through the Mature Age Entry Scheme (AES) include the use of a battery of aptitude tests. The battery is a modified version of what are known as Internationally Developed (I-D) tests. Specifically designed for use in Africa, these tests were originally developed in West Africa during the period 1960-64 under a project sponsored by the United States Agency for International Development (USAID). The project, which was built on research on testing and test development in developing countries, was implemented by the American Institute for Research (AIR). The objectives of the project, according to Schwarz and Krug (1972), were:

> first, to devise techniques of aptitude testing that could be applied in cultures in which standard ability tests are not fully effective; and then, to assist in the application of these techniques to human resources development programs in the developing countries. (p.v)

The project was carried out under the auspices of the West African Examinations Council (WAEC). In 1969, again through USAID and AIR, a new department of WAEC, namely the Test Development and Research Office (TEDRO), was formed. Its aims were: (a) to assist the Council to improve and expand its manpower testing and selection capability; (b) to assist the Council to expand its testing services to all its member countries; and (c) to develop within the member countries an institutional framework for the effective use of manpower testing and selection services by education and government institutions. The Council's member countries are Nigeria, Ghana, Sierra Leone, and the Gambia. Liberia joined the Council officially in 1969 as an associate member. Through TEDRO, the Council conducts a wide-ranging testing programme for selection of candidates for technical and professional training courses at all levels, as well as for selection for clerical, technical, managerial and supervisory positions in commerce, industry, and the civil service. It also undertakes research studies related to this programme.

DESCRIPTION OF THE INTERNATIONALLY DEVELOPED (I-D) TESTS

The I-D tests are standardised tests consisting of multiple-choice items. Their results are expressed in stanine scores. The original battery consists of 21 sub-tests (Snider, 1972). The administration time varies from 10 to 40 minutes, while the number of items ranges from 2 to 200. Some are power tests, while others are speed tests. Simple and effective administration instructions have been developed after many trials. The administration includes the use of some apparatus and visual aids. The tests can either be hand-scored or machine-scored. Three manuals have been developed for the tests: (a) an examiner's manual, which contains administration instructions; (b) a technical manual, containing reliability, validity, and other psychometric data on the tests; and (c) test norms, which provide information on standardisation procedures. There is also information on the methods of combining the tests into series for various selection purposes.

The 21 I-D tests, which measure technical, commercial, and scholastic aptitudes, may be used as a set of 'building blocks' from which many selection series can be constructed, the combination for a given series depending upon the kind of traits to be assessed. The tests measure several aptitudes and it is relatively easy to constitute a series to meet particular needs. The construction of a series involves three stages: (a) selection of tests relevant to the trait; (b) validation of the trial series; and (c) selection of the final series on the basis of the validity trial. If a series does not predict well, another combination of tests may be tried. Tests are designed for candidates with qualifications ranging from no formal schooling to more than eleven years of formal education.

At a finer level, the complete battery consists of reasoning, information, numerical, technical, clerical, and manual sub-tests. It has been shown that the tests measure complementary rather than overlapping abilities (Snider, 1972). This permits the construction of series with a minimum number of tests which assess aptitude with efficient prediction. It also enables users to obtain optimum information with minimum effort, expense, and time. A number of research studies have been carried out to establish the psychometric properties of the tests. Since the tests were developed for use over wide ability ranges, reliabilities and validities tend to be stable under a variety of testing conditions.

Scholastic Series

The scholastic series of the I-D aptitude tests, which is the focus of the present paper, comprises the following sub-tests:

(a) Verbal Analogies (VAL): a verbal reasoning test for people with six to eight years of formal education. It is used to predict success in school or in a job requiring formal studies. It is a power test that most examinees complete in the allotted time. It contains 40 test items. Administration time is 30 minutes.
(b) Verbal Analogies High (VAH): a more advanced form of the above test intended for people with nine to twelve years of formal education.
(c) Reading Comprehension (RDL): a test of ability to read and understand written material. It is used to predict academic potential of examinees with six to eight years of formal education. It is a power test that most examinees complete in the allotted time. It contains 40 items. Total time to administer the test is 30 minutes.
(d) Reading Comprehension (RDH): a more advanced form of the above test requiring reasoning as well as comprehension. It can be used up to university level.
(e) Memory (MEM): a test of the ability to learn and remember material organised in a meaningful way. It is used mainly for selection of secondary school

students. It is a partly speeded test with separately timed halves. It contains 80 items. Total time to administer the test is 20 minutes.

(f) Graphs (GPH): a test of facility in working with a complex graph and thereby of the more general ability to cope with a problem in which a number of variables must be considered and interrelated. It is used to predict success in post-secondary training and education. It is a partly speeded test with separately timed halves. It contains 60 items. Total time to administer the test is 25 minutes.

(g) Arithmetic (RTH): a test of speed and accuracy in doing simple computations. It is used whenever general facility with numbers is required. It is a speeded test with separately timed halves. It contains 150 items. Total time to administer the test is 20 minutes.

(h) Science Information (SCI): a test of interest in science, as shown by the examinee's knowledge of basic facts about a wide range of scientific topics. It is used mainly for selection or guidance into post-secondary science training. It is a power test that most examinees complete in the allotted time. It contains 40 items. Total time to administer the test is 30 minutes.

(i) World Information (WLD): a test of interest in business or public affairs, shown by the examinee's knowledge of current events, civic affairs, and elementary economics. It is used for selection or guidance into commerce, government, and similar fields. It is a power test that most examinees complete in the allotted time. It contains 40 test items. Total time to administer the test is 30 minutes.

The scholastic series exists at three academic levels. (a) The first level (Academic) consists of the sub-tests VAL, RDL, MEM, and RTH. It is appropriate for candidates with six to eight years formal education. Predictive validity coefficients range from .56 to .64, while the reliability coefficient is .91; (b) The sub-tests for the second level (Academic 2) are VAH, RDH, GPH, and RHT. The battery is designed for candidates with nine to ten years formal education. Its predictive validity coefficient is .62 while its coefficient of reliability is .90; (c) The highest level (Academic 3) consists of RDH, GPH, RHT, SCI, and WLD. It is appropriate for candidates with a minimum of 11 years formal education. The predictive validity coefficient is .61 while its coefficient of reliability is .87.

I-D tests have proved useful for the efficient selection of human resources by assisting in ensuring that the people who are given educational and occupational opportunity are those who will make the best use of it.

THE REGIONAL TESTING RESOURCE AND TRAINING CENTRE

The basic I-D test research and development work done in West Africa was followed by adaptation of the tests in Brazil, Korea, Thailand, Iran, Indonesia, and other locations. In 1965, a survey on educational and occupational testing needs in Malawi indicated that the I-D tests could be used in that country with only minor modifications. This led to the establishment of the Regional Testing Resource and Training Centre (RTRTC) in 1969. The Centre, which was funded by USAID, was a joint project between the governments of Malawi, Botswana, Lesotho, and Swaziland. The goal of the project, which was implemented by AIR, was to meet identified educational and occupational selection needs in the four member countries. The specific objectives of the Centre were (a) to develop a system of tests for selection of pupils into secondary education; (b) to advise ministries of education and universities on the development and use of testing programmes for educational and manpower utilisation systems; (c) to develop and implement a system of testing to supplement existing public service selection procedures; and (d) to perform a similar function for the private sector.

The I-D tests were slightly modified and renormed for the region served by RTRTC. The modification involved the following, among other things: (a) systematic omission of some items from certain sub-tests, leading to the shortening of administration time; (b) ample shortening of administration time without eliminating any items in some sub-tests; and (c) weeding out of some items which were obviously culturally unfair for the population served by the Centre. In general, however, the tests remained basically the same as the original battery in terms of format, content, and purpose.

In educational selection, RTRTC assisted in identifying individuals who had the potential for academic success, particularly at the secondary level and above. The Centre established the Secondary School Selection Testing programme which developed a system of ability tests for the Primary School Leaving Examinations' (PSLE) candidates.

The Regional Testing Resource and Training Centre administered I-D tests to diverse groups of candidates applying for occupations in industry, commerce, parastatal organisations, and the civil service, and for places in secondary and high schools, nursing schools, polytechnics, and universities. It provided wide-ranging consultations and professional expertise on the improvement of existing selection procedures. The Centre also provided services on data processing, analysis, and interpretation, and conducted a variety of research studies on testing.

In the mid-1970s, RTRTC ceased to operate as a regional organisation. More emphasis was placed on national centres. In Lesotho, however, the national centre never functioned, although the tests have continued to be used for selection purposes by some tertiary institutions. In other countries, the respective national centres were later amalgamated with other institutions. The Malawi centre was incorporated into the Malawi Examinations Board to form the present Malawi Certificate Examination and Testing Board. In Botswana, the national centre has become a section of the Department of Curriculum Development and Evaluation in the Ministry of Education. In Swaziland, the centre is operating under the Swaziland Educational Testing Programme. The work started by the RTRTC has continued to expand in these three countries. For example, in Botswana, studies on the predictive validity of the I-D test on high school performance have been carried out (Khama & Masie, 1981). The Swaziland Educational Testing Programme has developed the Swaziland Behavioural Assessment Test series which have adopted some I-D tests.

JUSTIFICATION FOR THE USE OF APTITUDE TESTS FOR SELECTION

According to Schwarz and Krug (1972), the use of achievement tests for selection of students into some higher-order training is based on three assumptions. First, the educational experiences that the applicants were provided with by their previous schooling were approximately the same. Second, differences in applicants' relative achievements, given these equivalent experiences, are the result of differences in their individual abilities and characteristics. And, third, advanced courses for which applicants are being selected will require the same abilities.

If these assumptions are justified, then we would expect that applicants should continue to achieve at different levels, just as before. It would thus be logical for, say, the university to admit the highest achievers by using achievement examination results such as those of the Cambridge Overseas School Certificate (COSC). However, in the case of Lesotho at any rate, while the third assumption might reasonably be accepted, the first and second assumptions cannot. Both the MAES and other candidates have varying levels of educational experiences. This is due to variations in quality among secondary and high schools in the country, in terms of instructional facilities and teachers' qualifications. It is conceivable that some students may be denied admission into higher education not because they have low scholastic ability but because they happen to have attended poor schools. This calls for the use of aptitude tests, which are less dependent on the quality of schooling but rather emphasise the potential of the student. The failure of the first assumption to hold may lead us to reject the use of achievement examinations as a sole selection instrument. One may further argue that the predictive value of COSC has not been empirically established, at least for Lesotho.

Other important areas in which aptitude testing plays an important role are manpower development, assessment, and utilisation. Scarce financial resources and a shortage of skilled manpower for development underline the need to identify potential candidates who can benefit most from certain courses of study or job opportunities. Aptitude tests can help in this endeavour. They can also assist in achieving optimum allocation and channelling of candidates into appropriate training programmes commensurate with the abilities and talents of the candidates concerned.

THE MATURE AGE ENTRY SCHEME

The Mature Age Entry Scheme (MAES) was launched in 1970/71 as an alternative route for entry into the then University of Botswana, Lesotho and

Swaziland (UBLS) for full-time study (Sebatane, 1975). The scheme was designed to identify those who had, in one way or another, been unable to meet the entrance requirements and offer them a chance to pursue university studies on equal terms with other students. Applicants had to be at least 25 years of age. Originally, a maximum of 10 places were reserved for MAES students from each of the three countries that were served by the university. Later the Lesotho Government stipulated that 20% of the annual intake should be MAES candidates.

After the break-up of UBLS, NUL continued to operate the scheme. The screening procedure for candidates seeking admission into NUL through MAES consists of the following components (in addition to letters of recommendation): performance on I-D tests; performance on an English test, which consists of an essay and comprehension; an interview by the admissions committee; and any other qualifications candidates may have.

The I-D series used is selected from the Academic 2 and Academic 3 levels of the scholastic aptitude tests, namely VAH, RDH, GPH, RTH and SCI. Performance on SCI is considered only for candidates who wish to pursue a B.Sc. or other science-related programme. The English test, on the other hand, is basically an achievement test.

MAES is based on the assumption that people with scholastic potential and relevant experience can achieve excellence without good high-school credentials. A more recent argument for alternative entry routes for degree programmes was that COSC results were deteriorating in Lesotho. If this trend continues, the university could find it difficult to meet its admission quota, particularly in science-related programmes.

Prior to 1978, the English scripts of only those candidates who had scored above a certain cut-off point in I-D tests were marked. The cut-off point itself was arbitrarily set and tended to change from year to year. To be admitted, a candidate had to both pass the English test and obtain a mark at or above the cut-off point in the I-D tests. Since 1978, changes have been introduced in some aspects of this selection model. First, it was decided that all English scripts should be marked. Second, the cut-off point for the I-D test results was fixed at 18, which is 50% of the possible total score (stanine of 36) for the battery. Third, all candidates with a score of 17 or better in the I-D tests are invited for interview. Fourth, any candidate with a score of 16 or below who passed the English test was also to be invited for interview. Lastly, any other evidence of having passed an English test of other recognised bodies or institutions would be taken into account. It is worth noting that 1978 was the year in which the part-time degree programme was temporarily offered at NUL. The candidates for this programme have been admitted mainly through MAES.

Some research studies on the predictive validity of the MAES selection tests were undertaken in the early 1970s, although these were limited by small sample sizes. Both the results of these studies and casual observation indicate that candidates who were admitted through MAES have tended to do well in their university work. Most of these students are also said to be industrious and to contribute to the social life of the university. Khama and Masie (1981) have shown that in Botswana the I-D scholastic series is a good predictor of academic success for the MAES students at the University of Botswana although one has to recognise that other selection factors contribute to the admission of candidates who later succeed in their studies at the university.

ATTEMPTS AT REVISIONS OF THE I-D TESTS

A scholastic aptitude test series from the I-D test package has been used at the National University of Lesotho for many years to select Mature Age Entry Scheme candidates. But the series has not been revised in any systematic and significant way. Standardised tests, however, should be revised regularly, particularly if the conditions in which they are administered change.

Another important issue is that the tests should be developed and standardised on populations for which they are intended to be used. The content, format, and administration directions of the tests should be geared to the conditions prevailing for the relevant population. This calls for the development of national/local norms. So far there are no national norms on the tests for Lesotho. Their absence has necessitated the use of internal standardisation. This means that the performance of a given candidate is compared to that of other candidates who take the tests in that particular year rather than to 'typical performance.' It is not uncommon to find that, for any one year, the performance of the highest scoring candidate is equal to that of the lowest scoring candidate in the previous year. However, that candidate has the highest chance of being selected for admission.

The use of internal standardisation has brought about the problem of setting a cut-off point. In this kind of situation it is not easy to establish a constant cut-off point, except arbitrarily as has been done by the NUL admissions committee. One has to shift the cut-off point around, depending on how the group of candidates have performed in a given year. Shifting of the cut-off point means, in effect, that one admits groups of candidates of varying abilities in different years. The situation for NUL MAES is further complicated by the fact that there is a quota on the number of candidates to be admitted each year. If, however, national norms were available it would be easy to decide whether a given candidate's score falls on, above, or below the average.

Towards the end of the 1980s, the NUL proposed the revision and improvement of the tests and also the development of national norms. Unfortunately, lack of financial resources did not permit full implementation of this important but ambitious project. All that could be done was to develop new sets of sub-tests and try them out on candidates who had applied for admission. The new sets of tests were tried out by administering them concurrently with the old battery. This procedure went on for three years, that is, for three testing sessions. The new battery was improved each time through item analysis and computation of parallel-form reliability.

Predictive validity has not yet been determined due, first of all, to the problems encountered in obtaining criterion data. The number of students admitted through the aptitude test package has been too small to allow calculation of coefficients. However, attempts are being made to determine validity estimates through other techniques. Momentum for the exercise has also been slowed by the fact that the university has temporarily suspended the MAES due to improvement in COSC results. Another reason is that the enrolment size in the university as a whole has been kept constant because of lack of accommodation, classroom, and laboratory space and priority is for the time being given to students entering the university through COSC. It is, however, likely that MAES will be reactivated when a proposed part-time degree programme is launched at the university. The majority of candidates for this programme will not qualify for admission through COSC.

REFERENCES

Irvine, S. H. (1966). Towards a rationale for testing attainments and abilities in Africa. *British Journal of Educational Psychology*, *36*, 24-32.

Khama, S. Y., & Masie, L. T. (1981, May). *Scholastic aptitude test series and achievement examination results in Botswana.* Paper presented at the BOLESWA Educational Research Seminar, Gaborone, Botswana.

Schwartz, P. A., & Krug, R. E. (1972). *Ability testing in developing countries: A handbook of principles and techniques*. New York: Praeger.

Sebatane, E. M. (1975, March). *Selection and admission procedures at the University of Botswana, Lesotho and Swaziland (UBLS).* Paper presented at the Annual Meeting of the American Education Research Association, Washington, DC.

Snider, J. G. (1972). Aptitude tests for West Africa. *West African Journal of Education*, *16*, 171-177.

19. THE SYSTEM OF ADMISSION TO NIGERIAN UNIVERSITIES

J. K. Majasan and A. Salami
The West African Examinations Council,
Lagos

Before Independence (1960), there was only one university, University College, Ibadan, in Nigeria. It was then an affiliate of the University of London and served the whole country as far as first degree courses were concerned. The first five years after independence saw a radical change in university education with the establishment of the University of Nigeria, Nsukka, Ahmadu Bello University, Zaria, and the Universities of Lagos and Ife (the latter now Obafemi Awolowo University). By the 1975/76 academic year, seven new universities had been established: eighteen more have been added since, bringing the total number of universities (including Universities of Technology and Agriculture) to thirty.

Admission to universities before 1978 was conducted by each individual university through entrance examinations. This procedure was found to result in multiple admissions, wastage of resources (particularly in the context of administering concessionary entrance examinations) as well as placing tremendous strain on applicants, particularly those who had to pay application fees to two or more universities only to find themselves not admitted by any in the end.

It was in recognition of these problems that a panel of experts was set up to examine the system of admission into Nigerian universities. The report of the panel led to the setting up of the National Committee on University Entrance in February 1977. The committee recommended, *inter alia,* the setting up of a joint matriculation board and this led to the promulgation of a decree which established the Joint Admissions and Matriculation Board (JAMB) in 1978.

The main responsibilities of JAMB were to control the conduct of matriculation examinations (JME) for admission into tertiary institutions (universities, polytechnics, and colleges of education) and to place qualified candidates in these institutions. The board has been performing these functions for the universities since April 1978.

This paper examines the admission guidelines as issued by the Federal Government of Nigeria regarding admission procedures employed by JAMB, including entry requirements, stages of admission, and the involvement of university authorities in the admission process. It also looks at the issue of combining two external examinations as criteria for admission purposes. The advantages and disadvantages of the system are highlighted and recommendations are made for the continued improvement of the system.

ADMISSION GUIDELINES

As a way of ensuring that admissions into tertiary institutions reflect the 'federal character' enunciated in the country's constitution, the Federal Government of Nigeria in 1981 issued guidelines to JAMB on admissions into all federal universities. The guidelines stipulate that first a percentage of the candidates should be selected on merit and another percentage on the basis that they are resident in the geographical or sociocultural area contiguous to the university. Second, a proportion of places is to be reserved for candidates from the educationally 'disadvantaged states' and foreign candidates. And third, disadvantaged groups such as female and handicapped candidates are also to be given special concessions in the form of lower cut-off points. Furthermore, the need for scientific and technological advancement gave rise to a policy which stipulates that admissions to science and arts should be in the ratio of 60:40 for all universities throughout the country.

Precise admission policies for all state universities are determined by the state governments concerned. Generally, most state universities offer a sizeable percentage of their admissions to native candidates of the state in which the university is located. It is, however, worth mentioning that the admission of qualified applicants to all universities by JAMB is normally undertaken with the full co-operation of the universities. It is the universities that send to JAMB the list of candidates they wish to recommend in compliance with the federal government's guidelines on admissions. Representatives from universities are also on the admission panel of JAMB. In fact, the Chair of the panel is usually a representative of one of the universities. Other members include the representatives of the National Universities Commission (NUC), admissions officers of the universities, and JAMB officials. Notwithstanding these guidelines, all candidates must meet minimum entry requirements before they are accepted by a university. Details of these minimum requirements for university admission are described below.

UNIVERSITY ENTRY REQUIREMENTS

Entry requirements for admission to Nigerian universities are basically in the form of credit passes in the terminal/certificate examinations conducted by the West

African Examinations Council (WAEC) or their equivalent. For candidates seeking admission through the Joint Matriculation Examination (JME), credit passes in at lest five subjects taken at not more than two sittings in the Senior School Certificate (SSC) or General Certificate of Education 'Ordinary' Level (GCE 'O' Level) are the basic requirements. The five subjects usually include the English language in the case of candidates applying for admission to courses in the Humanities and Mathematics plus one other science subject in the case of candidates seeking admission to degree programmes in the Sciences, Medicine, Agriculture, Engineering and other programmes with a scientific orientation (Candidates awaiting their SSC or GCE 'O' Level results are also eligible to apply for JME). It is important to note that candidates who do not satisfy the minimum entry requirements are not offered admission even if they score above the cut-off mark in the JME. The cut-off marks are determined for individual courses by each university taking the performance of candidates and the student quota for that particular course and year into account. The cut-off marks vary from year to year.

Candidates could also apply to the JAMB offering the results of the GCE A-level examination and be considered for admission on the basis of their results in that examination only. This mode of entry, known as direct entry, has declined in importance with the phasing out of the A-level examination.

PHASES OF ADMISSION

Admission to Nigerian universities is done in three phases, namely: first JME admissions; first direct entry admissions; and supplementary admissions.

In the first phase, candidates' scripts are scored and an aggregate score is calculated for each course in each university. An order of merit of candidates is drawn up by course and university of first choice. Other information contained in the computer print-out includes candidates' sex, state of origin, age, second and third choice universities, and second-choice course. Copies of the computer print-out are sent to the universities which are required to mark 'R' against the candidates they wish to recommend for admission. These recommendations are then considered by a panel constituted as already outlined above. The second phase differs only in the method of scoring the candidates. For instance, an A grade in the GCE A-level gives a candidate five points, B gives four points, and so on. A candidate who obtains grades on three papers at a single sitting receives one bonus point. The purpose of the third phase is to fill up vacancies in all courses. The computer print-out indicates universities and courses of candidates' second choice.

Applicants who fail to gain admission into any of the universities in a particular academic year are required to repeat the matriculation examination and compete on the same terms as other candidates in subsequent examinations.

Two questions arise in relation to the above admissions policies and procedures. Has the process of admission been fair, well-defined, and effective? And what are the advantages and limitations of using both the JME and the terminal school certificate to determine admissions to the universities?

ADVANTAGES AND DISADVANTAGES OF THE SYSTEM

The admissions system through the JME and SSCE/GCE has enabled applicants to enter university on the basis of their expressed preferences and level of performance in the examinations. However, there are usually some complications in meeting the general preferences of all candidates. For instance, an applicant who is not accepted by the university and course of first choice is often reluctant to accept an offer of the same course in the university of second choice. Such universities are usually those which are not the first choice of a sufficient number of applicants to fill their available places. It is not uncommon to find such candidates repeating the JME the following year with a view to renewing their application to the university of their first choice.

There have been some reported instances of applicants who, in spite of very good performance in the JME, are not accepted by the universities of their choice because they do not meet the minimum entry requirements. It also happens that applicants who meet the minimum requirements fail to gain admission because their results in the JME were not good enough. Indications from the universities to the JAMB are that about 90% of candidates whose scores qualify them for admission by the JME also satisfy minimum requirements. Table 19.1 gives the enrolment figures for four academic years.

TABLE 19.1

NUMBERS OF APPLICANTS, ADMISSIONS, AND ENROLMENTS FOR ALL NIGERIAN UNIVERSITIES, 1985/86 - 1989/90

Year	Applicants	Provisional Admissions	Actual Enrolments (%)
1985/86	212,114	35,163	16.5
1987/88	210,525	36,456	17.3
1988/89	191,482	41,700	21.8
1989/90	255,636	37,426	14.6

There is a high correlation between the assessment made by JAMB through JME and by WAEC through the GCE O-Level or the SSCE. In addition, the centrally controlled system of admission has been able to eliminate the problem of multiple admissions. JAMB offers only one admission to a candidate into just one of the

Nigerian universities. However, a very high proportion of qualified applicants is not accepted due to the number of places being limited by lack of facilities in the universities. It must be pointed out that the number of available places is determined not by the JAMB but by each university based on the approval received from government through the National Universities Commission. It will be noted that the proportion of offers to applications did not reach 25% in any year from 1985/86 to 1989/90, an indication of the very limited number of places in the universities (Table 19.1).

RECOMMENDATIONS FOR CONTINUED IMPROVEMENT OF THE SYSTEM

First, based on past performance of candidates on JME, JAMB should include in their bulletin information about the range of JME scores expected of applicants for a given course at a given university. Such information would guide an applicant in making a choice of course and university. The applicant would be able to relate expected examination performance to the expected scores for a given course and university.

Second, JAMB and the universities should use the information about choice of course and university in the best interests of applicants. In this connection, it is observed that the Board requires an applicant to make a choice of three courses and two universities. However, the universities have been known to be rather subjective in the use of the information supplied by applicants. For instance, for a given course in a university, the institution selects mostly from applicants who make the university and the course their first choice. Thus, an applicant with a good score who failed to be accepted by the university of first choice for a given course may not be accepted by the university of second choice even though he or she may have better results than some applicants who were accepted by that university on the basis of their making it their first choice.

Third, more efficient and well-defined guidelines should be drawn up for the admission system particularly insofar as the relationship between JAMB and the universities is concerned. There have been cases where candidates offered admission by JAMB are rejected by the universities concerned even when the candidates had the requisite qualifications.

20. SENIOR SECONDARY SCHOOL EXAMINATION RESULTS AND SELECTION IN NAMIBIA

Donton S.J. Mkandawire
University of Namibia,
Windhoek

SELECTION IN EDUCATION

The argument that the acceleration of economic and technological advancement of developing countries largely depends on its trained human resources logically leads to a demand for appropriate educational selection procedures. The need for good selection procedures is all the more pressing because the available resources are so limited. While higher education is seen as a primary means of upward mobility, it is impossible to educate and train all individuals who might be eligible for or could benefit from tertiary education because of limited resources. In the past, Biesheuvel (1962) and Taylor (1962) described the acute shortage of trained manpower and resources in developing countries. It remains important to obtain the maximum benefit from the limited educational opportunities currently available and from the resultant trained manpower.

The majority of developing nations accept, in their economic plans, the principle of optimum manpower utilisation. As a result, planning is based on the philosophy that it is individuals who are capable of benefiting that should be given the opportunity of higher education. Higher education institutions have invariably adopted selection procedures which are consistent with this view. Clarke (1959), together with many others interested in this question, suggested that, given their situation, the only way developing nations can meet their aspiration is to develop selection procedures that will identify the most suitable individuals for the relatively few places available.

Throughout the developing world, education authorities are developing selection procedures designed to select applicants for educational institutions. They have adopted the selection-rejection model which follows a standard format: applicants are given some form of examination or aptitude test and those who perform above a determined cut-off point are selected; the rest are rejected. Cronbach and Gleser (1965) call this a non-sequential testing strategy or a single-stage testing strategy. The model assumes that the applicants will be ranked from high to low on scores that have high predictive value. The highest ranked applicants are selected and go through similar educational programmes.

Hills (1971) has pointed out that an institution contemplating the establishment of a selection programme should take a number of factors into account. First, it should identify the benefits it expects from the programme. In an educational institution the immediate benefit from the selection programme might be the admission of applicants who have a high probability of success. However, the ultimate benefit in most cases is to have people who will be productive after they graduate. Second, the institution should decide whether the treatment, once applicants have been selected, will be fixed or adaptive. Where treatment is fixed, successful applicants go through a similar educational programme. By contrast, an adaptive treatment is one in which an educational programme is modified to accommodate the characteristics of the selected applicants in order to achieve the desired outcomes. The selection-rejection model tends to be used in fixed treatment systems which are used in most developing countries. Third, the nature of the applicant population must be determined. It will be necessary to know in advance whether everybody applying can be considered eligible, or whether some advance requirements have to be met by applicants. Fourth, the instruments to be used in making the selection decisions must be decided in advance. In most instances, end of secondary school examinations are used. Fifth, it is also necessary to know how the measures derived from different instruments or tests will be combined. A regression model is commonly used for this purpose. Finally, a decision must be made regarding the cut-off point on the measures included in the selection procedure.

In evaluating the benefits of a testing programme, Cronbach and Gleser (1965) have pointed out that criterion-related validity should not be the sole criterion. An institution's selection procedures should include, but should not be limited to, test performance.

APPLYING DECISION THEORY TO SELECTION

When examination results are used for selection, validity coefficients *per se* do not tell us how much gain is likely to accrue from the use of these results. A model that applies decision theory has been suggested as an alternative way of evaluating the worth of test results when used for educational selection. The main thrust of the decision theory approach is to provide a meaningful way of demonstrating the worth of test results. Cronbach and Gleser (1965) view the purpose of testing as one which helps educators to arrive at rational decisions about applicants.

Selection procedures in post-secondary school institutions in developing countries contain most of the elements that Cronbach and Gleser (1965, p.16) have proposed in their taxonomy. First, the benefits obtained from the decision to accept or reject an applicant are evaluated the same way for each individual. Examination or test results are used to aid in these institutional decisions. Second, in every selection problem, fixed quotas are assumed where only a certain number of applicants are accepted for study because of financial or other resource problems which limit access to higher education. This involves choosing a threshold ability cut-off point and accepting those who exceed this level. Free quota models used are hardly ever used in developing countries. Third, each individual selected is assigned to just one available treatment. Fourth, it is inherent in the model that some applicants are rejected. Fifth, it is assumed that the information used can be either univariate or multivariate in nature. Finally, single stage or non-sequential decision strategy is commonly practised.

There are three types of educational selection decisions frequently encountered in post-secondary education. First is the decision to admit some applicants to an academic institution and reject others who do not qualify. Second is the decision required when rejection is not an acceptable alternative. The decision required is to which one of several available academic programmes an applicant should be assigned (Rulon et al, 1967). The third type of decision involves assigning applicants to different levels of the same programme. A classical example of this kind of placement is the grouping of students into several courses or giving credit to students in accordance with their performance in an examination or an aptitude test. A decision maker will want to make decisions that will be as beneficial as possible to the institution he or she represents and to society at large. Where all of the necessary information is not available to the decision maker, one can only adopt a strategy which will work best on average.

A clear distinction between these three types of educational decisions is sometimes difficult because institutions often use the same test data for all of them. Some institutions in the U.S.A. also use relevant nontest measures as part of the selection process. Whitney (1991) has remarked that:

> It is both simplistic and inaccurate to assume that most institutions use admissions-test scores to rank applicants and then admit those with the highest scores. In fact, when making admissions and placement decisions, institutional officials nearly always consider a number of relevant nontest measures such as prior grades and courses, expressed educational needs, and background characteristics. It is also incorrect to assume that most placement decisions are made by simply using an established cut-off score on some valid test to assign students to alternative courses such as 'advanced' or 'introductory.' The institution is also usually concerned with the prior academic record and study goals of the student. (p. 515)

In some developing countries, such as Botswana, Lesotho, Swaziland, and Malawi, regional or ethnic distributions and mature age are factors which are taken into consideration.

The establishment of a criterion is a basic issue in the prediction of success. Once the criterion has been established it is necessary to identify predictors that are likely to be related to a suitable measure of success (Thorndike & Hagen, 1969). While the initial identification of potentially useful tests is made on rational grounds, the validation of the selection test battery is an empirical task that involves the determination of the statistical relationship between the scores on the selection instrument and measures of criterion performance, usually based on subsequent academic performance, in a third-level institution. On the basis of regression analysis, the most effective predictors are selected. Once evidence of statistical relationship has been demonstrated, a good validity coefficient established and cross-validated, a test procedure may be used year after year to select future students.

Ordinarily, in the basic selection model, a test or a test battery is used to select from a group of applicants those individuals who are likely to perform well at the university. This is the reason why some measure of university achievement is used as a criterion. The value of a test in this context has been judged traditionally simply by the accuracy with which it predicts this criterion.

The selection-rejection problem frequently encountered in educational selection is represented in Figure 20.1 (Wiggins, 1973). Examination data on applicants are collected, a rule (strategy) for arriving at the decision of whether to accept or reject is decided upon, then a decision is made. Applicants who meet the requirements are selected; others are rejected. The outcomes of these decisions to accept or to reject, in theory at any rate, are fourfold: O_A — a person who is accepted performs successfully; O_B — a person who is accepted performs unsuccessfully (fails); O_C — a person who is rejected is able to perform successfully; O_D — a person who is rejected is unable to perform successfully (fails).

FIGURE 20.1

MODEL OF DECISION PROCESS

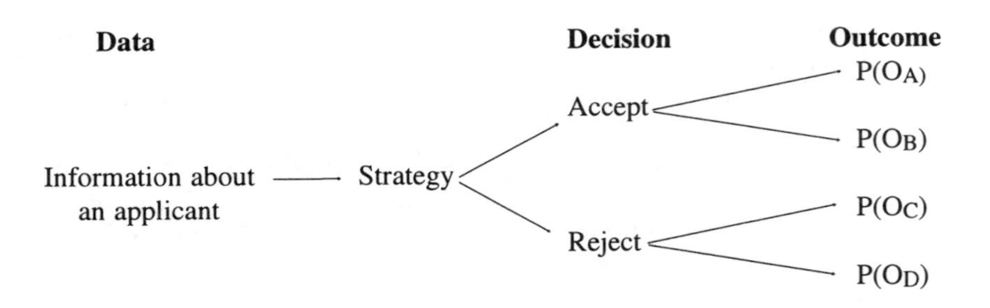

The likelihood of the occurrence of particular outcomes is usually expressed in probability forms. In the selection-rejection problem in Figure 20.1, there are probabilities associated with each of the four possible outcomes: $P(O_A)$ is the probability that a potential success is accepted; $P(O_B)$ is the probability that a potential failure is accepted; $P(O_C)$ is the probability that a potential success is rejected; and $P(O_D)$ is the probability that a potential failure is rejected.

Some authors have referred to outcome A as 'valid positive' (VP), outcome B as 'false positive' (FP), outcome C as 'false negative' (FN) and outcome D as 'valid negative' (VN).

AN INVESTIGATION OF THE PREDICTIVE VALIDITY OF SCHOOL-LEAVING EXAMINATIONS

In Namibia, senior secondary schools have followed a common subject syllabus designed by the Cape Education Department of South Africa which also administers school exit achievement examinations which are used both for certification and for the selection of applicants for tertiary educational institutions.

The minimum pass criterion in senior secondary school examinations is a pass in five subjects. To be awarded a matriculation certificate or its exemption — which serves as a qualification to enter the university — a candidate must pass with 40% in at least five subjects selected from appropriate subject groupings of not fewer than six subjects. A candidate is expected to attain a minimum of 20% in these subjects and to have a minimum aggregate score of 950 points.

Prior to 21 March 1990, when the country gained its independence, the education system operated on the basis of separate racial development resulting in severe disparities in the education infrastructure which in turn resulted in marked differentials in examination results. An examination of senior secondary school examination results provided by the Ministry of Education and Culture indicates that during the ten years before independence between 88 and 95% of students in white schools passed; between 38 and 79% of students in mixed schools passed and between 3 and 68% of students in black schools passed. After independence, when schools were integrated, 49% of students passed in 1990 and 42% in 1991. Thus, pass rates have been low on the whole except in the case of schools attended only by white students.

Admission decisions to the Faculty of Education at the University of Namibia are currently based solely on the results of the senior secondary school examinations taken at the conclusion of 12 years basic and secondary education. Because results are poor, very few candidates qualify to enter university and institutional resources continue to be underutilised. Furthermore, the examination system has produced very few university entrants from the black student population. In light of this situation, it was decided to carry out an investigation of the predictive validity of these secondary school results and the utility value of the selection decisions being made. The study addressed the following questions: (i) Do the examination results at conclusion of secondary school predict first year university performance in the Faculty of Education? (ii) Do education admissions based on school examination results only have a utility value in providing access to university education for the majority of senior secondary school leavers?

The data for the study were obtained from the 1990 and 1991 records of students admitted to the Faculty of Education. The precision model was used to evaluate the predictive value of the selection decision by examining the relationship between performance at the end of the first year and secondary school examination results. The academic performance of 174 and 142 students admitted in 1990 and 1991 respectively and who completed their first year in the Faculty of Education were obtained from the student records. A regression analysis using senior secondary school results as predictors and first year university academic performance as criteria was carried out. The regression coefficient between school examination results and performance at the end of first year in university was .30 for the 1990 cohort and .19 for the 1991 cohort.

The predictive value of the 1990 examination results was statistically significant at the .01 level of probability and for 1991 it was statistically significant at the .05 level. It should be noted, however, that since criterion data were not available for rejected applicants, these results were affected by restriction in range on the predictor variables; consequently, coefficents are likely to underestimate the strength of relationships (Gulliksen, 1950).

It should be pointed out that the utility value of the selection procedure is questionable since access to higher education is restricted to a few successful applicants from a few schools, the majority of which have hitherto accepted whites only but are now integrated. The majority of former black or mixed schools which cater for the majority of the secondary school population, do not yet have comparable infrastructures and until these schools are improved (which will take some time) in both human resources and physical infrastructure, the integrated school, which still take 90% of their students from the white population, will continue to produce better results (Mkandawire, 1992). Consequently using school-leaving examination results as the only criterion for selection could for some time deny access to higher education to the majority student population whose results are not good enough to qualify for entry to the Faculty of Education.

CONCLUSION

When faced with a selection problem for entry to higher education, decision makers frequently use secondary school exit examination results to aid them in their decisions whether to accept or reject applicants. Selection decisions are usually based on a single-stage decision strategy whose four possible outcomes have been identified. It has been suggested that the aim of selection is to make rational decisions which will bring the most benefit to the institution and society.

In Namibia what is of concern at the moment is the use of the secondary school exit achievement examination results as the only criterion for selection to the university. Although the results have reasonable predictive validity for university first year academic performance, the selection procedure needs to be reformed if false negatives are going to be turned into valid positives.

Increased access to university is a priority objective so that an increased number of secondary school leavers can benefit from the currently underutilised university places available. The university is considering several additional access routes. One will continue to be a direct route from secondary school after passing the International General Certificate of Secondary Education (IGCSE) which will replace the present examination. Other routes will provide prerequisite skills to adult learners through distance education or will require them to pass mature age aptitude tests. What will need to be done is to set threshold ability levels and admit all applicants whose scores exceed this level. The university and indeed the Faculty of Education has not at this stage reached a situation where the number of applicants exceeds the number of places. When institutional resources are underutilised the threshold ability levels should be used to help identify applicants with the potential for success as well as the current practice of using secondary school exit examination results to select and admit applicants most likely to succeed (Whitney, 1991). If the educational qualifications of adult applicants could be evaluated through threshold ability levels, enrolment to the Faculty of Education would be increased and would also provide many applicants with opportunities to gain a professional qualification hitherto denied to them. The university is also currently thinking of introducing bridging courses so as to enable potential applicants to reach the required standard for admission.

Whitney (1991) has argued that although admission test scores provide a 'common metre' to express an applicant's ability for post-secondary school education, many institutions also consider relevant nontest data such as background needs of the applicants, secondary school continuous assessment scores, and desired mix of geographical origins.

With the attainment of independence, one of Namibia's educational goals is to have high proportions of its citizens participate in post-secondary education. The majority of the secondary school population are crying out for equal educational opportunities at tertiary level in keeping with government policy of affirmative action programmes in all sectors.

Based on the foregoing arguments, it is recommended that for Namibia at this point in time selection decisions to the university should be based on threshold test ability levels, prior secondary school academic records, and mature age evaluation entry qualifications. The primary concern should be to admit students with a reasonable chance of success until such time as fixed quotas are introduced putting the university in the position of becoming even more rigorous in its selection procedures.

REFERENCES

Biesheuvel, S. (1962). The detection and fostering of ability among under-developed peoples. *Yearbook of Education*. (Pp. 337-352, 541). London: Evans.

Clarke, M.G. (1959). Secondary school selection in Northern Rhodesia. *Overseas Education, 31*, 99-101.

Cronbach, L.J., & Gleser, G.C. (1965). *Psychological tests and personnel decisions. (2nd ed.).* Urbana, IL: University of Illinois Press.

Gullicksen, H. (1950). *Theory of mental tests.* New York: Wiley.

Hills, J.R. (1971). Use of measurement in selection and placement. In R.L. Thorndike (Ed.), *Educational measurement (2nd ed.).* (Pp. 680-732). Washington, DC: American Council on Education.

Mkandawire, D.S.J. (1992). The academic achievement in liberal arts and science subjects of a fragmented Namibian secondary school system prior to independence. *Zimbabwe Journal of Educational Research, 4*(1), 17-31.

Rulon, P.J. et al. (1967). *Multivariate statistics for personnel classification.* New York: Wiley.

Taylor, A. (1962). *Educational and occupational selection in West Africa.* London: Oxford University Press.

Thorndike, R.L., & Hagen, E. (1969). *Measurement and evaluation in psychology and education (3rd ed.).* New York: Wiley.

Whitney, D.R. (1991). Educational admissions and placement. In R.L. Linn (Ed.), *Educational measurement (3rd ed.).* (Pp. 515-525). New York: Macmillan.

Wiggins, J.S. (1973). *Personality and prediction: Principles of personality assessment.* Reading, MA: Addison-Wesley.

21. THE ROLE OF THE JOINT ADMISSIONS BOARD IN UGANDA

David L. Ongom
Uganda National Examinations Board,
Kampala, Uganda

The education system of Uganda has three major segments: primary, secondary, and tertiary. The primary cycle lasts seven years, though there is a recommendation by the Education Policy Review Commission (EPRC, 1989) that this period be extended to eight years. At the end of primary education pupils who are successful in the Primary Leaving Examination (PLE) are admitted to secondary schools.

The secondary segment is divided into two cycles: a lower secondary cycle which currently lasts for four years (the EPRC recommends a reduction to three years), and the upper secondary cycle which lasts for two years. At the end of the lower secondary cycle, students sit for the Uganda Certificate of Education (UCE) examination, which is mainly a certification examination, although its results are used to select and admit students to A-level classes in upper secondary school. At the end of the upper secondary cycle, students sit for the Uganda Advanced Certificate of Education (UACE) examination (Uganda National Examinations Board, 1987).

TERTIARY (HIGHER) EDUCATION

In the EPRC (1989) report, higher education is defined as the system of advanced education which is offered to candidates who have successfully completed the full course in the two cycles of secondary education. It includes all third-level education, not just the university sector.

In the sector, there are: two national universities (Makerere University and Mbarara University of Science and Technology), one polytechnic, one national college of business studies, ten national teachers' colleges, four technical colleges, and four colleges of commerce which are fully funded by the government. All twenty-two institutions fall under the Ministry for Education and Sports. There is also a Muslim university at Mbale in Eastern Uganda and up to three other church universities may be established. There are several self-awarding and privately established colleges of higher education offering courses in vocational subjects but they do not have official recognition.

In the EPRC (1989) report, the functions of tertiary institutions are set out as teaching to produce high-level manpower such as doctors, engineers, accountants, teachers, and administrators; research, particularly to improve and develop production sectors; publication of books, journals, and research works; public service through a variety of extension activities; and service as a store of knowledge and centres of excellence. Tertiary educational institutions should not only generate advanced knowledge and innovation through research but should also adapt knowledge that is generated to local situations. They should develop the intellectual capacities of students to understand their local and national environment and to appreciate the development of the local environment. They should also promote the development of the indigenous scientific and technological capacity that is needed to tackle problems of development as well as equipping students with knowledge, skills, and attitudes to enable them to join the world of work as useful members of their communities and the nation at large. These functions indicate that tertiary (higher) education is assigned a crucial role in Uganda's social, economic, and cultural development.

UACE EXAMINATION RESULTS: THE BASIS FOR ADMISSION TO UNIVERSITIES AND OTHER TERTIARY INSTITUTIONS

Uganda Advanced Certificate of Education (UACE) examinations, conducted by the Uganda National Examinations Board (UNEB), form the basis for admission to universities and other tertiary institutions. They cover 25 subjects. Standard candidates, i.e., candidates presented by a registered or recognised school, are required to sit for a General paper and either four Principal subjects or three Principal subjects and one Subsidiary or two Principal and two Subsidiary subjects (see Uganda National Examinations Board, 1987).

Because of the unique role that UACE examination results play in the admission of candidates to higher institutions, UNEB tries to maintain uniform academic standards in examinations from year to year. This is done during the setting and moderation of the examination papers and at the time of awards.

UNEB is the only body which conducts UACE examinations. The issue of the comparability of standards between different examining boards, therefore, does not arise. At the same time, care is always taken to ensure that the questions that are set adequately cover the contents of the syllabus issued by the Board. The examinations are conducted under comparable conditions throughout the country, thus ensuring that no particular candidates are favoured.

UACE examination results for a subject offered at Principal level are awarded at one of seven letter grades A, B, C, D, E, O, and F. Grade A is the highest and grade E the lowest of the Principal passes. O indicates that a candidate has failed to pass at Principal level but has been allowed a pass at Subsidiary level. F is a fail. Subjects offered at Subsidiary level are graded from 1 to 9. Grade 1 is the highest and 9 the lowest. Grades 1 to 6 are passing grades; 7, 8, and 9 are failing grades.

ADMISSION TO FIRST DEGREE AND DIPLOMA COURSES AT UNIVERSITIES

Almost all candidates who attend A-level courses compete for a place at one or other of the two government-funded universities. In 1992 only 1,950 places were available for first degree courses, 75 for diploma courses, and 20 for the certificate in librarianship in Makerere University. The number of places on first year degree courses in Makerere increased from 1,000 in 1970 to 2,200 in 1990. Mbarara University admits about 50 candidates per year for Medicine only. Competition for available places is very keen and it is not uncommon for a few candidates to employ unfair means to gain admission to university.

Admission Requirements

Makerere University has three avenues for entry to first degree courses: direct entry, mature age entry, and diploma holders entry (Makerere University, 1990). For direct entry after an A-level course, the university considers candidates who have completed O-level courses and obtained at least five passes at one sitting of the UCE or an equivalent certificate and have two A-level passes or their equivalent at the same sitting. Only candidates who sat A-level examinations during the year of admission or in either of the previous two years are considered for direct entry. Candidates who sat UACE or equivalent examinations more than two years prior to the year of admission are eligible for consideration only if they have been engaged in academic work such as teaching.

Mature age entry applies to candidates who do not hold UACE or who may have attempted UACE examinations and not qualified for admission. They may seek entry to university by sitting and passing a Mature Age Entry Examination set by the university. Mature Age applicants must be at least 25 years of age and must have completed formal education five years previously.

A third mode of admission is available for candidates who hold diplomas awarded by Makerere University or by other recognised institutions. Candidates may be admitted to undergraduate degree courses provided they hold a diploma with a first or second class pass, have relevant work experience specified by the faculty to which they are applying, pass an oral examination, and have a strong recommendation from their employer. Only 5% of places available in each faculty are reserved for such entrants and in some faculties, the number is restricted to one or two entrants a year.

Method of Application

All candidates in final A-level classes who wish to be considered for admission to university must complete computerised application forms and pay an application fee of 3,000 Uganda shillings. Non-Ugandan applicants pay an application fee of 15 US dollars. Applications must reach the Academic Registrar (Admissions) by 31st March of the year for which admission is being sought. Each candidate may apply for a maximum of *eight* courses. Currently, Makerere University offers a total of 24 first year degree courses and five diploma courses, while Mbarara University of Science and Technology offers only one course in Medicine.

VACANCIES IN UNIVERSITIES

The university authority, in consultation with the Joint Admissions Board, fixes the number of vacancies available each year, taking into account the number of applicants who qualify for admission, as well as the teaching facilities (not accommodation facilities) available. Cut-off points on scores are then calculated.

Not all students admitted to the university turn up. The reasons are many and require urgent investigation. Some of the possible reasons may be financial or accommodation problems. The university has recently decided that not all the candidates admitted to the university can be accommodated. Some students who have been admitted but not offered accommodation might decide to opt out. Lack of adequate financial means could be another possible reason. In the past the government paid tuition fees for each student admitted as well as a textbook allowance, a stationery allowance, pocket money, and an allowance for travel to and from the university. All these allowances have been withdrawn.

Among the other reasons that students do not accept offers may be late receipt of a written offer, ill-health, simultaneous offers from more than one university, receipt of an offer of a place on a course not of the student's choice or to a non-university institution, and refusal by an employer to release a mature entry candidate.

THE JOINT ADMISSIONS BOARD

The EPRC (1989) report recommended, among other things, the establishment of a Joint Admissions Board (JAB). The functions of the board were surprisingly not defined by the Commission. The board was established in 1990 and was charged with responsibility for co-ordinating admissions to universities and other tertiary institutions.

It was noted that Joint Admissions Boards in other African countries serve institutions of similar or equal status. For example, the Joint Admissions and Matriculation Board (JAMB) in Nigeria serves 20 federal universities and nine state universities and degree-awarding polytechnics and colleges (Joint Admissions and Matriculation Board, 1988). In Tanzania, on the other hand, there is a Joint Admissions Board which does not meet until after the universities and university colleges have completed their selection of candidates. The admission lists are submitted to the JAB, which acts as a clearing house by going through the lists to ensure that no candidate is admitted to more than one college. The Tanzanian JAB also ensures that selection is carried out in accordance with procedures laid down by each institution.

The JAB proposed for Uganda falls between the Tanzanian and Nigerian models. It is designed to co-ordinate admissions into universities and other non-degree awarding institutions which cannot successfully compete with the universities in the conduct of admissions or finalise their admissions before the university admissions have been completed.

The Joint Admissions Board in Uganda plays a number of roles in university and tertiary admissions. First, it collects information on matters that are connected with admissions to tertiary institutions including the universities. Second, it enables the business of admissions to under-graduate degree and diploma courses in all the constituent Uganda institutions of tertiary education to be dealt with in an orderly and co-ordinated manner, taking into account the places available in those institutions, the requirements for admission into particular courses, having due regard to the freedom of individual candidates to make a responsible choice or indicate preference for particular institutions or course programmes and such other factors as may be relevant to the admissions process. Third, it acts as a clearing house for admission into tertiary institutions helping to avoid duplication of admissions and to fill all vacant places. Fourth, it compiles statistics of vacancies available in each college and the number of students admitted to all tertiary institutions. Finally, it organises and supervises admissions meetings at which the selection process to tertiary institutions is carried out.

The Process of JAB Selection

In its effort to streamline the process of admission, the Joint Admissions Board has prepared three documents. The first is an application form for the purpose of verifying Ugandan citizenship which must be completed by candidates who claim it and wish to be considered for admission to a third-level institution. The second is a document which gives information on the minimum requirements for admission and a list of courses on offer. The third document is an application form which must be completed in triplicate by candidates. One copy goes to the registrar of the institution of first choice, the second to the secretariat of JAB, and the third is retained at the candidate's school.

Members of the secretariat of the JAB attend university selection meetings held at Makerere University for university admissions. While they participate fully in the admissions process, the main purpose of their presence is to note the cut-off points for each faculty or school and hence determine the candidates who qualify for admission. This helps eliminate the problem of multiple offers. In the past, some candidates gained admission both to a university and a tertiary institution. They would attend lectures in the university at the beginning of the academic year and if they found the academic pressure too great would transfer to a diploma-awarding institution. With the establishment of JAB, this practice has been eliminated. The presence of JAB officers also ensures proper co-ordination of admission in the two national universities as well as enabling the secretariat to prepare accurate information for admission to diploma-awarding institutions. When the admission of candidates to the universities has been completed, JAB organises a meeting at which selection to the tertiary institutions is carried out. The meeting which lasts for five days is organised at Makerere University and is chaired by the academic registrar of the University. The meeting is attended by deans of the faculties of Education, Commerce, and Technology from Makerere University as well as the principals and registrars of the diploma-awarding institutions. The first task is to admit students to the Higher Diploma in Marketing (HDM) and Uganda Diploma in Business Studies (UDBS), which are the most popular among diploma courses. This is followed by admission of arts students for teacher education, as well as students to technical education institutions and to secretarial courses in Colleges of Commerce. Finally, admission is arranged to teachers' colleges for science, agriculture, home economics, and technical education, as well as for a few students who wish to study catering in colleges of commerce.

CONCLUSION

In Uganda, as in other developing countries, education is seen as a means of ensuring access to the very much cherished white-collar job. Many parents therefore invest very heavily in education. Allocation of places in universities and other tertiary institutions is a very sensitive undertaking which must be carried out with all possible transparency. Prior to the establishment of the Joint Admissions Board, admissions to other tertiary institutions were viewed with a lot of suspicion, often without clear proof. Unsubstantiated, but persistent, rumours abounded of preferential admission for students in a position to make a financial contribution to an institution. Allegations of this kind, however, have not been made about Makerere University. Apart from one recorded instance of political interference, admission to the university is decided on meritocratic grounds.

The present government has established the Joint Admissions Board as a means of extending the meritocratic admission that has long existed in the universities to the other tertiary institutions. From the experience of the past two years, this move is seen by the general public as very wise. JAB has played a very crucial role in co-ordinating admission to universities and other institutions of higher learning. It has in particular dealt with the problem of multiple admissions. Students also welcome the opportunity of being able to get assistance from a centralised agency. Tertiary institutions see the establishment of the JAB as a solution to the problem of allegations of unfair practice.

JAB has in the first two years of its operation produced clear records of the available places in tertiary institutions and compiled accurate lists of the students who have been admitted. It is now possible for a student to get information on admission from a central source. However, to enhance the efficiency of JAB, there is a pressing need for personal computers to be installed in JAB offices with properly trained computer personnel.

In conclusion, it is safe to say that the Joint Admissions Board has to date performed the delicate job of co-ordinating admissions to universities and other tertiary institutions in Uganda quite successfully.

REFERENCES

Education Policy Review Commission (EPRC). (1989). *Education for national integration and development. Report*. Kampala: Ministry of Education.

Joint Admissions and Matriculation Board. (1988). *Guidelines for admission to first degree courses in Nigerian universities*. Lagos: Author.

Makerere University. (1990). *Admission to first degree and diploma courses: Official guide*. Kampala: Author.

Uganda National Examinations Board. (1987). *Uganda Advanced Certificate of Education: Regulations and syllabuses*. Kampala: Author.

THE AMERICAS

22. ADMISSION POLICIES AND PRACTICES IN U.S. COLLEGES AND UNIVERSITIES

Cameron Fincher
Institute of Higher Education,
University of Georgia, Athens, GA

In 1903, Edwin Cornelius Broome wrote a doctoral dissertation entitled *A Historical and Critical Discussion of College Admission Requirements*. Because of its continuing relevance to college admissions, Broome's dissertation was reprinted in 1963 by the College Entrance Examination Board. Now, almost 30 years later and 100 years since Broome began his study, his dissertation remains a fascinating introduction to admission policies and practices in U.S. institutions of higher learning.

Following his remarkable discussion of admission practices in colonial and ante-bellum colleges, Broome gave a summary of the advances that had been made since 1870. Changes in entrance requirements were influenced, most of all, by the gradual transformation of colleges into universities and by the popular demand for advanced studies in public high schools (institutions that Broome referred to as 'the people's college'). By 1900, many new subjects were present in college entrance requirements. English, Mathematics, History, and Science had advanced considerably. Increasingly important in admission procedures were English composition, the solution of original problems in geometry, independent experimental work in science, and coursework involving the actual use of a foreign language. Some colleges still required Latin and Greek but they required higher standards and a broader exposure to the classics on which students were examined. Each of these interesting changes implied that examinations were becoming tests of 'power' rather than the mere acquisition of facts.

Broome did not doubt that he had witnessed a 'revolution in educational principles and practices.' The aim of education had become (or was becoming) the development of individual students and their preparation for life in its fullest most comprehensive sense. The most important problem, in his estimation, was the need for closer articulation between school and college. Good progress had been made toward uniformity in school curricula but that uniformity was impeded by the dual objectives of high schools. Not only were schools trying to prepare more students for college, they were trying to prepare other students for life in the world of work. To school leaders the two objectives were mutually exclusive; to Broome, the preparation of students for college should be the best way of preparing them for the world of work.

The conditions for an ideal connection between high schools and colleges are specified by Broome as: a fair degree of flexibility in both high school curricula and in college admission requirements; a reasonable degree of uniformity in high school standards and in college requirements for admission; and adequate and fair tests of the student's intellectual, moral, and physical fitness to begin college. Flexibility was not a cause for alarm, but (to Broome) high school curricula might go too far in their efforts to be flexible. Uniformity was increasing, but for high schools the move for uniform standards was mostly local or sectional; for colleges the quest for uniform admission requirements was national.

As for adequate and fair tests, there was a great diversity of opinion and practice. When tests were administered by local school teachers, standards were lowered by 'the eagerness of high-school principals to make a good showing' (Broome, 1903, p.151). And among students, standards were lowered by 'the deplorable desire ... to evade all thorough tests of accurate scholarship and of acquired mental power' (p.150). Broome quietly pleads for 'admission to college by examination, these to be thorough, fair, uniform, and judiciously administered by a board of national recognition' (p.152).

In many respects Broome's survey of the 19th century was a forerunner of much that has happened in the 20th century. Admission policies and requirements have continued to be a matter of on-and-off concern in relation to uniform curricula across the nation's diverse high schools, to consistency and flexibility in the application of college admission requirements, and in relation to academic standards when classrooms are opened to students who vary significantly in scholastic achievements, abilities, and interests. In retrospect, at least five waves of reform can be identified. Each included public debates about school/college relations, the use of standardised tests, uniform curricula, flexibility in dealing with pluralistic groups of students, and the diversity of academic programmes and courses.

The first wave of reform reflected an intensive concern with school and college relations as the 20th century opened. High schools were under great pressure to establish uniform curricula, to shake free of the tight grasp of the classical languages, and to provide instruction in English and modern foreign languages instead of Latin, Greek, and Hebrew. One mark of success in this first effort to reform the public schools was the establishment of the College Entrance Examination Board as a means of facilitating access to college for students who had previously been at the mercy of idiosyncratic college admission requirements (see Fuess, 1967).

The second wave included a subsequent concern with diversification of curricula and a loosening of college admission requirements. The villain in this plot was a rigid high school curriculum of English, Mathematics, foreign languages, Science, and History that did not meet the needs of students who would not attend college. The Progressive Education Association's Eight-Year Study proved to the satisfaction of many educators that good students could succeed in college irrespective of what they studied in high school. The advent of the Second World War prevented, no doubt, the Eight-Year Study from having greater impact on American schooling.

In the third wave following the Second World War, college admission standards and the purposes of education were the subject of intensive consideration. The GI Bill was instrumental in what has proved to be a continuing revolution in educational thought and discussion. President Harry S. Truman's Commission on Higher Education stated unequivocally that students with average intelligence should be able to benefit from one or two years of education beyond the high school. Incumbent upon colleges and universities was 'a much larger role in the national life.' High schools accepted the challenge of educating some students for higher or advanced learning and other students for employment and citizenship.

The post-Sputnik era, the fourth wave, moved the post-World War II baby boomers through high school and on to college campuses. This era produced an extraordinary effort at reforming school and college curricula to meet the changing demands and expectations of enormous numbers of students, and to cope with an unprecedented challenge to combine excellence with equality in educational opportunities. Some observers believe that it took the decade of the 1970s to ride out the shock waves that came with and/or produced the need for reform in American education (Fincher, 1977; Valentine, 1987).

In 1983, the fifth wave of reform was launched by a dozen or more commission reports that addressed the plight of public schooling and called for active national leadership in reforming secondary education while there was still time. In each of these reports there are major recommendations pertaining to more explicit requirements for high school graduation that are educationally relevant; admission policies that are definite about required or preferred pre-college curricula; and admission standards and academic criteria that are creditable and fair. In all such reports, there is a sense of urgency about the co-operation of schools and colleges in providing graduates with basic academic competencies; adequate foundations in science, mathematics, and other fields of disciplined inquiry; and literacy in the nation's history, its traditions, and its general culture (Fincher, 1985; 1991a, 1991b).

AN INTERNATIONAL CONTEXT

Admission policies in the U.S. have been influenced strongly by the series of tumultuous events that began in the 1950s and continued until the mid-1970s. The 'impending tidal wave' (of students born in the post-war era) is but one of the graphic terms that depicted the decade of the 1960s. In 1964, the first of the baby-boomers (born in 1946) enrolled in the nation's colleges and universities, and higher education has never been the same.

The increased demand for higher education was documented internationally in 1963 with the publication of a study conducted jointly by the United Nations Educational, Scientific, and Cultural Organisation (UNESCO) and the International Association of Universities (IAU). The study, directed by the president of the College Board (Frank Bowles), was conducted at a time when education throughout the world was being remoulded by unprecedented population growth, technology and specialisation, an explosion of knowledge, a 'revolution of rising expectations,' the democratisation of education, and the growing interdependence of nations and regions (Bowles, 1963).

When viewed from an international perspective, the problems and issues of college admissions were undoubtedly related to the political, economic, and social forces at play in the post-war world. Among the requirements for successful solutions were expanding and enriching institutional facilities at national level and through international co-operation; diversifying further the curricular offerings of secondary and higher education; easing the pressures on traditional forms of education while maintaining standards of quality; and serving the public interest by cultivating individual capacities for different economic, social, and intellectual opportunities and needs.

Running throughout the study is the conviction that 'every effort toward the discovery and the cultivation of human talent' (Bowles, 1963, p.15) should be made. The demand for education at all levels had risen to 'unprecedented heights' and the nations of the world had made a varying response to their particular educational needs. Educational facilities had been expanded at primary, secondary, and higher levels but no level of education had kept pace with the increased demand. With the expansion of facilities, there was a need for added programmes that would serve students from many diverse social origins. In many nations, universal education was required at the elementary level, as well as the provision of secondary facilities to take in as large a proportion as possible of those who finish elementary education. For higher education, the implication was quite direct: 'We must select those who show promise of being able to meet the intellectual challenge of higher education' (p.15). And perhaps not so apparent to many readers, 'generous financial assistance for needy students' should be an investment in mankind, avoiding thereby the tragedy of uneducated individuals and the social crime of wasting human talent.

Implicit in the assumptions, working premises, and findings of the study is an increasing recognition that universities are universal institutions that belong to the international community. A similar perspective is explicit in later studies that have addressed school and college relations (see Clark, 1985). Despite the great divergence that can be observed in the purposes and functions of secondary schools and universities, each influences the other in many subtle and complex ways. Schools continue to educate students for advanced or specialised learning at the university level, and universities continue to supply the principals, teachers, counsellors, and coaches who influence students in their choice of postsecondary or higher education. In schools and colleges seeking to educate students for participation in international communities, the lack of uniformity in school and college curricula and the inflexibility of college admission requirements continue to be major problems in school and college relations.

ADMISSION POLICIES AND FUNCTIONS

Admission policies and practices in the 1990s reflect the many changes that have taken place in American higher education since the 1960s. Embedded in the policies are social, economic, political, and cultural consequences that followed from three decades of rapid change and various efforts to experiment with new functions and procedures. Thus the admissions process in U.S. colleges and universities is far more complex now than it was in 1963 when Frank Bowles (1963) described the process as 'the series of selections to which students are subjected by their country's educational system through the entire period in which they mature to the age of entrance.' Indeed the process is now an elaborate series of choices and decisions that involve many admission specialists, such as counsellors, advisers, and assistant directors. As a result, the distinctive features of the overall process may be: the professionalisation of staff functions and the varied responsibilities of numerous staff specialists; the diffusion of policy and decision making at different levels of academic governance; and the involvement of policy makers far removed from college classrooms.

The arrival of the 'admissions officer' as a staff specialist was quite evident in the early 1960s. As statewide systems of public higher education adopted system-wide requirements for entry to their various units, the responsibilities of directors of admissions expanded accordingly. And as prestigious universities found themselves with far more applicants than classroom seats or dormitory beds, selective admissions became a provisional solution to educational problems that called for specialised or technical skills. In turn, the admissions process was increasingly directed by a specialist for whom admissions was his or her only responsibility. To give the position a title more in keeping with its academic duties, many directors became 'deans of admissions.'

Selective admission, one means of coping with increasing demands, was quickly seized as an opportunity to admit better prepared students. For most universities this meant high school averages and entrance examination scores that were appreciably higher than those recorded for students previously admitted. The outcome of many such efforts was an almost obsessive concern with multiple regression equations that combine high school averages and entrance examination scores to give the best prediction of academic performance. To improve the precision and accuracy of prediction, many institutions were captivated by freshmen grade-point averages as the most useful single index of achievement at the college level. Admission decisions thereby became a matter of selecting students on the basis of predicted performance.

Other institutions, seeking to reduce drop-out and failure rates, turned to personal interviews as a means of assessing the interests, attitudes, and motives of applicants. As a national survey indicated, 12% of the responding officials regarded personal interviews as the single most important factor in admission decisions. Another 51% believed personal interviews to be an important factor in admission. Less than a third were dubious about the merits of interviews (Hauser & Lazarsfeld, 1964).

Since the 1960s, numerous changes in federal regulations, state laws, governing board policies, and public expectations have altered the decision-making authority and responsibilities of admission officers. A study conducted by the College Board and the American Association of Collegiate Registrars and Admission Officers (AACRAO/CEEB, 1980) implies that admission officials are primarily responsible for specific admission policies in almost half (48%) of the nation's institutions, but admission committees have such responsibilities in more than a third (35%) of the institutions surveyed. General policy, in the form of broad guidelines, sometimes shared among two or more policymaking bodies, was found to be the responsibility of presidents (40%), governing boards (31%), state legislatures (13%), co-ordinating boards (8%), executive councils (25%), and faculty senates (12%) in other institutions. The diffusion of policy decisions reflects, no doubt, the political, legal, and economic struggles of U.S. institutions over the past 30 years. Significant variations are observed in public and private colleges, and in two-year and four-year colleges. It is significant, therefore, that general admission policies are more likely to be decided by admission committees in private four-year colleges (53%). Governing boards are likely to control policy in public four-year colleges (42%), and the influence of state legislatures is quite visible in public two-year colleges (33%).

In 1992, the recruitment, selection, and admission of U.S. college students can be described as energetic and aggressive. The posture of many universities and colleges is competitive, to say the least, and relatively effective, to say the obvious. Despite many gloomy predictions of enrolment decline since the early 1970s, national enrolment patterns reveal no precipitous decline in the number of applicants seeking admission to the nation's prestigious research universities and liberal arts colleges, to the state universities and landgrant institutions that educate the great majority of U.S. college students, or to the various community and/or technical colleges that offer short-term, career-related educational opportunities. Where enrolments have declined, the cause can usually be found in economic conditions, in a lessening demand for certain kinds of educational experiences, and in the attraction of other kinds of educational advantages and benefits.

In institutions where full-time, traditional college-age (18-24 years), male students have fallen in relative numbers, their classroom seats have often been filled by other students. Adult learners (over 25 years of age), women students (in traditionally male fields of study), minority students (identified by race or ethnic group), disadvantaged students (economically, socially, or culturally), handicapped students (especially those who are physically impaired), and students with special talents (art, music, drama, athletics) have participated in higher education at a higher rate as traditional college-age students have declined in relative numbers. In certain fields of study such as engineering, the increase in foreign students is quite noticeable. And with the innumerable and highly variable efforts of many institutions to establish extension centres, inservice programmes, and other forms of offcampus instruction, part-time, working and/or offcampus enrollees have replaced full-time, oncampus students.

REQUIREMENTS AND PROCEDURES

The ACCRAO/CEEB (1980) survey of admission practices and procedures suggests a relatively stable pattern for the nation's two-year and four-year public and private institutions of higher education. Admission requirements were reported to be 'about the same' in 1978 as they were in 1970, and responding admission officials did not anticipate significant changes through the mid-1980s. The kinds of factual data and information required by the 3500 colleges and universities vary greatly according to institutional mission, programmes, services, organised activities, and type of control. To be considered for admission, most applicants are required to submit transcripts of their high school records, entrance examination scores, and one or more letters of recommendation. Other kinds of information that may be required are achievement test scores, personal essays or brief biographies, portfolios, or other evidence of productivity, physical health statements, and other kinds of data that can be reported through questionnaires or checksheets. The uses of such information vary as greatly as the kinds of information gathered.

When specific requirements are made in high school subjects, the requirements usually pertain to units or credits earned and not to the grades earned in specific classes. A typical pattern of requirements is seen in four years of English, two years or less of Mathematics, one year or more of physical science, one year at most of biological science, and two years at most of a foreign language. For many candidates, two years of social science may be specified but the substance of this requirement is not always clear. Over a quarter (26%) of the responding officials regard the pattern of high school subjects as very important; for private, four-year colleges the corresponding figure is 38 percent. Almost a third (30%) of respondent institutions do not take the pattern of high school subjects in admission decisions into account, and at least 9% believe such patterns to be a minor factor.

A significant development in college admissions is the requirement of a college preparatory curriculum by statewide governing boards. In Georgia, for example, where all 34 institutions of public higher education are responsible to a single governing board, a specified number of high school courses is required in English (4), Science (3), Mathematics (3), Social Science (3), and a foreign language (2). Additional courses that are strongly recommended to high school students include computer technology, fine arts, and a third course in a foreign language. Each institution in the university system is authorised to require higher standards for admissions, and provisional admission policies have been approved for applicants from schools in which all requirements could not be met.

When high school grades and test scores are specified, they are likely to be minimum requirements which must be counterbalanced by other, more positive information on the qualifications of candidates. For example, the average minimum high school grade-point average of 2.0 (on a 4-point scale) is specified by 43% of the respondent public four-year institutions and by 58% of the private four-year institutions. An average minimum score of 740 (combined) for the Scholastic Aptitude Test (SAT) is specified by 39% of public four-year colleges and 750 is required by private four-year institutions. Comparable scores for the American College Testing (ACT) test are 16.2 for 30% of the public four-year colleges and 16.4 for 36% of the private four-year colleges.

The requirement of personal essays has increased significantly since the 1970s. They are of value in judging writing skills, and as a source of other information concerning personal qualities, they can often provide insights that are otherwise difficult to obtain. Relatively few (7%) of the respondents in the AACRAO/CEEB (1980) survey, however, regarded personal essays as very important. Much the same response was given on the importance of portfolios. Thirty percent of the respondents from private four-year institutions, however, regarded portfolios as one of several factors that would be considered in making admission decisions.

In brief, the findings of the AACRAO/CEEB survey suggest great variation in admission requirements and procedures when they are considered for public and private two-year and four-year institutions. The extent to which requirements vary is one of several reasons to believe that a lack of uniformity is in the public interest. The flexibility that is maintained in requirements may be lost, however, in the rigidity of admission procedures for many colleges. The pressure of annual cycles in recruitment, selection, admission, and enrolment are unlikely to permit a leisurely pace for reluctant applicants.

STANDARDS AND CRITERIA

The academic standards and criteria that dominate admission decisions and choices continue to be secondary preparation and standardised tests of academic ability. High school grade-point averages or rank in class are often used as a simplified measure of secondary preparation and are the most frequently used criteria of high school performance. The SAT and ACT continue to be the most frequently used measures of verbal and mathematical abilities, educational achievement, and academic promise at the college level. The academic standards that are employed in selective admissions are obscured by the lengthy process of recruitment, application, screening, selection, and acceptance. High school records and entrance examination scores are reduced to statistical indices that have acquired their own distinctive features. Some indices, such as SAT scores and high school averages (or rank in class), have been reified (or personified) because they are so widely accepted as the reasons why individual students are accepted or rejected by various colleges. It is both significant and alarming, therefore, that admission officials in the AACRAO/CEEB (1980) survey did not perceive extensive or pervasive change in admission practices during the decade of the 1970s. Well over half (61%) of responding officials saw no significant change in the importance of high school achievement as a criterion for use in admission decisions. Almost a third (31%) regarded the high school grade average (or class rank) as the single most important factor in making admission decisions. Where selective admission was more important, over four out of ten public four-year colleges (43%) and almost four out of ten private four-year colleges (39%) regarded grade averages or class rank as the most important single factor.

Very few (2%) of the responding institutions regard the SAT, ACT, or PSAT/NMQST as the single most important factor to consider in admission decisions. Over four out of ten (42%) regarded such standardised tests as a very important factor. The high regard for test scores increased when public four-year colleges (59%) and private four-year colleges (54%) were responding.

The use of academic standards and criteria in college admissions gives neither an encouraging nor disappointing picture of higher education in the 1990s. The findings of research give no credence to the opinions of critics (and the news media) who oppose the use of standardised tests in admission decisions. The high school average (or class rank) continues to be the best single predictor of college grades, but SAT scores continue to make a significant contribution to predictive efficiency in many colleges where the incremental validity of the SAT should be appreciated. Colleges dropping the SAT as an admission requirement will be praised in the news media, but editorial praise is but another indication of the controversy that has plagued testing, measurement, evaluation, and assessment for the past four decades.

Systematic and objective research has consistently demonstrated the incremental and differential usefulness of SAT scores in predicting freshmen grade-point averages (Willingham et al., 1990). No one listens, however, when friendly critics point out that prediction is the least satisfactory of solutions to educational problems. And no one bothers to ask about the significance and meaning of grade-point averages as an academic standard or criterion. Very few colleges make admission decisions on the basis of predicted performance. And no institution with a competent director of admissions will reject applicants solely on the basis of their SAT scores. On the contrary, two out of three (65%) AACRAO/CEEB (1980) survey respondents said that no predicted grade-point average was computed at their institution, and well over half (57%) had never conducted a validity study involving entrance examinations.

Among the minor tragedies of higher education is the consistency with which many administrative officials and faculty members use SAT (combined) scores, high school averages, and freshmen grade-point averages as absolute measures of ability and achievement. All three indices have merits that are relative to administrative, academic, and admission decisions but none is a standard that can stand as an absolute. In other words, educators – like the general public and the news media – often confuse criteria (SAT-V, SAT-M, HSA, and GPA) with standards of ability, achievement, or accomplishment that they have not bothered to define and cannot possibly defend.

As long as unusually high SAT scores are applauded by presidents, deans, and admission directors as a special accomplishment (and low scores cited as evidence of intellectual disability), critics should be less concerned about the predictability of grades from SAT scores and high school averages. And as long as honours graduates are selected on the basis of grade-point averages computed to the fourth decimal place, public leaders should worry less about grade inflation or the erosion of academic standards. The target of worry and concern should be the inability of educators to define academic standards that are more directly related to teaching and learning or to specify adequate criteria that would allow an informed public to recognise when academic standards have been met.

CONCLUSIONS AND IMPLICATIONS

At a time when school and college relations are undergoing rapid change it is necessary to again consider admission policies and practices. Another 'era of commission reports' has spurred a national interest in the assessment of educational outcomes as the most suitable way of meeting accreditation requirements and public demands for accountability. Public attention and concern are turning to national standards as one means of ensuring more uniformity in high school curricula and a higher standard of performance for graduating seniors. Organised interest groups, litigants in federal and state courts, and faculty dissidents embrace a specious ideology of multiculturalism to ensure flexibility in all matters pertaining to gender and minority group membership. Efforts to revise the SAT suggest that we are still searching for entrance examinations that are adequate and fair. In all such efforts, admission policies, standards, and criteria are expected to meet public expectations of uniformity, flexibility, and fairness without sacrificing academic quality or excellence. In other words, significant and enduring progress had been made in the admission policies and practices of U.S. colleges and universities, but they are still coping with conditions of flexibility, uniformity, and adequacy that Broome identified in 1903.

From the perspective a new century will provide, later generations of policy and decision makers will wonder why there was so little public accord about the purposes of education in the 1990s. They will understand why college admissions continued to be a crucial stage of transition in the lives of young adults, but will wonder about the inability of schools and colleges to speak a common language and to define acceptable standards and criteria that met public expectations. They will be perplexed about the great distance travelled in the 20th century without making better progress in education. Some of them will be astounded that we were still seeking a fair degree of flexibility in high school curricula and college admission requirements, a reasonable degree of uniformity in high school standards, and adequate and fair tests of the student's intellectual, moral, and physical fitness for higher education.

REFERENCES

AACRAO/CEEB. (1980). *Undergraduate admissions: The realities of institutional policies, practices, and procedures*. A report on a survey conducted by the American Association of Collegiate Registrars and Admissions Officers and The College Entance Examiantion Board. New York: College Entrance Examination Board.

Bowles, F. (1963). *The international study of university admissions: Access to higher education, Vol.1*. New York: Columbia University Press.

Broome, E. C. (1903). *A historical and critical discussion of college admission requirements*. Columbia University Contributions to Philosophy, Psychology, and Education, Vol. XI, Nos. 3-4. [Reprinted by College Entrance Examination Board, 1963].

Clark, B. R. (Ed.). (1985). *The school and the university: An international perspective*. Berkeley: University of California Press.

Fincher, C. (1977). Standardized tests, group differences, and public policy. *College Board Review, Spring*, 19-31.

Fincher, C. (1985, June-July). *The assessment uses of the SAT in the university system of Georgia*. Paper presented at the 11th annual conference of the International Association for Educational Assessment, Oxford, England.

Fincher, C. (1991a). *Assessment, improvement, and cooperation: The challenge of reform in higher education*. Athens: Institute of Higher Education, University of Georgia.

Fincher, C. (1991b). Social justice, public interest and the SAT. In A. J. M. Luijten (Ed.), *Issues in public examinations. A selection of the proceedings of the 1990 IAEA conference*. Utrecht: Lemma.

Fuess, C. M. (1967). *The college board: Its first fifty years*. New York: College Entrance Examination Board.

Hauser, J. A., & Lazarsfeld, P. F. (1964). *The admissions officer*. New York: College Entrance Examination Board.

Valentine, J. A. (1987). *The College Board and the school curriculum*. New York: The College Board.

Willingham, W. W. et al. (1990). *Predicting college grades: An analysis of institutional trends over two decades*. Princeton, NJ: Educational Testing Service.

23. CREDIT TRANSFER IN ADMISSIONS PROCESSES IN THE UNITED STATES

Sandra Johnson
Franklin College,
Lugano, Sorengo, Switzerland

Perhaps one of the greatest strengths of the United States higher education system, as seen by those outside it, is the opportunities it allows students to broaden their education by moving from one institution to another without penalty. While far from being problem free, the mechanism which makes this possible, credit transfer, is a valuable concept long overdue within the educational systems of other countries, and only now being gradually introduced into Europe on a large scale.

Before discussing the various forms of credit transfer which the system accommodates, and before exploring the kinds of decisions that arise, it might be useful to recall the form and structure of the U.S. undergraduate degree. While it is impossible to generalise about any aspect of education in the U.S., if we accept that for every statement about to be made exceptions will certainly exist, the picture looks roughly like the following.

The programme is modular and is usually based on a semester or quarter system. Individual courses are allocated a specific number of credit hours, reflecting the number of class-contact hours involved. Three contact hours each week throughout a semester would qualify the course as a 3-credit course (semesters are generally 15 weeks long, but can be shorter depending on the institution). Credits accumulate as courses are successfully completed, and typically 120 credits are required for graduation. Progress towards graduation, and hence current class status, is reflected in the number of credits accumulated to date. Up to 30 credits signifies freshman status; 31-60 credits indicates a sophomore; 61-90 a junior; and 91+ a senior.

Students studying full-time generally carry five courses per semester, though able students are usually allowed to carry six and less able students can opt to take four; part-time students can carry as few as they choose. On a 3-credit course system, students would normally expect to study for four years before graduating; able students, carrying six courses per semester and attending summer school sessions, can reduce this timescale considerably.

Degree programmes in their entirety generally offer some space for elective courses, especially in the lower division before specialisation towards a major begins. Indeed, in many institutions, especially traditional liberal arts colleges, the curriculum studied in the first two years of the programme will be very broadly based. A large proportion of the 3,500+ tertiary-level institutions in the U.S. are two-year junior or community colleges, which offer students Associate in Arts degrees with the possibility of later transfer into the upper division of a four-year institution to begin specialisation towards a bachelor's degree.

Courses are graded according to a common scale: A, B, C, D and F (fail), often with pluses and minuses on grades A to D. Grade C is a critical grade, universally interpreted as indicating satisfactory performance. Individual faculty have a great deal of autonomy with regard to grading. They choose their own modes of assessment, and they alone make the final grading decisions. Often, graduation will depend on the achievement of an average grade C throughout the programme, or at least for those courses constituting the major. Grades are not generally transferred from one institution to another, though credit transfer is typically allowed only for courses completed with a grade C or higher.

It is, of course, the modularity of programmes, together with the broad base of lower division work, which facilitates credit transfer. Modularity allows a greater possibility of similarity in content coverage at an individual course level than would be the case for an entire one-year non-modular programme, whilst avoiding an otherwise inevitable need to standardise curricula on a large scale. The broadly-based curriculum of the first two years increases the likelihood of content similarity when students apply for associated course exemption alongside their credit transfer.

The system, then, has a relatively flexible structure, which allows the possibility of credit transfer from one institution to another to an extent that would be difficult in any other system. But why should the system incorporate this possibility at all? What forms does credit transfer take? What, if any, are the difficulties inherent in operating it? These are the kinds of question this paper sets out to address.

TYPES OF ADMISSION

There are a number of different routes to admission to institutions in the U.S. system. Most potential students apply for admission from within the country, though there are also those who apply from outside it. Most apply directly from their secondary schools, but others apply after a period of time spent studying in another institution; some even apply after many years in paid employment or after bringing up a family. And then there is the admission agreement required from a potential host institution when students choose to take advantage of their system's study abroad possibility.

The majority of students in U.S. colleges and universities enter higher education directly from their high schools. The minimum requirement for admission is a high school diploma with recommendations from teachers. High school diplomas are awarded by individual high schools, and there is accepted to be little if any comparability in the grades achieved by students in different schools. In consequence, higher education institutions generally require further evidence of academic ability, and the almost universal indicator used for this is performance on the Scholastic Aptitude Test (SAT). Depending on their real quality, their perceived quality, the level of their fees, their general reputation, their location, and whatever other factors render them more or less attractive to potential students, different institutions will demand greater or lower SAT scores as additional minimum entry requirements.

But as indicated above, students graduating from U.S. high schools are not the only applicants to tertiary institutions. For decades the U.S. system has made available the possibility of admission to its institutions to individuals who have received their entire secondary education in the system of another country. In this field the U.S. has without question been a pioneer, and much research has been undertaken over the years by various bodies to provide guidelines to admissions officers on which foreign certificates can reasonably be considered equivalent to the U.S. high school diploma, and so qualify the applicant for consideration for admission. Applicants with native languages other than English are usually in addition required to achieve some minimum score on an English proficiency test, such as the Test of English as a Foreign Language (TOEFL).

Then there is the possibility of temporary or permanent transfer from one institution to another within the U.S., or from a foreign institution into one in the U.S. system. Temporary transfer would include those students who need to relocate for a while, perhaps for family reasons, as well as those who choose to study for a semester or a year abroad. Permanent transfer means what it says: some students, for whatever reason, might at some stage have no choice but to relocate, and so have to leave their original home institution on a permanent basis. Others will simply take advantage of the system's transfer possibility to broaden their education. Still others will be constrained to leave their home institution because of poor academic performance, and will look desperately for, and will generally eventually find, another institution of lower quality willing to allow them to continue their education.

All these different kinds of individual, whatever their status before application, can in principle qualify not only for admission but also for credit transfer and advanced placement or advanced standing in their future institutions.

For example, U.S. high school students can attempt one or other of the College Board Advanced Placement tests and in that way gain some credit advantage as soon as they begin college. Indeed, able pupils in schools in large towns in the U.S.

are particularly advantaged, since many large universities allow potential home students to attend regular college freshman courses during their senior year in high school, awarding credits for successful completion once the individuals concerned are eventually admitted.

Mature students can also take various commercial standardised tests which would allow them immediate credit on entry to higher education. In addition, in some institutions such individuals could be given credit, with or without test evidence, for past achievement of some relevant kind.

Students transferring from one college or university to another will rarely do so without the security of some credit transfer. Not all U.S. universities accept transfer of credit from other institutions, of course, and others accept from some institutions, with or without reservation, but not from all. Christensen (1990) offers a description of the variety of policies in operation today.

Some of the more prestigious universities do not accept credit transfer from any other American institutions, however prestigious they might be. Students can choose to transfer out of such universities without penalty, but others cannot transfer in, other than as freshmen. In less prestigious institutions the situation is more generous and less clearcut. Despite the fact that U.S. accreditation implies little about institutional academic quality, where institutions accept credit transfer at all they will usually, thought not always, do so without reservation from any institution accredited by one of the six regional accreditation boards. Even then, credit is often transferred only on a course by course basis.

For non-accredited institutions, or for those accredited by some organisation other than the regional boards, or for transfer within a business programme, credit transfer is either not allowed or is allowed only on a provisional basis. Provisional credit transfer means that a student will be given the transfer credit only after one or two semesters in the new home institution on condition the student manages to maintain a grade-point average of 2 or higher (i.e., an average grade C).

For credit transfer to be accompanied by exemption from required courses the courses successfully followed in the previous institution must be considered by relevant persons in the new institution to be sufficiently similar in content coverage and demand to warrant the exemption. Often this similarity is determined on nothing more than brief one-paragraph course descriptions, although the review can be a little more thorough, involving outline syllabuses and the names of textbooks used.

For foreign students the situation is more complex. In an effort to be as fair as possible, and as attractive as possible, to foreign students, U.S. institutions offer up to one full year of credit (30 credit hours) for most of the major European school leaving certificates, including the French *Baccalauréate*, the German *Abitur*, and the Italian *Maturità*. The rationale underlying this long-standing tradition is that while the U.S. primary and secondary system spans 12 years of full-time education, European school-leaving certificates often require 13 years of education. The thirteenth year is credited as equivalent to the first year of American college education. However, credit is not automatic, and can depend on grades achieved in the principal subjects contributing to the certificate. Where credit is accepted, appropriate course exemptions in U.S. system are relatively easily identified, since most foreign educational systems maintain a broad curriculum to the point of exit from secondary schooling.

The single most obvious exception to the rule is the British General Certificate of Education at Advanced level. The British system is, or has been, extremely selective by tradition, and has involved subject specialisation from a much earlier age than is the case in most other countries. As a consequence, academically able British students with three A-level passes would actually be awarded less credit transfer in total than their counterparts from other European countries, irrespective of grades achieved. They would also find difficulty gaining many specific course exemptions in the broadly-based U.S. system, given the limited range of subjects they had studied during their last years in secondary school. The problem is one of matching breadth with depth, an issue we will return to later.

For our final group of applicants, students studying in foreign colleges and universities who wish to transfer into the U.S. system, the guidelines are complex and credit transfer is often negotiated on an individual basis. Despite the potential difficulties, it is, ironically, still easier for many of these students to transfer from their own national systems into that of the United States with minimal penalty than it is to transfer from one institution to another within their own home countries.

DETERMINING EQUIVALENCES FOR CREDIT TRANSFER

The many U.S. and other organisations that have over the years, with the collaboration of academics, educational administrators, and politicians, produced numerous volumes describing the educational systems of the different countries in the world are to be congratulated. For the task is not an easy one. Each country has, over centuries, developed a system with features unique to itself. In every system, there is variety in type of education and of institution at every level. The picture is complex, as a browse through any volume of, for example, the World Education Series of the American Association of Collegiate Registrars and Admissions Officers will testify (see, e.g., Schuler, 1984, on the Netherlands; Mashiko, 1989, on Japan).

It is impossible to take account of all the complexity when comparing one system with another in attempts to determine equivalences. And it is understandable that among the various factors which determine whether educational experiences, and in particular academic achievements, are comparable, that of duration of study is the easiest to handle. Thus it is that if one national system requires students to undertake 13 years of education before awarding a school leaving certificate and the U.S. system requires only 12, then most people would be happy to accept that the additional year deserves some kind of recognition when students apply for admission to a U.S. college.

The problem that must be faced is how much credit to award, and on what basis it should be awarded. It is here that serious conceptual difficulties arise. For duration of education is clearly not of itself a sufficient criterion for determining equivalence of experience. The subjects studied and the content coverage within these are clearly also relevant, particularly when exemption from foundation-level courses on which more advanced study would normally build is at issue. In addition, there is level of demand to consider, as well as level of achievement.

As noted in Johnson (1991), relative demand levels and consequent relative achievement levels are topics rarely touched upon in placement guidelines, since informed comment would require a solid research base involving detailed scrutiny of syllabuses and examination papers. Indeed, one of the most observant discussions on this issue offered in the various publications on foreign educational systems and U.S. equivalence was included in a report on Norway (Sjorgren & Kerr, 1985), inspired perhaps by the fact that there is no longer a formal school leaving certificate awarded in that country which could be used for simplistic comparative statements.

Just as there is little if any comparability between the grades achieved in high school diplomas by students graduating from different high schools, there is similarly little comparability between the grades awarded within U.S. higher education institutions. Few working in the system would dispute that there is likely to be only a tenuous equivalence between the grades awarded to students in different higher education institutions following the same courses, or between the grades awarded to students in the same institution following different courses, or even to students following the same courses in the same institution at different times. As mentioned earlier, faculty in U.S. colleges use a variety of approaches to assessment, and decide their own component weightings when deciding final grades. Even when they use standardised, often textbook, tests, which many do, these alone will not determine overall course grades.

Given this, we are left wondering what the true significance of grade C as indicating 'satisfactory' performance is. What does 'satisfactory' mean? 'Satisfactory' with respect to what? To other students in the class? Probably. To other students in other institutions studying similar subject matter? Maybe. To some universal abstract and absolute criteria that all teachers are familiar with? Highly unlikely, given the British experience in grade comparability investigation (see, for example, Johnson & Cohen, 1983, 1984).

If grade C cannot be assumed comparable from one institution to another within the U.S. system, in terms of what it indicates about students' real educational experiences and achievements, how can it be used as a yardstick against which to measure foreign grading scales? And yet it is. Foreign grading scales, where these exist, are implicitly or explicitly 'equated' with the universal U.S. scale, the critical reference point for equivalence being whichever grade on the foreign system has the verbal description 'satisfactory.' *The Country Index* (Sepmeyer, 1986) is particularly guilty of this practice.

Without any consideration of the meaning of 'satisfactory' in the two systems, without any consideration of, for example, the percentages of an age-group in the two systems who achieve the various grades, how can such comparability claims be justified? Even as 'guidelines' for admissions officers, they are naive in the extreme. Perhaps the British A-level system has been among those that have suffered the most from this grade equivalence practice. In the past, A-level grades of A, B, or C have typically qualified an applicant to the U.S. system for nine credit hours per subject, with grades of D or E qualifying for less credit, even none at all in some institutions.

Given the very narrow range of percentage points known to separate grades B from D in the British A-level, how can this practice be maintained? It clearly cannot, and in the latest guidelines to be published featuring British certificates no reference is made to credit variation with regard to grades achieved; according to these placement recommendations, an applicant offering A-levels for entry 'may be considered for up to 1 year of advanced standing credit in each subject corresponding to an A-level pass' (Higashi, Weaver, & Margolis, 1991, p.49).

This is an improvement on earlier practice, since grades A to E all earn credit. Yet just six credits per A-level pass are recommended, still leaving A-level certificate holders with much less total credit transfer than any of their continental diploma-holding peers. Is this good enough? Does it do justice to the individual? Has depth of study been adequately rewarded in a system based on breadth? These are difficult questions to answer. Much time has been spent studying foreign systems, describing them in depth, and providing what are intended to be helpful guidelines to admissions officers. Yet there is room for improvement in the transfer of credit between national systems.

It would not be too difficult, for instance, to compile relevant statistics about the performances of examination candidates, statistics such as the percentages of students achieving each grade on national examinations, even maybe about the often arbitrary decisions about cut-off points that distinguish passes from failures, or 'satisfactory' grades from the rest. There would be risks in adopting such a strategy, it is true, especially the risk of undermining the confidence of the public in the absoluteness of examination grading. But in the interests of justice to the individual, maybe this is the direction we should be moving in now.

REFERENCES

Christensen, J. E. (Ed.). (1990). *Transfer credit practices of designated educational institutions: An information exchange, 1990-1992*. Washington DC: American Association of Collegiate Registrars and Admissions Officers.

Higashi, S. K., Weaver, R., & Margolis, A. (1991). *The educational system of the United Kingdom: The admission and placement of students from the United Kingdom and study abroad opportunities.* Washington, DC: American Association of Collegiate Registrars and Admissions Officers and NAFSA, Association of International Educators.

Johnson, S. (1991). Determining equivalence among European educational qualifications. In A. J. M. Luitjen (Ed.), *Issues in public examinations. A selection of the proceedings of the 1990 IAEA conference.* Utrecht: Lemma.

Johnson, S., & Cohen, L. (1983). *Investigating grade comparability through cross-moderation.* London: Schools Council.

Johnson, S., & Cohen, L. (1984). Cross-moderation: A useful comparative technique? *British Journal of Educational Research, 10,* 89-97.

Mashiko, E. E. (1989). *Japan.* (World Education Series). Washington, DC: American Association of Collegiate Registrars and Admissions Officers.

Sepmeyer, I. H. (1986). *The country index. Interpretations for use in the evaluation of foreign educational credentials.* Alhambra CA: Frank Severy Publishing.

Schuler, P. (1984). *The Netherlands.* (World Education Series). Washington, DC: American Association of Collegiate Registrars and Admissions Officers.

Sjogren, C. F., & Kerr, L. G. (1985). *Norway: A guide to the admission and placement of Norwegian students in North American colleges and universities.* New York: College Entrance Examination Board.

24. EQUITY AND SELECTIVE ACCESS TO HIGHER EDUCATION IN LATIN AMERICA

Benjamin Alvarez
Academy for Educational Development,
Washington DC

NEW CONTEXT FOR AN OLD DEBATE

The university, the most traditional institution of knowledge, has evolved through history and has adapted to changing needs and circumstances all over the world. But it has never been subjected to so many conflicting demands and intensive debates as today when participation rates in industrialised countries have reached one in three of the population in the 20- to 24-year age range. Issues related to the university's role, financing, admissions, and outcomes are particularly critical in developing nations, in which higher education systems have also grown very rapidly since 1960. As new opportunities became available and a great variety of institutions and programmes were created, expectations for higher education among youth increased dramatically. However, reassessment is at present taking place and society in general–governments, private enterprises, and families–is demanding that its publicly-supported institutions perform more efficiently. Meanwhile, severe economic constraints, radical shifts in the responsibility of the state in relation to education, and emerging global trends suggest a major new role for institutions devoted to knowledge generation and utilisation in all spheres of life.

In Latin America, for example, the tenfold expansion of higher education enrolment over the last three decades (Figure 24.1) has resulted in a complex, diversified, overpopulated, and poorly supported system. Several universities of the region, particularly the major public ones, exhibit severe signs of deterioration and inadequate funding which demand the design of alternative operational models and the formulation of new policies. Policy makers will have to take a fresh look at dilemmas faced by governments and the private sector in relation to the role of higher education in society. Some of the dilemmas have remained the same since Plato founded the Academy, the forerunner of our modern universities twenty-four centuries ago, but the context of the debate has changed substantially in recent years at both global and national levels.

FIGURE 24.1

HIGHER EDUCATION ENROLMENT RATIO BY REGION

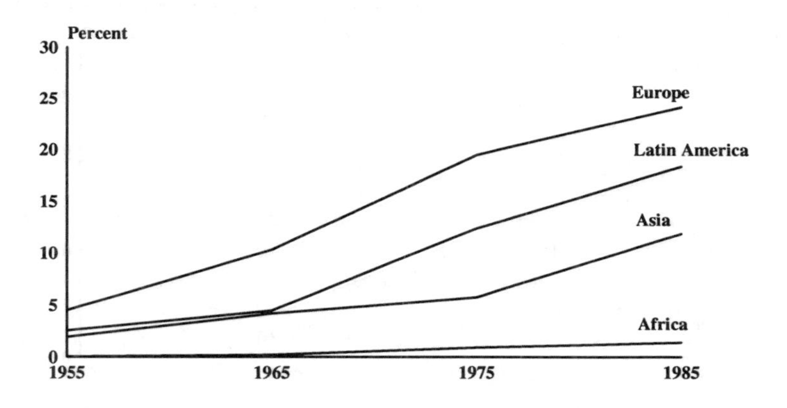

Source: Ramirez & Riddle (1991), p.96

Economic, political, and technological changes demand a reassessment of our current institutions of knowledge. Universities need to establish a balance between their search for knowledge and the exercise of power, between basic research and technology, between general and specialised instruction, between economic progress and social service, between access and equity, quantity and quality, and research and teaching. The balance of all these factors will determine curriculum patterns, research and educational outcomes, and student-selection mechanisms.

This paper analyzes some of the critical issues of higher education in Latin America through a consideration of admission policies, procedures, and results. General comments on prevailing policies in different countries are followed by examples of access systems reflecting alternative philosophical principles relating to the function of higher education in society. The application of such principles has produced partial solutions to the problems confronting higher education systems, problems which have, however, been exacerbated by profound changes in contemporary societies, resulting in the failure of systems that could not respond to unrealistic demands and increasing social expectations.

A continuation of current trends implies that during the next five years more students will be applying to universities in Latin America; new educational requirements for employment will be established by the productive and the social sectors; more rigorous standards of quality will be demanded from universities; less public resources will be available and more competition will be generated for places in both university and in non-university institutions of higher education.

Today's universities are part of a complex system of organisations devoted to the generation and utilisation of knowledge and high-level learning. Laboratories, research centres, scientific associations, foundations promoting science and technology, research departments in industry, consultancy groups, museums and specialised units in government share many features and goals of traditional academic centres. Other institutions less closely related to the development of research and teaching, such as business enterprises, are faced with the challenge of making increasingly complex goods which require the intensive use of knowledge, as well as training and retraining of their employees at all levels. The new alliances between universities and other institutions that are beginning to emerge may provide new possibilities for all partners involved and present unexpected problems for academic organisations, some of which will be related to access mechanisms.

In addition to the technical issues related to validity and reliability of the tools used, the admission procedures to higher education in Latin America will have to take account of developments such as the following: (a) the emergence of different patterns of relationships between universities, private enterprise, and governments; (b) growing competition from other institutions in the 'education and research market,' both in their own countries and abroad; (c) an increasing need for professional updating and the changing job requirements of the productive sector; (d) the availability of advanced technologies; (e) the recent trends towards a 'common market of knowledge' in a region; and (f) the qualitative changes that most countries are implementing in their school curricula.

The traditional concern of most Latin American and Caribbean countries regarding university admission has been to improve its democratic operation. Unfortunately, social inequities persist in the educational systems of the region. The implementation of alternative admission policies in universities as an instrument of social mobility has not provided evidence of the success of these policies.

INSTITUTIONS AND STUDENTS

Over six million students are currently registered at the 2,500 Latin American higher education institutions. The universities account for only one-fifth of those institutions; the rest are professional training centres, technological institutes, or vocational institutions.

Few universities offer post-graduate programmes (Figure 24.2). Most of the 150 that do are concentrated in five countries: Brazil, Mexico, Colombia, Chile, and

Argentina. The concept of a 'research university' is relatively new to the region as evidenced by the lack of long-term research efforts supported by doctoral programmes. Of the approximately 21,200 post-graduate programmes existing in Latin America and the Caribbean, only 215 are offered at the doctoral level.

FIGURE 24.2

HIGHER EDUCATION INSTITUTIONS IN LATIN AMERICA AND THE CARIBBEAN

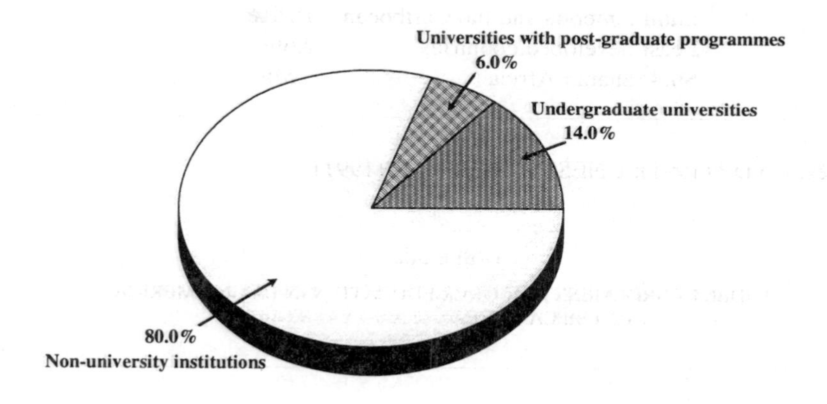

Source: IDRC, 1992; UNESCO-CRESALC, 1991

The participation rate in education of the population in the 20- to 24-year old age range for the region is 16.9%, a high figure in comparison with the average for developing countries (6.5%) or even the world average (12.2%) (Table 24.1). However, participation rates vary from 1.1% in Haiti to 41.6% in Uruguay, indicating the large variance between countries. The same observation can be made in relation to differences in educational opportunities within countries. Latin America and Caribbean countries can be classified in three groups according to participation rates in higher education: high (over 20%), medium (between 10 and 20%), and low (under 10%). There are approximately eight countries in each group (Table 24.2).

TABLE 24.1

PARTICIPATION RATES OF SCHOOL AGE POPULATION IN HIGHER EDUCATION (20-24 YEARS OLD)

The World	12.2%
Industrial countries	33.0%
Developing countries	6.5%
Latin America and the Caribbean	16.9%
Least developed countries	2.6%
Sub-Saharan Africa	1.5%

Sources: UNDP (1991); UNESCO-CRESALC (1991)

TABLE 24.2

STUDENT ENROLMENT IN HIGHER EDUCATION IN LATIN AMERICA AND THE CARIBBEAN (20-24 YEARS OLD)

High (more than 20%)		Medium (10% to 20%)		Low (less than 10%)	
Uruguay	41.6	Barbados	19.9	Paraguay	9.7
Argentina	38.4	Dominican R.	19.3	Honduras	9.5
Ecuador	33.1	Bolivia	19.0	Nicaragua	8.7
Panama	28.2	Chile	15.9	Guatemala	8.6
Venezuela	26.1	Mexico	15.7	Surinam	7.7
Peru	24.6	El Salvador	14.1	Trin. & Tob.	4.2
Costa Rica	23.8	Colombia	13.I	Jamaica	4.2
Cuba	22.5	Brazil	11.4	Guyana	2.1
				Haiti	1.1

Source: UNESCO-CRESALC (1991)

As institutional capacity develops, more students tend to stay in their own region to undertake their undergraduate and first level post-graduate education; currently only a few countries (Caribbean countries, except Cuba) send large proportions of university students abroad (Table 24.3).

TABLE 24.3

PERCENTAGE OF HIGHER EDUCATION STUDENTS ABROAD
(20-24 YEARS OLD)

High		Medium		Low	
Trin. & Tob	61.7	Nicaragua	9.9	Guatemala	1.9
Haiti	31.1	Honduras	3.7	El Salvador	1.9
Guyana	30.8	Panama	3.4	Bolivia	1.8
Jamaica	21.5			Costa Rica	1.8
Barbados	12.6			Chile	1.4
				Colombia	1.3
				Venezuela	1.1
				Paraguay	1.0
				Peru	0.8
				Dominican R.	0.7
				Ecuador	0.6
				Cuba	0.6
				Mexico	0.6
				Uruguay	0.6
				Brazil	0.5
				Argentina	0.3

Source: UNDP (1991)

ENTRANCE REQUIREMENTS

For a long time there has been a debate on who should and who should not have access to higher education. However, selection procedures have not changed substantially. In addition to a high-school diploma, some higher education institutions also take into account results on entrance examinations (usually standardised tests) or secondary education grades. Admission is also influenced by other external factors such as ability to pay tuition fees, previous learning experiences, and social class.

A summary of the prevailing formal requirements for higher education entrance throughout Latin America and Caribbean countries is presented in Table 24.4. These requirements are related to the characteristics of higher education in each country and to the country's history and social philosophy. Open access to higher education, for example, prevails in societies with strong state support for education. Classical examples include Uruguay and Argentina. Other countries, such as Chile, Costa Rica, Brazil, and especially Colombia, have developed a complex system of admissions to higher education, arising from the fact that they have a variety of institutions, with different objectives and characteristics.

TABLE 24.4

ACCESS REQUIREMENTS FOR HIGHER EDUCATION IN LATIN AMERICA AND THE CARIBBEAN

Countries	School grades	National Examination for all	Examination for some institutions	High school diploma
HIGH				
Uruguay				x
Argentina				x
Ecuador			x	x
Panama				x
Venezuela	x	x		x
Peru			x	x
Costa Rica			x	x
Cuba	x	x		x
MEDIUM				
Barbados	x			x
Dominican Rep.			x	x
Bolivia			x	x
Chile	x	x	x	x
Mexico		x	x	x
El Salvador				x
Colombia		x		x
Brazil		x		x
LOW				
Paraguay				x
Honduras				x
Nicaragua				x
Guatemala				x
Trin-Toba	x			x
Guyana	x	x		x
Haiti				x

Performance on national examinations is used in about one-third of the countries. In others, examinations are administered by individual institutions (particularly large private liberal arts colleges) or by certain schools within universities, such as Medicine or Engineering. High school grades are also considered as a selection criterion in Cuba, Guyana, and Venezuela (Garcia-Guadilla, 1992). Academic requirements and standards, legal procedures and schedules, and even basic information, vary so much that it is almost impossible for students to move from one country to another to begin university studies or to transfer credits from one institution to another within the same country.

OPEN ACCESS TO HIGHER EDUCATION: THE CASE OF URUGUAY

At first sight an effective way to solve the problem of educational inequalities might appear to be the elimination of selection procedures and fees. Uruguay, with its tradition of publicly supported educational institutions at all levels, adopted this approach. Until very recently there was only one university in the country: the University of the Republic, which has currently about 60,000 students. Now there is a private Catholic university with less than 1,000 students, as well as several technical schools and some graduate programmes affiliated to non-university institutions.

The University of the Republic has free tuition and follows a policy of professional training through independent schools which provide specific curricula aimed at preparing students for specific careers. From their first semester, students are trained for the occupation of accountant, notary public, lawyer, engineer, etc. Highly structured and uniform annual teaching programmes constitute the general rule. There are few research oriented activities and, with the exception of the university hospital, few community projects.

The Transition from High School to University

In Uruguay, the only requirement for entry to university is the high-school diploma. High-school curricula, however, are specialised and closely linked to professional programmes within the university. The last two years of high school follow schemes which vary according to the prospective careers that the students want to pursue. At an early age, during the 11th grade, students must select from among three alternatives: Humanities, Sciences, and Biology. At the 12th grade, they must choose between Law and Economics (for the Humanities alternative); Engineering and Architecture (for the scientific alternative); and Medicine and Agronomy (for the biological alternative). Students wishing to change their major areas of study in the university must go back to high school to satisfy the entry requirements for the new career.

Outcomes And Limitations Of The Open Access System

Several conclusions about the system of open access to higher education in Uruguay can be drawn; some are related to the demographic composition of the student body, others to university curricula, teachers' role, and management of the university as a whole. The most notable phenomenon is the massive student intake. Uruguay has the highest student participation rate of all Latin American countries (41.6%). In practice, however, students can be registered for several years without formally attending school. In order to respond to the demands of large-scale registration within a very limited budget, the university has to rely on mass teaching strategies (large classes in movie theatres, voluntary attendance, and an evaluation system based exclusively on essay-type examinations).

The student population is comparatively old. While in the United States only 15% of undergraduate students are older than 24 (Facts about higher education, 1989), in Uruguay the percentage is almost 50 (Universidad de la Republica del Uruguay, 1988). About one-fourth of students are older than 30. The mean age of undergraduate students is 25.3 years for men and 24.8 for women. The average age for university entrants is also relatively high: over 20 years. Non-completion rates are high. In theory, the concept of 'dropping-out' does not apply to university students in Uruguay, since students can stay for years without losing their academic status and there are no minimum requirements to continue at the university. The Census of 1988 showed that in a typical career of five years, about 42% of students had not completed 20% of required courses, meaning that they were in practical terms still freshmen. Although more than half of the students registered for the first year never attend classes in the second year (Errandonea, 1991), those who remain tend to stay in school for a long time as suggested by the fact that about 46% of those registered in 1988 had entered the school more than four years earlier.

The basic activities of teachers at the University of the Republic are lecturing and grading exams, which in practice are the only evaluation tool available. Examinations are usually based upon memorisation, and are of the essay type. There is no academic advisory system, nor even space for teachers' offices. The student services or *bedelías* are managed by clerks with practically no academic training. There are no computers to process student information nor is there a centralised data base.

Although there is a general awareness of the need to reassess its functions, procedures, and curricula, the university is too large and politically complex for radical shifts to be feasible. However, the quality of teaching, the absence of research, and problems relating to the recruitment and evaluation of students will be on the university agenda for a long time. While the open model has had predictable difficulties from the point of view of quality, one might expect greater success on the side of social equity. Recent studies have concluded that the opposite is the case. Errandonea (1991) suggests that the university is less efficient today than in 1960 in its role as an agent of social mobility; and at that time it was less efficient than during the first decades of the century. A comparative analysis of recent student demographic information and parallel data collected in 1960 indicates that the representation of lower social classes in the university has not increased as expected. Similar observations have been made in Argentina, which has also followed the open access model for higher education (Sigal, 1991).

Invisible selection mechanisms are in place in the model of open access to university in Latin America; some of these operate before and others after formal admissions and registration procedures. External pressures created by growing private competition and the inability of national governments to support the higher education system will have a major impact on the implementation of explicit selection strategies.

A FREE-MARKET MODEL: THE COLOMBIAN APPROACH

Higher education in Colombia has a long tradition going back to the 16th century when the first Catholic universities were founded. In the 19th century, the state created public universities. There is now a mixed system of private and public institutions of different kinds: national and regional public universities, religious and secular private universities, and public and private organisations which are not universities (technological and intermediate professional institutions). In 1960, only 2% of Colombians aged 20 to 24 years had access to higher education. Today, the figure is almost 15 percent. During the 1960s and 1970s there was a huge expansion in the availability of university places, and from 1983 correspondence courses, which began in both public and private universities, provided new opportunities and alternatives for access to students living outside metropolitan areas.

Selection Mechanisms for a Segmented Market

Admission requirements to universities include both the high-school diploma and the taking of state examinations, which are standardised tests designed to demonstrate knowledge and abilities. The universities decide on the minimum score required for each course of study. The National Testing Service, a department of ICFES (Colombian Institute for Higher Education), is responsible for the preparation, application, and processing of state examinations.

Universities may also establish other requirements for admission, such as interviews, additional examinations, and high-school grades. Different criteria and sources of information are combined for student selection. The predominant pattern for public universities is to give priority to test results in state examinations and additional achievement measures. For private universities, personal interviews are an important selection device. Of the 256 Colombian higher education institutions existing in 1992, 253 require that applicants present their scores on state examinations. In addition, 76 institutions apply their own tests and 161 interview each applicant. Sixteen of the latter also require some previous work experience. In general terms, admission to higher education is highly selective, particularly for the socially prestigious universities in which courses such as Medicine are much in demand. The institutes of technology, the intermediate professional entities, and the open universities or programmes are on the whole less selective. Different institutions tend to serve different segments of the higher education market. Obviously, the social prestige of qualifications varies from one institution to another.

Selection Devices

The state examinations cover the areas of Mathematics, Science, Social Studies, and Language. There is room for optional subjects to allow students from vocational or comprehensive schools to compete on equal terms. Although the system has been in operation for over two decades, few studies have focused on the validity and reliability of the tests that all high-school graduates must take. In two studies, the first conducted in 1977 in the Universidad del Valle and the second in the National University in 1988, a positive and significant correlation was found between the results obtained on the standardised tests developed by the universities and the tests provided by the National Testing Service (Mantilla, Giraldo, & Molina, 1991). The lack of research in this area contrasts with the social importance attributed to tests in the national context. In addition to their function as a higher education selection tool, state examinations have become a social indicator of secondary school performance. Each semester, there is a covert competition among the top schools in the country for the best student averages on public tests.

Outcomes and Limitations

The effects of the Colombian system are mixed and highly heterogeneous. Social inequalities are reinforced by the existence of parallel paths in higher education. Some of those paths lead students from good private bilingual high schools to well-established high quality universities; others lead to intermediate institutions or colleges lacking resources and social prestige. Government efforts aimed at controlling and monitoring the quality of higher education institutions and programmes through the establishment of ICFES (The Colombian Institute for Higher Education) have not been effective. There are more poor quality higher education institutions with 'official approval' than ever before.

Students are able to choose, at least theoretically, among a great variety of options. The universities can also choose among vast numbers of applicants. However, the development and application of measures meeting quality and equity criteria are the ultimate responsibility of each individual institution. Students with economic resources, good educational background, and family support have a better chance of entering and graduating from the centres of excellence than the majority from public high schools, rural areas, or poor environments.

LESSONS AND FUTURE CHALLENGES

Several lessons can be learned from the recent history of Latin American universities in their attempts to resolve the problem of securing equity in their access procedures. An obvious conclusion is that traditional approaches to the problem have not been very successful; the traditional rhetoric which considered universities as the main tool for social mobility and change does not seem to have strong empirical evidence to support it. Paradoxically, high levels of higher education development coexist with low attendance ratios at primary and secondary school and high illiteracy rates in the majority of the countries, as illustrated by the cases of Bolivia and the Dominican Republic, which have a higher education enrolment ratio of over 19%, but illiteracy rates of 21 and 16% respectively (UNDP, 1994).

In real terms, for Latin American children and youth, the selection process for higher education begins years before they reach the stage of meeting entry requirements. If social equity issues are not addressed at early stages of human development, there is little possibility that universities can change the social structure of the countries through their admissions systems.

To date, research on university admissions and school performance has not been very creative; the majority of studies carried out in the region on those issues tend to repeat analyses developed in advanced countries. Greater consideration now needs to be given to national evaluation or testing services. Evaluation tools should not be regarded as final products: a permanent research effort needs to be applied to the development of such programmes.

Despite past failures and current difficulties, the prospects for higher education in the region appear promising. As knowledge generation and utilisation become major concerns for all nations, new opportunities for innovation will emerge. Latin America has already a modest but basic social capital represented by institutions and human resources. We can expect the new relationships that universities are establishing with other institutions and sectors of society, the availability of advanced technological resources, and the needs that are emerging from the new economic and political environment to result in major innovations and adaptations of their admission and selection systems.

REFERENCES

Facts about higher education in the nation, the states, and D.C. (1989). *Chronicle of Higher Education Almanac, 36*(1), 1-96.

Errandonea, A. (1991, February). Los ciclos básicos como respuesta a la masificación universitaria en América Latina. *Revista de Ciencias Sociales*, pp.89-98.

García-Guadilla, C. (1992). Modelos de acceso y políticas de ingreso a la educación superior. El caso de América Latina y el Caribe. *Educación Superior y Sociedad*, *2*(2), 72-92.

IDRC (International Development Research Centre). (1992). *Postgrados en América Latina y el Caribe*. Montevideo: Author.

Mantilla, M., Giraldo, M., & Molina, M. (1991). *Quienes aspiran a la educación superior en Colombia*. Unpublished manuscript, Servicio Nacional de Pruebas, Bogotá.

Ramirez, F. O., & Riddle, P. (1991). The expansion of higher education. In P.G. Altbach (Ed.), *International higher education. An encyclopedia. Vol. 1*. New York: Garland.

Sigal, V. (1991). *Consideraciones sobre el ingreso irrestricto a la universidad*. Paper presented at Seminario de la Red Latinoamericana de Educación y Trabajo, CIID-CENEP, Buenos Aires.

UNESCO-CRESALC. (1991). *Visión cuantitativa de la educación superior en América Latina*. Caracas: Author.

UNDP. (1991). *Human development report*. New York: Oxford University Press.

UNDP. (1994). *Human development report*. New York: Oxford University Press.

Universidad de la Republica del Uruguay. (1988). *IV censo general de estudiantes universitarios*. Montevideo: Author.

25. THE ENROLMENT AND EXAMINATION SYSTEM TO HIGHER EDUCATION IN CHINA

Yang Xuewei
National Education Examinations Authority, Beijing

The institutions of higher education in China consist of two categories: the 'normal' and the 'adult'. Normal institutions offer undergraduate and special courses for students who have just completed secondary school. There are altogether 1,075 such colleges and universities in the country, enrolling annually about 600,000 students from 3,000,000 candidates. Graduates from such institutions are assigned by the government to various technical or management jobs. Adult institutions also offer undergraduate and special courses, admitting those who have worked for more than two years after graduation from secondary schools, vocational schools, technical secondary schools, or schools of technology. There are 1,333 such colleges, enrolling annually about 400,000 students from 1,300,000 candidates.

National entrance examinations are held for both categories of colleges separately. Besides, the normal colleges and universities also admit every year about 50,000 graduate students for master's degrees from 130,000 candidates. Common tests are given in the common subjects while special subjects are tested separately by the universities concerned. In the annual admission of nearly 3,000 postgraduate students for doctor's degree, candidates are tested by each university individually.

The entrance examination for the normal colleges and universities, which is referred to as the matriculation, is by far the most important of all examinations administered in China and can be regarded as a continuation of the imperial examination system which goes back more than 1000 years. Although it is an entrance examination to individual colleges and universities, it is actually administered on behalf of the government by the State Education Commission. The examination paper is ranked as top secret at state level and is protected by the Ministry of Public Security and the State Security Bureau. At the provincial level, an enrolment committee is formed consisting of the heads of the departments responsible for such services as education, personnel, public security, health care, communication, and commerce, under the leadership of one of the deputy governors of the province. Examination rooms are provided by the county and supervised by a vice-head of the county with the relevant responsibility. Test papers are printed by the printers approved by the Security Bureau and protected by armed police.

The matriculation examination is held on July 7, 8, and 9, days which by now have assumed the air of a festival. Accommodation arrangements are made in county towns for examinees from rural areas by their schools. Doctors are posted at examination centres, makeshift selling stalls are put up by shops, and temporary bus lines and stops are installed where necessary. Even catastrophic flooding in 1991 was not allowed to interfere with the conduct of the examination. Any attempted irregularities are fully investigated and, where appropriate, punished by law.

Before the founding of the People's Republic (PR) of China, the matriculation examination was generally held by individual colleges and universities. Beginning in 1952 following two years of discussions and trials, it was decided that all candidates for both the undergraduate courses and special courses at all normal colleges and universities in the country would have to take a nationwide matriculation examination administered by the government. The main points of the regulations governing the admission of students are laid down in a publication entitled *Regulations Regarding the Enrolment System of Normal Institutions of Higher Education* issued by the State Education Commission.

Anyone who is a citizen of PR China, under the age of 25, single, and has completed senior secondary school, can enter for the examination. (Those over the age of 25 can take the matriculation examination for adult colleges and universities.) The examination falls into two categories: liberal arts, and science and technology. The former tests such subjects as Chinese, mathematics, Politics, History, Geography, and a foreign language. The latter tests Chinese, Mathematics, Politics, Physics, Chemistry, Biology, and a foreign language. The test time for Chinese is 150 minutes. All other subjects are allotted 120 minutes.

Some colleges and universities enrol students from all over the country, while others enrol students from their own province or municipalities only. An examinee anywhere in the country can apply to five colleges and to five universities without having to take the examination where the colleges are located.

In the autonomous regions of the minority nationalities, colleges and universities which adopt their native languages as the working languages set the examination papers and administer the matriculation examination independently. Each provincial enrolment and testing organisation is responsible for the printing of examination papers, organising the administration of the examination and scoring the papers. The score is sent to each individual examinee.

If a graduate from a minority nationality secondary school applies to a college using the Chinese language, he/she must take the national matriculation examination, but in a different form. In this case, Chinese is tested by a special paper set by the State Education Commission which must be worked on in Chinese while in the other subjects, test papers are translated into the examinees' languages and may be worked on in these languages. A test of a candidate's own native language may be given along with a Chinese test.

The assessment of applicants for adult colleges and universities is done by a neighbourhood committee. The admission work is done by individual colleges and universities under the supervision of each provincial enrolment organisation. All candidates are assessed comprehensively according to standards laid down by the State Education Commission in terms of their political ideology and morality, test scores (in descending order of merit), and physical health, and an enrolment list is compiled for the agreed number of places. The list is checked by the provincial enrolment organisation and will be approved unless a violation of regulations is detected.

Priority is given to members of minority nationalities, people of exceptional moral character or outstanding sporting prowess, or people who achieve extremely high marks in relevant subjects. In some categories, individuals with low test scores may be admitted. Secondary school graduates who show all-round excellence morally, intellectually, and physically or who are extraordinarily outstanding in some respect or other may, within a limited quota, be recommended by their schools for direct admission to college. This is known as the enrolment system 'with examination as the chief means and recommendation as a subsidiary'.

As early as the 1950s many provincial education commissions had established some kind of standing organisation for the matriculation. However, in 1987, to improve the administration of the matriculation examination for both colleges and universities of the unified entrance examination for admission of graduate students for masters degrees, and of other national examinations, the State Education Commission set up a new organisation called the National Education Examinations Authority. This body was given responsibility for the development of tests, the administration of examinations, and conducting statistical analyses of the examination results.

The national matriculation examination since it was set up in 1952 has played an immensely positive role in selecting high quality students to higher institutions and in influencing teaching in secondary schools. At the same time, it has also had seriously negative effects, which, during the 'Cultural Revolution,' were used as an excuse for its abolition. Since the 'Cultural Revolution,' its negative effects have once again become a worrying problem for the education system. To maximise the positive contribution of the matriculation examination to the selection of the best students and to the improvement of teaching in secondary schools and at the same time to minimise its negative effects, the State Education Commission initiated two reforms in 1985. The first relates to high-school graduate certificate examinations, the second to standardised tests.

HIGH SCHOOL GRADUATE CERTIFICATE EXAMINATIONS

In the past, graduation examinations were administered by individual secondary schools. Now, according to regulations laid down by the State Education Commission, such examinations are to be replaced by a provincially unified examination organised by the provincial education commission. Each of nine required courses is tested according to the teaching programme whenever it is completed. A check is made on laboratory work in Physics, Chemistry, and Biology. Standards for the examination are formulated by provincial governments. Results are reported in four grades. If a student passes the examination, and performs satisfactorily on the moral and physical assessments, he or she will be awarded a graduation certificate by the provincial education commission. The certificate serves as a basis for the recruitment to jobs and to the army. Further, only individuals who have been awarded graduation certificates are eligible to take the matriculation examination.

Shanghai was the first to conduct a unified graduation examination in 1985; the examination is now administered all over the mainland except in Tibet.

The matriculation examination is a standardised norm-referenced test, based on the obligatory syllabus in the secondary school and the optional syllabus. Each examinee takes an examination only in those subjects that are closely related to the major subject to be studied in college.

THE STANDARDISATION OF TESTS

The term standardised examination does not refer to multiple-choice items only. Rather it refers to a test that on the one hand is based on the rich experience of China's examination traditions and on the other hand is designed to minimise errors by applying modern psychological measurement and educational statistical theory.

With a view to popularising the concept, Guangdong Province introduced the standardised examination in 1985. In 1989, the State Education Commission issued a publication entitled *Programme of Administering Standardised Examinations*, officially publicising it all over the country. The standardised examination differs in a number of ways from more traditional examinations. First, to guide the teaching programme, a publication called *Directions on the Examination* is issued which explains the nature and purpose of the examination, what kinds of knowledge and competence it will test, as well as item types, the proportion of each type that will appear in the examination, and sample tests. The *Directions* have taken much of the mystique out of the examination while at the same time guaranteeing the quality of test papers. They have been welcomed by both the teachers in secondary schools and the examinees.

Second, multiple-choice items are used only if they test the kind of knowledge and competence which the examiners are seeking to elicit. Such items usually amount to an average of 50% of all items and can vary from 80% in the case of English to about 30% in the case of Mathematics. The items are scored by an optical mark reader.

Third, statistical analyses are carried out to determine difficulty and discrimination indices of items, as well as the variance of test scores. These data are used to evaluate the quality of test papers and are published.

CONCLUSION

In China, competition in the matriculation examination is extremely keen. Those who are successful and are admitted to institutions of higher education amount to only 3% of an age cohort or 20% of all graduate senior secondary school students. Those who are admitted will have a great advantage in social status and material conditions over those who are not. This is especially so for candidates from rural areas. Among the problems which have caused difficulties for the administration of the matriculation and have aggravated its negative aspects are: excessive competition; the vast size of the country; the great disparity in achievements between different regions of the country; and the enormous numbers of examinees.

For the past 40 years, the most difficult problem facing the matriculation examination has been how to provide effective guidance to teachers preparing students for the examination without, at the same time, affecting the value of the examination as a selection instrument. The reforms I have considered, especially the High-school Graduation Certificate Examinations, have so far yielded good results. It can be expected that when the Programme Of Adminstering Standardised Examinations is completed, still better results will be achieved.

26. THE HIGHER EDUCATION ENTRANCE EXAMINATION IN CHINA

Han Ning
National Education Examinations Authority, Beijing

The People's Republic of China came into being in 1949. In order to adapt to the needs of the newborn socialist system, that was characterised chiefly by a planned economy, the system in which university enrolments were handled separately and independently by various higher educational institutions underwent gradual change. A unified national examination system, known as the Higher Education Entrance Examination, was established for the recruitment of students to universities and colleges. Except for the period of the 'Cultural Revolution' when college enrolment was suspended, this system has been in operation over the past 40 years. It has played a very useful role in recruiting competent young people to institutions of higher learning, in promoting and raising the quality of basic education, and in raising society's appreciation of learning.

However, because of the underdeveloped state of the economy and of the education system, the proportion of students admitted to the universities and colleges is very small. Only 20% of senior middle school graduates are successful in finding a third-level place. Further, because of limited employment opportunities, the relatively big gap between city and countryside, and the influence of the cultural heritage, competition for university admission is very acute. Some secondary schools, in response to the demand of a limited number of students, have adopted measures which go against good educational practice such as calling on students to learn by rote and placing excessive emphasis on problem solving with a view to improving their performance on examinations. Moreover, these schools provided separate courses in arts and science so that students intended for science studies do not learn History and Geography and those intended for liberal arts do not learn Physics and Chemistry.

The ordinary senior middle school is at the highest level in China's basic education system. Only about 10% of an age cohort are enrolled at this level. Education at this stage, of course, is designed not only at providing qualified recruits for institutions of higher learning but also qualified workers for the country's economy. For a long time, however, the graduation status of students destined to go directly into the workforce has not received adequate recognition, with the result that success in gaining admission to universities through the entrance examination became the sole criterion for measuring the quality of teaching in senior middle schools. Undue emphasis on university admission resulted in a grave waste in high school education: students who held promise for advanced study were overburdened with class assignments; courses lacked cohesion and were incomplete; and students with no hope of gaining admission to universities lacked motivation and entered society as 'losers'.

In view of this, the State Education Commission made a decision to make the High School Graduate Certificate Examination compulsory for all graduates of ordinary senior middle schools. The certificate examination, which is recognised by the state and held at provincial level, aims at testing the standards of high school graduates on cultural subjects. The examination, organised and conducted by the education department in the province, is designed to assess the entire range of cultural subjects prescribed for senior middle schools as well as some science-related subjects. Adhering strictly to the course requirements set out in the teaching programme, the test seeks to check on the level reached by graduates of senior grade in the programme. It also serves as a means of examining and evaluating the quality of teaching in senior middle schools. In 1985, Shanghai took the lead in introducing the certificate examination. This was followed by Zhejiang Province in 1988. By 1992, the examination had been made compulsory throughout the mainland, with the exception of Tibet.

Subjects which are externally examined are politics, Chinese language, Mathematics, foreign language, Physics, Chemistry, Biology, History, and Geography. A number of subjects are assessed at the school level. These assessments are monitored and include labour skills and laboratory work related to Physics, Chemistry, and Biology. Unified provincial arrangements operate in test development, administration, scoring, and result reporting. In some provinces, scoring is done at the regional level but practical measures must be adopted in this case to guard against scoring error.

The certificate examination, which is a criterion-referenced test, is a new development in China. Precisely because of this, some technical problems await urgent solution. The National Education Examinations Authority and provinces and municipalities have focused their research on two points. The first one concerns the standard for the unified national curriculum and the criteria for testing. Teaching plans and programmes for various courses are prescribed by the State Education Commission. Educational workers canvass the views of people of all walks of life and explain the evaluation standards for various subjects in determining a provincial norm for courses. Secondly, a system of scoring for the certificate examination, appropriate to China's national conditions, will be instituted and perfected.

This will include two aspects. The first refers to the reporting of results. At present, most provinces adopt the method of grade scoring, under which results are divided into four or five grades. In some places, however, the candidate's raw marks are reported on the basis of a 100 mark system. Generally speaking, the way the examination result is reported depends on the nature and function of the examination. The certificate examination serves as a way to test the standard of senior middle school students in order to determine whether or not they are qualified to take the university entrance examination. It also serves as a record of achievement in cultural subjects for a high school graduate when he or she applies for a job. We support the adoption of the system of grade marking. We also believe that the instructions for the examinations should clearly indicate the different connotations of different grades. The second aspect is the question of equivalence of examination results. As a criterion-referenced test, the level of results between the years should remain stable. We are studying the possibility of equating scores from year to year.

Implementation of the certificate examination has already had a number of consequences. It has enabled senior middle schools to shift from paying attention to the minority to the majority of students and ensured that the overwhelming majority of senior grade students measure up to graduation standard. Thus the standard set for the certificate examination has established a basic standard in senior middle school education and is expected to provide a comprehensive and practical evaluation of the quality of teaching in the senior middle school. It is also expected to prove beneficial to the all-round development of students morally, intellectually, and physically.

In view of the dual tasks of the senior middle schools and the implementation of the certificate examination, corresponding reform of the Higher Education Entrance Examination is required. Such reform may be reflected in three developments: the re-introduction of the grouping of subjects for the university entrance examination; ability testing; and introduction of new technologies for scoring examinations.

GROUPING OF SUBJECTS FOR THE UNIVERSITY ENTRANCE EXAMINATION

The basic pattern followed in China for the Higher Education Entrance Examination is to divide the test between the liberal arts group and the science group. Candidates who enter for liberal arts are tested in Politics, the Chinese language, Mathematics, History, Geography, and a foreign language; those entering for Science are tested in Politics, the Chinese language, Mathematics, Physics, Chemistry, Biology and a foreign language. The paper for the university entrance examination is based on the teaching programme for senior middle schools.

Information sought in the examination must not go beyond what is prescribed in the teaching programme; the main areas tested are the basic knowledge and skills of the various courses.

The large number of subjects required in entrance examinations places an excessive burden on students, even though only a small proportion of the subjects is required to assess suitability for university studies. Since the introduction of the certificate examination helps to ensure the basic education of students, the number of subjects included in the Higher Education Entrance Examination may be reduced, so that only those subjects closely associated with a student's proposed studies in college need be tested.

The decision that the number of subjects would be reduced was followed by heated debate regarding the subjects that should be included in the Higher Education Entrance Examination. When the certificate examination was introduced in Shanghai in 1988, a new system of subject grouping was also introduced. The new system provided for all candidates to take the examination in one of six groups according to the speciality which the student wished to pursue. The Chinese language, Mathematics, and a foreign language are common to all groups. Candidates are also examined in Politics, Physics, Chemistry, History, Geography, or Biology in accordance with the requirements of each speciality. In 1991, Hunan Province experimented with another scheme of subject groups. Under this scheme, candidates are divided into four groups according to their speciality. The courses to be examined for each group are: (1) Politics, Chinese language, History, and a foreign language; (2) Mathematics, Chinese language, Physics, and a foreign language; (3) Mathematics, Chemistry, Biology, and a foreign language; (4) Mathematics, Chinese language, Geography, and a foreign language. The State Education Commission is making a serious study of the positive and negative effects of the schemes in Shanghai and Hunan and will gather the opinions of all concerned. It is envisaged that a unified national scheme on subject group arrangements for the Higher Education Entrance Examination will be agreed.

ABILITY TESTING

While great importance is attached to the knowledge of entrants in the entrance examination, students' level of ability should also be considered. In the past, the main component in the university entrance examination was that of appraising the achievements of students. Because of sharp competition, students had to work extremely hard to cope with the examination. In this situation, a number of unwelcome tendencies could be detected. There was undue emphasis on rote learning. In teaching, emphasis was placed only on the accumulation of knowledge, while the cultivation of ability was neglected. Some students were known to commit a whole volume to memory. To deal with these problems, it is recommended that a test of ability be included in entrance examinations following the introduction of a unified test at the secondary stage.

Some measures are already being adopted to improve the quality of examinations. First, attention is being paid to the distribution of questions of various types. While the proportion of questions in which a student has to select a correct answer is being increased, a given proportion of questions in which a student has to compose an answer is being retained. New types of questions are also being developed. In the case of History, for instance, to test students' ability to analyse historical materials, students are required to analyse materials presented to them. Secondly, while examination questions do not go beyond what is prescribed in school programmes, items are being developed to test the ability of students to handle problems that have not been topics of instruction, using the know-how they have learned. Thirdly, in marking papers, effective measures are being taken to allocate marks for comprehension with a view to encouraging creativity.

NEW SCORING TECHNOLOGIES

At present, computers and optical-mark reading facilities are being widely applied in dealing with examination results. Technologies such as long-range digital correspondence and laser type-setting are also being gradually adopted. All have greatly increased the efficiency of the system.

CONCLUSION

The High School Graduate Certificate Examination in China is still in its initial period and the Higher Education Entrance Examination following the certificate examination is also at an experimental stage. The progress of reform in these two areas is likely to lead to great changes in the way middle schools of senior grade are run, and the mode of university enrolment can also be expected to change. This should lead to important reforms in the administration of examinations as well as in the system of general education.

27. EFFECTS OF THE JOINT ADMISSIONS SCHEME ON EDUCATION IN HONG KONG

Eva Poon Scott
Hong Kong Examinations Authority
Hong Kong

In September 1990, six tertiary institutions in Hong Kong which offer first degree courses started a scheme, the Joint University and Polytechnic Admissions System, that accepts joint applications from school students seeking admission to first degree courses in these institutions. This paper discusses some of the effects of this joint admissions scheme on education in Hong Kong.

The Joint University and Polytechnic Admissions System (JUPAS) operates on a two-year cycle. The scheme aims to make application procedures convenient for students by allowing them to apply to all six tertiary institutions at the same time, using one application form. In the 1990-92 cycle, 17,000 students applied for just over 10,000 places.

Applications for JUPAS must be made at the beginning of the Secondary 6 year (lower form of the two-year Advanced Level course) and may be made by all students attending local schools who wish to seek admission to one or more of the six institutions. Each applicant may select up to 12 degree programmes but not more than five from any single institution. Once students have submitted their applications, they are not allowed to change their list of degree choices.

One institution makes firm offers of about 1,300 places and accepts students before the start of the Secondary 7 year. The other five institutions make conditional offers to selected students at the end of the Secondary 6 year. The condition specifies the number of subject grades that must be obtained in the Hong Kong Advanced Level (AL) Examination which takes place at the end of the Secondary 7 year. Each institution considers applicants independently and sets its own conditions for acceptance to its degree programmes. Applicants are considered on the basis of a range of criteria, including their performance in the Hong Kong Certificate of Education (CE) Examination which is taken after Secondary 5, their school reports, which include other academic and extra-curricular achievements, and their performance in interviews or tests conducted by the individual institutions. An applicant may receive as many as 12 conditional offers from the six institutions and may accept up to three of them and place them in order of priority.

After the AL results are known, applicants who have satisfied the criteria in their conditional offers will be given a firm offer during an initial round. The aim of the scheme is to fill around 70% of degree places in this way. The remaining places will be filled by applicants who do not receive/accept any conditional offers, or fail to satisfy the conditions in any of the offers they receive. Firm offers are made to these applicants in which their results in the AL Examination are the main consideration. The scheme completed its first full cycle at the end of the 1992 school year and institutions admitted the first batch of students under the scheme in September/ October 1992.

The JUPAS scheme is a big step forward from previous practice whereby students had to apply to individual institutions and receive offers from them separately, often at different times. On the whole, the joint admissions scheme has run very smoothly. It is cheaper and more convenient for students. It also enables students to make more informed choices of tertiary institutions and degree courses. This paper discusses some possible effects of a system which is largely based on conditional offers on education in Hong Kong, highlighting those areas of the system where improvements could be made. The effects on students, secondary schools, tertiary institutions, and public examinations will be discussed in turn.

EFFECTS ON STUDENTS

Under the JUPAS scheme, students are asked at the very beginning of their Secondary 6 year to decide the degree choices they wish to study two years later. This may be too early to require students to make a choice which involves selecting not just a faculty/department in an institution but a specific degree course. Moreover, there is no provision in the scheme to cater for students who would wish to make a different choice in the light of their experience of Advanced Level courses. Some flexibility may, therefore, be needed.

The system of conditional offers was introduced to enable students to assess their chances of admission to a particular institution/degree course before they are required to make decisions on acceptance. However, the uncertainty regarding conditional offers, some of which may carry much tougher conditions than others, results in students having to face the difficult task of making a decision between a true preference and a safe choice. Also, as conditional offers are published at the end of the Secondary 6 year, the length of the waiting period between offer and acceptance may cause some anxiety and stress to students. Despite these drawbacks, the fact that institutions announce their offers simultaneously does help students in their choice of institution/degree course which they can make on the basis of knowledge of all offers received. This arrangement is the most welcome feature of the joint admissions system.

EFFECTS ON SECONDARY SCHOOLS

School principals and teachers are required to submit within six months of the start of the Secondary 6 year a school report on each student who has been made a conditional offer. This includes the student's academic and extra-curricular achievements. It allows the institutions to consider factors other than academic achievements in processing students' applications and is welcomed by schools. However, the time allowed is far too short for a school to prepare a detailed and thorough report on each student.

To help them in the task of selection, institutions may also conduct interviews and tests before conditional offers are made. This is considered necessary for some degree courses by institutions and is also seen by students as being fair, as it enables institutions to assess students on qualities not tested in the public examination, such as personality and communication skills. Unfortunately, these activities are carried out by all institutions in a short time-frame and often take place during school hours. This brings some disruption to classes during the Secondary 6 year. More co-ordination among institutions and schools may be needed.

Finally, schools would no doubt wish to be of maximum assistance to their students in making decisions or choices that will affect their academic future. The requirements for students to make application at the beginning of the Secondary 6 year does not allow enough time for schools to help their students to choose the degree programmes that best suit them. Also, as the offers are made directly to students and the time for students to reply is very short, it is difficult for schools to provide any guidance or counselling to their students in making decisions.

EFFECTS ON TERTIARY INSTITUTIONS

The JUPAS scheme was designed to co-ordinate the admissions of the six tertiary institutions in Hong Kong. Since the choices are open to all applicants at the same time and there is a limit to the total number of choices for each student, competition remains very keen among institutions to admit the 'best' students.

JUPAS aims to fill about 70% of degree places by conditional offers. However, it is extremely difficult for institutions to plan and predict entries based on conditional offers. Under this scheme, once an offer is made, it is up to the applicant to accept or decline. If an applicant accepts a conditional offer by an institution, that offer cannot be withdrawn unless the applicant fails to satisfy the associated conditions. Since all offers are made to applicants at the same time, but an applicant is only allowed to choose up to three conditional offers, the uncertainty of how applicants will choose makes it very hard for an institution to determine how many offers should be made in the first place. While on some degree programmes a 1,000 conditional offers may fail to fill 100 places, on others the number of acceptances can exceed the number of places available.

Each institution sets its own offer conditions. It is acknowledged that the setting of conditions is no easy task. Conditions which are too harsh will scare potential applicants away while those which are too easy may be perceived as soft options or may attract too many students ending up with available places being over-subscribed. While agreeing that institutional autonomy in the selection of applicants should be preserved, there could be more co-ordination among institutions in the setting of conditions, particularly for courses of a similar nature.

EFFECTS ON PUBLIC EXAMINATIONS

Due to the short time allowed for the preparation of school reports and the conduct of interviews and tests, Hong Kong Certificate of Education (CE) results of students have become the major criterion in the selection of students for conditional offers. The pressure to do well in the CE Examination has therefore increased. As a result, more students may prefer to repeat the CE in the hope of getting good conditional offers rather than starting the Advanced Level course with little hope of securing any conditional offer. The percentage of repeating students in CE (49% in 1992) is already very high and students should be encouraged not to repeat the examination when they have already obtained the qualifications to study the Advanced Level course.

For students who have received easy conditions in their offers, there is little motivation for them to do well in the AL Examination since they know that they do not have to excel in the examination to get a place. On the other hand, students without conditional offers may find it hard to prepare for the AL Examination as they are put under pressure and much uncertainty, knowing that many places would be gone before their AL results are even being considered. In view of the possible existence of these two groups of AL students the standards of students taking the AL Examination may need to be monitored more closely.

The CE and AL examinations are distinct milestones for students in Hong Kong and represent achievements at different levels. It is understandable that tertiary institutions have to choose students based on some kind of academic achievements and this usually is based on public examination results. However, the incentive for students taking examinations should really be to do well in the subject(s) they take as evidence of achievement and not to get a place in a tertiary institution. This applies in particular to the CE Examination which should not be the main mechanism to determine students' admission to tertiary education.

FUTURE DEVELOPMENT

The JUPAS system currently operates under a difficult situation since there are two points of entry to tertiary institutions, with one institution giving firm offers and accepting students at the end of Secondary 6 while other institutions accept students at the end of Secondary 7. The system of conditional offers provides a solution to this arrangement but has its drawbacks.

Starting in 1994, all institutions accept students only after they have completed the full Advanced Level course and this provides a good chance for JUPAS to go for a different system. Recently, the JUPAS Board announced that changes will be made to the scheme starting 1994. First, the scheme will be expanded to cover non-degree courses and private candidates. Second, the scheme will be shortened from the two-year cycle to one year and application will start at the beginning of the Secondary 7 year. Third, applicants will be allowed more choices (up to 20) with no limit for individual institutions and will be allowed to change their choices even after they have sat the AL Examination. Fourth, conditional offers will no longer be made and firm offers will be made by institutions after the AL results are known. Finally, offers will be made in order of merit by institutions and will be matched against the applicants' choice of priority before a final offer is made to the applicant.

The new joint admissions scheme will continue to assist students seeking admission to tertiary institutions. It will also remove some of the less desirable effects of the existing scheme. There will be more time for students to choose the degree courses they wish to apply for. Students will be able to make decisions on true preference rather than weighing up their chances of satisfying the offer conditions. Schools will be able to assist to a greater extent in preparing students for tertiary education and to run a less interrupted Advanced Level course. Institutions will be able to plan their admissions more accurately and to fill their degree places with students who are truly interested in and best qualified for them. The CE Examination will no longer be the main determinant of tertiary admissions.

Hong Kong has learnt a hard lesson from the conditional offer system. Changes have been proposed and it is recognised that further evolution will probably be needed. In the long term, greater co-operation and co-ordination will be required among institutions, particularly regarding selection criteria and offer procedures. More consultation with schools and students over admissions procedures will also be required, as well as closer monitoring of the scheme's operation. Finally, regular reviews, allowing flexibility and changes of the system as and when needed, will be required.

AUSTRALIA

28. ADMISSION TO HIGHER EDUCATION IN TWO NEIGHBOURING AUSTRALIAN STATES

Neil Baumgart
University of Western Sydney,
Nepean

Bruce McBryde
Tertiary Entrance Procedures Authority,
Queensland

As in a number of other countries, selection for higher education in Australia has been an increasingly vexed issue over the past two decades. The problem has been exacerbated by the interaction of two related factors: a dramatic increase in the retention rate to the end of secondary schooling (Year 12) and greater demand for places in higher education, with intense competition for some faculties.

Since schooling in Australia is managed at the state/territory level, comparisons across states/territories can provide insights into the relative effectiveness of different approaches to common problems. Since 1988, the Education Ministers have made significant strides in agreeing on a range of common policy directions, but selection for higher education remains an area where practices differ. In this paper, we have chosen to contrast Queensland's progressive approach with the more conservative one of New South Wales (NSW) over the past 20 years. To elucidate rationales for present practices in the two states, we trace the historical background within each state and describe current and proposed strategies for selection for higher education. From an analysis of common elements and points of divergence, we draw implications for future directions and comment on the extent to which each state is strategically placed to take on board the newer directions in curriculum and assessment implicit in collaborative national initiatives.

A COMMON STARTING POINT

Thirty years ago, entry to higher education in both Queensland and New South Wales was by matriculation, determined by passes in a minimum number of subjects on the external examinations leading to the Queensland Senior Certificate or the NSW Leaving Certificate. With ample places available in the few universities and teachers' colleges for all matriculants able to pay the fees and wishing to enrol, selection *per se* was not an issue. The Commonwealth Government provided scholarships which covered fees and provided a means-tested living allowance to encourage post-secondary studies. State governments and other potential employers also offered scholarships, fellowships, and other financial incentives as a means of recruiting graduates into the future workforce.

Over the years, retention rates in upper secondary schooling have continued to rise, with a consequent increase in the number of students seeking entry into higher education. Although the availability of places in higher education has also increased, at times quite dramatically, it has not kept up with the demand.

Because earlier changes in demand were readily extrapolated from trends over time, problems were tackled as they emerged. Solutions consisted of small, incremental shifts designed to address particular crises as they occurred rather than any fundamental re-examination of policies and practices. Then, as the cumulative effects of increasing enrolments became more significant, the states began to diverge in their strategies to accommodate them. Two major problems had to be addressed. First, the curriculum in Years 11-12, once seen as preparation for higher education, now had to cater for increasing proportions of students who would not enter higher education. Second, pressure for places in higher education was intense and fundamental questions were raised about equity and access (Baumgart, 1984; McGaw et al, 1986).

HISTORICAL CHANGES IN QUEENSLAND

It was not until the late 1960s that pressure for places at the University of Queensland stretched its capacity to enrol all matriculants. Prior to this, students were admitted if they passed a minimum number of Year 12 subjects, typically including English, Mathematics, and one or more Science subjects. Subsequently, under increased competition for places, students had to obtain better than pass grades in some if not all of their subjects. As entry requirements were raised, variations developed across institutions and a hierarchy developed. Following major reviews of upper secondary education in Queensland, changes occurred in curriculum, assessment, and reporting practices. Of these changes, three stand out as watersheds.

The first major change was a move to school-based assessment following the Radford (1970) report. With a broader range of students proceeding to Year 12, there was concern about the backwash effect of university entrance requirements, operationalised in external examinations, on school curricula. With the introduction of school-based assessment for school leavers in 1973, teachers had considerable autonomy in developing relevant local applications within the subjects devised by the Board of Secondary School Studies and were responsible for the setting and marking of examinations within their schools. Moderation meetings of teachers were held to establish comparability of standards across schools.

Although this first watershed decision did have the educationally desirable outcome of minimising the impact of university entrance on school curricula, it resulted in further pressure on selection decisions. Teachers attending moderation meetings faced a conflict in defending the assessment materials, standards, and grade distributions for students from their schools while reviewing those proposed by teachers of other schools. As teachers tried to accommodate both roles, one consequence was an inflation of grades across the system. While the moderation process may have achieved comparable grades across schools, the universities found they could not predict how many would qualify for entry and typically the number who met minimum entry levels exceeded planned enrolments.

A new selection method was introduced in 1974 (and used until 1991) whereby all eligible students were provided with a tertiary entrance (TE) score. The TE score resulted in a single ranking of candidates irrespective of school or subject combination. Achievement scores provided by schools were scaled against the Australian Scholastic Aptitude Test (ASAT) which was the only test completed by all students. (This process of course equating for students studying different combinations is used extensively in Australia; see Masters, 1988; Maxwell, 1987; Sadler, 1992). Where a common test such as ASAT is used, the course equating procedures are well known, but perceived bias within ASAT (e.g., on gender) has led to numerous criticisms, validations, reviews, and modifications in various states and territories (Adams, 1984; Daley, 1985; Masters & Beswick, 1986; McGaw, Warry, & McBryde, 1975; McGaw et al., 1986).

The assessments for all students in a subject at a school were scaled (mean = ASAT mean; Standard Deviation = 12). Each student's aggregate was obtained by adding the best adjusted scores for 20 semester units over Years 11-12, provided at least three subjects were studied over four semesters. The aggregate scores for all students in a school were finally scaled to yield a distribution with the mean and standard deviation corresponding to those of ASAT scores for all students receiving a TE score.

In ranking all students in the state, TE scores were assigned as percentile bands with the number of students in each band set at 0.5% of the number of 17-year olds in the state (except for the top band which contained 1%). The scale started at 990 and moved down in steps of 5 until all eligible students had been allocated a band. In the early years of the system, the lowest bands were around 750 but this drifted down over time to reach 465 in 1991 as the retention rates in senior secondary schooling increased. In a nutshell, the TE score provided a fine-grained scale which was convenient for universities because it allowed them to set and fill quotas without reference to additional information.

A second watershed in Queensland was a move from norm- to criterion-referenced assessment known as ROSBA, the acronym for a Review of School-Based Assessment (Scott et al., 1978). When school-based assessment was introduced in 1973, research studies found that the amount of assessment had increased, perhaps as teachers sought to justify their decisions in moderation meetings; school-based implementation of syllabuses showed an emphasis on content at the expense of process objectives; and the competitive nature of norm-referenced assessment at the school level was considered to affect student-teacher relationships (Campbell & Campbell, 1978; Campbell et al., 1976). The Scott Report recommended assessment based on defined performance criteria and reporting on a 5-point scale. In the first system-wide attempt in Australia to move from norm-referenced to criterion-referenced assessment, the Queensland system implemented the recommendations of the Scott Report, first on a trial basis, and then progressively until full implementation was achieved in 1986. The initiative required rewriting of syllabuses to emphasise outcomes and considerable professional development for teachers.

This second watershed decision, again highly desirable educationally, had virtually no impact on selection for higher education. Although the criterion-referenced assessments featured in the Senior Certificates issued to Year 12 graduates, the norm-referenced TE scores, statistically moderated with ASAT, provided an incongruous overlay and remained the basis for selection.

The third watershed involved a move towards profile reporting for selection purposes (see Baumgart, 1988). Although the TE score has provided universities with a low cost and objective method of filling their quotas, it has been the subject of widespread public criticism. The intensity of the criticism probably reflects the community's aspirations for higher education which have outstripped the ability of the sector to provide places. Thousands of qualified students are not being offered places, a problem further compounded when applicants who miss out apply again in subsequent years, having accepted places in courses with lower quota cut-off scores in an attempt to upgrade to their first choice. As a result, school leavers face even greater competition.

An important criticism of the TE score was whether a single aggregate can operate validly and fairly to select students for all courses. The construct validity of an aggregate can be challenged when not all components correlate similarly with the total score. Predictive validity studies indicate at best moderate correlations between TE scores and subsequent performance and considerable variation in coefficients when particular subjects are used as predictors. Anomalies such as the selection of students in Mathematics and Science courses in secondary school into Arts/Law courses ahead of students with high grades in Language/Humanities subjects, but lower TE scores, are cited as evidence of the irrationality of such procedures.

In 1986, a committee was established to review all aspects of entrance to tertiary institutions in Queensland and its report made 52 recommendations for change (Pitman, 1987). Although the committee was broadly representative of schools and universities, a number of universities baulked at the potential impact of the recommendations and subsequently criticised aspects of the report publicly. In the absence of support from all parties, and since it was undergoing a difficult time politically, the government of the day was not willing to press ahead and only two of the 52 recommendations were implemented.

A second review was initiated by the new Labour government which acted quickly to implement its recommendations (Viviani, 1990). The review endorsed the use of school-based assessment but recommended the replacement of the single fine-grained TE score with a student education profile to contain a number of coarse-grained scales, which could be used in different combinations for selection into different university courses. Professor Viviani described the system as 'horses for courses,' implying that the selection criteria for each university course should match the skills and prerequisite knowledge relevant to that course.

The student education profile provides two certificates. The Senior Certificate records student achievement in subjects studied in Years 11-12 as previously, together with a result on the new Core Skills Test, which replaces ASAT. The Core Skills Test, an omnibus test of four papers administered to all Year 12 students, is based on the skills and processes contained in the 40+ accredited subjects. Forty-nine curriculum elements have been identified for inclusion in the test. The criteria for inclusion are that a curriculum element must be covered in at least two subjects, that at least 95% of students have studied at least one of the subjects containing the element, and the element can be assessed using a written examination. A 5-point scale is used in reporting achievement for each subject or core skills reported on the Senior Certificate. Use of this profile of achievement by employers and universities in selecting applicants will start to bridge the gap which has developed over the past 20 years between certification and selection.

A second certificate, the Tertiary Entrance Statement, provides rank-order information for university selection. Students obtain an Overall Position (OP) but, in contrast to the TE rank, the OP is a coarse-grained 25-point scale. It is derived by averaging, with equal weights, the scaled scores on the best five subjects (usually out of six) for each student. In addition, supplementary information is provided on up to five field positions. The following skills are developed in a number of subjects across the curriculum.

Field A: Extended written expression involving complex analysis and synthesis of ideas.

Field B: Short written communication involving reading comprehension and expression in English or a foreign language.

Field C: Basic numeracy involving simple calculations and graphical and tabular interpretation.
Field D: Solving complex problems involving mathematical symbols and abstractions.
Field E: Substantial practical performance involving physical or creative arts or expressive skills.

Within each subject, a weighting is given for each field to reflect its emphasis in the assessment, as specified in the accredited syllabus. Student achievement in each subject is then weighted by these field weights in the calculation of field positions. If students' choice of subjects does not allow a minimum level of exposure to a field, no field position is assigned. Typically, students will be eligible for field positions in two or three of the five fields. Because of the coarse-grained nature of the OP, university faculties need to use additional information, including field positions, to select students at the margin. Individual university courses can use different field profiles for selection reflecting perceived prerequisite competencies.

HISTORICAL CHANGES IN NEW SOUTH WALES

Similar pressures for university places have also occurred in NSW. However, it is difficult to identify fundamental educational changes in NSW which might be labelled watershed decisions. Even where major reviews of secondary education have been conducted (e.g., Carrick, 1989; Swan & McKinnon, 1984), they have recommended only minor changes to the year 12 certificate, the Higher School Certificate (HSC), and the use of a selection aggregate for university entrance (Hester, 1990). Perhaps this is why the NSW Education and Youth Affairs Minister, Virginia Chadwick, in foreshadowing changes in the rules governing the HSC, was able to claim that 'the HSC is a credential of high public standing and has been a pillar of education in this State for a quarter of a century' (Chadwick, 1992).

Yet many changes have been implemented over the past 25 years by the controlling Board. In general, the changes have been incremental, usually aimed at increased precision, better communication, and greater equity. Many have arisen from in-house working papers or limited reviews on aspects of the statistical scaling process or on the formation of a Tertiary Entrance Score (TES). We provide a catalogue of the changes before contrasting them with those in Queensland.

Initially, when ample places were available to meet demand from matriculated applicants, an aggregate derived from NSW Leaving Certificate scores was used for the award of scholarships. It was based on five (Commonwealth Scholarships) or six (Teachers' College Scholarships) subjects, English was used as a benchmark, and scores in other subjects were adjusted for the IQ distribution of the candidature. By 1964, the Faculty of Medicine at the University of Sydney had introduced quotas and by the late 1960s other faculties and universities had followed. A significant change occurred in 1967 when the former Leaving Certificate, issued on the culmination of five years of secondary education, was replaced by the Higher School Certificate following six years of secondary schooling.

In 1976, earlier 'levels' within subjects were replaced by a Unit structure (of 1, 2, 3 and, in Mathematics and Science, 4 Units) where, for example, a 3-unit subject implied that students covered the 2-Unit work and then additional work in both scope and depth. From 1977 for several years, examination committees made judgments about the relative distributions of 2- and 3-Unit subjects. However, faced with some apparent anomalies and the subjectivity involved, the Board in the early 1980s introduced a common paper for 2- and 3-Unit students to facilitate scaling between Units.

Also at this time, in the absence of a common test for all students, a system of iterative scaling across subjects was introduced to allow for different average abilities of different candidatures in optional subjects. From a prescribed mean and standard deviation, adjustments were made for the abilities of different candidatures in different subject areas. Finally, the TES has been computed from scaled scores on the best 10 Units.

Major difficulties occurred when performance in other subjects could be questioned as a basis for estimating the achievement of candidates in the subject under scrutiny. Languages other than English (when the candidature will contain some native speakers) and Music are two examples. In these instances, chief examiners and supervisors of marking were given some latitude to negotiate score distributions with a consultative committee of the Board. The scaling of languages continued to cause concern and the issue was eventually resolved politically with the decision to peg mean achievement in other languages to that in French and German, the foreign languages historically taught in NSW schools.

Recognising the limitations of external examinations as the sole determinant of student achievement (Baumgart, 1984), the Board introduced a change in the late 1970s whereby 50% of the marks awarded were school-based. In contrast to school-based assessment in Queensland, however, schools were asked to furnish estimates (predictions) of likely external examinations results rather than report on their own assessment of students. The change was, therefore, designed more to improve reliability than validity. Schools used HSC trials to make their estimates and generally mirrored the external examinations.

To allow assessment of a broader range of objectives, the rules were further modified in 1986 and schools were asked to furnish 'assessments' rather than estimates. Although schools were encouraged to assess objectives not readily measured in the external examinations, with these examinations based on prescribed curriculum content and accounting for 50% of total marks, there was limited scope for schools to adapt the curriculum or modify assessment practices. Schools faced with a broader spectrum of students' aptitudes and interests because of rapid increases in retention rates did have the option of offering 'Other Approved Studies' courses, but these did not count in the selection aggregate. With the subjects of clearly different status, parental pressure often ensured that students opted for the university entrance-linked subjects so they could at least keep their options open.

A further change which occurred in 1986 was to report the school mark and the external mark separately on the Certificate, whereas previously only the combined mark was shown. This change removed some of the mystique associated with the scaling process and had the benefit of highlighting discrepancies between the two assessments, a basis on which students could seek a re-mark of the external examination. Since 1988, the Certificate has also included a decile band to report combined examination and assessment marks.

When the scaling process involved essentially a linear transformation requiring a specified mean and standard deviation overall and the same mean and standard deviation in the school assessment as the group obtained in the external examination, it was thought that examiners and/or schools on occasions sought to modify the shape of the distribution to give students an advantage. Presumably to counter such manipulations, additional 'rules' were introduced into the Board scaling. Thus, in a 2-Unit course, with the mean set at 60 and the standard deviation at 12.5, the following additional requirements are set: 100 is the maximum; 1-2% receive a mark of 90 or more; 20% receive a mark of 70 or more; 80% receive a mark of 50 or more; 1% receive a mark of less than 30 (New South Wales Board of Studies, 1990). In other words, the move to an area rather than a linear transformation of scores (although not to a normal distribution) was apparently designed to frustrate the practice of giving advantage. However, it does create one other effect, although whether or not this is an intended outcome is a matter for speculation. It is important to ask what meaning students, parents, employers, and others give to the 'marks' shown on the Certificate. The 'examination marks' and the school 'assessment marks' are shown as out of 100 for each 2-Unit subject. The choice of the mean and standard deviation and the other constraints placed on the distribution are such that the reported marks resemble percentage scores. To be fair, it must be acknowledged that the Board of Studies (1990) provides a full explanation of the scaling but the fact remains that many of the public view scores as familiar percentage marks, an interpretation encouraged by the scale and the language ('out of'; 'marks') used.

Courses with small numbers pose particular scaling problems. Various incremental changes have been made over the years to accommodate the difficulties. Currently, 2-Unit courses with fewer than 200 students are not bound by all of the rules above and the median rather than the mean is set at 60. Top and bottom marks are set by examiners. With fewer than 20 students in a 2-Unit course, examiners again set top and bottom marks and intermediate marks reflect the raw score distribution.

One other change that warrants mention is the membership of the Board controlling the HSC. At a time when there was a Board of Senior Secondary Studies, its membership, and hence syllabuses, were dominated by university people. The Swan & McKinnon (1984) Report recommended the formation of one Board for all of secondary education and this was implemented by Act of Parliament in 1987. The Carrick (1989) Committee then recommended a single Board of Studies for all of schooling and this was also duly implemented. As a consequence, the Board now has only two university representatives, just over one in ten of the membership.

Difficulties with the calculation of the TES have surfaced on a regular basis and the debate on scaling of languages was particularly heated. In 1987, the Board decided to distance itself from the TES, arguing that selection was the province of the universities. Scaling across subjects was abandoned, also a recommendation of the Swan and McKinnon (1984) Report, and scores for each course were reported on the same basis, without any attempt to adjust for the calibre of the candidature (although a Tertiary Entrance Score was still printed on the Certificate until 1989). The University of Sydney immediately picked up the inter-subject scaling and the calculation of the TES for its entrants. For one year in other universities, a TES formed without scaling across subjects was used but the following year most negotiated with the University of Sydney, through the Universities Admissions Centre (UAC), to return to a TES based on scores scaled across subjects. The current situation is that a TES is calculated first and then a Tertiary Entrance Rank (TER) is reported in percentile form, in steps of 0.05.

Although the Board has effectively distanced itself from any controversies associated with the TER, the tension between certification and selection is alive and well. The Carrick (1989) Report endorsed most of the current practice associated with the HSC but recommended that the TES should be deleted from the Certificate. This has now occurred (beginning in 1990) but students still receive their HSC Certificate and UAC's Tertiary Entrance Rank in the one envelope.

In addition to Board-determined HSC courses, there is provision for schools to develop Board-approved courses. Results from the latter are shown on the certificate but do not count towards the TES. The issue of standards-based assessment is also being addressed by the Board with attempts to provide statements of outcomes to accompany various syllabuses. However, this work is not yet well developed.

Finally, a number of new initiatives affecting the HSC and the TER are currently being proposed. In general, the intention is to introduce more flexibility into the credential and also into the pathways students might use to proceed to university study (New South Wales Board of Studies, 1992a) (see Figure 28.1). One proposal is that students will be able to accumulate the HSC over up to five years instead of within one year as at present. Courses taken over two consecutive years will count directly towards the TES but courses spanning two to five years will be discounted by 10 percent. The rationale for the discounting is difficult to understand conceptually if the intention is to focus on growth in, and demonstration of, competence as a prerequisite for further study. It does have the effect of emphasising the competitive nature of this pathway, this time with handicaps, but unlike sporting analogies, not for the best performers. (Interestingly, the University of Melbourne has decided to give bonus points to students who have studied languages at school.)

FIGURE 28.1

PATHWAYS TO UNIVERSITY ENTRANCE IN NEW SOUTH WALES

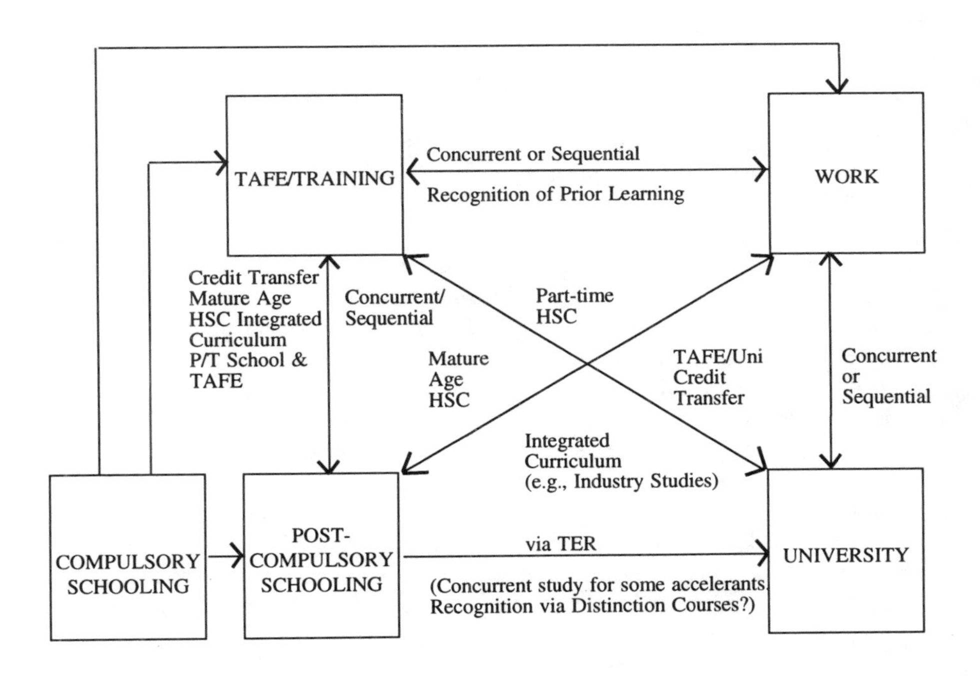

A further proposal is to place restrictions on the 10 Units to be used for the TES. Previously, the TES was based on the 'best 10 Units' unless particular faculties or universities specified particular Units. The proposal is that at least one Unit of English must be included; at least one Unit must come from each of Mathematics/Science/ Technology and Humanities/Social Sciences/Arts fields; and not more than 6 Units should come from any one field of study (defined in NSW as 'Key Learning Areas', of which there are eight). These proposed changes make educational sense in encouraging a comprehensive curriculum and further reducing the backwash effect of the TES on school curricula. But they can also be seen as a reaction to statistics cited for 1991 where 94% of medical students and 45% of law students entering the University of Sydney directly from the HSC included 4-Unit

Mathematics in their best 10 Units but less than half of these students included English in the TES. That a high proportion of these students also had Asian names is no coincidence.

Other proposed changes include basing school assessments on the final year (four terms) of study rather than on two years; the inclusion of credit transfer (e.g., from TAFE courses); the option to repeat individual subjects rather than the whole HSC; and the inclusion of 'Distinction' course for students able to accelerate through the school years.

THE WOOD AND THE TREES

The various attempts to separate the dual functions of certification and selection that have been attempted in Queensland and New South Wales have had only limited success. A backwash effect of university entrance requirements on upper secondary curricula and student choice of subjects still remains. Universities have seemed reluctant to use Year 12 certificates as screening devices and then a range of other information to make final selections. To a large extent, the increased demand for university places is a major factor and the recent approval of and funding for televised Open Learning courses is one strategic response by government. In contrast, though, a recent survey of NSW employers found that they rated the TER as less useful than other information on the certificate (subjects studied; examinations and school assessment marks) (New South Wales Board of Studies, 1992b).

Universities have long argued that students require appropriate prerequisite knowledge and skills but their method of using an aggregate based on a student's best subjects pays scant regard to such a requirement. The continued use of aggregate scores for selection purposes remains enigmatic. Baumgart & Low (1990) expressed the concerns as follows:

> The intention of statistical moderation and aggregation is grounded in concerns for equity and the removal of bias. The aim is to yield a criterion for entry which is not influenced by such factors as subjects selected...., teachers' whims in marking, school attended, and so on. ... The work which has gone into teasing out irregularities and suggesting further fine tuning to correct for them is to be applauded. But these refinements also seem to lead us further into the mire. Are we not simply creating an aura of objectivity which shrouds the more fundamental concerns of validity?

What lessons can be gleaned from the comparison of changes in the two states discussed in this paper? We have identified three major watershed decisions affecting assessment and selection in Queensland, namely, the move to school-based assessment, the use of a standards-based approach, and now the use of a profile approach to reporting in preference to a fine-grained aggregate. The first two were significant educational decisions but were constrained by having to co-exist with a single ranking for university selection. The third offers scope for more fundamental change in selection procedures since universities will be obliged to use additional information in selecting students at or near cut-off scores on the coarse-grained scale.

In NSW, while the most recent proposals are sound educationally, there is still a sense in which the system has lost the grand plot. The catalogue of changes in NSW is dominated by refinements and adjustments. The focus has been on increasing the precision of the HSC grading; ensuring equity in the TES as the major selection device for universities; minimising tinkering as a ploy to confer advantage; discouraging subject choice based on maximising the TES rather than inherent interest and career goals; building public confidence on objectivity rather than more elusive validity; and placating the occasional cries of 'foul' from special interest groups. In case this judgment appears too harsh, it should be stated that many of the decisions, including the most recent proposals, represent fair attempts to move in directions similar to those described for Queensland. It is just that the agenda has been dominated by the minor adjustments and one cannot really point to watershed decisions as in the case of the northern state. It is a classic case of finding it difficult to see the wood for the trees.

Viewed on a broader canvas, the current picture for university admission shows school leavers 'applying to gain entry to the most prestigious courses rather than the ones that best suit their intellectual and vocational aptitudes' (Elliott, Meade, Power, & Toomey, 1987, p.187). The 'prestige' in turn is a function of the hierarchy of courses resulting from selection processes tied to aggregate scores. Further indirect evidence that students apply for courses they perceive as prestigious comes from statistics on change of preferences after HSC results are known. In NSW in 1991, of 85,471 applicants to UAC, over 47% subsequently changed their preferences (Universities Admissions Centre, 1991).

On the other hand, a great many students already enter via pathways other than a recent HSC. Moreover, studies of mature age students in higher education have indicated that they make exemplary progress (West, Hore, Eaton, & Kermond, 1986). In 1992, 40% of the medical intake and 25% of the combined law intake at the University of Sydney were admitted on the basis of qualifications other than the most recent HSC (McNicol, 1992). In addition, following discussion over a decade of delaying entry to prestigious faculties to remove some of the pressure from the HSC (see Australia. Commonwealth Department of Education, 1986; Beswick, Schofield, Meek, & Masters, 1984; McGaw & Hannan, 1985), the University of Sydney now has a firm proposal for future graduate entry to Medicine. The University of Queensland admits Dentistry students into second year, on the basis of results in first year science or a related faculty. At UWS Nepean, 42% of the total undergraduate intake in 1992 were admitted with qualifications other than a recent HSC.

If we accept that the future points to much more flexibility in credentialling, lifelong learning, more learning in a workplace environment, and multiple pathways to higher education, we consider that the watershed changes in Queensland are the ones of greater significance. It is time in NSW to view the broader picture and in particular to address whether the fine-grained TER is still necessary and whether its continued presence inhibits the concurrent attempts at innovation. This decision is now squarely in the hands of the universities. Who is prepared to take the initiative?

REFERENCES

Adams, R. J. (1984). *Sex bias in ASAT?* Melbourne: Australian Council for Educational Research.

Australia. Commonwealth Department of Education. (1986). *Selection for higher education. A discussion of issues and possibilities by an education portfolio discussion group*. Canberra: Author.

Baumgart, N. (1984). Public examinations: Purposes and alternatives. *Current Affairs Bulletin, 60*(8), 22-31.

Baumgart, N. (1988). *Reports and records of achievement for school leavers*. Canberra: Australian College of Education.

Baumgart, N., & Low, B. (1990). A national overview. In B. Low & G. Withers (Eds.), *Developments in school and public assessmen. Australian Education Review 31*. Melbourne: Australian Council for Educational Research.

Beswick, D., Schofield, H., Meek, L., & Masters, G. (1984). *Selective admissions under pressure*. Melbourne: Centre for the Study of Higher Education, University of Melbourne.

Campbell, W. J., & Campbell, E. M. (1978). *School-based assessments: Aspirations and achievements of the Radford scheme in Queensland* (ERDC Report No. 7A). Canberra: Australian Government Publishing Service.

Campbell, W. J., et al. (1976). *Some consequences of the Radford scheme for schools, teachers and students in Queensland* (AACRDE Report No. 7). Canberra: Australian Government Publishing Service.

Carrick, J. (Chair) (1989). *Report of the Committee of Review of New South Wales Schools*. Sydney: NSW Government.

Chadwick, V. (1992). Minister's column. *School Education News, 2*(5), 2.

Daley, D. J. (1985). Standardizations by bivariate adjustment of internal assessments: Sex bias and other statistical matters. *Australian Journal of Education, 29*, 231-247.

Elliot, B., Meade, P., Power, C., & Toomey, R. (1987). Policy directions for the processes of selection for higher education in Australia. In R. Toomey (Ed.), *Passages from secondary school to higher education*. Hawthorn, Victoria: Australian Council for Educational Research.

Hester, D. (1990). Participation and tertiary selection. In G. Mullins (Ed.), *Breaking the mould.* Canberra: Higher Education Research and Development Society of Australasia.

Masters, G. (1988). Anchor tests, score equating and sex bias. *Australian Journal of Education, 32*, 25-43.

Masters, G. N., & Beswick, D. G. (1986). *The construction of tertiary entrance scores: Principles and issues* (Study commissioned by the ACT Schools Authority, the Australian National University and the Canberra College of Advanced Education). Melbourne: Centre for Study of Higher Education, University of Melbourne.

Maxwell, G. (1987). Scaling school-based assessments for calculating overall achievement positions. In Queensland Working Party on Tertiary Entrance, *Tertiary entrance in Queensland: A review* (Appendix 1, pp. 190-200). Brisbane: Board of Secondary School Studies and the Minister for Education's Joint Advisory Committee on Post-Secondary Education.

McGaw, B., & Hannan, B. (1985). *Certification in upper secondary education.* Canberra: Curriculum Development Centre and Commonwealth Schools Commission.

McGaw, B., Warry, R., & McBryde, B. (1975). Validation of aptitude measures for rescaling of school assessment. *Education Research and Perspectives*, 2, 20-34.

McGaw, B. et al. (1986). *Making admissions to higher education fairer. Report of the Committee for the Review of Tertiary Entrance Score Calculations in the Australian Capital Territory.* Canberra: ACT Schools Authority, The Australian National University and the Canberra College of Advanced Education.

McNicol, D. (1992). The HSC and university entry: Comment by the Vice-Chancellor. *The University of Sydney News, 24*(11), 1.

New South Wales Board of Studies. (1990). *HSC scaling. An explanation of the facts and procedures.* Sydney: Author.

New South Wales Board of Studies. (1992a). *Higher school certificate pathways. A consultation document issued by the Board of Studies NSW.* Sydney: Author.

New South Wales Board of Studies. (1992b). *The HSC. A study of employers' views.* Sydney: Author.

Pitman, J. (1987). *Tertiary entrance in Queensland: A review.* Brisbane: Board of Secondary School Studies and the Minister for Education's Joint Advisory Committee on Post-Secondary Education.

Radford, W. (1970). *Public examinations for Queensland secondary school students.* Brisbane: Department of Education, Queensland.

Sadler, D. R. (1992). Scaled school assessments: The effect of measurement errors in the scaling test. *Australian Journal of Education, 36*, 30-37.

Scott, E., Berkeley, G., Howell, M., Schuntner, L., Walker, R., & Winkle, L. (1978). *A review of school-based assessment in Queensland secondary schools.* Brisbane: Board of Secondary School Studies.

Swan, D., & McKinnon, K. (1984). *Future directions for secondary education: A report*. Sydney: NSW Education Department.

Universities Admissions Centre. (1991). *Twelfth annual report*. Sydney: Author.

Viviani, N. (1990). *The review of tertiary entrance in Queensland*. Report submitted to the Minister for Education. Brisbane: Queensland Department of Education.

West, L., Hore, T., Eaton, E., & Kermond, B. (1986). *The impact of higher education on mature age students*. Canberra: Commonwealth Tertiary Education Commission.

29. COMMON CURRICULUM ELEMENTS WITHIN A SCALING TEST FOR TERTIARY ENTRANCE IN AUSTRALIA

Doug McCurry
Australian Council for Educational Research, Camberwell, Victoria

ASSESSMENT FOR TERTIARY ENTRANCE IN AUSTRALIA

There is significant and sometimes very intense competition for tertiary entrance in Australia. This competition is generally dealt with by placing all candidates on a common scale to construct a single tertiary entrance (TE) score for each one. Once this overall rank ordering has been undertaken, tertiary selection can become a largely automatic process. Using such a rank, selection is made by finding the cut-off score which will fill the quota for a course with candidates who have undertaken the required prerequisites. The construction of TE scores is problematic and a matter of some controversy in the Australian educational community.

There are two broad kinds of assessment regime at the end of secondary schooling that are used to construct TE scores in Australia. First, there are syllabus-based examination systems which examine a centrally determined curriculum with subject-specific examinations. The schools teach the prescribed curriculum which the examinations assess. With varying components of school-based assessment, syllabus-based examinations are the most common arrangement for assessment at the end of secondary school and for the construction of TE scores. Second, there are school-based assessment systems which are moderated by a common test of skills or abilities that are not curriculum specific. Systems in some other countries also use subject-specific reference tests that are not curriculum-based. The Australian system (as distinct from the syllabus-based examination systems) use broadly cross-curricular tests which assess skills that are not parts of a specific or prescribed curriculum. Two states have systems which use such an assessment regime at the end of secondary school and for the construction of their TE scores.

These moderation tests are related to the Scholastic Aptitude Test (SAT) developed in the United States, but the use made of the Australian equivalent of the SAT, the Australian Scholastic Aptitude Test (ASAT) contrasts with the role of the SAT in the U.S. The ASAT is not used to generate scores for individuals. It is used to determine group parameters for the statistical moderation of school assessments. The basic aim of the process is to get a kind of comparability between different subjects within a school, and a kind of comparability between schools. ASAT is used for moderating or scaling school assessments in systems that do not have external examinations of the prescribed curriculum.

The examination systems are usually thought of as assessments of achievement in school subjects, and the moderating tests have been described as assessments of aptitude. However, these tests are probably more appropriately seen as tests of general or cross-curricular skills and abilities. In spite of its name, this is the way the ASAT is understood by the test developer, the Australian Council for Educational Research. (In 1992 the test was re-named the Australian Scaling Test to reflect more appropriately its nature and function.)

CRITICISMS OF EXAMINATION AND TESTS

Predictably, both the examination systems and the scaling tests have been subject to various criticisms. The examination systems are criticised by some because they are prescriptive and limit the choices available to schools. Defenders of the systems see them as requiring a common and worthwhile curriculum for all students. They see assessments made outside the school as equitable and reliable because they are set and marked externally.

The cross-curricular tests used for the moderation of school assessments are criticised on a number of grounds. The constructs or aptitudes they assess are challenged as being vague or ill-defined. Others complain that they are entry tests and predictors of future performance rather than assessments of school performance. They are also seen as favouring one or another group of candidates. Because the results of individual students are controlled during scaling by the performance of the cohort, some candidates do not take the test seriously and this is seen to weaken both validity and reliability. There is the further criticism that such tests cannot distinguish between students at the same level.

TERTIARY ENTRANCE AND THE QUEENSLAND CORE SKILLS TEST

Attempts have been made in the state of Queensland to develop a system of school-based assessment moderated by an external test so as to refine the process of selection for tertiary study and to meet the criticisms made of aptitude or cross-curricular tests.

In 1991, an incoming Labour government promised to reform the tertiary entrance system in the state of Queensland. Previously, selection for tertiary study was done on the basis of a TE score which gave each student a number on a single percentile rank order, extending from a score of 990 down. This number was a measure of a student's overall school achievement compared to other students in Queensland. Tertiary institutions filled their courses by running down this rank order list until the course quota was filled.

In a situation where there was considerable competition for tertiary entrance, many criticisms were voiced about the TE scores generated in Queensland. First, the single TE score was criticised as inadequate for an expanding and increasingly diverse cohort of students. Second, it was argued that the tertiary entrance system needed reform so that multiple criteria could be used in tertiary selection. Third, there was a desire to match students to particular courses rather than using a single rank order for selection. Fourth, questions about the comparability of school-based assessments and arguments against the moderating test, ASAT, led to advocacy of examinations or reference tests in different subjects. Fifth, it was claimed that the TE score made unjustifiably fine discriminations among candidates. The final and most telling criticism was that the test did not test student achievement in school, and doubts were expressed about the ability of the test to predict future performance.

In the context of such criticisms, a review of tertiary entrance was commissioned by the Minister for Education in Queensland, and undertaken by Professor Nancy Viviani (1990). Amongst other things it recommended were the abolition of the TE score; the introduction of a Student Education Profile to be prepared mainly for tertiary entrance purposes; the retention of the principle of scaling school assessments to a common test; reporting of individual student performance on this test; the establishment of a new Tertiary Entrance Procedures Authority to act as the interface between secondary and tertiary interests; tertiary selection on the basis of a 'two-gate process,' involving determination of an overall position for each candidate, and also specific field positions for use in entrance to particular tertiary courses.

These changes involved the development of a Core Skills Test (CS Test) which would be used to generate a range of assessments for what was to be called the Student Education Profile. By comparison with the TE score, this profile would offer substantially more, and new kinds of, information as a basis for tertiary selection.

THE THREE-PART METHOD FOR TERTIARY ENTRANCE

There are now three components within the new tertiary entrance procedures. First, there is a measure of overall student achievement at school expressed as a position in a rank order (the overall position or OP). This entails results for the best five subjects, which are scaled within schools and across schools and are reported on one of 25 bands. The OP, which is in some respects similar to the old TE score, is seen as the most reliable and valid indicator of student achievement.

The second component is a measure of student skill in five specific fields of study which is also expressed as a position in a rank order (the field position or FP). These performances show how well a student did in certain aspects of the senior curriculum. The five fields are extended written expression involving complex analysis and synthesis of ideas; short written communication involving reading comprehension and basic use of English or a foreign language; basic numeracy involving simple calculations and graphical and tabular interpretation; solving complex problems involving mathematical symbols and abstractions; and substantial practical performance involving physical or creative arts or expressive skills. An individual student's field positions will be determined on the basis of the extent to which each of these five fields or dimensions is reflected in each subject undertaken by an applicant for a particular kind of tertiary place. This means that applicants may have different positions in different fields as a result of the subjects they have studied. Weightings for individual subjects were determined by an extensive review of curriculum documents (detailed in Allen, 1991). FPs are needed and used to differentiate among students who are otherwise of equal calibre on the OP.

The third component in the entrance procedure are student's individual results in the new Core Skills Test (CS Test) which is to be taken by all Year 12 students desiring tertiary entrance, and reported on the Senior Certificate. This test will be described below.

It is expected that tertiary selection will be made on the basis of OPs, and the subsidiary information from FPs and CS Test results will be used if finer discrimination is needed between applicants for high demand courses. Because it is reported on an A-E scale, it is envisaged that the CS Test cannot be the major factor in selection, and will only be an additional piece of information.

The Credibility of the New System

It was argued in Viviani's (1990) *Review of Tertiary Entrance in Queensland* that public confidence in the new tertiary system would depend largely on two issues. The first is the extent to which successful applicants for tertiary courses are selected according to their suitability for the course, with this suitability being defined in terms of the applicants' subject choice during senior studies. The second is the extent to which the CS Test reflects the Queensland curriculum.

The Review recommended the creation of the Tertiary Entrance Procedures Authority (TEPA) to ensure that the new tertiary entrance system takes full account of these two factors. The functions of TEPA include the monitoring of selection procedures used by universities to ensure their fairness and appropriateness.

The *Review of Tertiary Entrance* also recommended the replacement of the current scaling devices (ASAT and a Writing Task) used to moderate school-based assessment in Queensland with the more comprehensive Core Skills Test. The Board of Senior Secondary School Studies (BSSSS), the assessing and certifying authority in Queensland, was charged with the development and administration of the CS Test. The purpose of the test is to provide group parameters (subject-group and school-group) which are independent of the subjects studied or school attended, for the scaling required in the calculation of OPs; group parameters on components of the test (yet to be identified) for the scaling required in the calculation of FPs, up to five per student; and individual results on a 5-point scale to be reported on the Senior Certificate.

The challenge to the Board was to develop a cross-curricular test which was grounded in the curriculum. The Board responded to this challenge by reviewing the senior school curriculum to identify the common underpinning elements.

The Common Curriculum Elements

The Common Curriculum Elements (CCE) are the basis of the CS Test. They are derived from the Queensland senior curriculum and are the basis on which each form of the test can be audited against the curriculum. They were identified from the Board syllabuses in terms of elements which are common to two or more syllabuses; required by the syllabuses to be included in work programmes; likely to be accessible to most students through the set of subjects they actually take; and testable through the formats available.

CCEs were identified through a seven-phase curriculum scan which involved extensive consultation with teachers about the identification, description, and occurrence of the elements. The process also involved consultation with teachers and test developers about test ability.

The 49 CCEs represent the common testable elements in the Queensland senior curriculum. The elements symbolise the unifying theme of the senior curriculum, and the CS Test is audited against the total list. As a result of this process, the Queensland Core Skills Test is a cross-curricular test that is grounded in the curriculum, but it is not an examination of any one syllabus nor a collection of them.

The Core Skills Test

According to test specifications, the Core Skills Test is a test of achievement in the common elements of the Queensland senior curriculum. It is not a test of subject-related achievement or of factual knowledge of a specific kind, nor is it an intelligence or aptitude test. It is not designed or aimed to predict university performance. It is, however, fully syllabus-based: it does not test core skills as a 'bolt-on extra,' but is intended to be accessible to all Year 12 students regardless of the subjects they may have studied in Years 11 and 12. It aims to be closely related to the skills taught in the senior curriculum, and it should be seen as derived from the curriculum rather than acting to set it. CCEs are designed to give construct validity to the test. It is assumed that the test is a test of developed abilities, and that students who achieve well overall in senior studies will generally perform well in the CS Test, (see Matters, 1991; O'Connor & Robotham, 1991).

The test assumes that students possess an elementary level of 'general knowledge' and a knowledge of vocabulary and mathematical operations at a level of sophistication consistent with that of a student with a sound general Year 10 education. Unless a particular question requires otherwise, any substantive vocabulary of a higher level of sophistication used, whose meaning cannot be determined from the context, will be glossed. Mathematical operations, including the basic arithmetic operations involved in calculation, also require knowledge of fundamental mathematical concepts such as percentage, ratio, area, and angle.

The test has four papers in three modes: a writing task; a multiple-choice test 1 (50 items); short-response items (30 items); and a multiple-choice test 2 (50 items).

The writing task is a continuation of the model already developed by the Board of Secondary School Studies and introduced in 1989. It is an interesting task because of the way it balances commonality and constraint by offering candidates choice about how they develop their writing from a common set of stimulus materials.

The task offers a loosely related set of such stimulus material that has a kind of common theme. Candidates are required to write a piece in response to one piece or a number of pieces of the stimulus material. They may choose the form of writing that seems most appropriate to them given the piece they intend to write. They are not required to answer a set question, although there are some prompts and suggestions embedded in the material that they may choose to consider.

It is a flexible and open format which places candidates in a common and comparable context to develop their piece of writing, and also allows them to determine directly the way they will develop it. The test design reconciles the potentially conflicting requirements for commonality and choice in writing test construction.

The multiple-choice items for the CS Test are usually developed in units which have a set or piece of stimulus material and a number of items related to it. These papers for the CS Test contrast with ASAT in that they are not based on the division of the earlier test into a quantitative half, containing maths and science units, and a verbal half, containing social science and humanities units. The key feature of these papers is the development of the items and the construction of the test on the basis of the 49 testable CCEs.

The introduction of open-ended items in which candidates produce short written responses is a major innovation of the CS Test. These Short Response Items (SRIs) aim to increase the validity of the test by expanding the range of testing formats beyond the multiple-choice items and the extended writing sample. SRIs are developed to complement the multiple-choice and writing tasks to give an integrated test; test a wide range of CCE; deal with the whole student ability range; reflect some school-based assessment practices; be open/closed; be convergent/divergent; involve generative thinking or the production of answers; involve the marking of the quality of responses/ conclusion and/or the accuracy of an answer; be marked according to pre-specified criteria and standards; have an effect on gender-linked discrepancies in performance.

The work done in developing the SRI paper is one of the most interesting and challenging aspects of the CS Test. All the items are developed with the CCE in mind. The aim was to diversify the range of the test, and to assess the kind of productive work not readily dealt with in the multiple-choice papers and the Writing Task.

DETERMINING GRADES ON THE CS TEST

The school-based assessment system in Queensland is a criterion- or standards-referenced regime. Consistent with this policy there has been an attempt to base the overall grades for candidates on the CS Test on a notion of criteria and standards rather than adopt norm-referenced procedures. There has also been consideration of the extent to which the test is multi-dimensional and this has prompted consideration of how to combine performance on different dimensions into a single grade.

Forty-nine CCEs have been tentatively grouped into a schedule for grading of the test. This schedule has three purposes: to provide a shorthand description of the test; to provide a set of criteria which can be elaborated into standards for defining the final grades; as an additional means of assessing the range and balance of the test.

The aim of this process is that the results of students, each expressed as one of five grades, are to be determined by a procedure which involves the use of a Grading Schedule. The intention is that students' results, expressed as one of five letter grades (from A to E) are determined by a process which reflects the distinct nature of the QCS Test.

The method incorporates traditional test-scoring techniques used elsewhere in the world together with appropriate aspects of the criterion-based assessment as practised in Queensland. The basis of the method for assigning grades on the QCS Test is the aggregate score on the total test. The distribution of grades is not predetermined but is based on student performance. The numerical cutoffs for the test are determined after analysis of student performance on five criteria, each of which represents some reasonably coherent set of related common curriculum elements (CCEs) which are being sampled across the whole test in any given year. The five criteria are: comprehend and collect; structure and sequence; analyse and assess; create and present; and apply procedures.

The Board of Senior Secondary School Studies defined the 49 testable Common Curriculum Elements as the basis for writing items and structuring a test. Through the Grading Schedule, the CCE are also involved in the criterion- and standards-referenced grading of the test. Items are assigned to criteria to allow the development of meaningful descriptions of student performance in the five criteria rather than the entire test. For each of the five criteria there is a verbal descriptor of an A-standard performance. This statement is expressed in terms of desirable features and is used to inform decisions about the cutoffs for the criterion. Decisions about the cutoffs for each criterion are also informed by the 'calibration' of sets of items in the criterion under consideration. This calibration involves the application of Item Response Theory to define the sort of skills high scoring students have (on a given criterion) that lower scoring students (on that same criterion) do not have. The A/B cutoff for the total test is determined by aggregating the A/B cutoffs on the five criteria. The B/C, C/D, D/E cutoffs are similarly determined. This is a compensatory model. It allows performances on the different levels to be traded off. There is a consistency between a student's grade on the test and that student's total score on the test. Obviously, given the multi-dimensional nature of the test, a student who is multi-skilled will obtain a high score.

These measures have meant that the Queensland Core Skills Test is an assessment of the Queensland curriculum without prescribing it. As a result of this process, the Test is a cross-curricular achievement test, one that is both curriculum-related and cross-curricular.

REFERENCES

Allen, R. (1991). *The Subject Weights Project*. Brisbane: Board of Senior Secondary School Studies.

Matters, G. N. (1991). *A design process for constructing the Queensland Core Skills Test*. Brisbane: Board of Senior Secondary School Studies.

O'Connor, C., & Robotham, M. A. (1991). *Towards equity in the Queensland Core Skills Test - The Queensland Sensitivity Review Process*. Brisbane: Board of Senior Secondary School Studies.

Viviani, N. (1990). *The review of tertiary entrance in Queensland*. Report submitted to the Minister for Education. Brisbane: Queensland Department of Education.

EUROPE

30. ADMISSION TO HIGHER EDUCATION IN THREE EASTERN EUROPEAN COUNTRIES

Karlheinz Ingenkamp[1]
University of Koblenz-Landau

The purpose of this paper is to provide a short account of procedures for admission to higher education in three Eastern European countries: Poland, the former Czech and Slovak Federal Republic (CSSR), and Hungary. The countries differ in history, culture, language, and industrial background but all had been occupied by the Soviet Union by the end of World War II and had communist governments from soon after the war until 1989. All communist governments and parties exercised a very strong influence on all stages of education, since they perceived the influence of education to be very important in building a new society.

For admission to universities in particular this approach had at least two consequences. First, the home background of students was taken into account in selection in an attempt to increase the small percentage of students from working-class backgrounds and decrease the percentage of students from middle- and upper-class backgrounds. Second, more weight was attached to communist loyalty than to aptitude and achievement in traditional subjects.

Research and teaching at the universities was required to serve the socialist society, and the communist party decided what was wrong or right according to marxist theory. We should keep in mind that academic freedom did not exist for 45 years. In fundamental questions, the party gave the directions, supported by many professions. Opposition to prescribed scientific orthodoxy frequently led to the loss of employment. Western literature was seldom available and only very few

1 For information on the systems of education in the countries discussed in this paper, I wish to thank Professor Zoltan Bathory, Budapest; Dr Attila Drescher, Szekszard (Hungary); Professor Miroslaw Szymanski, Warsaw; Dr Zuzana Tomaskova, Prague; and Dr Eliska Walterova, Prague.

university teachers could travel in the western world. All these restrictions were more severe in the CSSR than in Poland or Hungary.

What we have observed since 1989 is the greatest peaceful revolution in history. In more than one sixth of our planet a radical political change took place and an equally radical economic change is on the way. At present nobody can say whether the economic changes will result in an acceptable standard of living for society as a whole. Nobody can foresee either which practices in admission procedures to third-level education will survive after these first eventful years of change. There are, however, some indications of future trends for which we have to thank our colleagues in the CSSR, Hungary and Poland.

First, it would be useful to look briefly at the populations, the growth in student admissions and the relative proportion of students in the three countries concerned, as shown in Table 30.1. As one can see, the highly industrialised CSSR had the largest growth in the number of full-time students and the highest proportion of students compared to employees. Hungary, with still a strong rural background, had the lowest proportion of students compared to employees.

TABLE 30.1

POPULATION, EMPLOYEES, AND STUDENTS IN THREE EASTERN EUROPEAN COUNTRIES

Year		Poland	CSSR	Hungary
1975	Population	34,002,000	14,802,000	10,650,000
1975	Employees	16,946,000	7,435,000	5,085,000
1950	Students (full-time)	117,400	37,452	26,509
1960	1960	111,342	65,451	29,344
	as % of 1950	94.8%	174%	110.7%
1970	1970	209,846	102,015	53,821
	as % of 1950	178.7%	272.4%	203%
1980	No. of students per 10,000 employees 1970	138.3	145.0	108.1

Source: Hegedüs, Kopp, & Schmidt (1982)

POLAND

As in other socialist countries, family background was an important consideration in admission to academic courses at high school and in admission to universities in Poland. Policy for university entrance established the principle of limiting admissions in all subjects, according to the needs of the national economy, for a specific number of highly qualified specialists spread among the various branches of the economy and culture (Kietlinska, 1979). The requirements for university admission were: (i) the secondary school certificate, (ii) the university entrance examination, mostly comprising a traditional written and oral part, but sometimes including objective multiple-choice tests, and (iii) other criteria based on social background, secondary school performance, preuniversity periods of employment, and previous compulsory military service. These criteria facilitated the manipulation of admissions by reducing the importance of academic progress and examination results.

A short summary is available of longitudinal research in Poland on the prediction of higher education success on the basis of various factors, primarily the results of the university entrance examination and the Higher Secondary School Certificate (Kietlinska, 1979). The results indicate that neither factor is an adequate guide to a student's subsequent performance; that average marks in the Higher Secondary School Certificate and the last two years of secondary school are a more reliable guide than the entrance examination; and that the two factors taken together provide a substantially better guide than either taken separately. As far as additional criteria are concerned, the individual factors considered separately were not found to be a reliable guide to success in studies.

Following political change, many attempts were made to model higher education on systems in western democracies. The Higher Education Act of September 12th, 1990 refers to public, civil, and private universities. In 1990, some 400,000 students are reportedly enrolled in these institutions with staff of 60,347 academic teachers, including 5,344 professors (Poland. Ministry of National Education, 1990).

According to the ministry, the Higher Education Act of 1990 is based on the concept of autonomy and self-government of universities, manifested in freedom of research, artistic creation, and teaching, and recognises the extensive collective competencies of universities (Poland. Ministry of National Education, 1990). Among these competencies is the definition of special admission requirements and procedures as well as the scope of knowledge covered by entrance examinations in addition to the general requirement of a secondary school leaving certificate. If the senate of a university proposes to introduce a special entrance examination, the kind and duration of the examination has to be announced at least nine months before the beginning of the following academic year.

It is difficult at present to say what the future of the entrance examination will be. In Spring 1991, the Polytechnic University of Warsaw announced the abolition of entrance examinations from the summer of that year. Everybody expects other universities to follow. The public and the universities are perhaps tired of the compulsory entrance examination which was a feature of the communist regime. They may in the future look for alternative instruments to guide and select students.

CZECH AND SLOVAK FEDERAL REPUBLIC

The communist ideology had a particularly strong influence in the CSSR. Walterova (1992) described it as follows: 'The school system was unified and made uniform. It no longer allowed support for different learners' potentials, beliefs, interests, orientations. An ideological framework of curriculum was enforced based on the utilitarian philosophy of Marxist-Leninist morality, collectivism, the class struggle and on a concept of man subject to strict discipline. It was intolerant of any alternative thinking and feeling, particularly of thinking and feeling influenced by religion. Social credibility and the cultural status of education fell even further, particularly since the last educational reform in 1976 when the most repressive measures were adopted' (p.5).

In 1975, 12.5% of an age group passed the admission examination for universities. Because admission was centralised and completely organised according to communist ideology, failure to complete studies could be the result of bad admission procedures. Statistics have frequently been published to show how many students from the different high schools were successful in passing the examinations. It was a common belief that free admission to universities would lower university standards. Proposals to admit students who were willing to make private financial contributions were never likely to be accepted (Kopp, 1981).

Before 1989, the following components are believed to have contributed to a candidate's score for admission to the faculty of Mathematics and Physics in Prague: 0-25 points: marks of the secondary school; 0-25 points: result of the secondary school-leaving examination; 0-25 points: written examination in Mathematics; 0-25 points: written examination in Physics; 20 points: working-class background; and 15 points: living in the northern frontier region. In this scheme, working-class background and living in the northern frontier region (the border with Germany, settled by many Germans until 1945) contributed much to admission and could more than compensate for a complete failure in the school-leaving examination or in one written paper. The importance of these two components was not made public before 1989.

Prior to 1989, universities used their own written examinations which were constructed according to central regulations. No common tests or intelligence tests were used. Written examinations covered papers in the main subjects, relevant to the selected branch of studies.

Oral examinations focused on a so-called general knowledge of facts. These included basic theses of Marxism-Leninism, questions of interior and foreign politics, resolutions of the congresses of the communist parties of the Soviet Union and the CSSR. Questions were prepared by superior party bodies. Their influence was very strong after the 'Prague spring' in 1968, especially between 1971 and 1980. But the administration of orals depended partly on the members of the local admission board and their convictions.

Regulations for admission to higher education can be summarised as follows. First, the number of admissions was set by government. The ministry determined enrolments for higher education by establishing numerical limits (*numerus clausus*); the number of students with working-class background to be admitted was fixed. Preference was given to members of the organisations of the communist party. In addition to the secondary school-leaving examination and its marks, a written entrance examination was held.

The predictive validity of these admission procedures was largely unknown. Consequently, after the change of 1989, not only curricula but also the organisational structure of the educational system have been altered. Secondary education has become more differentiated, and for the graduates of some secondary schools there are postsecondary and preparatory courses in higher education.

As in Poland, the Higher Education Act of 1990 in the CSSR tried to remove existing restrictions to higher education admission. At present admission is based on the secondary school-leaving certificate. It is sufficient on its own for some faculties. Other faculties require an entrance examination. Each institution has the right to decide upon its admission procedures. The academic senate of the institution decides upon the dean's proposals. The results of the admission examinations are made public and candidates may appeal against the decision. The admission procedure is still selective (CSSR. Institute for Information and Prognoses of Education, Youth and Sport, 1991).

Oral examinations susceptible to political influence have been abolished but some faculties still use orals to test students' interest in subject content. The written examinations are very similar to those used before 1989. Some faculties require three papers. A paper in the Czech language is now the only compulsory examination; Russian is no longer compulsory. The effect of the formal separation of the Czech and Slovak republics on admission to higher education is not yet known.

HUNGARY

Up to the end of World War II, secondary schools in Hungary catered for a very small proportion of the age group and were highly elitist in structure. Graduation from the academic high school was based on teachers' subjective marks and admission to university was the decision of university bodies usually based on graduation marks. There were no entrance examinations.

A short period of democracy from 1945 to 1948 was followed by communist dictatorship. The state planned and controlled not only the economic but also the education system. It prescribed how many young people from different parts of the country and from different social classes could enter certain institutions of higher education and could study specified subjects designated by the state. The so-called educational target figures ruled out any individual choice outside that prescribed by the state. Individual achievement was less important than working-class background. These practices resulted in a growing discontent among the middle and upper classes and led to a decline in educational standards (Lukacs, 1989).

After the revolution of 1956 had been suppressed, the Hungarian communist party tried to gain more acceptance. During their congress in 1962, the party declared a new policy on professionals and intellectuals and abolished quotas based on social background in secondary school and university admissions. Only the secondary school-leaving examination and the university entrance examination would determine admissions. But in 1964 the admission committees were also allowed to take into account candidates' behaviour, talent, fitness and aptitude for higher education in addition to examination results (Lukacs, 1989). Again the door was slightly open to manipulate admission for political or individual purposes. From 1972 to 1978, several measures were taken to increase the percentage of students from a working-class background, including the introduction of non-academic subjects into entrance examinations.

Since the early 1980s, a reorientation of the economic system took place. Central planning decreased and market orientation increased more and more. In education, achievement gained higher priority, and the desire for professional excellence rather than egalitarianism in education was often expressed in the newspapers. At the end of the 1980s, and even today, admission took the form of a two-stage examination. The high school graduation examination based on marks in five primary subjects could yield a maximum of 60 credit points. The selected subjects depend mainly on the nature of a student's proposed study. For the study of Engineering, physical sciences count, while for language study a second language is more significant. The high school can also take into account additional qualifications such as external language courses and success in nationwide contests.

In the university entrance examination one could also achieve 60 points. The university examinations consisted of a written and an oral part. The written part was sometimes constructed as a kind of informal test. If the candidate's result exceeded 50 points and if he/she got fewer points from the high school, then the university points could be doubled for purposes of calculating his/her total admission score. I could not find any research on the predictive validity of the parts of the examination. Even in an article dealing with research in Hungary with regard to admission to higher education (Haber, 1979), no such research is mentioned.

Since the political changes in 1989, a fundamental reform of university structures has been under way. The 1992 proposals of the Ministry of Culture for a new higher education law designates high school graduation as a requirement for admission to the first four years of university study. The university may prescribe additional requirements two years in advance. Such requirements could include entrance examinations, job experience, or practicals. The ministry also proposes that the universities should be responsible for entrance examinations and that all or part of these examinations could be organised jointly by several universities.

A working group, invited by the Ministry of Culture, published a number of proposals for educational policies in the 1990s, some of which deal with higher education. Among the more important are the following. The examination system must provide an objective assessment of students' proficiency so as to enable individuals, families, employers and the various higher grades of schools to get a picture of their skills, abilities, and likely future performance. Accordingly, the examination system should be separated from the activity of teaching, i.e., it should be independent of the schools. There should be legislation regulating the examination system. The organisation of examinations should be put under the supervision of bodies that are under public control. Several examination bodies, in co-operation with each other, should be set up in the country (for example, in regional units or in university centres). The examination requirements should be formulated by experts appointed by the examination bodies, who would also ensure that the examinations were conducted in a professional way (Halacs & Lukacs, 1990).

Hungary's higher education structure today consists of 60 state and 16 church institutions, with 17,300 teaching staff and 103,500 students. In the 53 faculties of the country's 25 universities there are 41,560 full-time students, and in its 50 colleges, 35,000 full-time students. Nearly half the number of university and college students live in halls of residence, and 95% receive regular financial support from the state (Bakos, 1991).

The draft law for higher education has not yet been passed and new regulations are still in the planning stage. Consequently, no research information is available as yet. However, discussions and plans leave little doubt that the new arrangements will not only be more democratic but will also provide for international comparability.

CONCLUSION

Developments in Poland, the former Czech and Slovak Republic, and Hungary, as well as in other countries of the same region, are quite similar as far as admission to higher education is concerned. Before 1989, the communist governments laid down strict central regulations to keep university studies in line with political goals. The number of students was fixed, as well as the number in each subject. Students with a working-class background were given preference. The individual university had little or no influence on admission practices. The secondary school-leaving certificate and central university entrance examinations were the formal requirements. The predictive validity of different selection instruments has seldom been subject to research. The value of the criteria depended primarily on their political importance.

Since 1989, in all Eastern European countries, the political conditions for admission to higher education have been removed. In order to give the universities more freedom, each university can now handle admissions on its own. All central examinations are abolished. There is still a *numerus clausus*, and the secondary school-leaving certificate plays the decisive role. There are some experiments with the use of other kinds of tests, but objective instruments are seldom used. No research findings on the new procedures are as yet available. Everything is still in an experimental stage.

REFERENCES

Bakos, I. (Ed.). (1991). *Concept for higher education development in Hungary.* Budapest: Co-ordination Office for Higher Education.

CSSR. Institute for Information and Prognoses of Education, Youth and Sport. (1991). *Higher education in the Czech and Slovak Federal Republic.* Bratislava, Mimeographed paper.

Haber, J. (1979). Research in Hungary with regard to admission to higher education. In W. Mitter (Ed.), *The use of tests and interviews for admission to higher education.* Windsor: NFER.

Halacs, G., & Lukacs, P. (1990). *Educational policies for the nineties.* Budapest: Hungarian Institute for Educational Research.

Hegedüs, L., v. Kopp, B., & Schmidt, G. (1982). *Hochschulstudium und Berufseingliederung in Sozialistischen Staaten.* (Higher education and entering a profession within the socialistic states). Köln: Böhlau.

Kietlinska, Z. (1979). Research on criteria for admission to higher education in Poland. In W. Mitter (Ed.), *The use of tests and interviews for admission to higher education.* Windsor: NFER.

Kopp, v., B. (1981). *Hochschulen in der CSSR.* (Higher education in the CSSR). Weinheim: Beltz.

Lukacs, P. (1989). Changes in selection policy in Hungary: The case of the admission system in higher education. *Comparative Education, 25,* 219-228.

Poland. Ministry for National Education. (1990). *Higher education in Poland.* Warsaw, Mimeographed paper..

Walterova, E. (1992). *Secondary school curriculum in the framework of the current educational reform. Problems, trends, priorities in Czechoslovakia.* Strasbourg: Council of Europe.

31. ADMISSION TO HIGHER EDUCATION IN ENGLAND AND WALES: RETROSPECT AND PROSPECT

G. M. Forrest
Joint Matriculation Board, Manchester

The GCE Advanced level examination, introduced in 1951, is the direct descendant of the Higher School Certificate (HSC) which from its start in 1918 was clearly a sixth-form examination.

> .... the school course should, in these two years, provide for more concentrated study of a connected group of subjects combined with the study of one or more subsidiary subjects from outside the group (Great Britain. Board of Education, 1914).

Unlike HSC, in Advanced level there are no group requirements: a certificate is issued for one or more subject successes.

In 1918 there were 1,410 entries to the HSC. Between 1932 and 1941 the total (for England and Wales) fluctuated a little around 13,000 candidates. Because of the requirements for the award of a certificate, not all of these would have been successful. In 1938, 9,518 of the 13,201 entrants were fully certificated, of whom Petch (1946) estimates 44% entered university.

As the Second World War came to an end, entries rose dramatically: in 1946, there were 23,063. In the first year of Advanced level there were 103,803 subject entries from 36,677 candidates. In 1992, there were 730,212 subject entries (including Northern Ireland data).

PRESSURES FOR REFORM

Dissatisfaction was expressed about HSC in the 1930s. In 1937, the investigators appointed by the Secondary School Examinations Council (SSEC) drew attention to the dual function of the HSC examination:

> to act as a test for admission to universities and to be a suitable school examination (i.e., a test of two useful years of post-School Certificate work) (Secondary School Examinations Council, 1939, p. 6).

In more than 40 years, GCE Advanced level has not, of course, been static. For example, subjects have changed in popularity, a rising proportion of candidates are female, and there is a tendency for increasing numbers of candidates to offer a mix of subjects across the Arts, Science, and Social Science groupings. Curricular changes have taken place. The examining boards have constantly reviewed and revised their syllabuses so as to ensure that the needs of schools, colleges, and society in general are being met.

However, over the last 30 years or so various attempts to reduce specialisation and broaden the curriculum of the sixth form have not met with approval. In 1985, the introduction of Advanced Supplementary (AS) examinations, to start in 1989, was announced (Great Britain. Department of Education and Science and the Welsh Office, 1984). AS examinations were aimed at broadening the curriculum (Great Britain. Department of Education and Science and the Welsh Office, 1986). Despite the agreement of the universities to regard two AS subjects as equivalent to one A-level subject, entries are still low except for General Studies and Mathematics and it seems clear that the intentions of the ministry are being thwarted by the practices of schools. More recent proposals for 'leaner and tougher' Advanced levels (Great Britain. Department of Education and Science and the Welsh Office, 1988) came to nought. Government regarded the existing GCE Advanced level examination as 'the gold standard'.

None of the attempts to change Advanced Level addressed the dilemma first pointed out in 1939, and regularly repeated, that the examination was attempting to fulfil two conflicting functions. Christie and Forrest (1981), and more recently Kingdon (1991), drew attention to the problem that had become even more acute with increasing numbers of candidates.

A TEST OF ACADEMIC APTITUDE

The Robbins Report (Great Britain. Ministry of Education, 1963) recommended that research be carried out 'into the extent to which aptitude tests might supplement other features of the selection process' (p.277). The Committee made it clear that such tests were not intended to replace academic examinations which, along with school records, were seen to play an essential part in the selection process.

> But if some of the predictive load could be shifted from examinations, the pressure for candidates to cram for them would be less; and selection is likely to be more efficient if based on performance in more than one type of test. (Great Britain. Ministry of Education, 1963, para. 233)

The Investigation into Supplementary Predictive Information for University Admission (ISPIUA) was set up in 1966 by the Committee of Vice-Chancellors and

Principals of the Universities of the United Kingdom and the active co-operation of the two largest examining boards was gained. The first Test of Academic Aptitude (TAA), taken in 1967 by pupils in the fourth term of their two-year sixth-form course, was based on Oliver's (1966) Scholastic Aptitude Test. In the following years more tests were constructed. These were never used operationally and can no longer be regarded as valid instruments.

Of the 27,315 Advanced-level candidates in the sample, 7,080 entered university in 1968. Detailed information was collected on this group of undergraduates, the analysis of which formed the basis of a report compiled by staff of the National Foundation for Educational Research. The main finding of the study was as follows:

> For most courses the best predictors of first year performances assessed by the university and of final degree results were GCE A-level grades. This may be surprising when one considers that the advanced level examination was never designed to play this role. It must also be noted that although GCE A-level predicts better than the other available data, the correlations of A-level grades are still very low, ranging usually between 0.2 and 0.4. It would be difficult to justify the use of such a weak predictor if better measures were available (Choppin, Orr, Kurle, Fara, & James, 1973, p.63).

A close relationship between performance in this experimental Test of Academic Aptitude and performance in the Advanced-level General Studies examination was established but it did not help (Forrest, Smith, & Brown, 1970). It was impossible politically to decide that all aspiring university applicants should take an examination of a particular examining board when the UK examination system is based on the principle of choice of board. Choppin and Orr (1976) in a summary of the project point out that, even if the TAA did not earn a place in the regular selection process, such a test would be useful for those candidates with non-standard entrance qualifications as well as those wishing to join faculties for which there is no equivalent Advanced-level subject.

INITIATIVES FOR NEW QUALIFICATIONS

Smithers and Robinson (1989) estimate that in the late 1980s about 90% and 70% of those accepted for university and polytechnic places respectively did not have the normal academic qualifications. Admissions tutors are already accustomed to the International Baccalaureate and those in the old polytechnics are familiar with a range of vocational examinations, such as those of the City and Guilds of London Institute. The government's intentions for the future are clear (Great Britain, 1991): parity of esteem between academic and vocational qualifications will be ensured by the setting up of a system of national vocational qualifications (NVQs) so that other existing qualifications can be accredited within the new structure. Five levels of equivalence are planned, from Level 1 (lower grade GCSEs) to Level 5 (higher education). Young people still in full-time education will take General NVQs (gNVQs), which will not be specific to a particular job or type of work, like ordinary NVQs.

There are plans also for Ordinary and Advanced Diplomas, applicants for the former requiring some GCSE grades, a gNVQ at Level 2, and an occupationally-specific NVQ and for the latter, two Advanced-level passes and the same elements as for the Ordinary Diploma but at level 3. These developments mean that, in a very short time, thousands of aspiring university applicants will be offering qualifications other than Advanced level, thereby making the task of providing equal treatment for all very difficult.

UNIVERSITY EXPANSION

Despite post-war expansion of places, a reducing percentage of those who were 'qualified' – in the sense that they had the necessary entrance qualifications – actually entered university in the late 1950s (Great Britain. Ministry of Education, 1963, p.12). In the 1960s, the number of university places was again increased. Existing universities were expanded, six new ones were founded and full university status was granted to Colleges of Advanced Technology. In 1992, the polytechnics were up-graded and were given the status of universities. Although there has been some opposition, in general there has been great support for this

> A new pattern of higher education, common but various, had to be created to match the changed circumstances of the 1990s, on the edge of the 21st century. (Leader in *Times Higher Education Supplement,* 19 June 1992)

DISCUSSION

GCE Advanced-level performance up to now has been the best single predictor of degree success (Forrest, 1989). However, not only are preuniversity courses and their associated examinations undergoing great change, but the universities too are providing instruction in subjects and areas which until very recently were considered novel. Increasing numbers of aspiring university applicants are going to find that there is a mismatch between what they have been exposed to in school and what they wish to study at university. For more and more students the predictive level of their school results is going to fall.

The use of an achievement examinations for selection purposes throws up one problem: females have been shown in many countries to be disadvantaged by objectively-marked items in question papers. Moreover, in many cultures females shun the sciences, in which subjects there is evidence to suggest that male Advanced-level candidates consistently achieve higher grades than females (Forrest, 1992).

Recently there has been much talk about falling standards, be it the GCSE or grades at GCE Advanced level. It is so easy to say that standards have fallen, but it is extremely difficult to demonstrate whether or not they have. The only empirical study in England and Wales of comparability over time at Advanced level was a pilot experiment which was never repeated (Christie & Forrest, 1980). One thing stands out from this study, even if the results have to be regarded with caution: a radical change in a subject's syllabus over a span of years makes the demonstration of comparability almost impossible. The Chemistry on which candidates had answered questions on 1963 was very different from the Chemistry taught in 1973. If such comparisons are so difficult to make, it is scarcely logical to say that standards have fallen, and by the same token it is not possible to assert that they have risen.

There is another difference which may be rather significant. Recent (unpublished) work at the University of Manchester by Dr I. S. Peers, has broken new ground. Using meta-analysis of 20 studies of UK university and polytechnic students who graduated between 1954 and 1983, two main conclusions were drawn. First, the predictive validity of Advanced level was greater for universities than for polytechnics; second, prediction varied among degree subjects, a finding not unique to this analysis. Generally speaking, predictive validity was poorer in the Social Sciences than in the Arts in both universities and polytechnics. Predictive validity was highest for science courses in the universities.

One way of solving the problem caused by the two roles which the GCE Advanced-level examination is expected to fulfil would be for all applicants who wished to do so to enter the university of their choice. University courses, even with the previous polytechnics coming into the system, would have to change radically and would be required to cover a whole range of new subjects. The first year drop-out rate would be very high, thereby adding to the administrative difficulties which such a suggestion would produce. The costs of changing to this form of higher education would be so tremendous that, even if given the approval of society, no government is likely to accept the economic implications involved.

Alternatively, an academic aptitude test idea could be revived: aspiring university applicants would take a special examination and their acceptance would depend on the results. Although the ISPIUA Test of Academic Aptitude of more than 20 years ago failed, it is suggested that a new attempt to create valid university aptitude tests is urgent. The needs of both the established universities as well as the newly-designated ones would be met if each applicant were to have provided for him/her (along with a record of successes in a wide range of endeavours as well as examination results) standardised scores on an aptitude test taken by all applicants. Advances in computing technology since the 1960s mean that the software and the networks are available to ease the administration of an admissions system which would include a single national test each year. Such a system cannot be set up overnight. However, funds should be made available to develop the tests as well as the administrative structure required. Were a decision to go along this path taken today, it is not unreasonable to anticipate that acceptable tests and the administrative structure required could be in place by the turn of the century.

Failure to act now will mean that, not only will consistent comparisons among applicants with the newer qualifications become extremely difficult, but also GCE Advanced level will continue to be criticised for failing to do what it was never intended that it should do.

REFERENCES

Choppin, B., & Orr, L. (1976). *Aptitude testing at eighteen-plus*. Windsor: NFER.

Choppin, B. H. L., Orr, L., Kurle, S. D. M., Fara, P., & James, G. (1973). *The prediction of academic success*. Windsor: NFER.

Christie, T., & Forrest, G. M. (1980). *Standards at GCE A-Level: 1963 and 1973*. London: Macmillan Education.

Christie, T., & Forrest, G. M. (1981). *Defining public examination standards*. London: Macmillan Education.

Forrest, G. M. (1989). *The relationship between GCE Advanced level grades and university results in the UK: Past and future*. Paper presented at the 15th Annual Conference of the International Association for Educational Assessment, Sydney.

Forrest, G. M. (1992). Gender differences in school science examinations. *Studies in Science Education*, *20*, 87-121.

Forrest, G. M., Smith, G. A., & Brown, H. M. (1970). *General Studies (Advanced) and academic aptitude*. Occasional Publication 34. Manchester: Joint Matriculation Board.

Great Britain. (1991). *Education and training for the 21st century*. White Paper. Cm 1536. London: HMSO.

Great Britain. Board of Education. (1914). *Examinations in secondary schools. Proposals of the Board of Education (Circular 849)*. London: HMSO.

Great Britain. Department of Education and Science and the Welsh Office. (1984). *AS Levels*. Proposals by the Secretaries of State for Education and Science and the Welsh Office for a broader examination for A-level Students. London: HMSO.

Great Britain. Department of Education and Science and the Welsh Office. (1986). *Better schools*. London: HMSO.

Great Britain. Department of Education and Science and the Welsh Office. (1988). *Advancing A levels*. Report of a Committee appointed by the Secretary of State for Education and Science and the Secretary of State for Wales (Higginson Report). London: HMSO.

Great Britain. Ministry of Education. (1963). *Higher education*. Report of the Committee appointed by the Prime Minister (Robbins Report). London: HMSO.

Kingdon, M. (1991). *The reform of Advanced Level*. London: Hodder & Stoughton.

Oliver, R. A. C. (1966). *Scholastic aptitude test*. Manchester: University of Manchester.

Petch, J. A. (1946). *Some aspects of the growth of secondary school examinations.* Manchester: Manchester Statistical Society.

Secondary School Examinations Council. (1939). *The Higher School Certificate Examination. Being the report of the investigators appointed by the Secondary School Examinations Council to enquire into the eight approved Higher School Certificate examinations held in the summer of 1937.* London: HMSO.

Smithers, A., & Robinson, P. (1989). *Increasing participation in higher education.* Manchester: School of Education, University of Manchester.

32. THE DEVELOPMENT OF MODULAR A-LEVEL COURSES IN ENGLAND AND WALES

Mary Hayden
School of Education,
University of Bath

Since its introduction in the 1950s, the Advanced (or A) level examination has been a cause for concern in some quarters as a result of the specialisation it allows at the age of 16. The possibility of broadening the A-level curriculum was considered in 1988 by the Higginson Committee, which made a recommendation (promptly rejected by government) that students' A-level programmes should be broadened to include five subjects (Great Britain. Department of Education and Science, 1988). The Advanced Supplementary (AS) examination, designed to be of A-level standard but the equivalent of 'half an A-level' in terms of breadth, and to be taught over a two-year period, was greeted by many as a positive step that might encourage students specialising in one area of the curriculum to broaden their experience by studying an AS subject in a 'complementary' area. The uptake of AS has, however, been disappointing and it has not proved to be the instrument for increasing breadth which many had hoped. Among the likely reasons for its low take-up are the logistical difficulties experienced by schools in offering a course of half the content of A-level over a two-year period and the resource implications of delivering such courses to what may be small numbers of students.

One means of increasing the number of AS subjects within schools has been to teach AS and A-level courses together. Such combination, difficult to implement with traditional courses, which are assessed largely by written examinations at the end of two years, could be facilitated by the organisation of courses on a modular basis. This would allow AS and A-level students to be taught individual modules in the same class. Though not the only rationale for the development of a number of modular AS/A-level courses in recent years, the possibility of increasing the uptake of AS and thus broadening the curriculum for this age range was undoubtedly a factor in the development of the two modular schemes on which this paper is based. Both are offered by the University of London Examinations and

Assessment Council (ULEAC) to a limited number of candidates over a pilot phase of five years. The first is the Ridgeway Scheme which takes its name from the Ridgeway School in Swindon, where eight modular AS/A-level syllabuses were initially developed in Biology, Economics, English, English Literature, French, Geography, History, and Religious Studies (University of London Examinations and Assessment Council, 1992b). The second modular scheme consists of one subject only, Business Studies (University of London Examinations and Assessment Council, 1992a). This was developed by the National Design and Technology Education Foundation (NDTEF) and is certificated by ULEAC, which takes particular responsibility for assessment procedures. The issues highlighted in this paper are those which have appeared during the course of a recently completed two-year evaluation by ULEAC of both schemes to be amongst the most fundamental with respect to the distinction between modular schemes and the more traditional type of A-level course.

NUMBER OF MODULES

One of the first decisions to be made in developing a modular curriculum is the number of modules which should constitute the programme. The NDTEF scheme opted for a ten-module course, which for A-level was based on two compulsory 'core' modules (one each year) plus four optional modules per year. The AS course consists of five modules, consisting of a core module and four optional modules. The Ridgeway scheme, on the other hand, opted for six compulsory modules for the A-level curriculum (one to be taught and assessed per term of the school year), with three to be taken for AS. The conditions imposed with respect to the combinations of modules acceptable for the AS course vary between subjects. For French, for instance, only one combination is possible, while other subjects vary in terms of the amount of flexibility allowed. Moreover, the requirement to teach one module per term can cause problems since the sixth term of the two-year course tends to be disrupted by other A-level examinations. The fact that Colleges of Further Education tend to finish the academic year earlier than schools also means that, while schools are keen that assessment of summer term modules should take place as late as possible, colleges would generally prefer assessment to take place somewhat earlier.

ASSESSMENT OF COURSE CONTENT

It could be argued that a scheme should only be described as modular if each module is a self-contained unit, with assessment taking place at the end of the module. The Ridgeway Scheme, on the whole, fits this description. In most cases, each module is assessed at the end of the school term, with the marks gained by the student accounting for one-sixth of his/her total for the A-level course (or one-third for AS). The NDTEF scheme also fits this description in theory, with ten units of assessment for A-level and five for AS. A major issue in this context is the extent to which there should be overlap between modules in content and/or assessment. In a course consisting entirely of compulsory modules, it may be considered acceptable to assess each item of content or skill once only. Where there is choice, however, as in the NDTEF AS and A-level programmes, and in the Ridgeway AS programme, complications arise. Attempts to balance flexibility and choice with the need to ensure that important areas of content and skills are not bypassed by some students can lead to a tendency to over-assess, as the same knowledge and skills are included in a number of modules to ensure that every student encounters them at least once.

In the Ridgeway scheme, approaches to this issue vary between subjects. The assessment of English Literature, for example, consists of six components (one per module), some of which consist of a written paper and some of coursework. In French, on the other hand, each one of four language skills (working with recorded texts, working with written texts, active discourse oral skills, and independent writing) is assessed in every module. In addition, modules five and six include a component based on the interpretation of topic-related literature. It could be argued that such a blanket coverage of all skills in each module leads to unnecessary pressure being placed on students.

ASSESSMENT MODES

In the case of Ridgeway French, at least one component of each module is assessed by the teacher. In English Literature, some modules are assessed totally by the teacher, some totally by written examination. The means by which other Ridgeway subjects are assessed vary from subject to subject, as does the balance between the externally-assessed components (including, for instance, traditional unseen written examination papers, 'seen' examination papers, and practical tests) and the teacher-assessed components (including, for example, oral skills in French and fieldwork in Geography). The different weightings assigned to these components in each module lead to very different overall balances of assessment mode across subjects. For example, the weighting of the internally assessed component in Geography is as low as 20%, while in English it is as high as 50 percent. In between are the other subjects such as French, where the overall ratio between external and internal assessment is .612 to .388. In all subjects except Economics, the balance between external and internal assessment remains the same at AS regardless of the combination of modules selected.

The NDTEF Business Studies scheme is different from most other A-level subjects in that assessment is completely internal. For each module, students are assessed on a portfolio of their own work, as well as on their participation in group work with other students. Assessment criteria are provided for teachers, who assess each student's achievement on his/her own work in each module on a scale of 1-4 in the five areas of Investigation, Analysis, Evaluation, Decision-making, and Communication. For group work, teachers assess students (again on a scale of 1-4) on the criteria of Contribution, Co-operation, and Production. In addition, each student assesses his/her own group work and that of his/her fellow students, although peer assessments do not contribute to the overall mark. In theory according to the same criteria each NDTEF module is assessed at its end to the extent that teachers are required to submit their assessments only at the end of each of the two years of the course. Although they are advised to assess each module in turn, before moving on to the next, the extent to which this advice is followed is not monitored. It could be argued that if modules are not studied and assessed as separate units, then the course cannot truly be considered modular.

MODERATION OF ASSESSMENT

The process of bringing the assessment of all teachers to a common standard is carried out for Ridgeway subjects according to a traditional model of Chief Examiners sampling the assessment of each teacher and making adjustments as necessary. The assessment of students' portfolios in the NDTEF scheme is moderated by a system of consensus moderation, which had its origins in the Certificate of Secondary Education (CSE) examinations in England and Wales. The main feature of consensus moderation is that each teacher's assessment is essentially moderated by other teachers. Groups of teachers meet together at the end of the year, by region, under the chairmanship of a Regional Assessor. By moderating samples of each other's assessment, the group arrives at an overall 'consensus' with respect to standards. Samples of teachers' assessment in each region are then submitted to the Chief Assessor, who may adjust all the marks from a region if he or she feels that assessment has been either too severe or too lenient.

One of the issues arising in relation to this form of moderation is the extent to which it is sufficiently precise as a means of adjusting marks which account for the vast majority of the student's overall score. New teachers in particular can experience difficulties in applying the criteria and differentiating between the levels to be awarded, and the fact that time constraints may restrict the number of teachers who moderate a given teacher's assessment to one or possibly two also gives rise to concern. Consensus moderation meetings, however, clearly play an important part in teachers' professional development by making possible detailed discussion of the application of the assessment criteria.

It has not proved possible to devise a moderation scheme for the group work component of the NDTEF scheme, since the only means by which the Chief Assessor could make a judgment about the teacher's assessment of these skills would be by visiting each school to observe group work in action over a period of time. Assessment of group work has consequently been unmoderated to date, both in respect of the teacher assessment and of the student's self-assessment. Concerns about the validity of accepting marks with no guarantee of parity of standards led to a decision to withdraw the assessment of group work completely from this scheme in September 1992.

COHERENCE AND MATURATION

Concern is often expressed that dividing a syllabus into units can lead to fragmentation, by encouraging the treatment of modules as separate units which may be taught, assessed, and then forgotten. The experience of Ridgeway and NDTEF has suggested that, while this is potentially a problem, it can be avoided. The role of the teacher is crucial in this connection and it would seem to be the extent to which the teacher draws the content of the modules together, or treats them all as discrete units, that determines whether or not a modular course forms a coherent overall programme.

Maturation is probably one of the major issues associated with modular syllabuses. On the one hand, if an AS or A-level course is to have credibility in the eyes of, for example, employers and higher education admissions officers, the assessment of all modules must be seen to be of A-level standard. On the other hand, it could be argued that it is not reasonable to assess at A-level standard a student who has had only one term's teaching since completing GCSE courses. Opinions differ as to how this issue should be treated. In Ridgeway English Literature and Economics, the issue is dealt with by covering, in the first module of the course, introductory 'core' topics which are drawn upon throughout the remainder of the course but which are not assessed until the end of the programme. A student's first assessment, therefore, takes place at the end of the second term, when the issue of maturation is arguably not of such concern. Only Ridgeway French has addressed the issue of maturation by building in differential weightings: the total marks available for the three pairs of modules 1 and 2, 3 and 4, 5 and 6 are in the ratio of 1 : 2 : 3. However, consideration of mark distributions to date in all Ridgeway subjects has not suggested a trend towards better performance in later modules; any differences would appear to be related to the mode of assessment employed rather than to the timing of the assessment.

COMPARABILITY

A major issue in relation to the development of any new style of programme is that of comparability of standards with more traditional, or 'Mode 1', subjects. In both Ridgeway and NDTEF schemes, ULEAC has made provision for the involvement in all modular subjects of Chief Examiners, Moderators (who have an overall responsibility for standards), Subject Officers, and other permanent staff who also have experience of Mode 1 subjects. As yet, the number of candidate entries has been too small to allow statistical comparison of results that would provide evidence of the extent to which standards of modular and Mode 1 courses are comparable.

CONCLUSION

The evidence of the last three years would suggest that the introduction of the two modular courses considered in this paper has not satisfied one of its aims, that of leading to an increased uptake of AS. AS entries in Ridgeway subjects have been very low, and in the NDTEF scheme only slightly higher. While disappointing perhaps, some features of the modular schemes are clearly valued by teachers and students.

It is too early to judge the reactions of higher education institutions to these modular schemes. However, anecdotal evidence from the small numbers who have so far completed the courses and proceeded to higher education suggests that admissions officers have not been unduly concerned about the style of assessment leading to the AS or A-level grades awarded.

Finally, reference must be made to the major changes impending for modular AS and A-level courses, since the publication in March 1992 by the School Examinations and Assessment Council (1992) of its principles for Advanced and Advanced Supplementary Examinations. Changes to result from these principles include the restriction of coursework in most cases to a maximum of 20% of the total mark, and the introduction of an end-of-course examination, accounting for a minimum of 50% of the total marks. Clearly the restructuring required to conform to these principles will lead to both Ridgeway and NDTEF Business Studies schemes taking on a very different appearance in the future.

REFERENCES

Great Britain. Department of Education and Science. (1988). *Advancing A levels.* Report of a Committee chaired by Professor G. Higginson. London: HMSO.

School Examinations and Assessment Council. (1992). *Principles for Advanced and Advanced Supplementary examinations.* London: Author.

University of London Examinations and Assessment Council. (1992a). *Business Studies (NDTEF) Mode 2 AS/A Level evaluation. Report to SEAC.* London: Author.

University of London Examinations and Assessment Council. (1992b). *Ridgeway Mode 2 AS/A Level evaluation. Report to SEAC.* London: Author.

33. THE REPORT OF THE HOWIE COMMITTEE AND UPPER SECONDARY EDUCATION IN SCOTLAND

Peter Kimber
Scottish Examination Board, Dalkeith, Midlothian

In this paper, recent proposals for reforming post-compulsory education and certification in Scotland are examined in the context of entrance qualifications for tertiary education. Perhaps it is inevitable that the paper will contrast the quite diverse approaches to this issue in Scotland and in the rest of Britain. There is a tendency for Scots to compare themselves favourably with whatever happens in England. But a recent report by Professor Howie has obliged Scottish education to be less parochial; to look more widely at practice in Europe and to draw comparisons with Denmark, France, and Germany (*Upper secondary education,* 1992). This exercise has left Scots feeling less complacent than previously.

Two separate approaches to qualification for tertiary education are taken in England and Scotland. (In this paper reference to England includes Wales and Northern Ireland which share the same features.) The difference between the systems in Scotland and England in post-compulsory education, i.e., 16+, may be summed up in the following way. In Scotland, the goal of university entrance can best be approached on a broad curricular base, in an 'incremental' way, offering a series of relatively short-term goals which accumulate to the necessary standard. In England, the goal of university entrance can best be approached through a narrowly specialised curriculum, offering students a two-year integrated 'block' course with a long-term prospect of success.

The result of these two separate approaches, which may be called the block approach (A Level) and the incremental approach (Higher) is that a larger proportion of the age cohort goes to university in Scotland than in England and Scottish students are, broadly speaking, as successful as their English counterparts. It is claimed that the better staying-on rates at second level in Scotland are a result of offering students the short-term goal of one-year Higher courses compared with the more specialised two-year courses for A Level. The fact that Highers as a qualifying certificate for university entrance have been in existence for 104 years suggests, if nothing else, that the Scots see merit in the *status quo* and will need much persuasion before discarding it.

The proposals of the Howie report contain some characteristics of both approaches but also go beyond them. They offer an incremental approach for vocational education and a three-year block course in some 10 subjects for more academically inclined students. The purpose of this paper is to look at the merits of these diverse approaches to qualification for tertiary education and to propose alternatives to Howie's recommendations.

An issue raised by the Howie report which is of wide significance is the relative worth of academic as opposed to vocational education. There has long been an elitist view in Scotland, and elsewhere, that academic education is intrinsically superior to vocational education, and that since only a certain proportion of the population can benefit from academic courses they should be segregated from the rest at as early a stage as possible. On the other hand, there has been passionate opposition to this elitism and premature categorisation of ability. The battle between the two views has smouldered for many years with occasional outbursts of controversy. The Howie report asserts that one of its aims was to promote parity of esteem between academic and vocational courses. Indeed it is part of government policy to raise public appreciation of vocational education and training. One issue to be addressed in this paper is whether the sort of approach taken by Howie is likely to be successful or whether there are better ways of achieving parity of esteem.

The issues which this paper will address may be expressed in the form of two basic questions. Are secondary school students best served by a block approach to certification for tertiary education or by an incremental approach which allows accumulation of qualifications? And what is the best way of promoting parity of esteem for academic and vocational courses?

STRENGTHS AND WEAKNESSES OF THE SCOTTISH SYSTEM

There are a number of strengths in the Scottish tradition which it is important to preserve. As previously mentioned, staying on rates in Scotland are significantly higher than in England, with a majority of students remaining beyond the end of compulsory schooling. In broad figures, 62% of 16-year olds are in full-time education compared with 53% in Britain as a whole. By presenting students for some Highers in S5 and for others in S6, in addition to the fact that some students resit the exams, Scottish students have a chance to progress towards university qualification in a piecemeal way which gives opportunities to gain confidence and accumulate qualifications, albeit in a possibly disorderly way.

The mixture of modular, vocational courses and academic Higher Grade courses offers post-16 students a strong chance to add to qualifications in a step-by-step manner, as opposed to a group certificate or a two-year course, both of which may deter the less able and reduce staying-on rates. The proportion of school leavers with entry qualifications for university from Scotland is currently 26 percent. This compares with current figures of between 30 and 35% in Denmark, Germany, and France. The Scottish figure is expected to rise to 35% by the year 2000. It is not easy to obtain comparable figures for the rest of Britain, but Scottish rates seem to be a couple of percentage points higher where direct comparisons can be made.

There are also several weaknesses in the current system which prompted the Government to set up the Howie Committee including the following. First, there are only about two terms of teaching time to cover Higher courses after Standard Grade. This leads to exam-driven courses with inadequate opportunity to develop individual study skills. Second, the increasing numbers of pupils staying on into S5 have not found Higher to be an entirely suitable provision. Many have left at the end of S5 with few or even no Highers. Third, although the S5 curriculum is broader than in England, it is narrower than in some European countries. Fourth, the wide choice of subjects available to students often leads to a lack of coherence in their choices. This is particularly true of vocational education where modular provision allows almost unlimited combinations of courses. Finally, the range of choices in S5 and S6 leads to a process of what Howie called 'winnowing and sifting.' Students in choosing subjects for study attempt to collect sufficient awards for further or higher education.

THE HOWIE PROPOSALS

The Howie report has made proposals including the following which, it claims, are 'radical.' First, there is seen to be a 'plateau' in the pace of learning in the P7 to S2 years. If the pace of learning were increased at this stage, it would be possible to bring forward Standard Grade examinations from S4 to S3, i.e., from age 16 to age 15. Second, university entrance should be based on a SCOTBAC award at the end of S6. This, together with the previous suggestion, would allow a three-year interval between Standard Grade and university entrance certification, which would facilitate a more gradual 'gradient' of learning than the two-term dash of the present Higher arrangements. Third, the SCOTBAC would be a group certificate, as opposed to the single-subject accumulation of the present Highers, with a compulsory core including English, Mathematics, a modern language, Science, Social Subjects, Music or History of Art or Information Technology, plus four options spread over the three-year course. Students would be required to cover a wide range of subjects and to pursue a few of them in considerable depth. The subjects chosen would ensure adequate coverage of basic skills. The award would be based on accumulating points for awards at the equivalent of Higher or Certificate of Sixth Year Studies. A predetermined points threshold would be the basis for a group award.

Fourth, a parallel course of study of a mainly vocational kind would lead to the Scottish Certificate (SCOTCERT). This would be either a one-year course leading to SCOTCERT Part One, or a two-year course leading to SCOTCERT Part Two. These courses would be made up of 40-hour modules chosen in one of 10 'occupational sectors' such as Engineering, Catering, Business Administration, plus two general educational awards. All SCOTCERT courses would include essential 'core skills'. Fifth, students would have to decide at the end of S3, on the basis of Standard Grade results, whether to embark on a vocational or academic course, albeit with a series of 'ladders and bridges' to avoid trapping students prematurely in one kind of course or the other. Sixth, to avoid the premature foreclosure of subject choice, 'modal courses' should be developed. These would be mainly in science and the social subjects. From S1 to S6 students would follow a science course which combined Biology, Chemistry and Physics. Similarly in the social subjects there would be unified courses with an amalgam of Geography, History, Economics, and Politics.

These are the broad outlines of the Howie report's proposals, although for the purposes of this paper most attention has been focused on SCOTBAC for university entrance rather than SCOTCERT. Consultation on the Report showed considerable interest in the criticisms of the current arrangements and the proposals for reform, but there were several serious reservations.

CURRICULAR OBJECTIONS TO THE HOWIE PROPOSALS

First, the twin-track approach with its clear distinction between the academic and the vocational is in conflict with the avowed aim of giving parity of esteem to both types of course. Moreover, the proposed bridges and ladders between the two seem unlikely to span the division effectively. Second, SCOTCERT courses would be modular while SCOTBAC courses would be unitary. This is likely to accentuate the distinction between the two. Third, the separation of courses at age 15 will, if implemented, have a number of serious consequences. Errors of inclusion will affect many children who through teacher uncertainty or parental pressure will be entered for the more demanding course on the grounds that it is easier to move from a SCOTBAC course to a SCOTCERT than *vice versa*. There will also be errors of exclusion, if only because predictions are grossly inaccurate, as previous experience suggests. Fourth, Howie recommends the development and introduction of modal courses right through to SCOTBAC. The main ones would be in science and the social subjects. This would mean a major reconstruction of existing courses throughout secondary education and it is not clear that students would benefit. It would also mean major retraining of teachers.

Fifth, the very demanding nature of SCOTBAC as an entrance qualification will, by the report's own admission, reduce the number of students meeting the qualification. This would be unfortunate. At present, Britain in general has a high completion rate for students in higher education. In Scotland, a greater proportion of the age cohort than in England, goes to university and the completion rate is virtually the same. It would be a retrograde step to raise the level of entry qualifications, thus debarring people who are perfectly capable of completing a degree course successfully. The point was made above that Scottish students are persuaded to aim for tertiary education, not by making it a conscious goal at age 15, but by incremental steps in S5 and S6.

Sixth, Howie uses conflicting arguments about staying-on rates for SCOTBAC and SCOTCERT students. He assumes that the former will be motivated by the prospect of a three-year course, while the latter will be motivated by numerous short-term goals in a number of modular courses. This is dubious psychology. It may be questioned whether there are in fact two distinct groups of students who can safely be assigned to contrasting courses at age 15. Seventh, Howie proposes some narrowing of the curriculum which, he maintains, offers an unnecessary breadth of choice at present. The range of subjects offered at Ordinary Grade was reduced from 45 subjects and 52 syllabuses to 34 subjects and syllabuses at Standard Grade. Yet Howie recommends reducing this still further at the expense of new and very popular subjects such as Technological Studies, Physical Education, and Drama.

Finally, the Howie report proposes that for students embarking on a SCOTBAC course the only exit points would be either a group award at the end of S6 or a 'bridge' into a SCOTCERT course. The proportion of the cohort willing to commit themselves to this length of course is a matter for conjecture, but A-Level experience is not encouraging. Although there would be recognition of partial achievement at the end of S6, it is a weakness of the proposals that there would be no recognition at an S5 exit point. It would be difficult to convince students that a SCOTCERT award is of equal worth if it is the only option for failed SCOTBAC students.

ALTERNATIVES TO HOWIE

If the Howie report as it stands is not the best solution to the problems it identified, what is? A number of points are worth considering: for one thing, evolution is preferable to revolution. Scottish secondary education has just experienced a major upheaval through the development of Standard Grade at age 16, Revised Higher at 17, and Revised CSYS. Teachers are battle-scarred and weary with little appetite for more change. Further, new proposals should be demonstrably superior to existing arrangements. If a one plus one, incremental approach has produced proportionately more graduates in Scotland than in England, why move towards something that threatens to be a retrograde step towards a more restrictive and unnecessarily elitist qualification?

If existing Higher courses which are notionally of 120 hours' duration give insufficient time to develop appropriate study skills, Higher courses could be extended to, say, 160 hours. This would allow a candidate to take, say, three Highers in S5 and two in S6 at a more leisurely pace. Alternatively a Higher course could be end-on to existing CSYS courses and could be spread over two years. It would also allow a judicious mixture of Higher and modular courses according to the abilities and inclinations of the candidate.

The goal of a group certificate is worth establishing for those able to attain it. While a group certificate has advantages for encouraging - or indeed obliging - students to follow a broad and balanced curriculum it should not be the only basis for university entrance since market forces will determine whether or not candidates are admitted to the course of their choice. Entrance will in practice be awarded to holders of lesser qualifications if the number of places available exceeds applicants, which is likely to be the case at a time of falling rolls.

There should be provision for exit points from the system, with recognition of attainment, when required. In general, individually certificated courses which allow curricula of mixed academic and vocational subjects where appropriate would seem desirable. Exit points can also be entry points for mature students. The evidence is that this encourages students to aim for more immediate goals and that short-term success encourages efforts to achieve more demanding goals.

A possible scenario for reforming upper secondary education in Scotland might take the following lines. First, Standard Grade would continue to be taken by most students at the end of S4 and would be certificated as at present. However, the balance of internal and external assessment could shift substantially toward internal assessment, making use of centrally prepared banks of test materials. (This system is currently in operation for primary education and the materials have been welcomed by teachers.) Second, presentation for Standard Grade examinations is currently tied to S4 and only exceptionally may candidates be presented before this stage. However Standard Grade would no longer be tied to S4, but instead students could be entered for one or more subjects when the school considered them to be ready for it. This would become increasingly easy as the balance shifts towards internal assessment. Third, Higher courses would be extended to take a notional 160 hours instead of 120. A majority of candidates might then take three subjects in S5 (480 hours) and two in S6. Additionally, 160 hours is also the recommended teaching time for four modules. In principle, equivalence between modular and Higher courses could be established where appropriate.

CSYS courses would be merged with Higher courses and become part of the Certificate of Education so students could follow a course to Higher level or to the current CSYS level. Certification would be possible at the end of S5 for those who chose to go no further, but there would be a strong encouragement for students to stay on to S6 through the prospect of a group award at the end of S6. This would retain the advantages of Howie's SCOTBAC proposal while also offering an exit point from S5 for those who wanted it.

Instead of Howie's modal courses in science or social sciences, students would be required to follow a balanced course by taking at least one subject (at either Higher grade or a short course) in each mode. For example, at least one social subject (e.g., History, Geography, Economics) would be studied instead of an amalgam of all three. This would ensure *inter alia* that essential skills, such as literacy, numeracy, problem solving, languages, and information technology were properly covered. For the purposes of a group certificate, a points system related to a fully graded examination would be required with SCOTBAC requiring a predetermined number of points as recommended by the Howie report.

At present the Scottish Technical and Vocational Examining Council (SCOTVEC) and the Scottish Examination Board (SEB) produce separate certificates based on separate syllabuses and assessment arrangements. If awards from both bodies were issued on the same certificate, candidates could follow a mixture of vocational and academic courses in line with their abilities and have both on a common certificate.

The existing Higher and CSYS courses and examinations could be immediately incorporated into a Howie system without requiring time-consuming and expensive development. Howie estimated that the first SCOTBAC awards would be made in 2001 at the earliest. Using the sort of evolutionary approach outlined above the first awards could be made in 1996 or 1997.

CONCLUSION

The Howie report takes two conflicting approaches to the issue of adopting a 'block' or an 'incremental' approach to qualifications at the end of secondary schooling. On the one hand, it assumes that an incremental approach will persuade students aiming for SCOTCERT vocational awards to persist with modular courses leading to awards at either Part One or Part Two of SCOTCERT. On the other hand, it assumes that a three-year SCOTBAC course will persuade students to stay on for a highly structured, broadly based group award in 10 subjects. The basic assumption must therefore be that there are two very distinct categories of students and that these two groups have manifested their proclivities by the middle of S3, when they are 14 or 15. All experience suggests that this is a false assumption. Neither does the existence of 'bridges and ladders' between SCOTCERT AND SCOTBAC courses remove anxieties about students who make ill-judged initial choices.

As far as the issue of parity of esteem for academic and vocational courses is concerned, the measures proposed in this paper, namely to allow common certification for both academic and vocational awards, should help diminish difference of esteem between academic and vocational courses and awards. Such a move would encourage students to pursue mixtures of courses without being placed in either an academic or a vocational category. These distinctions would not be made within schools and parental pressure to enter students for courses for which they are ill-suited would be removed. Such an approach would fit well with a Scottish tradition which has encouraged an incremental approach to qualification, an approach which builds on success and encourages participation.

REFERENCES

Upper secondary education in Scotland. (1992). Report of the Committee to Review Curriculum and Examinations in the fifth and sixth years of Secondary Education in Scotland. (Howie Report)

34. SELECTION TO HIGHER EDUCATION IN SWEDEN

Ingemar Wedman
Department of Education,
University of Umeå

During the last three decades the higher education system in Sweden has been the focus of a number of commissions and committees as well as being of great interest in the general debate about education in the country. Many changes have taken place during that time. Part of the debate about the higher education system has specifically dealt with problems of selection, i.e., how admission to higher education is organised and what rules and instruments characterise the selection process.

In this paper, selection to higher education in Sweden is examined against the background of developments that have taken place during the last three decades. Following some statistics about Sweden in general and the Swedish higher education system in particular the paper deals with the commissions, committees, and debate concerning the two basic instruments used today in the admission process, school marks and the Swedish Scholastic Aptitude Test (SweSAT). Then the SweSAT is briefly described and commented upon. The next part discusses experiments being conducted with alternative selection instruments. Finally, the paper deals with the future of selection to higher education both in terms of organisational changes that are already decided upon and those that may be expected.

Sweden is a rather small country with 8.6 million inhabitants. The standard of living is quite high although today the economy is under severe pressure with an unemployment rate of about 7% that is increasing.

There are six universities, six specialised university institutions, and 16 colleges in the country. The difference between universities and colleges lies in the fact that the former offer both undergraduate and graduate programmes while the latter offer undergraduate programmes only.

Each year, about 50,000 students are admitted to programmes offered by the universities and colleges. For quite a few of these programmes there are many more applicants than available places. While the government has increased the number of places, it still does not match the increase in the number of applicants. Therefore, selection for many programmes is necessary and for some the competition is very stiff. Rising unemployment contributes to the level of competition for places.

CHANGES IN THE ADMISSION SYSTEM FROM 1965 TO 1991

Concern with the question of selection for higher education goes back to 1965 when the government appointed a Commission of Competence. The task of the commission was to reform the whole organisation of higher education, including admission procedures. The commission had the aim of broadening the possibilities of access to higher education, i.e., to move from the then position where access was available only to young people studying theoretical subjects at upper secondary education and to create the possibility of access for older individuals who had not had the opportunity to study at the upper secondary level in their younger days. In order to determine which individuals from the latter group should be accepted, a common selection instrument was required. A suggestion was made to develop a test battery similar to the American Scholastic Aptitude Test.

At the same time there was discussion about the selection instrument in use for all other applicants, namely, marks given at upper secondary school. It was argued that for some students at least, the marking system was unfair and that an admission test would provide a second chance for students to get access to higher education. During the period form the mid-1960s to the early 1970s, the idea of developing an admission test got strong support from many interest groups. However, there was much discussion about how the test should actually be used. The point at issue was whether the test should be used for all applicants or should be limited, for example, to older people who were deemed worthy of a chance to get access to higher education. This question was referred to a new committee appointed in 1972, the Committee of Competence, which was given the task of carrying forward the suggestion made by the earlier commission. The use to which the test should be put was not at all clear initially. The main issue was, as pointed out above, whether the test should be used for all applicants or limited only to older people who wanted access to university. In the end, the suggestion was made to limit the test to persons of at least 25 years of age who had at least four years of work experience. The suggestion was accepted by parliament.

The first version of the admissions test was administered in May 1977, when about 6,000 eligible applicants took the test. A further 4,000 took the test the following October. Up to 1988, about 10,000 applicants took the test each year at spring and autumn sittings.

At the beginning of the 1980s, the system of admission to higher education became the focus of attention for a number of reasons and began to be criticised as being unfair. The government decided to appoint another commission in 1982 called the Commission on Access to Higher Education to examine the system. Its aim was to examine the admission procedure then in use to see if the impact on the selection process of the marks used for the main group of applicants could be reduced.

In 1985, the commission proposed that the impact of school marks on the selection process should be reduced and that the test should be more widely used in the selection process, thereby endorsing some of the proposals already made in the mid-1960s. The decision made by parliament was pretty much in line with the commission's suggestions and since 1991 the system of selection for higher education has been based on marks or results from the SweSAT. The effect on the SweSAT has been dramatic. While about 10,000 applicants took the test each year prior to 1989, today about 130,000 applicants take the test each year between the two sittings, 13 times as many applicants as previously.

Thus, selection to higher education has radically changed during the last three decades. Whereas previously the only way to get access to universities was through the marks obtained at the upper secondary school, now almost half the places are allocated on the results obtained on the Swedish Scholastic Aptitude Testing programme.

I now turn to the interest of the politicians and the general public in the other part of the selection process, namely, the marks obtained at the upper secondary school.

THE MARKING SYSTEM AT THE UPPER SECONDARY LEVEL IN SWEDEN

Side by side with the discussions on the use of SweSAT, a debate on the use of the marks obtained at the upper secondary school took place. Before dealing with the political aspects, it might be of interest to outline developments since the 1960s in the marking system used in Swedish schools.

In contrast to most other countries Sweden uses a marking system based explicitly on a norm-referenced procedure, specifically on the normal distribution curve. Before 1940, a system of selection for further education based on tests of some sort existed. At that time, however, it was argued that marks from the elementary school were as effective as the test used. Investigations, even empirical ones, confirmed this. Following some further commissions and investigations, the decision was made to drop the entrance test and use instead the marks from the elementary school for selection. However, it was further decided that if such marks were to be used in this way, standardised tests in a number of subjects would have to be developed and given to all applicants in a certain grade to establish the level of achievement of the individual class in each subject.

In 1962, such a situation was formally established. Since then Sweden has had a marking system based explicitly on a norm-referenced principle, implying that the marks given are, at least in theory, based on the level of each individual class compared with all other classes in the same subject all over Sweden. That marking system took about 20 years to develop but had only been in use for a few years before it began to be severely criticised. Since the late 60s a number of commissions and committees, similar to those described above, have been appointed to determine whether norm-referencing should be replaced by criterion-referencing.

In the late 1960s, the National Board of Education established a committee with the aim of examining the possibilities of replacing the norm-referenced marking system by a criterion-referenced system. They concluded that that would be possible only if a very well documented specification of the curricula for individual subjects was introduced. More than 30 working groups all over Sweden were appointed to specify the curricula for each subject. This led to the production of some fairly weighty documents. When word got out of the working groups' proposals, a national debate started about the consequences of developing such specified curricula for each individual subject. The debate ended with a decision from the director of the National Board to abolish all the working groups with the result that the impetus for changing from a norm-referenced to a criterion-referenced system was lost.

Criticism of the norm-referenced marking system did not, however, cease. Further arguments were presented for replacing it and, as a result, the government appointed a parliamentary commission with the aim of trying to find a new marking system that most people could agree on. In 1977, the commission proposed the substitution of the existing system by a criterion-referenced marking system. By this time almost all interest groups within the education area, including all political parties, were agreed about the disadvantages of the norm-referenced system. However, the commission had not discussed the use of a criterion-referenced marking system for selection. Because of reservations on that score, the government decided against its adoption. Another commission reported in 1981 and again recommended the replacement of the norm-referenced system by a criterion-referenced system but again the government decided against it.

At this time the selection process as a whole began to be discussed. As pointed out above, a commission was set up in 1985 with a view to finding a procedure that would lessen the impact of school marks in the selection process. As has been said, the commission recommended that marks from the upper secondary school should be complemented by the results of the SweSAT. That suggestion was supported by all political parties and that is the situation today: selection is based on average school marks and results on the SweSAT.

Criticism of the norm-referenced system remained, however, and a new commission was appointed to examine the marking system for the vocational part of the upper secondary school in 1986. That commission proposed the replacement of the norm-referenced marking system with a criterion-referenced system. For the first time since 1970 the government accepted the proposal and suggested the replacement of the existing norm-referenced grading system for the vocational part of the upper secondary school. However, the government realised that they could not replace one system with another without looking at the consequences for selection in the event that students in the vocational upper secondary school would wish to continue their studies at a higher level. Therefore, they appointed a special committee composed of members from the Swedish National Board of Education and the Swedish National Board of Universities and Colleges. After deliberating for a year the committee came to the conclusion that it accepted a criterion-referenced marking system but it did not agree that it should be used for selection purposes. The committee suggested instead that for students in the vocational part of upper secondary school, selection should be based on the marks gained in the academic subjects taken. However, it is interesting to note that this was the first time since 1970 that a government took a decision to change from a norm-referenced to a criterion-referenced system.

With regard to the other part of the upper secondary school, a group was appointed by the government with the aim of trying to find another way of assessing the achievements of students. That commission presented its findings in September 1990 and again a change from a norm-referenced to a criterion-referenced system was recommended. A new parliamentary commission was appointed to examine the implications of the proposed change. The commission suggested a criterion-referenced marking system that finally was agreed by parliament.

THE SweSAT PROGRAMME

In the context of changes to the system of higher education in the 1960s, an expert group led by Professor Sten Henrysson began investigating the possibilities of developing an entrance test to be used for all applicants to higher education. A great number of tests in use internationally were examined and tried out. The main reason for developing an entrance test at the time was the politically acceptable idea of enabling older people with work experience to gain access to higher education and the test was seen as a means of comparing their achievements with those of other groups of applicants.

In 1975, parliament decided that the admission system would be changed from autumn 1977. However, the decision limited the use of the test to applicants over 25 years of age and with at least four years' work experience. It may be noted that the test prototype used then, with minor changes, still forms the basis of the test known as the SweSAT.

As has been pointed out, the use of the SweSAT following the report in 1985 of the government commission on access increased dramatically. The commission suggested that the SweSAT should be open to all applicants including those leaving the upper secondary school. It also suggested that from 1991 selection to higher education should be based on marks from the upper secondary school *or* results on the SweSAT. So far, about 60% of available places on study programmes that have a limited number of places have been selected on the basis of average school marks and about 40% on the basis of SweSAT performance.

The system of admission is so arranged that applicants who offer both school marks and test results will be judged on the better performance. This has meant that most applicants, so far, have chosen to take the test. At the administration in May 1992 some 104,000 applied for the test.

The Content of the SweSAT

A range of contents and cognitive levels are covered by the SweSAT. Content categories represent the subject areas of Swedish university studies. The cognitive categories correspond broadly to those described in Bloom's (1956) *Taxonomy of Educational Objectives*.

The content of the present test is almost the same as the content of the 1977 version. The main difference is the addition of an English Reading Comprehension subtest which was introduced in 1991 to measure the study skills involved in finding information through many different registers and indexes. The subtest was developed by a research group at the Department of Education in the University of Gothenburg which specialises in measuring knowledge and skills in modern languages.

The test takes about four hours. No subtest is supposed to depend on speed of functioning though some testers find that this is the case in at least some subtests. Older persons in particular and, to some extent, women sometimes complain that the time limits set for some subtests are inadequate.

The SweSAT consists of six subtests which measure both verbal and nonverbal abilities, the capacity to make use of information, and knowledge of a general character. The subtest WORD (30 items) measures understanding of words and concepts and consists of items where the task is to identify which of five presented words has the same meaning as a given word. Both Swedish and foreign words are included in the test. The Quantitative Reasoning (DS) subtest (20 items) aims to measure numerical reasoning ability. In each item a problem is presented, and the task is to decide if the information presented is sufficient to allow solution of the problem. The response format is fixed, so that each item presents the same five alternatives. The test is designed to put as little premium as possible on mathematical knowledge and skills, in favour of problem-solving and reasoning. This format has been used in the Scholastic Aptitude test in the U.S. (Angoff, 1971).

The Reading Comprehension (READ) subtest (24 items) measures reading comprehension in a wide sense. In the original form of the subtest, examinees were presented with four texts, and six multiple-choice questions in relation to each text. The format of the subtest was recently changed to six tests, each of which is followed by four items. Each text comprises about one printed page. Some items ask about particular pieces of information but most are designed to require understanding of larger parts of the text or of the text in its entirety. The Interpretation of Diagrams, Tables, and Maps (DTM) subtest (20 items) consists of ten collections of tables, graphs, and/or maps which present information about a topic, with two multiple-choice questions on each collection. The degree of complexity of the items varies from simply reading off a graph to problem-solving using information from different sources.

The General Information (GI) subtest (30 items) measures knowledge and information from many different areas. The test is broader than traditional school achievement tests and looks for information that a person may acquire over an extended period of time in different contexts such as work, education, or social, cultural, and political activities. The English Reading Comprehension (ELF) subtest (24 items) is of the same general type as the Reading Comprehension subtest. However, in this test there is much more variability as to both the texts and item format used. The test consists of eight to ten texts of different length. Most texts are followed by one or more multiple-choice questions with four alternatives. In one of the texts, some words are omitted and the testee is required to select the words from four alternatives presented alongside the text.

Basic Function of SweSAT

The inclusion of separate subtests is dictated by the different requirements that a university admission test has to fulfil. SweSAT is designed to be used when selections are made for different types of university courses, and therefore has to measure the general aptitude of candidates for undertaking such courses. Since SweSAT is a selection test it should be able to rank the applicants as fairly as possible according to their likelihood of achieving academic success at university.

It should, however, also satisfy other criteria. It should be in line with the general aims, curricula and content of higher education; it should not have a negative effect on the courses which precede it; it should be possible to correct the test quickly, cheaply, and as objectively as possible; it should not be possible for individuals to improve their test results by means of mechanical exercises or by learning special principles for solving the problems set; it should be seen as meaningful by candidates and as a suitable instrument for selecting students for admission to higher education; and it should not discriminate against any candidate or group of candidates on the grounds of, for example, gender or social class. All subtests, but especially the proficiency and general information subtests, should cover a large number of different subject areas so as not to favour or damage the chances of any particular group. Furthermore, the tasks which are set should be of such a kind as to demand mental activity at different cognitive levels. Thus, the test should not be limited to questions intended to elicit purely factual knowledge.

Some Administrative Characteristics of the SweSAT

The Swedish National Board of Universities and Colleges has overall responsibility for the administration of the SweSAT and other matters connected with it. The actual construction of the test has been delegated to the Department of Education (Division of Educational Measurement) at Umeå University. The research and development work was initiated at the end of the 1960s and started on a large scale in 1973. There are two basic tasks: (i) developing the test itself and (ii) carrying out research and development work connected with it. A completely new test is set for each sitting which is held at the same time all over the country and always on a Saturday. To register for the test, candidates must pay a registration fee.

EXPERIMENTAL ACTIVITIES IN SELECTION TO HIGHER EDUCATION

Side by side with its decision to introduce the aptitude test in 1977, the government agreed to remain open to the possibility of finding alternative selection instruments to school marks and the aptitude test. They also agreed that each university or college should be free to suggest alternatives which, however, would require government approval prior to their adoption. Today there are at least four actual or potential alternatives. Two medical schools, one in Stockholm (Karolinska Institutet) and the other in Linköping (TEMA Linköping) use an alternative selection procedure to fill a proportion of their places.

On the basis of performance on the aptitude test, a number of applicants equal to about twice the number of available places are invited to write an essay and to attend for interview, the purpose of which is to assess a student's aptitude for dealing with clients and patients. Two independent interviewers from the staff of the relevant departments try to assess such personal qualities as empathy and interpersonal skills. Following evaluation, a decision will be taken about the formal incorporation into the selection process of these activities.

In a similar experiment, applicants for courses in architecture are being asked to take an adapted form of the SweSAT which includes additional subtests designed to provide a more searching test of spatial ability and of the ability to interpret numerical data. This experiment has been going on for five years and is being evaluated. A special selection procedure for applicants for journalism was not finally introduced because it seemed likely to prove too expensive. It may be pointed out that the government in giving institutions freedom to devise their own selection procedures also made it clear that any associated costs would have to be borne by the institutions themselves. In practice, considerations of cost have proved a limiting factor on institutional experimentation in this field so far. However, it is expected in the near future that other departments and universities will try out alternatives for selecting students.

THE FUTURE OF SELECTION FOR HIGHER EDUCATION IN SWEDEN

It is difficult to say what the future holds for higher education selection systems. However, we know that Sweden is moving from a centralised to a decentralised system for the organisation of universities and colleges. Since July 1993, this decentralisation allowed for the possibility of each individual university and college devising its own admission programme. The expectation nevertheless is that most of them will try, at least in the immediate future, to adhere, at least partly, to the present admission system so that for the next few years the situation should not change dramatically. It is, however, also the expectation that institutions and universities other than those mentioned above will try new ways of selecting students for their study programmes and that those alternatives will be sensitive to the knowledge and skills which students will need in their chosen third-level studies.

Ever since the Commission on Access to Higher Education put forward its proposals in 1985 there has been much debate on a move from the existing admission system to a more differentiated and more specific one, which would be more adjusted to the specific study programmes offered in universities and colleges. Technical schools and medical schools in particular have put forward arguments for changing the present system to a more differentiated one. An alternative proposal has been not to change the system but to add a specific component which matches more closely the content of the study programmes in medical and technical schools. Today, there are also research activities directed at developing separate admission systems for individual courses. However, we know from experience both at home and abroad that it is difficult and expensive to develop admission systems which are adjusted for many different student programmes and which will be much more discriminating than the general scholastic aptitude testing of today. Since the beginning of the 1990s, the trend in discussions has been towards a two-step admission procedure, where the first step would involve the use of the results obtained from a general instrument such as the SweSAT and the second would involve a more specific component that fits better with the content of individual third-level study programmes. What those specific components would contain is hard to say at this point. One may be a component that will take into account the more or less specific abilities that are relevant to particular study programmes; the other could be a more subject-oriented component such as the ones connected to the Scholastic Aptitude Test in the United States.

REFERENCES

Angoff, W.H. (Ed.). (1971). *The College Board admission testing program: A technical report on research and development activities relating to the Scholastic Aptitude Test and Achievement Tests.* New York: College Entrance Examination Board.

Bloom, B. S. (Ed.). (1956). *Taxonomy of educational objectives. The classification of educational goals. Handbook 1. Cognitive domain.* London: Longmans.

CONCLUSION

35. CONCLUSION

Thomas Kellaghan
Educational Research Centre
St Patrick's College, Dublin

No attempt will be made in this concluding chapter to summarise the many and varied contributions to this volume. However, the experiences represented in the papers, spanning six continents, do invite some reflection on the similarity of issues and the range of practices that are described. I shall address these issues and practices and conclude by identifying some directions in the development of selection procedures for higher education which they point to.

Although the educational contexts in which contributors address issues relating to admission to higher education vary considerably, there are some issues which seem to be universal. In all countries, with some exceptions for some courses, there are more applicants than places in higher education. Further, competition for places is increasing as provision for higher education lags behind provision for second-level education. The inevitable consequence of these conditions is that some method of selection is required to allocate places in higher education to those who seek admission. Even in countries in which a relatively large number of places is available, competition and selection occur for institutions and courses that are considered to be desirable and prestigious (see, for example, Baumgart & McBryde in this volume).

In all countries too, despite variation in practice, it seems reasonable to assume that selection procedures enjoy a high level of public confidence and legitimacy (see Cresswell in this volume). This would appear to be so even in the absence of intimate knowledge about the examination system or its quality, which of course is difficult to obtain because of the secrecy that surrounds the operation of many examination systems. In this context, one commentator has argued that the legitimacy accorded an examination in a society may have nothing to do with the merit of the examination process itself and that 'irrespective of "what knowledge is deemed of most worth," the major sociological trick is to convince consumers of the legitimacy of the evaluative process' (Foster, 1992, p.122). It is unlikely that many people involved in examinations or selection procedures would set out to play tricks, sociological or otherwise, on consumers. Certainly, contributors to this volume bear ample testimony to the efforts of those concerned with examinations to improve their quality in the interest both of equity and of more accurate prediction. Further, Hayden, Richards and Thompson in their paper point out that unless an assessment system is believed to be reliable and valid, it will soon lose currency within the higher education sector. When confidence in examination and selection systems breaks down and legitimacy is eroded, serious consequences for the ordering of society can ensue (see Greaney & Kellaghan, 1996). Less severe breakdown, as seems to have occurred in Victoria, Australia, may lead to a search for alternatives (see Withers in this volume).

A further common feature of examination and selection systems is that they seem to operate on the basis of meritocratic principles, though the principles may take somewhat different forms in different countries. This is not surprising when one considers that one of the reasons for the introduction of external examinations in the first place was to deal with problems of privilege and nepotism and to promote fairness in the distribution of occupational and educational benefits (see Eckstein & Noah, 1993; Greaney & Kellaghan, 1996). Commitment to meritocratic principles when applied to social groups, however, does not ensure equality of access or participation for members of those groups in any country. Indeed, the differential representation in higher education institutions of students from differing socioeconomic or ethnic backgrounds, as well as differences in gender representation, are persistent causes of concern in educational systems which aspire to equality of opportunity for all students. The concern is considered in several contributions to this volume and is found in developing and industrialised countries.

Concern is due to the fact that, despite the considerable expansion of participation in education, participation rates of students from varying socioeconomic backgrounds in higher education have not changed radically in several countries for which statistics are available. While there has been a slight narrowing in rates of participation, the proportion of students from higher socioeconomic backgrounds continues to be significantly higher than the proportion from lower socioeconomic backgrounds. Further, when increases are recorded in the participation rates of students from lower socioeconomic groups, they tend to occur in the less prestigious programmes of the higher education sector. Differences in participation relating to gender in industrialised countries are much smaller than differences between socioeconomic groups but continue to be a problem in some developing countries.

Conributions to this volume provide examples of several procedures that have been adopted to deal with the unequal representation of social groups in higher education. Providing a 'second chance' for mature students has been reported for several countries (see Baumgart & McBryde, Esezobor, Halsey, Johnson, Kimber, Mkandawire, Sebatane, Yang). There seems to be general agreement that students over a certain age can successfully complete higher education courses even when they do not meet the entrance requirements in place for students who have just left school. While mature students do not necessarily come from under-represented social groups, it is likely that many do.

Forms of 'affirmative action' which employ quota systems are also reported for several countries. Under such systems, all available places are not awarded on the same criteria. Thus, a certain proportion is reserved for students of a particular gender, race, ethnic background, family background, or place of residence, whether or not candidates reach the same level of achievement as candidates in other categories. Quotas established on the basis of race have been in operation in the United States for many years. In Nigeria, quotas are reserved for residents of the area in which a university is located (see Majasan & Salami in this volume). Efforts to increase the small percentage of students from working-class backgrounds in higher education led to the establishment of quotas for such students in former communist countries in Eastern Europe (see Ingenkamp in this volume).

Affirmative action policies have been the subject of much debate. The basic problem is to reconcile equity for individuals with equity for groups. It is not surprising if individual candidates are aggrieved to see students from other groups with poorer academic qualifications than they possess admitted to higher education institutions while they are not. Although in a 1978 opinion of the Supreme Court in the United States, attainment of a diverse student body was perceived as a constitutionally permissible goal for an institution of higher education, there have been, and continue to be, many challenges to the constitutionality of discrimination on grounds of race, whatever race benefits.

Issues relating to the unequal participation rates of social groups and efforts to address them are likely to continue as long as members of particular social groups fail to meet the entrance requirements of higher education institutions. To a large extent, however, the problem is outside the control of these institutions, since differences in achievement between social groups manifest themselves long before the point of entry to higher education. What is important from the point of view of selection procedures is to ensure, as far as possible, that inequalities in the system are not attributable to those procedures. In the future, we might reasonably expect greater diversification in higher educational provision, increasing numbers, and a broader and more relevant definition of the knowledge and skills that are considered necessary for further education than generally exists today to lead to an improvement of participation among groups that are currently under-represented in third-level educational institutions.

VARIATION BETWEEN COUNTRIES IN SELECTION PRACTICES

Despite similarities in issues relating to selection practices for higher education across the world, there are considerable differences in practice so that students' experiences, aspirations, and expectations in their later teenage years can vary very considerably from country to country. There are a number of reasons for these differences. One is the level of economic development of a country which is a major determinant of the resources available for higher education and of demand on the labour market for its products. Variation in the social philosophies of countries also affects selection to higher education. This variation is apparent in differences in the emphasis placed on individual development or selection in the organisation of the educational system which are reflected in the extent to which selection procedures are centralised and standardised (see Hooper, 1977). The traditions of a country also play a role in determining the kind of selection practices used. For example, a close relationship can be observed between examination and selection systems in African countries and systems in the European countries that colonised them. Thus, countries in Francophone Africa use the French *Baccalauréat* and *Concours* systems, while Anglophone African countries model their examination systems on those of British examination boards (Kellaghan & Greaney, 1992). In the following sections, variations in the practice of selection as represented in the contributions to this volume are described.

Open Entry

A number of countries (e.g., France, Germany) have a tradition of open access to higher education. That is, no selection procedure is operated prior to entry for students who possess certain minimum educational qualifications (see Alvarez and Trost in this volume). In these cases, students need only hold a high-school diploma or have obtained a school-leaving certificate to be admitted to study in a higher education institution. Open entry can operate only when the secondary school system is selective (Kallen, 1992). In this situation, the secondary school performs the selection at an earlier stage by allowing only those students who are performing well academically to reach the leaving certificate level. Moreover, with open entry, a further point of selection is introduced at a later point in the students' educational career, usually during the first or second year in college or university. In practice, pressure on places has meant that it has been necessary in a number of countries where open entry exists in theory to introduce a *numerus clausus* provision which has the effect of making students compete for entry.

Although open admission, since it gives all students who wish an opportunity to display their capacity for education for a period in a higher education institution, may appear a more equitable solution than selection before admission, there are a number of problems associated with the practice which have been outlined by Beller in this volume. These include the cost of maintaining a large number of students in the college or university, overcrowding, extreme competitiveness between students for the limited number of places in subsequent years, and the inevitable rejection of some students whose performance is satisfactory.

Pre-Entry Selection

Since a higher education institution will try to reduce the cost of failure, both to itself and to students (see Beller), it is not surprising that open entry does not operate in many countries. The more usual procedure is to operate some method of selection prior to entry. Selection at this stage, of course, does not alleviate all of the problems associated with open entry, such as competitiveness and the rejection of students who might well be capable of making satisfactory progress in higher education. Besides, pre-entry selection may create additional problems, such as the impact it has on second-level curricula.

It is clear from contributors to this volume, as well as from other sources, that when selection to higher education takes place before entry, a variety of approaches is used. Sometimes an approach operates uniformly for all students and for all higher education institutions in a country. In other cases, it does not: procedures vary for different institutions and, in some cases, alternative procedures coexist. Ways in which approaches differ from country to country (or from state to state in some countries) include whether selection is based on scholastic aptitude or scholastic achievement; the extent to which the procedure used for selection is external to the school or involves school-based assessment; whether a single measure or a combination of measures is used, in particular, the extent to which measures designed to assess aspects of candidates' performance other than scholastic achievement or aptitude are used; and whether selection is based on a dedicated measure or on a measure that is used for purposes other than selection.

Selection on the Basis of Scholastic Aptitude

Selection may be based on an assessment of scholastic aptitude or on an assessment of scholastic achievement. While the term 'achievement' is used to describe the knowledge and skills that students have acquired during courses of instruction which they have already undergone, the term 'aptitude' is used to describe 'capacity' or 'potential' to benefit from future instruction. The main focus of aptitude then is on prediction, and tests of aptitude are used to select those students that are most likely to be successful in a higher education institution.

The distinction between aptitude and achievement, however, may not be as clear-cut as this description suggests. First, the knowledge and skills assessed in an aptitude test depend on students' prior learning experiences just as do the knowledge and skills assessed in an achievement test. And secondly, aptitude tests may not predict later performance any better than achievement tests. In a number of studies in Britain and Ireland, achievement tests based on school syllabi have predicted performance in higher education institutions better than scholastic aptitude tests (Choppin & Orr, 1976; Christie & Mills, 1973; O'Rourke, Martin, & Hurley, 1989).

Aptitude tests may still be of value in certain situations. For example, since they are less sensitive than achievement tests to the differential opportunities of students to learn, they may be useful when school inputs and facilities vary widely (Heyneman, 1987). They may also be appropriate in countries, such as the United States where they are widely used, in which curricula are not closely prescribed at a national or state level. It has also been argued that their use allows schools to adopt more experimental approaches in teaching (Heyneman, 1987).

Scholastic aptitude tests may have a greater role to play in the future if, as has been described in this volume (see McCurry, Wedman), the concept of aptitude is more clearly focused on the knowledge and skills presumed necessary to learn in a third-level institution. Thus, in place of the verbal and numerical reasoning which current tests of aptitude assess, we might expect to see tests that assess such characteristics as students' capacity to read a body of material and to engage in analysis, evaluation, and synthesis.

Selection on the Basis of Scholastic Achievement

School-Leaving Examinations. It is much more common to base selection for higher education on a measure of students' scholastic achievements than on a measure of scholastic aptitude. A variety of methods is used to assess achievement, the most common of which in the contributions to this volume are school-leaving examinations. Such examinations are more or less formalised procedures, usually separated from the classroom situation, in which a candidate has to answer questions, based on externally devised syllabi, to demonstrate that he or she possesses certain knowledge and skills. The examinations are organised in terms of traditional subject-matter content (e.g., mathematics, science, language) and involve written essay-type questions, though in some countries multiple-choice questions and oral examining also feature. On the basis of examination performance, a candidate is awarded a certificate or diploma which, in addition to testifying to his or her satisfactory performance in an examination in a particular subject or groups of subjects, may also confer certain rights, such as the right to be considered for some sector of the social, professional, or educational world.

Marks (or grades) across five or six individual examination subjects are usually aggregated to provide a total, and students with the highest totals are selected for entry to higher education. Sometimes, the procedure is more complex and performance in a specific area of the curriculum is accorded additional weight for admission to particular courses. For example, a candidate may be required to obtain a specified minimum grade in Mathematics in the school-leaving examination if he or she is to study Engineering. In Australia, performance in five specific fields of study are used to construct a profile of student achievement (see Baumgart & McBryde and McCurry in this volume). Additional examinations may also be set by university departments. For example, in Sweden, a test of competence relating to the individual programme to which a candidate is applying is required. This might involve writing an essay or attending an interview to have interpersonal skills assessed (see Wedman in this volume).

In many countries, reliance solely on performance on an external examination as a basis for school certification or selection is increasingly being questioned.

Probably to a considerable extent as a response to expanding participation rates in education, which were accompanied by an increase in variance in the achievements, aptitudes, interests, and needs of students, a need has been perceived for changing the form and content of traditional assessment procedures as well as the curricula on which examinations are based. Today, many view the formal and academic nature of traditional examinations (particularly written terminal ones) as unsuitable for the assessment of many candidates and curricular areas. Furthermore, a criticism of external examinations, which has been consistently made during their history relating to their narrowing effects on students' educational experiences, achieved a new level of significance and relevance when the question of submitting total populations to traditional examination procedures arose.

School-Based Assessment. Either in place of external examinations or as part of them, increasing emphasis is being placed on the need for some form of school-based assessment in selection procedures for higher education. The arguments for school-based assessment seem compelling. Ideally, it involves a wide sampling of student achievements, based on diverse and multiple sampling of assessment tasks; it is spread over an extended time period by contrast with examinations which are conducted in a limited time frame at the end of a period of study; it is carried out under normal conditions by teachers who know the student well; and it relies on the observation of 'real performance' and can attend to areas of achievement other than ones involving the display of propositional knowledge. Important among those areas are problem solving and the application of knowledge and skills in new areas.

A strong advocacy for school-based assessment is presented by Withers in this volume. However, it has to be accepted that such assessment also has a downside. Whether results are used for certification or selection, problems of comparability between teachers and schools inevitably arise. Further, teachers, especially in small communities, are likely to come under pressure from parents, giving rise to the possibility of corruption. Efforts to deal with such problems through a variety of moderation procedures cannot be regarded as unproblematic (see, for example, Elley & Livingstone, 1972), leading, as Cresswell has observed in this volume, to a retrenchment towards less naturalistic assessment techniques.

Combining Assessments for Selection

The problems associated with reliance on one source of assessment information for admitting students to higher education has led to the use in some countries of several sources. Here, it should be acknowledged that in a sense external examinations involve more than one source since final scores or points considered for admission are usually based on an aggregate of scores derived from examinations in a number of subject areas. However, there are cases in which efforts are made to take into account a more varied range of information in making selection decisions. For example, higher educational institutions in the United States combine information from students' high schools (e.g., rank in class, grade-point average) with scholastic aptitude test information in making decisions about student admissions. In other countries also, teacher recommendations, references, or school reports on academic and extra-curricular activities may play a role (see Johnson, Ongom, Trost, Yang in this volume). Even when not generally required, such information may be obtained for selection to professional courses, such as teaching.

Interviews are used in conjunction with other assessment procedures in many countries for admission to some courses to help identify candidates that are likely to drop out or fail, or in some cases, to assess communication skills if the student is applying for a course leading to a profession in which such skills are important (see Alvarez, Beller, Esezobar, Fincher, Poon Scott, Sebatane, Trost, Wedman, Withers in this volume). Perhaps because of their expense and low predictive validity, not to mention the sheer volume of students now applying to higher education insittutions, the practice of interviewing applicants seems to be declining.

The Use of a Dedicated Measure or One Used for Other Purposes

In most of the countries considered in this volume, the school-leaving examinations which are used as a basis for selection for further education also serve other functions. There are countries, however, in which dedicated examinations are held to select students. These examinations may be the responsibility of a private non-governmental organisation, as is the case in the United States, or of a ministry of education, which is the case in European countries where such a system exists (Greece, Portugal, Spain). In both cases, data on candidate performance are provided to individual higher educational institutions. Dedicated entrance examinations that are separate from school-leaving ones seem to be more common in countries in which there is not a national or state school-leaving examination with a major external component, though there are countries in which university entrants are accepted on the basis of performance on a school-based diploma (e.g., Belgium) (Madaus & Kellaghan, 1991).

Most countries do not have dedicated entrance examinations for higher education. Rather, entrance decisions are made on the basis of performance on examinations that are intended to serve a variety of functions (see Cresswell in this volume and Ingenkamp, 1977). These functions include, as well as selection, certification, which provides formal evidence of educational achievement for students at the end of secondary schooling, and the control of curricula in schools. Examinations are also perceived to serve the function of unifying teaching efforts throughout a country around common goals and so can be particularly important when many schools are under private management (Kellaghan, 1992). It is also assumed that they motivate students and teachers to greater effort and in some situations may serve an accountability function by providing evidence of standards attained by individual teachers and schools.

When examinations have competing objectives, it is likely that one will dominate. In a study of 14 African countries, for example, the primary function of almost all external examinations was reported to be selection (Kellaghan & Greaney, 1992). Cresswell (this volume) also notes the close relationship between school-leaving examinations and selection in England and cites the argument that recent developments in that country relating to assessment techniques can be understood more easily when considered in the context of the demands made on examinations as selection instruments.

When the selection function dominates, the quality of the examination for other purposes is likely to suffer. Of particular importance among other functions is that of certification. Many students completing secondary education will not proceed to higher education and so require, and deserve, adequate certification of their achievements. However, examinations that are used primarily for selection are likely to emphasise discrimination between students rather than certification of achievements. As a consequence, the level of difficulty of the examination may be too high for low-achieving students. Further, use of the examinations for university selection will inevitably mean that they have a strong academic orientation; otherwise, universities would be unlikely to accept them. This orientation will inevitably be reflected in school curricula, again placing at a disadvantage low-achieving students or ones with greater aptitude for, and interest in, less academic pursuits. Attempts to separate the functions of selection and certification have had only limited success (see Baumgart & McBryde, this volume).

FUTURE DIRECTIONS

While the diverse selection systems in many of the countries described in this volume have been in place for many years, there is also ample evidence that systems are not static. A consciousness of problems in the present systems and of a need to review and possibly change them is evident in many contributions. Many changes have, in fact, occurred over the past two decades. These have often focused on improving the efficiency of the examination and selection processes, by for example introducing multiple-choice tests or machine scoring of answers or improving prediction. However, there is also evidence of much more radical change in some countries. These changes may be taken as signals of a number of the issues that those responsible for selection procedures to higher education will inevitably have to address in the coming years.

Increasing participation rates in secondary and higher education, which as already noted are reflected in an increase in the range of abilities, interests, and needs of students, raise questions about the appropriateness of using a single measure of achievement for all applicants to higher education. In this context, we may expect the concept of multiple pathways, which is already being given consideration in some countries (see Halsey in this volume), to receive increasing attention.

In considering pathways to higher education, it would seem that a broader view will have to be taken of achievement than has traditionally been the case in selection procedures. Today, one frequently hears criticism of the extent to which schools are successful in fostering the development in students of the knowledge and skills required in contemporary economies. The knowledge and skills are variously described as involving observation, problem identification, problem solving, reasoning, the application of what is learned in school, and taking initiative in and responsibility for learning. The extent to which selection instruments currently in use assess these abilities is questionable. Indeed, commentators argue that not only are current methods of assessment unsuccessful in this task, but may exacerbate the gap between what goes on in schools and desirable goals and accomplishments of educators.

In response to the needs of the changing workplace, as well as to accommodate the needs of students, curricula are already changing in secondary and tertiary institutions. The implications of these changes for assessment are already being considered (see Macintosh in this volume). There is a great danger, however, that failure to take action to adjust assessment procedures on a wider scale will inhibit the development of more relevant curricula in secondary schools. In developing new assessment procedures, it should be borne in mind that when high stakes such as selection to higher education are attached to them, they can have a serious negative impact on teaching and learning in schools (see, for example, Baumgart & McBryde, Han in this volume). It will be a daunting task to devise selection procedures that do not impact on learning and teaching in the way many existing procedures do: narrowing curricula, leading to an overemphasis on rote learning, encouraging the strategic selection of subjects by students, and actually contributing to the corruption of the assessment instrument itself (see Kellaghan & Greaney, 1992; Madaus, 1988; Madaus & Kellaghan, 1992). A start to addressing these problems is already evident in recent efforts at reform described in this volume which show greater sensitivity than has been the case in the past to the problems posed by high-stakes examinations. Solutions, however, are far from clear.

A further trend with implications for selection already in evidence in some countries is the changing age profile of students in higher education institutions (see Fincher in this volume). As more mature students, with diverse kinds of experience, enter higher education, the need for alternative procedures of selection will become more pressing since clearly the type of examination used at the end of secondary schooling will not be adequate for assessing the achievements or aptitudes of such students.

A final factor with implications for selection that is likely to achieve greater salience in the future is student transfer from one institution to another at the undergraduate level. In some countries, in the United States for example despite the number of institutions involved, this is relatively easy (see Johnson in this volume). In others, for example in Latin America, transfer is almost impossible because of differences in academic requirements and standards, legal procedures, schedules, and even availability of information (see Alvarez in this volume). Whatever the difficulties, student transfer seems set to become increasingly more common. At present, programmes supported by the European Union encourage student mobility between countries. As the practice becomes more widespread, issues about the comparability not only of selection procedures but also of courses in higher education institutions will inevitably become more prominent.

REFERENCES

Choppin, B. H. L., & Orr, L. (1976). *Aptitude testing at eighteen-plus*. Windsor, Berks: NFER Publishing Co.

Christie, T., & Mills, J. (1973). *The use of a scholastic aptitude test in university selection*. Manchester: Department of Education, University of Manchester.

Eckstein, M. A., & Noah, H. J. (1993). *Secondary school examinations. International perspectives on policies and practice*. New Haven CN: Yale University Press.

Elley, W. B., & Livingstone, I. D. (1972). *External examinations and internal assessments*. Wellington: New Zealand Council for Educational Research.

Foster, P. J. (1992). Commentary. In M. A. Eckstein & H. J. Noah (Eds.), *Examinations: Comparative and international studies*. (pp.121-126). Oxford: Pergamon.

Greaney, V., & Kellaghan, T. (1996). The integrity of public examinations in developing countries. In H. Goldstein & T. Lewis (Eds.), *Assessment: Problems, developments and statistical issues*. (pp.167-188). Chichester: Wiley.

Heyneman, S. (1987). Uses of examinations in developing countries: Selection, research, and education sector management. *International Journal of Educational Development*, *7*, 251-263.

Hopper, E. I. (1977). A typology for the classification of educational systems. (pp. 153-166). In J. Karabel & A. H. Halsey (Eds.), *Power and ideology in education*. New York: Oxford University Press.

Ingenkamp, K. (1977). *Educational assessment*. Windsor, Berks: NFER Publishing Co.

Kallen, D. (1992). Access to higher learning. In B. F. Clark & G. R. Neave (Eds.), *The encyclopedia of higher education. Vol 3. Analytical perspectives*. (pp. 1547-1557). Oxford: Pergamon.

Kellaghan, T. (1992). Examination systems in Africa: Between internationalization and indigenizatioin. In M. A. Eckstein & H. J. Noah (Eds.), *Examinations: Comparative and international studies*. (pp.95-104). Oxford: Pergamon.

Kellaghan, T., & Greaney, V. (1992). *Using examinations to improve education. A study in fourteen African countries*. Washington DC: World Bank.

Madaus, G. F. (1988). The influence of testing on the curriculum. In L. N. Tanner (Ed.), *Critical issues in curriculum. Eighty-seventh Yearbook of the National Society for the Study of Education, Part I*. (pp.83-121). Chicago: NSSE.

Madaus, G. F., & Kellaghan, T. (1991). Student examination systems in the European Community: Lessons for the United States. In G. Kulm & S. M. Malcom (Eds.), *Science assessment in the service of reform*. (pp.189-232). Washington DC: American Association for the Advancement of Science.

Madaus, G. F., & Kellaghan, T. (1992). Curriculum evaluation and assessment. In P. W. Jackson (Ed.), *Handbook of research on curriculum*. (pp.119-154). New York: Macmillan.

O'Rourke, B., Martin, M. O., & Hurley, J. J. (1989). The Scholastic Aptitude Test as a predictor of third-level academic performance. *Irish Journal of Education*, *23*, 22-39.

INDEX

W

Y

Z